Social History of the
United States

Titles in ABC-CLIO's
Social History of the United States

Social History of the United States
The 1900s

Brian Greenberg
Linda S. Watts

Series Editors
Daniel J. Walkowitz and Daniel E. Bender

A B C CLIO

Santa Barbara, California   Denver, Colorado   Oxford, England

Library of Congress Cataloging-in-Publication Data

Greenberg, Brian.
    Social history of the United States. The 1900s / Brian Greenberg and Linda S. Watts.
    p.   cm.
    Includes bibliographical references and index.
    ISBN 978-1-85109-903-0 (alk. paper) — ISBN 978-1-59884-127-5 (set)
    EISBN 978-1-85109-904-7 (ebook)
    1. United States—Social conditions—1865–1918.   2. United States—Economic
conditions—1865–1918.   I. Watts, Linda S., 1960–   II. Title.   III. Title: 1900s.
    HN57.G6925   2009
    306.0973'09041—dc22   2008021619

12 11 10 09   1 2 3 4 5

Production Editor: Kristine Swift
Production Manager: Don Schmidt
Media Editor: Julie Dunbar
Media Resources Manager: Caroline Price
File Management Coordinator: Paula Gerard

This book is also available on the World Wide Web as an eBook.
Visit www.abc-clio.com for details.

ABC-CLIO, Inc.
130 Cremona Drive, P.O. Box 1911
Santa Barbara, California 93116–1911

This book is printed on acid-free paper ∞
Manufactured in the United States of America

Contents

Contents

Series Introduction

Ordinary people make history. They do so in ways that are different from the ways presidents, generals, business moguls, or celebrities make history; nevertheless, the history of ordinary people is just as profound, just as enduring. Immigration in the early decades of the 20th century was more than numbers and government policy; it was a collective experience of millions of men, women, and children whose political beliefs, vernacular cultural expression, discontent, and dreams transformed the United States. Likewise, during the Great Depression of the 1930s, President Franklin Delano Roosevelt advanced a broad spectrum of new social policies, but as historians have argued, ordinary Americans "made" the New Deal at the workplace, at the ballot box, on the picket lines, and on the city streets. They engaged in new types of consumer behavior, shifted political allegiances, and joined new, more aggressive trade unions. World War II and the Cold War were more than diplomatic maneuvering and military strategy; social upheavals changed the employment patterns, family relations, and daily life of ordinary people. More recently, the rise of the Christian Right in the last few decades is the expression of changing demographics and emerging social movements, not merely the efforts of a few distinct leaders.

These examples, which are drawn directly from the volumes in this series, highlight some of the essential themes of social history. Social history shifts the historical focus away from the famous and the political or economic elite to issues of everyday life. It explores the experiences ordinary Americans—native-born and immigrant, poor and rich, employed and unemployed, men and women, white and black—at home, at work, and at play. In the process, it focuses new attention on the significance of social movements, the behavior and meanings of consumerism, and the changing expression of popular culture.

In many ways, social history is not new. American historians early in the 20th century appreciated the importance of labor, immigration, religion, and urbanization in the study of society. However, early studies shared with political history the emphasis on leaders and major institutions and described a history that was mostly white and male—in other words, a history of those who held power. Several cultural shifts combined to transform how social history was understood and written in the last half of the 20th century: the democratization of higher education after World War II with the GI Bill and the expansion of public and land grant universities; the entry of women, children of immigrants, and racial minorities into the universities and the ranks of historians; and the social movements of the 1960s. Historians created new subjects for social history, casting it as "from the bottom." They realized that much was missing from familiar narratives that stressed the significance of "great men"—presidents, industrialists, and other usually white, usually male notables. Instead, women, working people, and ethnic and racial minorities have become integral parts of the American story along with work, leisure, and social movements.

The result has not simply been additive: ordinary people made history. The story of historical change is located in their lives and their struggles with and against others in power. Historians began to transform the central narrative of American history. They realized that—in the words of a popular 1930s folk cantata, "Ballad for Americans"—the "'etceteras' and the 'and so forths' that do the work" have a role in shaping their own lives, in transforming politics, and in recreating economics. Older themes of study, from industrialization to imperial expansion, from party politics to urbanization, were revisited through the inclusion of new actors, agents, and voices. These took their place alongside such new topics as social movements, popular culture, consumption, and community. But social history remains socially engaged scholarship; contemporary social issues continue to shape social historians' research and thinking. Historians in the 1970s and 1980s who focused on the experiences of working people, for instance, were challenged by the reality of deindustrialization. Likewise, historians in the 1990s who focused on popular culture and consumer behavior were influenced by the explosion of consumerism and new forms of cultural expression. Today's historians explore the antecedents to contemporary globalization as well as the roots of conservatism.

The transformation of the questions and agendas of each new era has made it apparent to historians that the boundaries of historical inquiry are not discrete. Social history, therefore, engages with other kinds of history. Social history reinterprets older narratives of politics and political economy and overlaps both areas. Social historians argue that politics is not restricted to ballot boxes or legislatures; politics is broad popular engagement with ideas about material wealth, social justice, moral values, and civil and human rights. Social historians, naturally, remain interested in changing political affiliations. They have, for example, examined the changing political allegiances of African Americans during the 1930s and the civil rights movement of the 1960s. So too have they examined the relationship of socialist and communist parties to working-class and immigrant communities. At the same time, social historians measure change by looking at such issues as family structure, popular culture, and consumer behavior.

For the social historian, the economy extends far beyond statistical data about production, gross domestic product, or employment. Rather, the economy is a lived experience. Wealthy or poor, Americans have negotiated the changing reality of economic life. Social historians ask questions about how different groups of Americans experienced and resisted major economic transformations and how they have grappled with economic uncertainty. The Great Depression of the 1930s, for example, left both urban workers and rural farmers perilously close to starvation. During the 1970s and 1980s, factories in the Rust Belt of the Midwest and Northeast shuttered or moved, and many Americans began laboring in new parts of the country and working new kinds of jobs, especially in the service sector. Americans have also grappled with the unequal distribution of wealth; some people advanced new ideas and engaged with emerging ideologies that challenged economic injustice, but others jealously guarded their privilege.

As social history has broadened its purview, it has transformed our sense of how historical change occurs. Social history changes our conception of chronology; change does not correspond to presidential election cycles. Social history also changes how we understand sources of power; power is constituted in and challenged by diverse peoples with different resources. Social historians, then, look at the long history of the 20th century in the United States and examine how the terrain has shifted under our feet, sometimes slowly and sometimes dramatically and abruptly. Social historians measure change in complex ways, including but also transcending demographic and geographic expansion and political transformation. How, for example, did the institution of the family change in the face of successive waves of immigration that often left spouses and children separated by national borders and oceans? Or during years of war with rising rates of women's wage and salary employment? Or following moralist reaction that celebrated imagined traditional values, and social movements that focused on issues of sexuality, birth control, homosexuality, and liberation? Historical change can also be measured by engagement with popular culture as Americans shifted their attention from vaudeville and pulp novels to radio, silent films, talkies, television, and finally the Internet and video games. The volumes in this series, divided by decades, trace all these changes.

To make sense of this complex and broadened field of inquiry, social historians often talk about how the categories by which we understand the past have been "invented," "contested," and "constructed." The nation has generally been divided along lines of race, class, gender, sexuality, and ethnicity. However, historians have also realized that analysts—whether in public or professional discourse—define these "categories of analysis" in different ways at different moments. Waves of immigration have reconfigured understandings of race and ethnicity, and more recent social movements have challenged the meanings of gender. Similarly, to be working class at the dawn of the age of industry in the 1900s meant something very different from being working class in the post-industrial landscape of the 1990s. How women or African Americans—to cite only two groups—understand their own identity can mean something different than how white men categorize them. Social historians, therefore, trace how Americans have always been divided about the direction of their lives and their nation, how they have consistently challenged and rethought social and cultural values and sought to renegotiate relationships of power, whether in the family, the workplace, the university, or the military. Actors do this armed with differing forms of power to authorize their view.

To examine these contestations, social historians have explored the way Americans articulated and defended numerous identities—as immigrants, citizens, workers, Christians, or feminists, for example. A post–World War II male chemical worker may have thought of himself as a worker and trade unionist at the factory, a veteran and a Democrat in his civic community, a husband and father at home, and as a white, middle-class homeowner. A female civil rights worker in the South in the 1960s may have seen herself as an African American when in the midst of a protest march or when refused service in a restaurant, as working class during a day job as a domestic worker or nurse, and as a woman when struggling to claim a leadership role in an activist organization.

Social historians have revisited older sources and mined rich new veins of information on the daily lives of ordinary people. Social historians engage with a host of materials—from government documents to census reports, from literature to oral histories, and from autobiographies to immigrant and foreign-language newspapers—to illuminate the lives, ideas, and activities of those who have been hidden from history. Social historians have also brought a broad "toolbox" of new methodologies to shed light on these sources. These methodologies are well represented in this series and illustrate the innovations of history from the bottom up. These volumes offer many tables and charts, which demonstrate the ways historians have made creative use of statistical analysis. Furthermore, the volumes are rich in illustrations as examples of the new ways that social historians "read" such images as cartoons or photographs.

The volumes in this series reflect the new subject matter, debates, and methodologies that have composed the writing of the United States' 20th-century social history. The volumes have unique features that make them particularly valuable for students and teachers; they are hybrids that combine the narrative advantages of the monograph with the specific focus of the encyclopedia. Each volume has been authored or co-authored by established social historians. Where the work has been collaborative, the authors have shared the writing and worked to sustain a narrative voice and conceptual flow in the volume. Authors have written the social history for the decade of their expertise and most have also taught its history. Each volume begins with a volume introduction by the author or authors that lays out the major themes of the decade and the big picture—how the social changes of the era transformed the lives of Americans. The author then synthesizes the best and most path-breaking new works in social history. In the case of the last three volumes, which cover the post-1970 era, scholarship remains in its relative infancy. In particular, these three volumes are major original efforts to both define the field and draw upon the considerable body of original research that has already been completed.

The ten volumes in the series divide the century by its decades. This is an avowedly neutral principle of organization that does not privilege economic, political, or cultural transformations; this allows readers to develop their own sense of a moment and their own sense of change. While it remains to be seen how the most recent decades will be taught and studied, in cases such as the 1920s, the 1930s, and the 1960s, this decadal organization replicates how historians frequently study and teach history. The Progressive Era (ca. 1890–1920) and postwar America (ca. 1945–1960) have less often been divided by decades. This highlights the neutrality of this division. In truth, all divisions are imposed: we speak of long decades or short centuries, and so forth. When historians teach the 1960s, they often reach back into the 1950s and ahead into the 1970s. The authors and editors of these volumes recognize that social processes, movements, ideas, and leaders do not rise and fall with the turn of the calendar; therefore, they have worked to knit the volumes together as a unit.

Readers can examine these texts individually or collectively. The texts can be used to provide information on significant events or individuals. They can provide an overview of a pivotal decade. At the same time, these texts are designed to allow readers to follow changing themes over time and to develop their own sense of chronology. The authors regularly spoke with one another and with the series editors to establish the major themes and subthemes in the social history of the century and to sustain story lines across the volumes. Each volume divides the material into six or seven chapters that discuss major themes such as labor or work; urban, suburban, and rural life; private life; politics; economy; culture; and social movements. Each chapter begins with an overview essay and then explores four to six major topics. The discrete essays at the heart of each volume give readers focus on a social movement, a social idea, a case study, a social institution, and so forth. Unlike traditional encyclopedias, however, the narrative coherence of the single-authored text permits authors to break the decade bubble with discussions on the background or effects of a social event.

There are several other features that distinguish this series.

- Many chapters include capsules on major debates in the social history of the era. Even as social historians strive to build on the best scholarship available, social history remains incomplete and contested; readers can benefit from studying this tension.

- The arguments in these volumes are supported by many tables and graphics. Social history has mobilized demographic evidence and—like its sister field, cultural history—has increasingly turned to visual evidence, both for the social history of media and culture and as evidence of social conditions. These materials are not presented simply as illustrations but as social evidence to be studied.

- Timelines at the head of every chapter highlight for readers all the major events and moments in the social history that follows.

- A series of biographical sketches at the end of every chapter highlights the lives of major figures more often overlooked in histories of the era. Readers can find ample biographical material on more prominent figures in other sources; here the authors have targeted lesser known but no less interesting and important subjects.

- Bibliographies include references to electronic sources and guide readers to material for further study.

- Three indices—one for each volume, one for the entire series, and one for all the people and events in the series—are provided in each volume. Readers can easily follow any of the major themes across the volumes.

Finally, we end with thanks for the supportive assistance of Ron Boehm and Kristin Gibson at ABC-CLIO, and especially to Dr. Alex Mikaberidze and Dr. Kim Kennedy White, who helped edit the manuscripts for the press. But of course, these volumes are the product of the extraordinary group of historians to whom we are particularly indebted:

The 1900s: Brian Greenberg and Linda S. Watts
The 1910s: Gordon Reavley
The 1920s: Linda S. Watts, Alice L. George, and Scott Beekman
The 1930s: Cecelia Bucki
The 1940s: Mark Ciabattari
The 1950s: John C. Stoner and Alice L. George
The 1960s: Troy D. Paino
The 1970s: Laurie Mercier
The 1980s: Peter C. Holloran and Andrew Hunt
The 1990s: Nancy Cohen

Daniel J. Walkowitz, Series Editor
Daniel E. Bender, Series Associate Editor

Volume Introduction

THE MAKING OF MODERN AMERICA

"What is reform?" This is often asked at the beginning of class discussion of the late 19th and early 20th centuries, a period identified by historians as the Progressive era. Students invariably respond, "Change." When asked if this means any kind of change, they answer, "Change for the better." But better according to whom? Did Americans agree on what needed to be changed, or on how to effect change? And, above all, why did so many Americans at the outset of the 20th century appear to agree that reform was necessary?

One way to illustrate the complexity of these questions is to hand out for discussion a picture of downtown Chicago in 1905. In the picture, crowds of people on street corners frame a crossroads filled with a tangle of electric streetcars, horse-drawn trucks and other vehicles, a mounted policeman, and a few brave souls attempting to navigate the interchange. When asked to characterize the scene, most of the students reply, "Chaos." For them—as for most Americans in the early 1900s—the disorder of this scene exemplifies what, in *The Search for Order, 1877–1920,* the historian Robert Wiebe calls "a crisis in the community" (Wiebe 1967, 44). Wiebe portrays Americans during the late 19th century as viscerally sharing a sense of dislocation and bewilderment brought on by the sweeping changes that accompanied "the process of modernization" (Wiebe 1967, xiii–xiv). According to historians and social scientists, modernization encompassed intensified mechanization, the rise of giant corporations, and the movement of people from distant lands and from the farms of rural America into the nation's proliferating urban centers.

Industrial production in the United States boomed in the wake of the Civil War. Even though as late as the end of the 1860s water rather than steam still powered half of America's factories and the number of wage earners per manufactory averaged 8.15 workers, the direction of change was clearly toward large-scale industrial production. Overall, between 1860 and 1900, industrial production in the United States increased by more than five times, and the number of industrial workers quadrupled, becoming almost one-quarter of the nation's total workforce. The basic industries—coal, iron, and steel—experienced spectacular growth. In steel, for example, as output increased by more than 700 percent, capital investment rose by almost the same percentage, and the number of wage earners per steel mill increased by five times to average 330 workers. Whereas only a minority of the total firms in the United States employed more than 100 wage earners at the end of the 19th century, by 1909 more than 60 percent of the firms did so, with 28 percent of them each hiring more than 500 workers.

Large-scale industrialization meant more than big, highly mechanized factories that employed substantial numbers of semiskilled wage laborers. In mid-19th-century America, most businesses were family-owned operations that produced a small quantity of goods that they sold locally. Before 1880, the meatpacking industry, for example, was composed of a number of highly competitive small companies that shipped cattle east to be slaughtered near the towns where the meat would be consumed. However, after the Chicago meatpacker Gustavus Swift financed improvements in refrigeration technology and opened his own network of refrigerated warehouses, sales offices, and retail stores, he succeeded in centralizing the slaughter of cattle in Chicago and then shipping the "dressed beef" to markets in Eastern cities. Whereas in 1886, Swift owned a single plant that employed 1,600 workers, by 1903 Swift and Company operated seven packing houses that employed 23,000 people. Moreover, Swift developed a complex big business organization that brought together under his control every process of marketing and production. Each operation was coordinated through separate departments administered from the corporate headquarters in Chicago (Warner 1972, 96; Licht 1995, 133, 143–144). Even before the end of the 19th century, Swift and Philip Armour, along with other major meatpackers, led what was publicly denounced as the "Beef Trust."

Having taken on the functions of warehousing, transporting, and marketing in addition to slaughtering and processing, Swift had created a meatpacking empire through vertical integration. By the early 20th century, many other important industries were also dominated by a few large corporations or trusts. In the oil refinery industry, John D. Rockefeller successfully pioneered horizontal integration, the combining of competitors to form much larger enterprises that controlled one step in the production or sale of their products. In a wave of mergers in the half decade spanning the end of the 19th century and the beginning of the 20th, there were more than 300 such combinations involving more than

2,000 companies with total assets of almost $7 billion. In 1901, under the guiding hand of the financier J. P. Morgan, the Carnegie steel mills were combined with hundreds of other steel producers to form the largest of these mergers, the United States Steel Company. The nation's largest corporation, U.S. Steel controlled almost two-thirds of steel production in the United States (Hays 1957, 50). By 1904, some 300 corporations controlled more than two-fifths of all manufacturing, affecting the operations of about four-fifths of the nation's industries (Trachtenberg 1982, 4).

Many Americans regarded the formation of institutions of such concentrated economic power as a threat to the nation's cherished faith in itself as a land of opportunity. The "fate of each person" seemed increasingly determined by "distant forces" that the individual could neither see, understand, nor control (Link and McCormick 1983, 11). The loss of autonomy and the feeling of anxiety shared by many Americans, which are invoked by Wiebe, were vividly captured by the writer Theodore Dreiser in his novel *Sister Carrie* (1900). The novel's central character, Caroline Meeber, comes to Chicago in 1889 fresh from the Wisconsin countryside. Wandering the city's business district looking for work, Carrie is overwhelmed by a sense of helplessness brought on by the evidence of power and force in "the vast buildings" that surround her. Dreiser describes her confusion: "These strange energies and huge interests—for what purposes were they there? She could have understood the meaning of a little stonecutter's yard at Columbia City, whittling little pieces of marble for individual use, but when the yards of some huge stone corporation came into view, filled with spur tracks and flat cars, transpierced by docks from the river and traversed by immense trundling cranes of wood and steel overhead, it lost all significance and applicability to her world" (Dreiser [1900] 1981, 17). The triumph of big business and large-scale industrial capitalism in the 30 years or so after the end of the Civil War was accompanied by massive social changes that Americans grappled with in the 20th century's first decade and beyond.

By the early 20th century, virtually all manufacturing in the United States took place in cities. During the 1880s, as the value of production in manufacturing surpassed agriculture, roughly 100 cities, mostly located north of the Ohio River and east of the Mississippi, more than doubled in size, and the manufacturing centers of New York, Chicago, and Philadelphia all topped one million in population (Fink 2001, 116). The vast enterprises and expanded workforces these cities attracted fueled a radical transformation of urban America that went beyond increases in population and in physical space (Warner 1972, 98).

The late-antebellum city was a walking city, a place of shops, warehouses, factories, and homes where merchants, manufacturers, and laborers worked and lived within a physically compact and densely populated area. Relations among the social classes tended to be face-to-face personal contact. The community institutions and associations that these early city dwellers developed emphasized reciprocal connections and reinforced a sense of common good, bringing together members from the city's diverse social classes. In contrast, the 20th-century industrial metropolis was more spread out geographically and areas within the city took on specialized functions. In some 300 cities across the United States, urban technology, in particular the development of streetcar lines, enabled this spatial transformation. Outside the workplace, members of different social groups were no longer likely to share a common space. The old core of the city became the central business district—the industrial, commercial, and communications center of the metropolitan region. Those who could not afford to leave it remained crowded within the city's center while those more fortunate took advantage of the streetcar and other new forms of transportation, to live more comfortably in single-family homes in the suburbs. Contained within a square mile of downtown Chicago, an area which had so mystified Sister Carrie, could be found railway terminals and the city's business and professional offices, the wholesale and jobbing businesses, elaborate department stores and entertainment centers, hotels and many other features of early-20th-century urban life in America. For the new suburbanites, the older center city became a place in which to make money and to play.

The evolution of Boston as an urban metropolis exemplifies the fundamental changes that were remaking cities in the late 19th century. The industrial metropolis of Boston in 1900 was, according to the urban historian Sam Bass Warner, a divided city. The lower-income half of the population lived in the crowded older settlement, which also contained the main business institutions of the region. Outer areas differentiated by income and composed almost exclusively of single-family homes surrounded the central business district (Warner 1978, 1–3). To Wiebe, the physical expansion of the United States caused by development of a national system of railroads and other big enterprises had created a distended society, a nation without a core. No agency emerged that proved effective in replacing the power of the local community to manage people's lives (Wiebe 1967, 12). Warner describes a similar process that appears to have overtaken Boston. As life in modern Boston became increasingly more complex, community life, Warner concludes, became ever more fragmented and privatized. The new metropolis would prove incapable of responding to the general needs of the populace (Warner 1978, 12, 159–160). As a result, urban improvement to alleviate the worst consequences of modernization became the focus of reformers' efforts in the early 20th century.

Many of the poor who lived and worked in the older, core areas of the expanding cities were recently arrived immigrants. The pace of immigration greatly intensified beginning in the 1880s, reaching its apex in the first decade of the 20th century when some 8.8 million foreigners journeyed to the United States. By 1910, about three-quarters of these immigrants lived in cities; 50 percent of the industrial workforce was foreign-born, some two-thirds of whom came from southern and eastern Europe (Kraut 2001, 45). These immigrant newcomers represented a shift from the immigrants of northern and western European origin who had earlier characterized immigration to the United States. Both the vastly increased numbers and the more pronounced cultural differences of the Hungarians, Russians, Slavs, Greeks, Jews, and other "new" immigrants to the United States unsettled many native-born Americans.

The economic dislocations of the 1880s and 1890s led to an upswing in anti-immigrant sentiment. Many Americans, especially in the aftermath of the alleged anarchist Haymarket riots in Chicago in 1886, the growing wave of strikes during the final decades of the 19th century, and the assassination of President William F. McKinley by the foreign-born anarchist Leon Czolgosz in 1901, began to view the foreign-born as an "alien menace," subversive to the established order. Because nativists assumed that the immigrants' cultural backgrounds represented inherent, even racial, differences, they believed that these newcomers were incapable of adopting basic American values.

But not all Americans responded to the rising tide of immigration after 1880 with apprehension. For these Americans, the solution to the problem of the immigrants' foreignness was "Americanization," an understanding that viewed immigrants as capable of giving up their Old World values and being absorbed into the mainstream of American life. This process can be seen in the commencement exercises of the Ford Motor Company's English School. During this ceremony, an immigrant ship was represented on the stage of the largest hall in Detroit. Members of the motor company's diverse immigrant groups, dressed in their national garb, moved down a gangplank into a huge Ford melting pot set at the front of the stage. Then, using long ladles, the English School teachers stirred the contents of the pot. Soon the pot began to boil, and out came the immigrant workers now dressed in their American best and waving American flags (Daniels 1997, 93). Americanization in this formulation meant foreigners' divesting themselves of their past entirely and taking on the social and cultural habits of their adopted homeland.

Immigrants, however, were not simply victims of either nativists' antipathy or reformers' zeal to remake them according to an accepted American ideal. The reality of the immigrants' adjustment to life in the United States was more complex. Even as they adapted to a new way of life, immigrants often made choices that reflected their desire to retain their traditional values and patterns of behavior. Nor was the process of cultural transmission only one way, from the native-born to the immigrant, for what most Americans at the turn of the century took to be their unique cultural heritage was itself a product of interaction among the waves of immigrants that began well before the nation's founding. Still, behavior that may have been reasonable in the countryside or small towns of Italy, for example, did not necessarily make sense in the industrial cities of America. As the historian Virginia Yans-McLaughlin has shown, Italian men in Buffalo, New York, consciously chose more seasonal types of work—day laborer jobs that left them free to join their wives and children in the canning industry during the summers—over steadier and better-paying employment as unskilled workers in the city's steel mills. For Buffalo's Italian immigrants, the values associated with a family economy took precedence over the "American" value of maximizing individual opportunity (Yans-McLaughlin 1982, 41).

Intensified industrialization and the incorporation of big business, the swelling urban populations that expanded old cities and created new ones, and the massive migrations of newcomers to the United States had not only led to the breakdown of the familiar world of the small town "island communities" but also contained the seeds of a modern order (Wiebe 1967, xiii). A new middle class of physicians, lawyers, businessmen, scientists, engineers, industrial managers, and social workers arose that proved to be the key actors in the dissemination of a bureaucratic ethos that promoted a revolution in values based on professionalism, social scientific expertise, efficiency, and rationality (Rodgers 1982, 117–119). In the early decades of the 20th century, this middle class, which appears to have been an almost inevitable consequence of the rise of large-scale organization, sought to impose order and to address the problems caused by modernization by bureaucratic means (Wiebe 1967).

Wiebe's new middle class is portrayed very differently from the same groups that Richard Hofstadter views as members of a declining middle class, an older generation who found themselves overshadowed by a new governing elite of political bosses allied with railroad magnates and other corporate executives and financiers (Hofstadter 1955). Hofstadter offers a rather bleak portrait of the beleaguered white Anglo-Saxon Protestant progressive reformers. His middle-class progressives were not, as Wiebe would have it, exercising their newfound authority in large-scale organizations and professional associations but were instead victims of an upheaval in status who undertook reform to solve personal rather than societal problems (Link and McCormick 1983, 5–6).

Hofstader built his interpretation of progressivism on the work of his contemporaries, the historians George Mowry and Alfred Chandler, who had identified the older middle-class businessmen, lawyers, and other professionals as the main sources of progressivism. Their urban, middle-class interpretation of progressivism stood in stark contrast to the work of the early historians of the movement, who had been progressives themselves. To Charles A. and Mary Beard, Vernon Louis Parrington, and other progressive historians, the reform movement of the early 20th century represented a triumphant uprising of ordinary Americans against overweening wealth and privilege. In the 1960s, the New Left historians turned the tables on the older progressive interpretation. Instead of viewing progressivism as a victory of "the people" against "the interests," Gabriel Kolko and James Weinstein placed corporate leaders at the forefront of the progressive reform movement (Kolko 1963; Weinstein 1968). In their view, "corporate liberal" big business leaders, having abandoned their former faith in the laissez-faire doctrine of minimum government, encouraged and were the main beneficiaries of the regulatory legislation of the early 20th century (Link and McCormick 1983, 4–6).

Historians' conflicting interpretations about who the progressives were, as well as about their motives and objectives, led Peter Filene to declare in the *American Quarterly* "An Obituary for 'The Progressive Movement'" (1970). Filene correctly highlights the fluidity of progressive ideas and the lack of a coherent reform agenda. But he and the others who would bury progressivism cannot ignore the fact that there were Americans in the early 20th century who referred to themselves as "progressives" or who thought that their ideas were progressive. Historians persist in using this term as the common reference point to identify the first two decades of the 20th century. But as they continue their search for an elusive "Progressive Era," historians appear willing to embrace rather than fault the period's lack of coherence.

What cannot be contested was the growing consensus among Americans in the early 1900s that they needed both to constrain the highly individualistic laissez-faire order and to respond to the economic, political, social, and cultural changes that had been accumulating through the later decades of the 19th century. It is in this context that reform, broadly conceived, became the normative concept of the first decade of the 20th century. However, as has been noted, agreement on the need for reform did not mean consensus either on the nature of the problem or on its solution.

Progressivism's lack of coherence is evident in significant reform victories, the Pure Food and Drug Law and the Meat Inspection Act, both of which President Theodore Roosevelt signed into law on the same day in 1906. The former empowered the secretary of agriculture to imprison and to impose fines on producers caught selling adulterated or misbranded goods, and the latter authorized inspectors from the Department of Agriculture to go into the packinghouses to prevent bad meat from coming to market in the first place. The traditional story of this legislation credits Roosevelt with responding to an outraged public aroused by the publication earlier that year of *The Jungle,* Upton Sinclair's best-selling novel.

Yet a complete account of what lay behind these two regulatory reform laws is much more complicated. Sinclair, as a young socialist, wrote the novel as an indictment of the existing order, not as a call for public sympathy for reform legislation. As for Roosevelt, he was not just responding to the public outcry. He had not forgotten that in the late 1890s, during the Spanish-American War, his Rough Rider troops had suffered and even died from eating the rotten and impure "embalmed" beef that the packers had sold to the American army. Moreover, reform was not necessarily being imposed on a reluctant industry. When kept within proper guidelines, government regulation, such as represented by these two acts, could provide direct benefits to corporate enterprise. First, as early as the 1870s, European governments had banned importation of what they found to be unhealthy American meat. Earlier efforts to establish meat inspection in the United States had failed to change industry practices and open the European markets. But in 1906, U.S. meatpackers expected that once the sanitary

conditions imposed by the new legislation were certified by government inspectors, the world markets would again accept their products. Second, recall
that meatpackers like Swift and Armour had formed trusts as a means of limiting competition. Because regulatory legislation imposed a higher cost on doing
business, the laws served the interests of the large-scale corporate meatpackers
who could more easily absorb the greater costs and thereby undercut competitors who could not. Also, by appearing to embrace rather than resist regulation, the meatpackers could show the public that corporate enterprises were
capable of being "good citizens" and thus could forestall more restrictive legislation that might actually interfere with the internal operations of their business.
Less a victory for the people or for Roosevelt as their champion, the final "reform" laws reflected compromises that gave all interested parties—Roosevelt,
the public, and the corporations—some but not all of their objectives (Davidson
and Lytle 1982, 240–270). The history of this legislation enables us to respect
the dynamic aspect of progressive ideas so that we can better appreciate the contending social and political forces that shifted so rapidly around them (Rodgers
1982, 127).

Each of the themes to be explored in this volume accepts that the response of
Americans in the first decade of the 20th century to the social, political, economic, and cultural changes wrought by modernization was complex and dynamic. To explain the expectations and goals of business leaders, workers, social
reformers, African Americans, or any of the other diverse actors in this story,
the starting point will always be their own understanding of what they were doing. We begin by examining the restructuring of business and industry in the
United States. The emergence and rise to preeminence of giant corporations and
factories changed not only how business was conducted, as has been noted,
but also the way of life of all Americans. Efficiency and rationality became the
standard by which all institutions would be judged. Mirroring the bureaucratic
structure created to manage large-scale enterprise, the United States emerged as
a more tightly organized society "with new hierarchies of control that challenged
conceptions of America itself" (Trachtenberg 1982, 3–4). Even so fundamental
an American concept as mobility, the possibility to improve one's material conditions by becoming economically independent, was redefined in the process.

The changes brought on by the rise of corporate organization in the late 19th
century transformed the workplace and the nature of work itself. The composition of the working class became increasing synonymous with the blue-collar
wage worker in a factory, mill, coal mine, or sweatshop. Mechanization frequently
displaced older skills as workers became machine tenders. At the same time,
the bureaucratization of modern institutions and the emergence of new special-
izations, which fostered the rise of the new middle class that Wiebe puts at the
center of change, created white-collar jobs for managers, efficiency experts, store
clerks, and office workers. A struggle for control between industrial workers and
corporate capitalists evolved in the first decade of the 20th century as new asso-

ciations of labor emerged, especially industrial unions organized by immigrant workers. In addition, cigar makers, printers, and skilled workers in the building and other craft trades who had long belonged to the unions that made up the American Federation of Labor continued to fight for union recognition and collective bargaining. Life in immigrant, working-class neighborhoods was often dirty and hard. Nevertheless, both on the job and with their families at home, industrial workers resisted the bosses' efforts to assert control over them as they strove to build a better life.

The sociologist David Riesman has observed about the United States that "no other large industrial society has substituted color and ethnicity for social class as the basis for stratification and hence tension" (Dubofsky 1975, 9). Great waves of immigrants came to the United States during the latter decades of the 19th century through World War I. Historians of immigration speak of push and pull, those factors that compelled the immigrants to leave their homelands and those that attracted the immigrants to come to the United States. Migration, moreover, needs to be understood not as simply a one-way journey; many immigrants returned to their homelands rather than stay in America. Having brought with them expectations and a worldview based on their divergent homeland experiences and traditions, immigrants settled in the United States and made decisions about their new lives that balanced their need to adjust to the conditions they faced in modern America with their desire to retain traditional values derived from their heritage. Nationality-based social, cultural, economic, and political associations became primary agencies for the new immigrants' adjustment to life in America.

Beginning in the 1880s, immigrants to the industrial cities were joined by a migration from the cities and farms of the South. Finding themselves trapped in a cycle of continued dependency, racism, and violence, African Americans pushed out of the South in hopes of making a better life in Chicago, Detroit, Newark, New York, and other Midwestern and Northeastern cities. By 1900, 32 cities in the United States contained 10,000 or more African Americans. Victims of discrimination, these migrants frequently found factory doors closed to them. Nevertheless, their struggle for dignity continued, aided by the development of communal institutions and, in 1909, by the establishment of the National Association for the Advancement of Colored People (NAACP).

The city as a place to live and work was transformed in the early 20th century. As cities became more numerous, with greater populations, and physically larger, an urban way of life was created with its own institutions and associations. Cities could be fun. By the early 20th century, giant department stores that had become "palaces of consumption," ballparks for professional baseball teams, dance halls, amusement parks such as Coney Island in New York City, museums and other cultural institutions, legitimate and somewhat less so theaters, saloons, and other public establishments had emerged to entertain the nation's urban and suburban populations. The new urban environment also produced many challenges, such as how to house and provide basic public services to their vast and diverse populations. To meet these and other pressing needs, progressive reformers during the first decade of the 20th century worked together as members of countless voluntary associations and organized political movements that sought new laws or changes in policy.

As has already been established, progressivism is a hard concept to pin down. Yet even though they usually disagreed on means and on outcomes, the social reformers of the early 20th century each shared a faith in the possibility of ameliorating the worst consequences of modernization. Reformers also tended to see people as products of their environment. One impulse that motivated reform in these years emphasized coercion, the imposition of standards of behavior that reinforced the traditional moral values of sobriety and steady habits. Anti-drink reformers identified the liquor traffic and "Demon Rum" as the main source of disorder in America and joined the Anti-Saloon League (ASL) and other temperance movements that demanded that state and local governments restrict the sale and production of "spirituous liquors." Reform movements like the ASL relied on coercion as a way of achieving social control. For other progressives in the early 20th century, however, the poverty and harsh living conditions that the poor suffered in America's cities resulted from the inequities of the present order. These social progressives looked to provide the poor with more positive means to improve themselves. They opened settlement houses in the immigrant neighborhoods that provided clubs, classes, nurseries, and many programs that they intended, in the words of Jane Addams, the reformer most associated with this movement, as an "experimental effort to aid in the solution of the social and industrial problems which are engendered by the modern conditions of life in a great city" (Addams 1999, 95). Temperance and the settlement house are just two prime examples of movements that need to be looked at to understand Americans' reformist activism in the early 20th century.

A more radical challenge to the basic structure of modern industrial society was led by a diverse group of insurgents at the turn of the 20th century. For some, particularly the bohemians who collected in Greenwich Village early in the century, insurgency represented less a coherent movement than it did the adoption of an informal, more communal way of life as a self-conscious alternative to the accepted standards of personal and social behavior. Also sometimes informal but usually more well organized was the related assault on Victorian views on gender, especially on the role of women in society. At the core of the movement to gain suffrage rights for women in these years lay challenges to the accepted notions of domesticity and of men and women functioning in separate spheres. Still other insurgents viewed the injustices suffered by the working class to be a direct consequence of the basic social and economic arrangements of the capitalist system. The formation of the Socialist Party of the United States in 1901 and the organization of the Industrial Workers of the World four years later represent distinct efforts to transcend the prevailing capitalist political and economic order, efforts that found a receptive audience among a broad cross section of Americans in the first decade of the 20th century.

The flood of consumer goods that flowed out of America's factories produced a more standardized, mass consumption–oriented culture that challenged older values. Expectations changed as goods that once had been available only to a very narrow segment of society became mass produced, cheaper, and more accessible. Long-held ideas about leisure, about frugality and self-sacrifice, and about the good life were transformed by the new emphasis on consumerism. And this shift affected elite behavior and beliefs as much as it did the masses. Mass consumption, mass culture, and mass media became the accepted, if still contested, norm.

In the first decade of the 20th century, Americans confronted a host of problems brought on by modernization. As these changes are discussed in classes on the rise of modern America, students always notice that many of the core issues of those years—economic inequality, racism, the desire for a meaningful work experience, the concentration of economic power and privilege, gender relations, consumerism—remain with us today. Attempting to come to terms with what happened as the 20th century began can seem very much like a trip back to the future.

REFERENCES AND FURTHER READINGS

Addams, Jane. 1999. *Twenty Years at Hull-House*. Boston: Bedford/St. Martin's.

Chambers, John Whiteclay II. 1992. *The Tyranny of Change: America in the Progressive Era, 1890–1929*. New York: St. Martin's Press.

Chandler, Alfred D. 1959. "The Beginnings of 'Big Business' in American Industry." *Business History Review* 33 (Spring): 1–31.

Daniels, Roger. 1997. *Not Like Us: Immigrants and Minorities in America, 1890–1924*. Chicago: Ivan R. Dee.

Davidson, James West, and Mark Hamilton Lytle. 1982. *After the Fact: The Art of Historical Detection*. Vol. 2, 2nd ed. New York: Alfred A. Knopf.

Diner, Steven J. 1998. *A Very Different Age: Americans of the Progressive Era*. New York: Hill and Wang.

Dreiser, Theodore. 1981. *Sister Carrie*. New York: Penguin Books.

Dubofsky, Melvyn. 1975. *Industrialism and the American Worker, 1865–1920*. Arlington Heights, Ill.: Harlan Davidson.

Filene, Peter. 1970. "An Obituary for 'The Progressive Movement.'" *American Quarterly* 22:20–34.

Fink, Leon, ed. 2001. *Major Problems in the Gilded Age and the Progressive Era: Documents and Essays,* 2nd ed. Boston: Houghton Mifflin Company.

Harris, Neil. 1990. *Cultural Excursions: Marketing Appetites and Cultural Taste in Modern America.* Chicago: University of Chicago Press.

Hays, Samuel P. 1957. *The Response to Industrialism, 1665–1914.* Chicago: University of Chicago Press.

Hofstadter, Richard. 1955. *Age of Reform: From Bryan to FDR.* New York: Knopf.

Kolko, Gabriel. 1963. *Triumph of Conservatism: A Reinterpretation of American History, 1900–1916.* New York: Free Press.

Kraut, Alan M. 2001. *The Huddled Masses: The Immigrant in American Society, 1880–1921,* 2nd ed. Wheeling, Ill.: Harlan Davidson.

Licht, Walter. 1995. *Industrializing America: The Nineteenth Century.* Baltimore: Johns Hopkins University Press.

Link, Arthur S., and Richard L. McCormick. 1983. *Progressivism.* Arlington Heights, Ill.: Harland Davidson.

Porter, Glenn. 1973. *The Rise of Big Business, 1860–1910.* Arlington Heights, Ill.: AHM Publishing Corporation.

Rodgers, Daniel T. 1982. "In Search of Progressivism." *Reviews in American History* 10 (December): 113–132.

Trachtenberg, Alan. 1982. *The Incorporation of America: Culture and Society in the Gilded Age.* New York: Hill and Wang.

Warner, Sam Bass, Jr. 1978. *Streetcar Suburbs: The Process of Growth in Boston, 1870–1900.* Cambridge: Harvard University Press.

Warner, Sam Bass, Jr. 1972. *The Urban Wilderness: A History of the American City.* New York: Harper and Row.

Weinstein, James. 1968. *The Corporate Ideal in the Liberal State: 1900–1918.* Boston: Beacon Press.

Wiebe, Robert H. 1967. *The Search for Order, 1877–1920.* New York: Hill and Wang.

Yans-McLaughlin, Virginia. 1982. *Family and Community: Italian Immigrants in Buffalo, 1880–1930.* Urbana: University of Illinois Press.

Acknowledgments

I would like to express my deepest appreciation to many individuals for their time and assistance during the course of my researching and writing this book. In particular, I want to thank Donald Schmidt, Julie Dunbar, and Alex Mikaberidze at ABC-CLIO for their conscientious work on the manuscript; Kathy Shapiro, for finding many of the images I used in the book; and Danny Walkowitz and Dan Bender, for conceiving of the social history series and trying to keep me on track. At Monmouth University, Katie Parkin, Hettie Williams, and the librarians at the Guggenheim Library were especially helpful. I also owe a debt to Jules Plangere for all his help through the years and especially for his support, which enabled me to purchase many of the books I relied on to produce this book. As always, Susan Greenberg made certain I was clear in my writing and happy in my life.

DEDICATION

To the memory of Harry and Faye Greenberg, whose love for each other has always sustained me, and to Joseph and Anne Kofsky, for their enduring love for me and my family

Issues of the 20th Century

Corporate Capital in the Morgan Era

OVERVIEW

On the evening of December 15, 1880, New York's social elite gathered at an inauguration ball to celebrate the completion of the city's newest armory. In the aftermath of the Great Railroad Strike of 1877, New York and other cities across the nation constructed massive fortresses to preserve the public order and protect the homes of the upper classes against an expected threat from urban mobs. Located to be readily accessible to the wealthy members of the Seventh New York Regiment, the "rich man's regiment," the new armory functioned as an elaborate social club. Since their military training required "only a few hours each year," the regiment used the armory to hold frequent dances, teas, and polo matches to attract new members, or just gathered in the Tiffany-designed reception rooms to converse about the affairs of the day as they might do in the city's best private clubs. In an era that venerated the idea of laissez-faire, or limited state regulation, the new armory represented the willingness of the elite to use government for their own benefit. The Seventh Regiment's armory is just one example of the unprecedented influence that businessmen exerted over public policy and institutions during the late 19th century (Beckert 1993).

Class lines in the United States hardened in the aftermath of the Great Strike of 1877. Although outbreaks of labor strife had certainly been common in the United States before this time, these conflicts had largely been local brushfires. The 1877 strike, however, engaged hundreds of thousands of railway and other

1

workers and their supporters in communities across the nation, and marked the beginning of a new age of industrial conflict.

Historians refer to the decades after the railway strike as the Great Upheaval. During these years, strikes by U.S. workers averaged three per day. As they had in 1877, employers frequently responded by using both private and public forces against strikers. A reliance on armed force reflected the heightened class awareness among big business leaders in the United States. Paradoxically, the capitalists' willingness to utilize their economic and political power to serve their ends is at the same time evidence of their greater vulnerability. The very power that enabled the elite to employ the state to defend their economic interests created as well a crisis of legitimacy. During the 1880s and 1890s, both the militant nationwide labor movement and farmers in the South and West, along with their outspoken middle-class allies, rose in protest against the tremendous concentration of economic and political power wielded by large-scale corporations. By the final decade of the 19th century the established elite found themselves in a state of crisis, alarmed by an inherent instability in the order that they had created (Beckert 1993, 320–321).

Business leaders discovered that the giant combinations and pools that they had organized failed to contain the relentless competitive pressures that would come to a head in the depression of the 1890s, the worst the nation had yet experienced (Beckert 1993, 321–324). Between 1870 and 1900, the United States encountered more years of economic contraction than of economic growth. The House of Morgan, the financial empire headed by J. P. Morgan, led the effort during the final decade of the 19th century and the first decade of the 20th to bring the competitive market under control in what business and economic historians refer to as the "Morgan Era." Using the economic resources of his vast financial empire, Morgan, along with his allies from other leading New York banks, gained effective control over the business practices of many giant industries (Galambos and Pratt 1988, 5–16).

Although Morgan became the single most important force behind the merger movement that took place during the late 19th and early 20th centuries, the investment capitalist was less engaged by the effort to shape the administrative structure of the giant corporations that he helped to create. In modern enterprise, as Alfred Chandler, the dean of American business historians, has aptly observed, "the visible hand of management replaced what Adam Smith referred to as the invisible hand of market forces" (Chandler 1977, 1). Having displaced the small family-run firm, modern business was administered by a burgeoning corps of salaried managers. According to the 1901 annual report of the National Biscuit Company, formed four years earlier by the merger of three major biscuit producers, "when the company started it was an aggregation of plants. It is now an organized business." Rather than engage in a ruinous war with the competition, "we turned our attention and bent our energies to improving the internal management of our business" (Chandler 1959, 12).

Table 1.1. Manufacturing Output, 1890–1910 (metric tons)

Year	Pig iron (thousands)	Steel (thousands)	Coal (thousands)
1890	9,350	4,346	143,128
1900	14,011	10,352	244,653
1910	27,742	26,514	455,653

Source: B.R. Mitchell, International Historical Statistics (1983), 399–402, 453–454, 457. Adapted from Shifflett, 1996, 48.

A "managerial revolution" resulted from the structural changes in the organization of large-scale corporations during the late 19th and early 20th centuries. Internally, over a period of many years, the new giant corporations underwent a process of consolidation of administrative authority. Managerial functions that had previously been performed by owners were now carried out by specialists as part of a hierarchically arranged and permanent bureaucracy. These salaried managers—members of the "new middle class" that Robert Wiebe placed at the heart of progressivism—formed a new corporate elite. Yet these corporate managers served more as the servants of power in American life than as its masters.

Viewing themselves as professionals trained in the science of administration, these "scientific" managers sought to bring order and efficiency to all corporate operations but especially to production. In the decades spanning the onset of the 20th century, Frederick Winslow Taylor, frequently referred to as the "father of scientific management," publicized a blueprint for industrial efficiency, outlining the "one best way" that he had determined work must be performed. Even though corporate managers never fully implemented Taylor's elaborate system, they shared his goal of "scientifically" adjusting and controlling production.

Externally, local centers—the "island communities" that Wiebe has described—experienced a decline relative to the concentration of economic power in a score of interlocking metropolitan centers. For example, the National Biscuit Company spent the next several years after the merger not only improving the coordination of its manufacturing and marketing but also centralizing production in large-scale operations in New York and Chicago. In fact, Chicago's rise to become the nation's "second city" during the latter decades of the 19th century owed more to the city's financial ties to Eastern capital than to any physical advantages corresponding to its location (Cronon 1991, 82).

Outside interests tied to the House of Morgan also fueled the economic expansion of Milwaukee, another Midwestern city that had undergone rapid growth by the end of the 19th century. An integration of management, sometimes abetted by marriages among Milwaukee's leading families, took place at the same time as the city experienced a centralization of production. In Milwaukee and other industrial cities across the nation, the "best people" allied with

Eastern financial interests to form a national business elite. Increasingly what occurred in cities like Milwaukee, especially in, but not limited to, a city's economic sphere, would be a consequence of decisions reached in the corporate boardrooms of major companies such as International Harvester and U.S. Steel, and in the House of Morgan.

With Morgan's rise to power, after 1890 new values supplanted previously accepted ideas about the political economy. During the early post–Civil War decades, the industrialists John D. Rockefeller and Andrew Carnegie embraced Social Darwinism, the belief that human beings progressed through competition for survival. Rockefeller, in a sermon to a Sunday School class, avowed that "the growth of a large business . . . is merely the survival of the fittest, the working out of a law of nature and a law of God" (Trachtenberg 1982, 84–85). Similarly, in "Wealth," an essay he published in the *North American Review* in 1889, Carnegie pronounced that the law of competition "is here; we cannot evade it; no substitutes for it have been found; and while the law may sometimes be hard for the individual, it is best for the race, because it insures the survival of the fittest in every department" (Carnegie, 1889, 655). Having built their oil and steel empires to mitigate the negative consequences of excessive competition, these captains of the new corporate order still venerated a society built on the strong individual and the exercise of personal power.

Under Morgan's influence, cooperation replaced competition as the highest value among the business elite. Morgan looked to unite communities of interest among firms within the same industry as a means of restraining unbridled competition. The financial titan's business strategy rested on controlling price, competition, and production, thereby determining profits. In an address to the American Iron and Steel Institute in 1910, Elbert Gary, chair of the board of U.S. Steel and a Morgan associate, spoke of the manifold benefits of "enlightened" competition. Gary had founded the institute, whose members represented some 90 percent of American iron and steel makers, to establish mutual trust and cooperation. Gary noted that it was sometimes said that their effort to maintain "reasonable prices" was "opposed to the law of supply and demand." Not so. "Real, hearty, cheerful and continued cooperation on the part of the members" made much greater sense than "destructive competition" (Garraty 1960, 216).

Accepting the demise of the ruthless competitive entrepreneur and looking to develop a more stable economic environment through coordination and cooperation, leaders of large-scale corporations, many allied with the House of Morgan, came together in 1900 to launch the National Civic Federation (NCF). The NCF was the brainchild of Ralph Easley, a journalist and former schoolteacher who had converted from Populism and socialism to embrace the idea that a prosperous and democratic America could be built through the cooperation of labor and capital. Prominent in the NCF were corporate leaders, including several partners of Morgan, and such labor leaders as John Mitchell, the head of the United Mine Workers' Union, and Samuel Gompers, president of the American Federation of Labor and the NCF vice president until his death in 1924. In 1904, after unsuccessful efforts to develop mechanisms to mediate differences between business and labor, the NCF began promoting welfare capitalism, that is, nonwage benefits such as cleaner and safer workplaces, recreational and educational programs, and pecuniary rewards like profit sharing and pensions. Over the next decade, some 1,500 firms, mainly large corporations, devised some type of welfare work scheme.

Complex motives lay behind big business's endorsement of welfare capitalism. In the first decade of the 20th century, the newly created business trusts faced persistent and growing efforts by reformers to engage the government in either breaking up or, failing that, regulating these "soulless" corporations. Corporate leaders envisioned that the liberal benefits provided through welfare plans would create a more positive, "good trust," image for their business empires. The National Cash Register Corporation, a pioneer in these efforts, titled its welfare pamphlet *The Human Side of Industry* and adopted as the program's slogan "welfare work is the heart of business" (Marchand 1998, 18). Moreover, at the same time as reformers censured corporations for their antisocial practices, a militant labor movement demanded union recognition and better wages and working conditions. Corporate owners hoped that their welfare initiatives would deter "loyal" workers from joining unions. A 1909 letter from George Perkins to the NCF highlights the multifaceted appeal of the comprehensive welfare program that he had instituted at International Harvester: "If, as many of us have come to believe, co-operation in business is taking and should take the place of ruthless competition,—if this new order of things is better for capital and better for the consumer, then in order to succeed permanently it must demonstrate that it is better for the laborer; and if profit sharing, pensions, insurance, and the like mean anything, they must mean co-operation between capital and labor,—co-operation in the broadest, most helpful and enduring form" (Ozanne 1967, 73). In the early 20th century, the leaders of big business like Perkins adopted welfare practices both to resolve the crisis in industrial relations and to legitimize the new corporate economic order (Beckert 1993, 325–326).

Corporate capital advanced welfare work as a private means of forestalling state regulation. Yet as big business leaders demonstrated in their willingness to turn to government to quell "labor troubles," they could also endorse state action when such policies might be made to serve their ends. By the first decade of the 20th century, the ideal of cooperation eulogized by Perkins and other big business members of the NCF included not only the private welfare programs undertaken by corporations such as International Harvester and U.S. Steel but also the political campaigns on behalf of public programs such as the workmen's compensation laws that most states outside the South passed before World War I. Still wary of ceding control to government, the NCF was, nevertheless, willing to engage the state on behalf of those reforms that would further stabilize the system of large corporations and legitimize the authority of the corporate capitalist class.

TIMELINE

1901   The National Civic Foundation (NCF) is founded.

U.S. Steel is organized; Charles Schwab is the company's first president.

1903   International Harvester is formed.

U.S. Steel's profit-sharing plan is instituted.

Maryland enacts the first state workmen's compensation law; it is declared unconstitutional in 1904.

Streetcar conductors strike in Terre Haute, Indiana.

1904   *Shop Management* by Frederick Winslow Taylor is published.

Gertrude Beeks becomes the first director of the National Civic Federation's Welfare Department.

Elbert H. Gary is named chair of U.S. Steel's board of directors.

1905   National Civic Federation holds the first Conference on Welfare Work.

1907   J. P. Morgan organizes the financial resources to stabilize the U.S. economy in the wake of the Panic of 1907.

1908   George Perkins delivers a lecture, "The Modern Corporation."

The Harvard Business School is founded.

A workmen's compensation system is established for civilian employees working for the federal government.

1909   Scientific management is introduced at the Watertown Arsenal, Massachusetts.

THE MORGAN ERA

Between 1892 and 1902, John Pierpont Morgan masterminded the mergers that led to the formation of General Electric, American Telephone and Telegraph, and International Harvester. But the crowning achievement of Morgan's financial career was the formation in 1901 of U.S. Steel, the nation's first billion-dollar corporation. The year before, Morgan had heard Charles Schwab, president of Carnegie Steel, present his vision of the economic benefits that would be derived from a unified steel industry guided by a single huge producer. Inspired, Morgan questioned Schwab and expressed interest in purchasing Carnegie Steel. Andrew Carnegie agreed to sell his company to Morgan for $492 million dollars, and Morgan then acquired eight of Carnegie's largest competitors as well. Next, Morgan reorganized these acquisitions into U.S. Steel. The new giant company comprised 156 major factories and controlled some two-thirds of steel production in the United States (Heilbroner and Singer 1999).

Born in 1837 in Hartford, Connecticut, Morgan came of age in the family-centered and more personal business environment of 19th-century entrepreneurial capitalism. His grandfather Joseph Morgan III had invested in many businesses that contributed to making Hartford a transportation hub. J. P.'s father, Junius Spencer Morgan, was connected early in his career with Howe and Mather, a firm that engaged in wholesale dry goods merchandising and had ties to the growing cotton economy of the South. Morgan worked in his father's firm, transacting business whose success depended on personal contact and mutual trust. Howe and Mather was typical of entrepreneurial firms of the era, where decisions were made by one or two owners, who usually had used their own savings to start the business and who relied on personal connections to local banks to finance its growing operations. In 1835, J. S. Morgan earned the family name a reputation for trustworthiness when his Aetna Fire Insurance Company paid every claim on a fire that razed 17 blocks of New York's financial district (Galambos and Pratt 1988, 17–18).

After the Civil War, the need for capital to support an expanding economy made banking a key industry. In 1850, there were some 800 to 900 banks in the United States; by 1900, the industry had reached 13,000 banks, and that number would more than double in the next decade. The increasing influence of financial men in the economy accompanied the growth of banks. Through the 1880s, the New York Stock Exchange listed few industrial companies; even the largest, Carnegie Steel, was privately owned. Although there was no Dow Jones Industrial Average until the mid-1890s, 1,000 companies were publicly traded by 1901.

In 1871, J. P. Morgan became a partner in the investment bank of Drexel, Morgan and Company, which would be reorganized in 1895 as J. P. Morgan and Company. During the 1880s and 1890s, Morgan-connected investment banks helped finance the consolidation of the nation's rail industry. In negotiating mergers among major rail systems, Morgan looked to stabilize the industry by minimizing ruinous rate wars and rail line competition. As a member of the board of directors of the merged companies, Morgan, at the end of the 1890s, presided over a rail empire that covered one-sixth of the nation's rail lines (Fraser 2005, 166). By 1904, some 1,040 separate American rail lines had been unified into six huge combinations that controlled almost $10 billion of American capital (Cochran and Miller 1961, 191).

Having encouraged corporate consolidation among railroads, Morgan and other leaders of what reformers labeled the "Money Trust" orchestrated, during

Caricature of J. P. Morgan as a bull blowing bubbles labeled "inflated values," from a 1901 issue of Puck. *Morgan helped to create some of the largest trusts and monopolies during his lifetime, which gave companies control over prices and competition. (Library of Congress)*

the last years of the 19th century and the opening of the 20th, the merger movement that combined rival companies into giant new corporations that dominated their industries. For underwriting these mergers, Morgan took home about 20 percent of the more than $4 billion in new securities. By 1904, the House of Morgan and its allies from other leading New York banks controlled 341 directorships in 112 corporations whose total resources, in 1912, were more than $22 billion—more than the assessed value of all property in the 22 states and territories west of the Mississippi. The "great monopoly" in the United States, Woodrow Wilson proclaimed, was "a monopoly of big credits. So long as that exists, our old variety and freedom and individual energy of development are out of the question" (Cochran and Miller 1961, 193). Wilson was expressing the anxiety shared by many Americans that the monopoly control by the Money Trust was dramatically altering the dynamic by which power and authority were exercised in the United States.

Morganization and the Island Community

Robert Wiebe has described the loss of control many Americans felt as they experienced the transformation of their local communities that accompanied the

Table 1.2. Employed in Occupations, 1890–1910

Occupation	1890	%	1900	%	1910	%
Agriculture, Forestry, and Fishing	10,170	(42.8)	10,920	(37.6)	11,590	(31.6)
Extractive Industries	480	(2.0)	760	(2.6)	1,050	(2.9)
Manufacturing	4,750	(20.0)	6,340	(21.8)	8,230	(22.4)
Construction	1,440	(6.1)	1,660	(5.7)	2,300	(6.3)
Commerce and Finance	1,990	(8.4)	2,760	(9.5)	3,890	(10.6)
Transportation and Communications	1,530	(6.4)	2,100	(7.2)	3,190	(8.7)
Services	3,210	(13.5)	4,160	(14.3)	5,880	(16.0)
Other	170	(0.7)	370	(1.3)	600	(1.6)
Total	23,740	(100)	29,070	(100)	36,730	(100)

Source: International Historical Statistics, 154. Adapted from Shifflett 1996, 54.

growing consolidation of industry and wealth during the late 19th century. A typical "island community" was Terre Haute, Indiana, a small, pre-industrial city located on the banks of the Wabash River. Between 1850 and 1870, Terre Haute's population had soared by 300 percent. Five different railroads serviced the town, which ranked 5th of 92 counties in Indiana in manufacturing. For many years, the local elite's substantial political and economic power rested on close personal ties and a shared faith in democratic ideals. But in 1870, Terre Haute stood poised on the edge of dramatic change (Salvatore 1982, 12).

A native son of Terre Haute, born on November 5, 1855, Eugene V. Debs was a four-time Socialist Party candidate for president and the leader of an insurgent movement against corporate capital. Having absorbed the lessons of hard work, industry, and individual success at home and in school, Debs entered the workforce as a paint scraper for the Vandalia Railroad, a company owned by William Riley McKeen and other local investors. Debs rose quickly and soon became a fireman for the railroad. In 1873, he signed up as a charter member of Vigo Lodge No. 16 of the Brotherhood of Locomotive Firemen. Elected and reelected as an officer of the lodge, in 1883 Debs became the secretary-treasurer of the national union and editor of its journal.

McKeen, one of Terre Haute's leading citizens, owned numerous local enterprises and was quite active in the community's religious and cultural associations. At this point, both Debs and McKeen believed in the moral qualities of "manhood," that is, a shared a faith in the potential of each individual to secure the promises of American life, and the conviction that a harmony of interests existed among all members of the community (Salvatore 1982, 13–17). McKeen became Debs's patron and encouraged the young man's success. The railroad president loaned Debs $1,000 to rebuild the Brotherhood after the 1877 strike,

Russell Conwell: "Acres of Diamonds"

In 1908 at age 65, Russell Conwell, a Civil War veteran, attorney, clergyman, and noted public lecturer, embarked on a speaking tour that took him across the country where he addressed audiences in 17 states some 62 times. In at least 10 communities, Conwell, the pastor of Grace Baptist Church in Philadelphia and founder and president of Grace Temple College (now Temple University), delivered his most popular lecture, "Acres of Diamonds." Having first given this lecture to a Civil War veterans group 35 years earlier, Conwell is said to have presented "Acres of Diamonds" more than 6,000 times during his lifetime. In one rural community, his local guide reported that the audience "just sat in amazement. . . . I don't know of anything to be more inspiring than his lecture on 'Acres of Diamonds'" (Carter 1981, 655–669).

Before Conwell's death in December 1925, millions heard his inspirational lecture from pulpits and public platforms as well as on the radio. "Acres" was a parable of the success that Conwell believed was within the grasp of the self-made man in America. Conwell urged his listeners to take advantage of the "acres of diamonds" that could be found "in your own backyard" rather than search for riches in far-off places. He preached that it was one's "Christian and godly duty" to become rich. His numerous stories retell the example of a poor man who makes millions "accidentally" by transforming readily available materials into a popular toy or by inventing useful things, such as the pencil eraser. During the sermon, Conwell would mention his many "pious brethren" who ask him why he does not just preach the gospel rather than preach about making money, to whom he would reply, "Because to make money honestly is to preach the gospel." He insisted that 98 out of every 100 rich men were honest, which is why "they are trusted with money." Yet he agreed that a selfish person who simply idolizes money, "who refuses to invest it where it will do the world good," is evil. The wealthy were only stewards of the riches entrusted to them by God; they must use their money for holy purposes. "Money is power," he preached, "and you ought to be reasonably ambitious to have it . . . because you can do more good with it than you could without it" (Conwell 1975, 26). Although Conwell made a fortune from "Acres of Diamonds," he used much of his earnings to help needy students, to found Temple College, and to support his church.

and, in 1880, he guaranteed the union leader's bond when Debs became secretary of the association.

McKeen's commitment to the ideal of a common citizenship of all members of the local community faded as he developed relationships with extra-local industrial and financial interests. Between 1880 and 1900, Terre Haute's population increased by some 40 percent, and corporations were formed to provide the growing city with water service, electricity, and both intra- and interurban transportation. Although an expansion fever fueled by the discovery of oil—"a perfect gusher" within the city's limits—proved to be short-lived, the investment opportunities forged further links between the local elite and outside financial interests (Salvatore 1982, 86). In 1877, McKeen had been one of the few local businessmen who had ties to significant corporations; by 1900, as local investors in the city's infrastructure sold out their interests to corporations based in Chicago and Boston, such contacts became far more numerous among Terre Haute's elite.

During the late 1880s and 1890s, Debs's worldview also underwent a radical transformation. Strikes that he led against the Chicago, Burlington & Quincy Railroad in 1888 and the Pullman Palace Car Corporation in 1894 convinced Debs that a new corporate power had emerged in the United States that threatened the traditional community values of 19th-century America. Over the next two decades, Debs became a catalyst for those forces resisting the revolutionary changes being wrought by an industrial capitalist system presided over by powerful national corporations and financial institutions.

By 1900, Terre Haute had become fully integrated into the ascendant industrial capitalist order in the United States. The city's industries, including the railroad, a new large machine shop, the ironworks, and even the local streetcar company, were now owned by nonresident investors. A strike by streetcar conductors in 1902 exposed the growing class divide between the local elite allied with outside corporate interests and Terre Haute's working-class citizens. Even before the strike began, McKeen and other local businessmen had founded the Citizens' Protective League to oppose unions and protect league members and the community from labor strife. The conductors walked out after Stone and Webster, the Boston-based owners of the streetcar company, fired union leaders who had requested a reduction in the 12-hour workday. The conductors quickly called on Debs and asked him to direct their strike. Debs denounced McKeen and the league for its support of the streetcar company's refusal to negotiate. The three-month-long strike ended in a bitter defeat for the union. By the first years of the 20th century, in Terre Haute, as in many other cities and towns across the United States, local civic leaders had become fully integrated into a national elite. A consequence was the loss of formerly acknowledged reciprocal obligations of community. By 1902, Debs and McKeen were class enemies (Salvatore 1982, 181–182).

George W. Perkins and "The Modern Corporation"

In December 1907, as the recent financial panic was receding, Columbia University announced a series of lectures intended to provide the public with "a better understanding of the situation" (Garraty 1960, 216). After lectures by prominent Wall Street figures on such topics as the stock exchange and banking, the last talk, "The Modern Corporation," was given by George W. Perkins, a banker and insurance industry executive and a Morgan partner. An outspoken critic of the evils of competition, Perkins extolled the advantages of cooperation in business. His biographer, John A. Garraty, has summarized Perkins's approach to free enterprise: "Competition is cruel, wasteful, destructive, outmoded; co-operation, inherent in any theory of a well-ordered Universe, is humane, efficient, inevitable, and 'modern'" (Garraty 1960, 216).

Perkins often used language reminiscent of Charles Darwin's theory of evolution to support his own theory that the modern corporation represented the highest stage of development. For Perkins, the modern corporation—that is, the present organization of business—was simply a fact of life, "the working of natural causes of evolution" (Perkins 1908). The days when business was a local affair were long gone, displaced by the development that accompanied steam and electricity, and the "inevitable" expansion of trade. Yet, according to Perkins, the "real cause of the corporation" was not the "selfish aims of a few men," but the "imperative necessities of all men" (Perkins 1908).

Perkins described the first stage of corporate development as destructive competition: "A invaded B's territory and B retaliated. The fighting became faster and more furious" (Perkins 1908). Labor suffered and the public suffered. As the cost of doing business escalated, the great corporation came into existence to prevent waste by raising the standard of efficiency. The need for efficient administration of the modern corporation ensured that rather than those persons who had the greatest influence rising to the top only those with "the highest order of ability" would meet the "supreme test of fitness" (Perkins 1908).

Yet despite these advances, the modern corporation was still only in its formative state. Two courses are open to us, Perkins observed, either "to kill it or to keep it." But, he added, no one suggests that corporations be abolished; instead, "we have bent our energies towards regulating and controlling them." Ever the exponent of the ideal of the "good trust," Perkins did not deny the need to take a "broader view" of the management of corporations from "the standpoint of the community of interest principle." Managers, he recommended, must think of themselves as "semi-public servants, responsible not only to their stockholders, but to the public as well." Ownership of the corporations of the future should be "widespread among the public" and treat labor "fairly and equitably" so that the public would look upon these enterprises as "its friend and protector rather than as an ever-present enemy." Thus, the modern corporation, by the "cooperative principle," would be more "humane" and "uplifting" for all (Perkins 1908). A sophisticated and dedicated exponent of welfare capitalism, Perkins encouraged corporate leaders to accept the social responsibility that attached to their dominate position in society.

J. P. Morgan and the Panic of 1907

The system of banking in the United States proved to be highly susceptible to financial panics. Often triggered when depositors suddenly withdrew their assets, forcing the banks to quickly sell their securities, panics occurred with some regularity. In 1895, with the country mired in an economic depression, J. P. Morgan formed a syndicate that restored confidence in the nation's financial system by underwriting the sale of U.S. bonds. In 1907, when a run on banks caused by a stock market panic on October 16 threatened to wreak havoc on banks and corporations, Morgan again organized the resources of the banking and investment community to stabilize the country's financial system.

Office of J. P. Morgan & Co., New York, ca. 1900–1906. (Library of Congress)

At a midnight meeting in his New York City mansion, Morgan is said to have announced, "This, then, is the place to stop this trouble" (Cochran 1957, 83). Thereupon he decided which institutions would be saved and which would be allowed to fail. Morgan strong-armed reluctant bank presidents into subscribing funds for emergency loans and used a large reserve authorized by the secretary of the treasury to supply liquid funds for "approved" banks and trust companies.

Although at the time many Americans expressed gratitude for Morgan's intervention, his actions confirmed the suspicions others had of the inordinate power held by the Money Trust, and the critics demanded banking reform. Chaired by Sen. Nelson Aldrich of Rhode Island, in 1911 the National Monetary Commission conducted studies of federal banking policies. The commission's recommendations led to the creation, two years later, of the Federal Reserve System.

THE LEISURE CLASS

On February 10, 1897, about 700 persons prominent in the "society circles" from cities across the nation gathered in New York City to attend a fancy costume ball at the Waldorf-Astoria Hotel. The hosts, Bradley Martin, a prominent lawyer, and his wife, Cornelia, who wore a necklace said to have been owned by Marie Antoinette, greeted such prominent guests as J. P. Morgan, who was dressed as

Metropolitan Opera House, New York, ca. 1908. (Library of Congress)

the French playwright Molière, the real estate mogul John Jacob Astor, who came wearing a Henry of Navarre costume, and Caroline Astor, who had gems worth $250,000 sewn into her dress. The Martin Ball's ostentatious display represented, according to *The New York Times,* "the climax" of these forms of entertainment put on by the "society of the metropolis" (Beckert 1993, 1). Such wasteful extravagance in the midst of the widespread deprivation generated by the Panic of 1893 led to sweeping condemnation and forced the Martins into permanent exile in England.

Conjoining economic wealth with unprecedented social, cultural, and political power, a self-conscious upper class developed during the final decades of the 19th century. John D. Rockefeller and J. P. Morgan founded family dynasties whose social leadership and cultural prestige were advanced through intermarriage with fellow members of the social and political elite. A Rockefeller daughter married the younger son of Cyrus McCormick, whose company in Chicago dominated the agricultural implements industry, and, in 1901, John D. Rockefeller Jr. wed Abby Aldrich, the daughter of Rhode Island senator Nelson Aldrich. Designated the "Boss of the United States" by the muckraking author Lincoln Steffens, Aldrich chaired the Senate's finance committee from 1899 to

1911, the years during which the upper house was known as the "Millionaires' Club" because as many as one-third of its members were that wealthy (Dawley 2005, 154–157).

By the early 20th century, business tycoons such as Morgan, Rockefeller, and Carnegie had for some time applied their great fortunes to endowing museums, libraries, and orchestras. New York's Metropolitan Museum of Art, founded in 1870 by members of the elite Union Club, built its collections through gifts from wealthy benefactors. Morgan, who was president of the Metropolitan Museum from 1901 until his death in 1913, donated his own collection of medieval and Renaissance works to the museum. In 1880, the established Knickerbocker elite at the New York Academy of Music turned down William H. Vanderbilt's offer of $30,000 for a box at the opera house. In retaliation, Vanderbilt, joined by Morgan, William Rockefeller, Jay Gould, and other members of New York's fashionable society, built the opulent Metropolitan Opera House, which opened in 1883. With space for 70 plush private boxes, the new opera house quickly supplanted the Academy of Music, forcing it to close.

Conspicuous Consumption

Thorstein Veblen published *The Theory of the Leisure Class* in 1899 as a scathing satire of such upper-class frivolity as the Martin Ball, which had occurred two years earlier. To Veblen, costly entertainments like costume balls epitomized conspicuous consumption, the purchase of goods that takes place not for the pleasure or the satisfaction of the consumer, but to confirm one as the possessor of wealth. The leisure class, Veblen observed in *Theory* "stands at the head of the social structure in point of reputability" (Veblen 1899, 63). The way in which "good repute in any highly organized industrial community ultimately rests is pecuniary strength; and the means of showing pecuniary strength" (Veblen 1899, 63–64). Just as "a cheap coat makes a cheap man," so too does the purchase of an expensive and nonessential good demonstrate privilege. The wealthy choose clothing not for comfort but for display, as evidence of their pecuniary standing. With clearly intended irony, Veblen discusses the "honorific" value of owning domestic animals like cats, dogs, or fast horses. Domestic animals, he observed, "owe their place" to their "non-lucrative character alone." For being less wasteful, a cat is less reputable, whereas a dog has the "advantage in the way of uselessness. . . . The dog, then, commends himself to our favor by affording play to our propensity for mastery, and as he is also an item of expense, and commonly serves no industrial purpose, he holds a well-assured place in men's regard as a thing of good repute" (Veblen 1899, 103–104).

Born in Wisconsin in June 1857, Veblen taught at a number of colleges, including the University of Chicago (1892–1906). In addition to *The Theory of the Leisure Class,* he published many works critical of classical economic theory. In

1973, the economist John Kenneth Galbraith called *Theory* one of the two books by American economists of the 19th century that was still read. Because he wrote about the leisure class as if he were examining the customs of an exotic and primitive culture, Veblen is said to have approached the American scene as though he were an anthropologist. Veblen anticipated that an emergent "new class" of salaried technicians and professionals would displace this fading aristocracy. By incorporating the values of the professional and managerial classes, the "leisure class" revitalized itself and proved itself capable of adapting to change and retaining its power.

Custodians of Culture

Although the elites' involvement in building cultural institutions may have been more self-consciously earnest than their participation in costume balls, the social functions of the two endeavors were not all that dissimilar. The cultural critic Lewis Mumford has described the patronage of museums in the late 19th century "by the ruling metropolitan oligarchy of financiers" as "ostentatious and grasping," an attempt to "establish their own claims to culture" (Harris 1962, 546). Earlier in the 19th century, rather than construct temples of prestige and privilege, the patrons of cultural institutions had desired that these enterprises be popular. For example, less interested in making the museum a treasure house of original masterpieces, the founders of one of the first public museums, the Boston Fine Arts Museum, which was incorporated in 1870, used reproductions "to bring these [works] within the reach of our people" (Harris 1962, 553). The museum was an immediate popular success, attracting in its first year 17,000 paid visitors and more than 140,000 free visitors. Still earlier in the century, art unions enrolled tens of thousands and offered their members the chance to enter lotteries for engraved copies of the most prized artworks. The emphasis was on participation.

In the latter decades of the 19th century, however, members of the emergent financial and industrial class became the custodians of culture, creating elaborate and exclusive institutions as a means of fortifying their position in society. Their wealthy patrons insisted that the museums, opera houses, and symphonies they established be run in a businesslike manner. Control over these cultural institutions was invested in trustee boards. The Board of Trustees of the Boston Symphony, for example, adopted time schedules and enforced discipline, including threats to dismiss resistant musicians. Disparaged for their motley appearance earlier, symphony audiences, consisting of the well bred and middling to wealthy, became more decorous. "Full-dress" was now the required costume for attendance at symphonies. For the elite, sovereignty over cultural institutions was transformed into a means of demonstrating social standing, their badge of membership in an exclusive ruling class rather than in an inclusive municipal community.

In the 1880s and 1890s, private boarding schools such as Groton (1884), the Hotchkiss School (1897), St. George's School (1896), Choate (1896), Middlesex School (1902), and the Kent School (1906) emerged as institutions for socializing the children of the corporate elite from all regions of the country. The nature of the socialization that the trustees of these "prep schools" expected to take place underwent significant change. Still aimed at preparing the sons of the privileged elite for rule, the founders of the Groton School chose George Peabody as the school's first head. Peabody instituted a Spartan discipline intended to restore the physical and moral will that many feared was being lost among the families of the "leisured" rich (Lears 2005, 193–196). In a series of lectures that would be published in 1900, Theodore Roosevelt, a product of New York's privileged elite, preached against a life of "ignoble ease" of the type consecrated by the Martin Ball, insisting instead that the "highest form of success" comes only from a life marked by "strenuous endeavor" (Roosevelt 1899). For the corporate elite, the privileged prep school became the first step on a career path that led through an Ivy League college into an executive position in a blue chip corporation, top investment house, or prominent law firm.

By the turn of the 19th century, education, especially in private academies, colleges, and universities, had become a distinctive badge for the corporate elite. In the last third of the century, when few Americans attended college, 40 percent of the corporate elite had had some college education (Cochran 1972, 160–161). For the sons of the wealthy, the "old school tie," that is, the opportunity to meet and form friendships with others from their social class from across the nation, was a primary motivator for attending college, particularly an elite college such as Harvard or Yale. Yet wealthy students had attended these elite schools for much the same reason earlier in the century. What had changed was that the student body of these institutions had become more broadly national. In 1889, Jack Morgan, the son of J. P., became the first member of his family to graduate from Harvard. He was soon joined by the sons of the Roosevelts and the

The Low Library, Columbia University, New York, ca. 1900–1910. During the early 20th century Columbia, like other elite colleges, practiced selective admissions to maintain an upper-class student body. (Library of Congress)

Fishes, families whose members had traditionally attended New York's Columbia College. To reverse this trend, Columbia, in the early 20th century under its president, Nicholas Murray Butler, pioneered in establishing selective admissions policies intended to make the school more appealing to its "natural constituency" among the native-born elite, as well as to restrict entry of "socially backward" groups like Eastern European Jews (Wechsler 1977).

In addition to functioning as social networks, elite colleges and universities began to prepare the scions of upper-class families to assume their rightful place as leaders of modern corporate America. As early as 1885, President Charles Eliot of Harvard argued that the college should offer more training and guidance for students who increasingly were choosing to enter careers in industry and finance rather than pursue more traditional careers in the ministry, law, medicine, and education. Under Eliot's prodding, the Harvard Business School was founded in 1908 to provide the necessary technical training for students aspiring to the corporate aristocracy. The business school's first dean, Edwin F. Gay, developed many of the practices that informed business school education in the United States. The chair of General Electric, Owen D. Young, apparently wondered why Harvard had waited so long: "Is one to conclude that Harvard was fearful of an illiterate ministry in 1636 but was not apprehensive of an illiterate ministry of business until 1908?" (Commons 1935).

THE MANAGERIAL REVOLUTION

Colleges and universities in the late 19th century functioned as the training ground for members of the "new middle class" in business and the professions that Wiebe placed at the center of 20th-century urban-industrial society. In a speech to the American Bar Association in 1910, rather than mark the triumph of a trained technical elite in the United States, Woodrow Wilson chose to address the loss of individuality that he and many of his contemporaries believed accompanied the rise of the financial oligarchy led by the House of Morgan: "There is more individual power than ever, but those who exercise it are few and formidable, and the mass of men are mere pawns in the game" (Cochran and Miller 1961, 194). Between 1890 and 1915, about 250,000 men formed the core of those executives who ran big business in the United States. In addition to these policy-making executives, the restructuring of large-scale corporate enterprise created a career path for the managerial and professional middle class that, if it did not achieve the autonomy that Wiebe assigned to it, nevertheless opened up opportunities for advancement for the children (mainly the sons) of small-town and old-stock families (Bendix 1956, 226–229).

Middle-class managers—the leaders of functional departments and other specialized operations within the organizational structure of the giant enterprises—

served as subordinates to the ultimate authority of the owners. In any large-scale organization such as a big business corporation, the "bureaucratic official" is always, the sociologist Max Weber observed, appointed by and subject to "a higher functionary" (Miller 1952, 288–89). Typical of the bureaucrats who climbed the ladder to the top, Charles S. Mellen had begun his career as a clerk in the cashier's office of the Northern New Hampshire Railroad. From this humble start, he spent almost the next quarter of a century moving up through successive positions with various New England railroads to become vice president of the New York, New Haven, and Hartford. In 1897, he became president of the Northern Pacific Railroad only to return seven years later to the New Haven as president. Regarded as "The Railroad Lord of New England," Mellen proudly attributed his success to his loyalty to his superiors: "I took orders from J. P. Morgan, Sr. I did as I was told." After Morgan died in 1913, Mellen, not unexpectedly, lost his presidency of the New Haven line. Mellen and men like George F. Baer, Morgan's personal lawyer, represented the new type of "captive professionals," executives who retained strong ties to financial benefactors such as Morgan, and who became the top business leaders in the early 20th century. During the 1902 anthracite miners' strike, Baer declared that the rights of laboring men "would be best protected" not by labor agitators but "by the Christian men to whom God in his infinite wisdom has given control of the property interests of the country" (Miller 1952, 286–292; Cochran 1972; Fraser 2005, 179).

The claim that a managerial revolution took place in corporate America during the late 19th and early 20th centuries assumes that effective control within the modern corporation shifted to an independent managerial and professional class. Such autonomy presumed that these employees exercised a collective authority as members of an organized society, such as the Society for the Promotion of the Science of Management, founded in 1911, and had achieved an individual independence based on their training and specialized knowledge. But in reality "scientific" managers and professionals working within the bureaucratic enterprise had to make necessary compromises with their desire for autonomy. This tension is readily apparent in the vast expansion of engineering during the decades that frame the turn of the new century.

Men at the Top

The road to the top in the world of business increasingly ran through service in the vast bureaucratic structures set up to more efficiently administer the giant enterprises forged at the turn of the 20th century. As a percentage of the labor force, the number of professional employees and managerial employees together, although still less than six percent of the total, increased by almost 50 percent between 1880 and 1910. Whereas the urban middle class of 1850 was largely composed of independent professionals, mercantile proprietors, artisans, and only a few managerial employees, by 1910 business careerists, either as mangers or specialists, made up about half of this class. By the early 20th century, a "new" style of business executive had emerged, less a captain of industry than a corporate bureaucrat.

A study of the biographies of more than 1,000 prominent businessmen found that while less than a third of business leaders born between 1861 and 1890 became chief executives by moving up through their company's bureaucracy, nearly half of the company heads born between 1891 and 1920 had risen up through the ranks of the modern industrial enterprise. William Miller, in his study of 185 members of the business elite in the first decade of the 20th century, found that 47 percent had climbed the bureaucratic ladder to get to the top. Of these "bureaucrats," he determined that more than 80 percent had never headed an enterprise, that is, had never been a sole owner, a partner, a president, or a chairman. Among the remainder of these leaders of big business, 27 percent inherited their high positions through family ties, 14 percent obtained their key positions through connections to firms that were involved in mergers or by using available capital from another enterprise, and 12 percent had been lawyers. Rather than having experienced the risks of founding their own enterprises, these new captains of industry had, according to Miller, exercised the art of negotiation.

The Visible Hand: Alfred D. Chandler Jr. and Business History

During his career, Alfred D. Chandler Jr. published 4 major books and more than 70 essays on the rise of business organization in the United States, including the Pulitzer Prize–winning *Visible Hand: The Managerial Revolution in American Business* (1977). Unlike previous historians, who labeled early big business leaders like Andrew Carnegie and John D. Rockefeller as "Robber Barons," Chandler, as one of his students suggested, "establish[ed] business history as an independent and important area of study" (McCraw 1987, 168). Heavily influenced by the idea of structural functionalism associated with his mentor, the sociologist Talcott Parsons, who assigned principal importance to the impersonal forces that produced stability and order in society, Chandler identified as the "dynamic factors in the growth of the American economy and its business system during the late nineteenth and early twentieth centuries" the expansion of the railroad, the establishment of an extended urban market, and the advent of such new technologies as electrification and the internal combustion engine, as well as the formation of corporate research and development laboratories (McCraw 1987, 169). For Chandler, the emergence of the vertically integrated, multiunit business enterprise at the turn of the century gave rise to the separation of management from ownership and produced a new class of full-time, salaried, career middle managers who, rather than corporate executives, were the main actors in the unfolding drama of the modern corporate capital economy in America. Chandler never questioned the essential beneficence of the rise of the giant company in these years.

In Chandler's unblinking acceptance of the inevitable development of the corporate capital system there exists a kind of economic and technological determinism that dismisses the actions of individuals as representing conscious choice. Concerned with how institutions change, Chandler ignores people. As Oliver Zunz notes in *Making America Corporate, 1870–1920,* Chandler focuses "on management, not managers," on the "middle-level executive" as "simply a stage in an organizational flow chart" but not as "a specific person in specific social circumstances" (Zunz 1990, 6–7). Similarly, Steven Usselman observes that in Chandler's hands the railroad, the telegraph, the telephone, and the array of heavy machines associated with large-scale industry apparently emerged autonomously, but "What about labor? What about society? What about politics?" (Usselman 2006, 589–591). In the 1960s and 1970s, an alternative to Chandler's understanding of the actions of America's leaders of big business was offered by William Appleman Williams, Gabriel Kolko, and James Weinstein. These "New Left" historians insisted that politics—specifically the tacit approval that the largest corporations provided for government intervention, usually federal regulation—intended to ensure the stability of corporate capitalist order (Weinstein 1968, x). In similar terms, David Noble's *America by Design* (1977) challenges technological determinism. Rather than view technical changes as the principal cause of industrialization, Noble centers technological innovation in the desire of corporate leaders and a rising class of scientists and engineers for control. Although Chandler's organizational approach offers a coherent structure for understanding the rise and development of big business, his work ignores how America's corporate leaders wielded power to achieve their economic and political objectives.

The Engineer in Modern America

Known as the "golden age for the application of science to American industry," the end of the 19th and the beginning of the 20th century witnessed the engineering profession increase by almost 2,000 percent, from 7,000 to 136,000 engineers. New technical specialists in metallurgical, mining, mechanical, electrical, and chemical engineering emerged to meet the demands of industry. Specialized training in institutions of higher learning was critical to the advance of the engineering profession. In 1870, 21 engineering colleges awarded 866 degrees; by 1896, the number of engineering colleges had reached 110. Between 1890 and 1900, the number of students in the field experienced a tenfold increase, from 1,000 to 10,000.

The engineer in the early 20th century functioned as both scientist and businessman. Although the scientific training of engineers and the growing demand for their expertise should have facilitated their autonomy, their work within the bureaucratic structure of corporate enterprises impinged on their professionalism. Because employers assumed that undivided loyalty to the company facilitated success, they expected that the engineer would, like any employee, follow orders. As a result, no issue was purely a technical matter for the engineer; economic considerations always had to be taken into account. In an address to students in 1896, the president of the Stevens Alumni Association advised the young engineers that they must remember that "the financial side of engineering is always the most important; . . . [the engineer] must always be subservient to those who represent the money invested in the enterprise" (Noble 1977, 34–35). As the historian of technology Edward Layton has noted, when faced with the competing demands of professional independence and company loyalty the engineer tended to favor accommodation with the needs of business (Layton 1971, 1–8).

Many engineers finished their careers as part of management. To be successful financially and socially, the engineer had to leave the engineering of materials for the engineering of people, that is, leave engineering proper for a management or executive position (Calvert 1967, 231). One study in the 1920s of the career paths of engineering graduates since 1884 found "a healthy progression through technical work toward the responsibilities of management" (Noble 1977, 41). During the previous 40 years, roughly two-thirds of engineering graduates had become managers within 15 years of their leaving college. Along with business leaders, engineers who moved into management also had considerable influence as college trustees, on alumni boards, and as members of engineering societies.

At the beginning of the 20th century, engineers instituted research laboratories both within industrial corporations and outside in research foundations, government bureaus, and the science and engineering departments of universities. The General Electric Laboratory, formally organized in 1900, was the first research laboratory established in American industry. The lab expanded quickly. Eight were on its staff in 1901; by 1906, the lab's employees numbered 102. Willis R. Whitney, a former professor of physical chemistry at MIT, understood that GE's lab had to produce practical results, "had to pay for itself," but as director, he was determined that it also contribute to "fundamental scientific discovery." Nevertheless, calls to the lab from GE's production men for assistance to meet customers' needs always took precedence (Noble 1977, 113–114).

The evolution of the patent system in these years also reinforced the control by private corporations over the process of invention. For a century after the first United States Patent Law of 1790, inventors alone benefited from the protections offered by the patent system. Yet by the end of the 19th century, corporations had begun to establish a monopoly over patents. In 1906, Edwin J. Prindle, a mechanical engineer and patent lawyer, recommended that corporations secure the patent rights to their employees' inventions as part of their employment contracts. In science-based industries like General Electric, such contracts would soon become standard and compulsory (Noble 1977, 84–109).

The career of the engineer epitomizes the transition from the old mercantile and agrarian middle class of the 19th century to the new professional and business specialist middle class of the 20th century. A survey of first-year students admitted to engineering schools in 1924 found that many of their parents were owners or proprietors of small enterprises or farms. More than 90 percent of the students had been born in the United States; their grandparents had mostly emigrated from the British Isles or northwestern Europe. Only 13 percent of the fathers had a college degree, but 40 percent had graduated from high school. Most of the students' families lived in small towns or villages, or on farms. Slightly more than one-third came from cities with a population of more than 25,000 (Layton 1971, 9–10). Like other members of the modern managerial middle class, engineers had an opportunity to hold onto or, for a favored few, improve, their social and economic standing.

THE "ONE BEST WAY"

The scientifically trained professional engineer came into prominence with the emergence of large organizations in the United States. The needs of managers in corporate enterprise for better information merged with business owners' long-standing attention to costs to raise awareness of efficiency. The effort to more carefully measure performance came to be known as "scientific management," a movement closely associated with the engineer and industrial manager Frederick Winslow Taylor. Taylor's principles of management concentrated on how to reorganize business to make work more efficient. Most companies resisted full implementation of his system. Nevertheless, Taylorism reflects an ethos of control that spread rapidly through business in the first decade of the 20th century (Layton 1971, 1–8; Galambos and Pratt 1988, 75).

Frederick Winslow Taylor developed the concept of scientific management. Through the use of time-study experiments, he sought to standardize work under the control of management. Despite the resistance of both workers and managers, Taylor's theories had a profound effect on the management of business in America. (Library of Congress)

Scientific Management and the Systematization of Work

In *The Principles of Scientific Management* (1911) Taylor chronicled the defiance he confronted when he worked as a gang boss at Midvale Steel, "As was usual then . . . the shop was really run by the workmen, and not by the bosses." Relying on their traditional knowledge and the physical skills they learned on the job, skilled craftsmen determined among themselves how fast they would work; each new worker quickly assimilated these "rules." Taylor called these practices *systematic soldiering,* a direct consequence, he reasoned, of management's ignorance of what constituted a fair day's work. To break workers' hold, Taylor argued that management had to "scientifically" determine through time study experiments the most efficient pace at which a worker could do a task. "Functional foremen," each with different specialized responsibilities, could then provide detailed instructions and supervise each worker's performance. Taylor expected that wage incentives would induce workers to abandon their restrictive practices and willingly agree to do what they were told: "It is only through *enforced* standardization of methods, *enforced* adoption of the best implements and working conditions, and *enforced* cooperation that this faster work can be assured. And the duty of enforcing the adoption of standards and enforcing this cooperation rests with the *management* alone" (Taylor 1947, 83). Taylor placed responsibility for enforcement in a centralized planning department. His essential goal, as Harry Braverman, a critic of Taylorism has put it, was to separate the conception of the job from its execution (Braverman 1974, 114).

The essential features of scientific management are captured in an "experiment" Taylor conducted while working at the Bethlehem Iron Company. Taylor's largely apocryphal account involved a pig iron handler he named "Schmidt." A pig iron handler's job required hand loading onto cars cast iron ingots weighing about 92 pounds. The standard pace at the time was 12.5 tons per man per day. Taylor had determined that a first-class iron handler could move 47 to 48 tons per day. After carefully studying about 75 handlers, he "scientifically selected" a Pennsylvania Dutchman, Schmidt, to illustrate how his system would operate. Schmidt appealed to Taylor because he had a reputation for being "exceedingly close, that is, placing a high value on a dollar" (Taylor 1947, 44). In Taylor's account, Schmidt was asked, "Are you a high-priced man?" After some haggling over what that meant, Schmidt was informed that if he did exactly as he was told, "with no back talk," he would be paid $1.85 a day instead of the $1.15 a day he then received. He agreed to the experiment. The next day, Schmidt started to work, and all day long he was told, "Now pick up the pig and walk. Now sit down and rest" (Taylor 1947, 47). At end of the day, Schmidt received 60 percent more for his day's work, having moved 47.5 tons of steel. Although Taylor offered different versions of this story, the pig iron "experiment" reveals the essence of scientific management: time study to determine the most efficient way to do a job, careful selection of the workman, incentives

Frederick Winslow Taylor, the "Father" of Scientific Management

Born on March 20, 1856, in Germantown, a suburb of Philadelphia, Frederick Winslow Taylor, the second son of Quaker parents, planned to attend Harvard University and become a lawyer. Taylor passed Harvard's entrance exam with honors, but severe headaches, probably caused by problems with his eyesight, forced him to abandon his plans. Instead of going to Harvard, Taylor became an apprentice pattern maker in 1875 for a local Philadelphia steam pump company, Enterprise Hydraulic Works. Although he was required to read complicated mechanical drawings, Taylor's eye problems apparently had cleared up.

After his apprenticeship, Taylor, then 22 years old, went to work as a machine-shop laborer at Midvale Steel Company, a local plant partly owned by a family friend. At Midvale, Taylor became successively a shop clerk, machinist, gang boss, foreman, maintenance foreman, head of the drawing office, and chief engineer. He also took home-study courses in physics and mathematics in his spare time, eventually earning a degree in mechanical engineering from Stevens Institute of Technology. Before Taylor left Midvale in 1890 he had begun conducting time studies and experimenting with pay incentive systems to increase workers' output. After a brief stint as the general manager of the Manufacturing Investment Company, Taylor, by then a consulting engineer, refined his system while working for numerous industrial clients. In 1901, Taylor retired, spending the rest of his life promoting and publicizing his basic ideas of scientific management.

for the "first-class workman" through a differential piece rate, and finally, training and help for the workman in how to do the job according to the scientific method.

After 1901, Taylor lectured at public gatherings, wrote for popular audiences, and, in general, advertised his system to the public at large. In 1906, the American Society of Mechanical Engineers (ASME) elected Taylor its president. He published all his major papers in the society's journal, *Transactions*. He also continued in his efforts to persuade businessmen to adopt the Taylor system of management. Strongly opposed to direct solicitation, he would invite businessmen to stay at his home in Philadelphia. During their visit, he would lecture them for about three hours on his "Principles" and then conduct a tour of a local "Taylorized" plant. Potential clients would then be referred to an "expert," usually a disciple of Taylor's. Once the expert had been chosen, Taylor became an active advocate, writing letters encouraging the client to be patient and to give the expert the greatest freedom to pursue his work.

As a theory of control over the factors of production, including labor, Taylorism had broad appeal among business leaders. Yet in actual practice, its impact was

Unmasking Schmidt:
Henry Noll and Scientific Management

Almost 100 years have passed since the publication of *The Principles of Scientific Management* (1911). Yet articles and textbooks on management and industrial psychology still cite Frederick Winslow Taylor's account of the 1899 experiment in scientific management conducted with the pig-iron handler "Schmidt" at Bethlehem Iron Company. Schmidt was the pseudonym that Taylor used for Henry Noll (or Knolle as he appeared in company records). The account in Taylor's book, however, is only one version of a story that Taylor offered through the years in published and unpublished form. When he discussed the experiment before the American Society of Mechanical Engineers (ASME) in 1901, Taylor emphasized two aspects of the story: the worker's physical characteristics, noting that the pig-iron handler was "a man properly built for that work," and scientific management's economic advantages to the company in both lower cost and greater output per ton. In 1903, Taylor incorporated the pig-iron story into a paper he delivered at the ASME's annual meeting. In this account, he discarded the reference to the worker's physique and stressed instead the necessity of scientifically determining the elements of the task before selecting "a laborer." Taylor also mentioned for the first time that he knew that the "the workman" was building a house and "needed money" and that he was, as well, "independent" and "very anxious to succeed." (Taylor does not appear to have specified "Schmidt" in either this or his previous account to the ASME.) Beginning in 1904 and continuing to 1912, many people heard the story of Henry Noll (Taylor used his real name in these talks) during visits to Boxly, Taylor's home in Philadelphia. In lectures that lasted nonstop for two hours, Taylor standardized his account of the pig-iron experiment to the point that the tale appeared to be spontaneous. In those talks he spoke of having "picked out a Pennsylvania Dutchman" and asked him, "Noll, are you a high-priced man?" At Boxly, as in *Scientific Management,* Taylor presented Noll as being "stupid" and only slowly won over into becoming "a high-priced man."

The original record of the pig-iron experiment, "Report on the Establishment of Piecework in Connection with the Loading of Pig-Iron, at the works of the Bethlehem Iron Co., South Bethlehem, Pennsylvania," compiled by James Gillespie and Hartley C. Wolle in 1899, differs markedly from Taylor's account in *Scientific Management.* Taylor had designated Gillespie and his assistant, Wolle, to observe the men and time their work. In his book, Taylor emphasizes the "scientific" selection of Schmidt. However, in their report, Gillespie and Wolle note that they first approached a work gang of Hungarian pig-iron handlers about the experiment but that these men refused to work under piecework. When Taylor learned that the Hungarians had defied his orders, he had them discharged. Gillespie and Wolle then asked for volunteers, and Noll, who was a physically slight man, was among the five men who responded. The men performed the work according to the instructions provided by Gillespie and Wolle over the course of five days, and Noll was simply the only man not to quit. It is possible that during this time Taylor took

Unmasking Schmidt:
Henry Noll and Scientific Management, Continued

Noll aside and encouraged him to prove that he was "a high-priced man." Furthermore, Taylor states in the book that after careful study he concluded that a first-class handler could move between 47 and 48 tons of pig iron per day. But Gillespie and Wolle came up with a figure of 45 tons based on their observation of 10 of the "best" pig-iron handlers at the plant. They had found that a first-class man, working at the maximum, could load 75 tons in 10 hours. To allow for rest and other contingencies, Gillespie and Wolle then simply reduced that amount by 40 percent. In addition, unlike Taylor, Gillespie and Wolle gave full credit to "Knolle" for his effort, praising him for demonstrating that "a good day's wages" could be made "by a good man." Other differences between Gillespie and Wolle's report and Taylor's account of the pig-iron experiment include a description of the usual method of loading pig iron (two men working together, not a man working alone as the Schmidt account makes it appear).

Who was Schmidt? Henry Noll was a Pennsylvania Dutchman born May 9, 1871, in Shimersville, Pennsylvania. He married a few years after the 1899 experiment but divorced not long after that, possibly because of his reputed fondness for drink and women. He did build a house not far from the mill, one that remained standing until 1960. Little else is known about Noll. In 1912, Taylor testified before a special committee of the House of Representatives called to investigate Taylor's and other systems of shop management. Shortly before his appearance, in anticipation of possibly being asked "Whatever happened to Schmidt?" Taylor resolved to find Noll and to have a doctor examine him and declare him fit. At Taylor's behest, an investigator located Noll, who was working as a teamster for another company and, apparently, in good physical health. However, in his report to Taylor the investigator also noted that Noll, who was in his early 40s, appeared "old," as did "most men" of his class and age. Taylor, believing that his critics would pounce on just such a statement, had the report retyped with that comment removed. He kept signed copies of the edited report with him ready to be used whenever necessary. Taylor continued to promote his principles of scientific management until his death on March 21, 1915. Almost ten years later, on February 25, 1925, Noll died and was buried in Bethlehem Memorial Park (Wrege and Perroni 1974, 6–27).

limited. Estimates vary over how many companies instituted Taylor's system. In 1912, an ASME committee reported 52 industries in which one or more companies had introduced "labor saving" management; a critic of this report identified 169 American industrial plants, located mostly in New England and the Middle Atlantic states (Nelson 1975, 69). More recently, a historian determined that at least 46 industrial firms and 2 government manufacturing plants had introduced Taylorism between 1901 and 1917 (Kanigel 1999, 486–503). Yet U.S.

Steel, International Harvester, and other new industrial giants showed little interest in installing Taylor's system. When Charles Schwab took charge of Bethlehem Steel in 1901, he fired Taylor's experts and the costly 60 specialized foremen.

Taylor's system never worked as well as Taylor claimed. Unions resisted it, often through strikes, and individual workers sabotaged Taylor's time studies. Workers at the Watertown Arsenal, a federal facility in Massachusetts that introduced Taylorism in 1909, walked out in opposition, especially to the use of the stopwatch and to the bonus system. Resistance to Taylorism also came from managers and foremen who were equally wary of losing traditional prerogatives. Foremen had no interest in seeing their jobs fragmented into eight "functional" parts or in losing the power that they had long held over hiring and discipline. Scientific management also constrained the authority of managers, assigning key responsibilities instead to the planning department. Taylorism was complicated, and Taylor fought any modification. He mandated that each manager be confined to the performance of a single function. Any show of initiative, be it by managers or workers, was in his view a "fatal" error. Managers fought Taylor's schemes because, like him, they knew "best" how to structure work and manage their departments (Rodgers 1978, 53–57).

Although wary of Taylor, most large enterprises, nevertheless, eagerly tried to assert control in a more systematic way throughout the entire firm. Industrial managers grew more alert to the "science" of management. The New York Public Library's collection of books on management increased during the first decade of the 20th century by almost 1,000 percent over the previous 20 years. The Harvard Business School accepted the Taylor system as the final word in management. Tighter managerial controls became more common (Lescohier 1935, 308–309). One area of Taylorism's greatest success was in centralizing the foremen's functions in the planning and personnel departments. The foreman became a representative of management rather than a boss on his own. Also, the rise of Taylorism paralleled a transition in industrial labor that gradually eliminated the skills of craft workers. In the steel industry, for example, the impulse for economy, that is, management's desire to produce steel at the lowest possible cost, fostered changes in technology and in the treatment of labor. Undercut by mechanization, the highly skilled steelworker who had learned his trade after long years in the mill was supplanted by a semiskilled worker who quickly mastered the requirements of tending the new machines. As the control over work previously exercised by skilled labor diminished, management was able to impose a more disciplined work regimen.

Taylorism engaged in circular reasoning. The system rested on the certainty that each worker would respond to an incentive wage, "scientifically" determined. From a gang of 75 pig iron handlers at Bethlehem Steel, Taylor had chosen Schmidt because of the Pennsylvania Dutchman's "closeness," because to Schmidt "a penny looks like the size of a cartwheel" (Taylor 1947, 44). Yet, workers had long resisted speeding up the pace for two reasons: a desire to assert their independence and an understanding that faster work would inevitably result in fewer workers. The Schmidt "experiment" shows that they had good reason to be concerned. Taylor found that seven of the eight workers on the pig iron gang were not physically capable of maintaining the faster pace maintained by Schmidt. Such "incompetent men," Taylor asserted, should be laid off as an "object lesson" for the others to keep pace (Taylor 1947, 74; Commons, 1935, 308). Taylor assumed that all workers wanted to be "high-priced men" and that they would willingly do what they were told. For this to happen, employers would have to populate factories with individuals like Schmidt. Instead, workers resisted Taylorism, valuing their collective needs over the narrow self-interest that Taylor had taken for granted.

Still eager to assert greater control over their workforces, many of the big firms, even as they resisted Taylorism, experimented with alternative reward systems known as welfare work. Although Taylor considered welfare programs to be "a joke," the leaders of giant companies like U.S. Steel and International Harvester came to believe that securing workers' cooperation required benefits beyond the wage incentive.

"Taylorizing the Shopgirl"

A. T. Stewart's and Macy's in New York, Strawbridge and Clothier's and Wanamaker's in Philadelphia, Jordon Marsh in Boston, and Marshall Field in Chicago became elaborately appointed "palaces of consumption" in the early 20th century. Physically as monumental as many leading industrial enterprises, department stores also had vast workforces. In 1900, Jordon Marsh was the fourth largest employer in New England. And, by 1904, two years after Marshall Field opened his Chicago emporium, the store had a workforce of between 8,000 and 10,000 employees to handle the up to one-quarter of a million customers who passed through the 12-story building every day (Benson 1988, 34).

Like their counterparts in industry, store managers wanted to be able to supervise an efficient and tractable workforce. Frederick Winslow Taylor proposed to eliminate workers' autonomy and place managers in control over all decisions made in the course of doing a job to yield a "scientifically" determined optimal output. To achieve this, store managers relied on training programs that included uplift courses intended to impart to the sales force an air of polish and efficient competence, courses in merchandizing that merged greater knowledge about the goods with high culture experiences such as visits to museums, and courses in salesmanship intended to socialize the clerks to be more conscious of fashion and sensitive to meeting their customers' needs. Yet because a sales clerk's output ultimately rested on her social interaction with people instead of with the manipulation of inanimate objects, Taylorism proved to be an imperfect fit for the department store.

In sales, productivity was not the primary measure of success. According to one industry observer, "the central problem" in department store selling was that the best salesperson "is *not necessarily* the one that *has the largest book*," that is, the clerk with the highest total of daily sales (Benson 1988, 127). After all, what good was a sale if the customer went away dissatisfied with the service and unlikely to return? Department store managers needed their clerks not merely to sell the most merchandise they could as quickly as possible but also to establish long-term relationships with their customers. The key figures in Taylor's system were the functional foremen who constantly monitored each worker's performance. Yet in a department store, such close supervision could jeopardize a sale.

The relationship between the salesclerk and the customer rested on intangibles that could be neither quantified nor "scientifically" determined. Taylor's goal was to eliminate initiative: "Under our system the workman is told minutely just what he is to do and how he is to do it; any improvement which he makes upon the orders given him is fatal to success." But, as store managers recognized, an effective sales clerk had to respond to the moment; she had to be able to adjust her approach based on her interaction with the customer before her. Empathy and flexibility constituted the irreducible core of skilled selling. Christine Frederick, the doyen of household scientific management, urged retailers to concentrate on "*making a customer*" rather than "*making a sale*" (Benson 1988, 95). Furthermore, although department store managers store may have wished to have an obedient workforce that passively accepted its subordinate role, they also understood that a clerk's success depended on her employing initiative and independent judgment. Whereas Taylor developed a time study to eliminate the impact that the worker's skill had on output, a successful outcome in the department store could come only if the salesclerk retained control over her work. In seeking to develop a sales force that was at once loyal and deferential but still capable of exhibiting initiative and independent judgment, store managers faced an impossible task (Benson 1988, 114–116).

WELFARE CAPITALISM

Founded in 1884 in Dayton, Ohio, the National Cash Register Company (NCR) grew quickly. Less than 20 years later, NCR's more than 1,000 employees produced 15,000 cash registers annually. Rapid expansion led to labor problems as management grew distant. "When the business was smaller . . . I used to travel about through the shops a great deal, knowing everyone, and taking pains to ask them if they had anything to suggest," John Patterson, founder and president of NCR, recalled to his biographer. (Mandell 2002, 1) In 1892, Patterson learned that an order for $50,000 worth of cash registers had been returned from

Historians' Views: Corporate Welfare

Historians disagree about employers' motivations for welfare capitalism. Some scholars such as Irving Bernstein, in his study of the labor movement in the 1920s, *The Lean Years* (1960), see employers' opposition to unions as the impetus for corporate welfare programs. Bernstein's insights have been further developed by Stephen Meyer, *The Five Dollar Day* (1981); Gerard Zahavi, *Workers, Managers, and Welfare Capitalism* (1988); and Lizabeth Cohen, *Making a New Deal* (1990); while others like Daniel Nelson, *Managers and Workers* (1975), and Sanford Jacoby, *Employing* Bureaucracy (1985), regard welfare plans as efforts by management to secure greater control over the labor process. Still other scholars, for example, Andrea Tone, *The Business of Benevolence* (1997), argue that the employers' main goal was to preempt state regulation of business (Mandell 2002, 4–6). Essentially, these objectives should be understood as complementary rather than contradictory. The main issue for the employers came down to "Who's in charge?" Employers preferred to appear to be offering benefits voluntarily, as a reward to "loyal" employees rather than as an employment right conceded to a union. For Elbert H. Gary, a lawyer and steel industrialist, U.S. Steel's welfare work program promised to transform contentious labor–management relations into a harmonious partnership. Company-designed programs such as accident relief stood as a "rebuke and a rebuttal" to the notion that "workmen get nothing except by contest and struggle" (Edwards 1979, 94). But during the Progressive Era an increasingly skeptical public also supported more government regulation of corporate behavior. To forestall state action, business leaders such as the J. P. Morgan ally George H. Perkins promoted welfare capitalism as the "labor program of 'good trust.'" Facing an investigation by the federal Bureau of Corporations in 1906 and searching for ways to create a more positive image for International Harvester, Perkins counted on welfare work to convince the public and the government that International Harvester was a trust that did "good" instead of "evil" (Ozanne 1967, 73).

England because of defective workmanship. The following year, employee sabotage resulted in three fires being set in the factory. Convinced that by taking more interest in their employees the company could create "an ideal class of workers—'enthusiastic, loyal, and intelligent,'" NCR pioneered in the development of welfare work (Mandell 2002, 2). By 1900, NCR offered its employees such benefits as subsidized housing, profit-sharing plans, and a company library and reading room; the firm also ran a Sunday School, choral societies, and the N.C.R. House, which served as a club house and model workman's home. To oversee NCR's welfare program, Patterson, in 1897, hired Lena Harvey, a religious worker in Dayton. Calculating that the cost of these programs yielded a

Tool room of the National Cash Register Co., Dayton, Ohio, ca. 1904. (Library of Congress)

profit of from 5 to 10 percent in increased output, Patterson insisted that welfare work "paid" (Mandell 2002, 1–3).

Patterson looked to create a loyal and industrious workforce by developing "family-like" bonds through NCR's welfare programs. Some connection beyond the wage was needed to convince workers of the corporation's concern for their personal well-being. Although the growth in the size and scale of production in the late 19th and early 20th centuries had resulted in an even greater separation of owner and worker, the problem of workers' diligence was not entirely new. Prior to 1830, when his textile mills grew too large to personally manage, Samuel Slater, long distrustful of "absentee owners," had insisted that "it is in this triple capacity of money lender, employer and laborer that our most successful manufacturers have succeeded" (Tucker 1984, 103). Long before 1900, employers had devised a variety of means to create more personal ties intended to counter the loss of personal contact with their workers. In mid-19th-century Albany, New York, for example, owners of the leading businesses sponsored volunteer militia corps among their employees. Each year, the employers paid for an excursion for the volunteer corps members that they also attended. The outing featured a target-shooting competition for a long list of prizes followed by an elaborate dinner. Albany's employers hoped that such events would build a sense of camaraderie and thereby encourage greater effort among their workers (Greenberg 1985, 30–31).

The intense labor conflicts of the Great Upheaval that continued into the early 20th century encouraged corporate leaders to experiment with ways to gain the loyalty of their workforce. Even Taylor had recognized the need to provide a human connection; the men should be encouraged by the managers to discuss with them any problems they had "either in the works or outside" (Calvert 1967, 239–240). During the first decades of the 20th century, more than 1,500 private companies, especially firms with the largest number of employees, followed NCR's example and voluntarily offered to their workers a wide range of benefit programs. Only 20 percent of American firms had 1,000 or more workers, but 80 percent of these companies had welfare plans. This approach to labor–management relations epitomized welfare capitalism. Welfare programs encompassed workplace reforms that resulted in a cleaner and safer work environment; leisure programs such as recreation activities or classes to improve the home environment; and nonwage pecuniary benefits such as pensions, stock options, profit sharing, and loan programs for home ownership.

In 1902, George Perkins had arranged the merger between the McCormick Harvesting Machine Company and other major agricultural implements manufacturers to form International Harvester. Under Cyrus Hall McCormick Jr., the son of its founder, the McCormick Company had first become interested in "betterment" work in 1901, when the firm built a twine mill in Chicago. Up to then, the McCormick Works' nearly 5,000 factory employees had been male. The twine mill, however, employed 400 women, who were managed mainly by male supervisors. Concerned with both the health and the morality of the mill's female workers, McCormick hired Gertrude Beeks as a "social secretary." Beeks had been working for the Civic Federation of Chicago, an organization devoted to government reform. Under Beeks, the McCormick Company provided the women working in the mill with dressing rooms with mirrors, opened employee lunchrooms, and improved ventilation to remove the excess dust. Beeks soon made the entire McCormick Works her concern. One of her first ventures was

Two women sitting in the "rest room" at the McCormick Reaper Works, 1899. (Wisconsin Historical Society, Image ID 12008)

Gertrude Beeks and Welfare Work

In the years leading up to World War I, Gertrude Beeks was the person who employers and the public most associated with the new field of welfare work. Born in Greenville, Tennessee, in 1867, she was educated in the public schools in Fort Wayne, Indiana, and Chicago, Illinois. She was a protégé of Jane Addams, the founder of the Hull House settlement house in Chicago. Before becoming the first "social agent" at McCormick Harvesting Machine Company in 1901, Beeks was active in Chicago reform and business and women's organizations. In 1903, Beeks helped inaugurate the welfare department of the National Civic Federation (NCF) and became its first director. As department secretary, she investigated factories and other workplaces, published dozens of articles and pamphlets, and regularly gave lectures to women's clubs, employer associations, and labor organizations. Employers usually relied on her recommendation when their companies hired welfare managers. Frequently consulted by business leaders on how to establish welfare programs in their companies, Beeks was paid $100 a day plus expenses, a considerable sum in these years, especially for a woman. President Theodore Roosevelt and Secretary of War William H. Taft sent Beeks to Panama in 1907 to investigate the living conditions of American employees working on the canal and recommend improvements.

In 1917, she married Ralph Easley, the founder of the NCF. Together they were active in antisocialist, anticommunist, and other conservative movements. Easley died in 1939, but Gertrude Beeks Easley kept the NCF going until, facing growing debts, she was forced to declare bankruptcy in 1950 and the federation closed its doors. She died later that same year.

As a pioneer in social welfare, Beeks helped articulate the movement's basic principles. In an interview, Beeks defined welfare work as simply "the improving of working and living conditions of employees by employers" (Comstock 1913, 446). Special attention was given to programs that enhanced the safety, health, and comfort of employees in the workplace and the quality of the employees' home life. Work and home, in Beeks's view, were inextricably linked. But the key was for employers to take the initiative. At a time of intense labor conflict, Beeks saw company welfare benefits programs as the best way to "civilize" the relations between capital and labor. The press celebrated Beeks as an "Anti-Strike 'Social Agent'" (Ozanne 1967, 32). But real labor peace, she insisted, necessitated that employers pay workers a living wage. The "foundation" for welfare work required, Beeks wrote to Stanley McCormick in 1902, that International Harvester pay workers a just and reasonable wage: "I cannot say enough to emphasize the necessity of a fair wage scale" (Mandell 2002, 39). Although by 1910 welfare work was accepted practice in many large companies, Beeks was never able to get employers to concede the centrality of high wages.

In seeking to bring harmony to the relations of employer and employee, Beeks was not so much antilabor as she was convinced that voluntary action by businessmen was far preferable to state-mandated welfare legislation. Private welfare

Gertrude Beeks and Welfare Work, Continued

programs, in her view, protected workers' independence. Rather than "charity," workers "earned" the benefits provided them through company-sponsored welfare programs (Tone 1997, 40–43). Yet, she warned employers, the "spirit" of welfare work could be perverted by employer paternalism. Asked if welfare benefits cut strikes, Beeks replied not "if injustices underlie" workers' grievances. "The American workman," she admonished, "won't get down upon his knees to thank an employer for decent surroundings, but he appreciates them none the less. And he is now developed to the point where he demands them." For Beeks, social legislation burdened government with the high cost of charity and encouraged dependence on the state. Welfare work was "infinitely better" because these programs promoted "a self-respecting citizenship" among the workers (*New York Times*, November 17, 1912).

At the 1904 conference on welfare work sponsored by the NCF, Beeks noted that "scientific" welfare workers objected to the term "Social Secretary." The more appropriate term, the one more "descriptive of their duties," was "Welfare Manager." From the beginning, Beeks sought to professionalize welfare work (Mandell 2002, 92–93). Each year the NCF's welfare department sponsored conferences featuring speeches by prominent welfare managers on topics such as "guarding against accidents" and "a complete factory plan." In frequent publications the department circulated core ideas and defined professional standards. In 1904, Beeks attempted to get Harvard University to include welfare work courses in its curriculum. After failing at Harvard and, in 1909, at Columbia University, Beeks finally was able, in 1913, to offer her own course on welfare work at New York University's School of Commerce. Beeks designed the course to offer training to students in both the theoretical and the practical dimensions of welfare work. Beeks's own lectures were supplemented by talks from "prominent welfare workers, practical businessmen, and scientists as well as experts in the fields of welfare activity." Beeks had long experienced industrial managers' disdain for welfare work as a product of "female intuition" and not business expertise. She acknowledged this attitude in her course description in the university bulletin, which characterized welfare work as "a phase of business activity . . . not to be confused with philanthropic and social service." Beeks was careful to note that welfare work required not only sensitivity on the part of the practitioner but also rigorous formal training (Tone 1997, 233–234).

Looking at the role of female voluntary associations that focused on child welfare policy in these years, the historian Robin Muncy found that the women who led these groups created a "female dominion." Emphasizing the unique female ways of being a professional, such associations as the Children's Bureau sought to convince the public that only women possessed the special knowledge needed to administer child welfare policies. Beeks, however, rejected claims that women were uniquely qualified to be welfare managers. Good welfare managers, she

Continued on next page

Gertrude Beeks and Welfare Work, Continued

insisted, required tact, common sense, and executive ability. Although she had been wary at first in administering programs for men, she quickly dismissed the notion that welfare work was simply an extension of women's maternal activities or feminine instinct. Welfare workers were disciplined, efficient, and systematic managers who shared employers' goals of higher profits and productivity. Beeks also viewed the proper realm for welfare work to be within the corporation and not the public sphere. She spent her career attempting, albeit without much success, to convince business owners and managers of welfare workers' professional competency and to solidify welfare workers' place within the corporate bureaucracy.

to get the company to dig a new well to supply McCormick Works with pure drinking water. She also ran Sunday outings, organized a choral group, and staged an operetta for McCormick workers (Ozanne 1967, 31–36).

Beeks remained welfare secretary at McCormick Company and its successor, International Harvester, for only 18 months. Unable to convince International

Company housing at U.S. Steel, ca. 1900–1910. (Library of Congress)

"Garyism" and the Safety Campaign in Steel

"Garyism," which refers to the labor policies and business practices of Elbert H. Gary, is sometimes used synonymously as a reference to welfare capitalism. When the negotiations for the merger that created U.S. Steel were completed, Gary was named chairman of the board. Known as "the Judge" for his two brief terms as a county judge in Illinois, Gary was an outspoken proponent of the distinction between "good" and "bad" trusts. "The essence" of the Gary policy, according to *Fortune* magazine, was to "avoid the appearance of monopoly while keeping as much as possible the reality" (Serrin 1993, 131).

Although at the time of the steel corporation's formation the Amalgamated Association of Iron, Steel, and Tin Workers represented fewer than 5 percent of the nation's steel workers, the union on August 10, 1901, called a general strike against U.S. Steel. This misguided action failed after only one month. Gary insisted that the corporation be run without unions, that is, as an "open shop." In place of employment rights, Garyism posited paternalistic control. He reminded his fellow steel executives that they had the responsibility to see that "the workmen and their families are appropriately and efficiently cared for, drawing the line so that you are just and generous and yet at the same time . . . keeping the whole affair in your own hands" (Serrin 1993, 139). Gary's welfare policies included a stock purchase plan for employees, increased safety measures, employees' housing, and other benefits.

On December 31, 1902, Gary gave what the muckraking author Ida Tarbell called "a New Year's gift" to U.S. Steel's workers—a stock plan that enabled workers to buy corporation stock at below-market prices. Established in collaboration with George Perkins, who was chair of the corporation's finance committee, the stock plan demonstrated, according to Gary, that the "interests of capital and labor will be more closely and permanently together" (Edwards 1979, 94). More than 26,000 workers signed up for the stock plan in January 1903 alone. Moreover, U.S. Steel improved plant sanitation and introduced ventilating and heating systems. The corporation also sponsored employee baseball and football teams that played their games on corporation-built fields. Such generosity on U.S. Steel's part obviated the need for unions. Judge Gary noted that while "workmen may not have been treated justly" in the past, there was "no benefit or advantage" from joining unions now other than to the "union labor leaders" (Brody 1969, 175). On June 1, 1909, U.S. Steel posted notices that the corporation would no longer recognize the Amalgamated Association at the 12 mills where the union still had members. Although a subsequent strike lasted more than a year, when it ended U.S. Steel was a fully open shop.

Steelmaking was a dangerous job. In just one year, 195 men were killed in Pittsburgh's iron and steel mills. In November 1907, *Everybody's Magazine* published an investigative article on U.S. Steel's South Chicago plant, "Making Steel and Killing Men." The author, William Hard, found that in 1906 there had been 46

Continued on next page

"Garyism" and the Safety Campaign in Steel, Continued

fatalities and some 2,000 injuries at the plant. Judge Gary was ready to move, instructing subsidiary companies that "the safety and the welfare of the workmen is of the greatest concern" (Lescohier 1935, 367) In 1908, the corporation formed a central committee on safety composed of five officers from subsidiary companies; the committee was empowered to appoint inspectors, conduct investigations, and devise safety measures. Under the banner "Safety First," U.S. Steel's education campaign spread the safety message on bulletin boards and in pay envelopes. Signs in several languages warned of danger spots, and plant magazines reported accidents when they occurred. In 1914, the company claimed to have spent $10 million on its safety program and to have reduced serious accidents by 40 percent.

Increased safety in the mills facilitated the steel corporation's willingness to compensate workers for on-the-job accidents. Under the common-law understanding of accident liability accepted until the beginning of the 20th century, employees had full responsibility for any risk associated with their jobs. But as the size of factories increased and the pace of work intensified, the political and legal environment began to change and giant corporations like U.S. Steel more readily accepted responsibility for the hazards of employment. In 1910, U.S. Steel introduced a workmen's compensation plan called "Voluntary Accident Relief." As the plan's name underscores, the steel corporation wanted government officials and the public to understand that it was not acting in response to "any demand" by its employees, nor was it concerned about establishing liability. The plan provided generous benefits—35 percent of weekly wages for an injured single worker, 50 percent for a married worker, and an extra 5 percent for each child over five years of age of an injured worker. Modeled on workmen's compensation laws in Germany and other European countries, the U.S. Steel plan cost, according to the company, about $2 million a year.

Harvester executives to centralize welfare work in a special department, Beeks resigned. Yet the McCormick family continued to be interested in welfare work. In 1901, Cyrus McCormick, based on the recommendation of his son, Stanley, promoted the idea of making an outright gift totaling $1.5 million to all Harvester employees, including factory laborers. Whatever altruism had prompted this idea was quickly undone, however, following a strike in 1903 at International Harvester's Chicago Deering Works. At a special plant meeting held to forestall workers in the McCormick Works from joining the strike, top company executives promised the workers that their "faithful service" would be "remembered" by some sort of bonus plan. At the end of the strike, which the McCormick workers did not join, the McCormick family confirmed the $1.5 million stock offer, and included a pension system for older employees and stock for em-

The National Civic Federation and Welfare Capitalism

Although U.S. Steel emphasized the "voluntary" nature of its accident relief plan, workmen's compensation was one ingredient of welfare capitalism in which large-scale employers welcomed state action. By the early 20th century, injured workers had begun winning significant liability judgments, and the cost to big business for liability insurance had risen from $200,000 in 1887 to $35 million a quarter century later. In 1908, the federal government enacted a law that, although weak, granted certain designated employees the right to compensation for injuries suffered on the job. That same year the National Civic Federation made workmen's compensation a prime legislative objective. The NCF drew up model compensation bills and then lobbied state legislatures and governors for their approval. Between 1909 and 1913, 33 states either appointed investigative commissions or passed workmen's compensation legislation. By the end of the second decade of the 20th century, all states except 6 in the South had workmen's compensation systems in operation.

As the 20th century began to unfold, corporate capitalists came under greater scrutiny from both the government and the public. In response to this challenge, many big businesses joined the National Civic Federation. At first, as part of a strategy to "harmonize" the interests of capital and labor, the NCF promoted mediation in labor disputes. Working through its Committee on Conciliation, the NCF intervened in the 1901 U.S. Steel strike, the great anthracite coal strike of 1902, a strike against bituminous coal owners in 1903, and several other major clashes in these years. Although mediation appealed to NCF leaders as a mechanism for reducing class warfare in the United States, influential figures such as Gary remained adamantly opposed to recognizing unions in their own industries. In 1904, the NCF established a welfare department. Headed by Gertrude Beeks, the welfare department had as its stated goals to educate the public as to the real meaning of welfare work, to interest employers not engaged in welfare work to consider their "moral obligation to give consideration to the general welfare of employees," and to be a clearinghouse for companies engaged in welfare work (*Conference on Welfare Work* 1904, v–xv). NCF business leaders looked to welfarism as a substitute for unions to promote conciliation with workers and to convince the public and government that they were responsible and caring employers. The department promoted reforms in five key areas: sanitation, recreation, education, pensions and insurance, and housing. At its founding, the welfare department had 125 members; by 1911 membership exceeded 500.

Historians differ on the degree to which the NCF after 1908 modified corporate capital's long-held preference for self-regulation and endorsed state action in support of workmen's compensation legislation and child labor laws, as well as, in 1914, for the federal legislation that established the Federal Trade Commission.

Continued on next page

The National Civic Federation and Welfare Capitalism, Continued

In *The Business of Benevolence* (1997), Andrea Tone emphasizes the antistatist impulse behind welfare capitalism. She believes that by winning public approval for its agenda the NCF succeeded in shaping conservative legislation in place of more sweeping regulations. These were also the objectives of Perkins, who used his staunch support for the Republican Party to gain access to Roosevelt's White House. Perkins kept Roosevelt abreast of International Harvester's "good trust" welfare programs. For his part, Roosevelt, in 1907, expressed public regret that "our present laws" failed to discriminate between "those combinations which do good and those combinations which do evil" (Ozanne 1967, 73). But an appeal for government action could be a two-edged sword. For example, during the 1902 anthracite miners' strike, the NCF encouraged the mine operators to accept arbitration by a commission appointed by President Roosevelt. In one of its recommendations, one unlikely to have had the support of NCF members who favored the open shop, the commission established a conciliation board on which the operators and the union were equally represented.

Nevertheless, it is fair to say that the NCF's venture into state action was tentative at best. After the coal strike ended, the NCF abandoned mediation and supported welfare work initiatives controlled and directed by each corporation. Business leaders' enthusiasm for welfare programs blew hot and cold. Like Beeks, most welfare secretaries working for corporations did not keep their jobs for long, and foremen resisted ceding control over personnel matters. Furthermore, only the biggest corporations—those with large numbers of female employees—introduced extensive welfare programs in the opening decades of the 20th century. Too often, welfare plans at this time benefited only a few selected workers. After World War I, business leaders' modest welfare work efforts would be replaced by a more extensive and professional industrial relations movement. The same mode of thinking that led corporate capitalists like Morgan, Perkins, and Gary to seek to end ruinous cutthroat competition through co-operation in the free market influenced their approach to labor relations. In each instance, managerial control and stability became paramount virtues.

ployees with three and four years of service. Among those McCormick workers who met the five-year requirement, 20 union officials and activists nevertheless did not get stock certificates, having failed to qualify as "faithful" employees (Ozanne 1967, 36–40).

In 1905, two years after Beeks left, International Harvester introduced a separate welfare department, choosing one of its own, C. W. Price, as the manager. Price, who served from 1905 to 1911, appointed Mary Goss as his assistant in charge of women's welfare activities. Under Price's leadership, International Harvester employees participated in a welfare training course run by Graham

Taylor, a minister and educator, at his Chicago settlement house. Elaborate notes were kept of the lectures, and copies were sent to management personnel at various Harvester plants. In 1908, Harvester started a liberal sickness and accident plan and an even more extensive pension plan. The amount of the pension was related to the worker's wage and to length of service; the company assumed the full cost. Prior to Harvester's adopting the pension plan, McCormick family members often supported "old hands" with monthly gifts. The company's first pension plan provided employees 70 years of age who had 20 years of service benefits of at least $18 a month to a maximum of $100 a month.

Workers resisted welfare capitalist initiatives much as they had Taylorism. Although membership in labor unions leveled off after reaching a high point in 1904, the first decade of the 20th century witnessed the establishment of the Industrial Workers of the World—a radical alternative to the American Federation of Labor—and a vibrant socialist movement. But even unorganized workers resisted the paternalist ethos inherent in welfare capitalism. What made "betterment" work "pay," according to NCR president John Patterson, was workers' acceptance of their "mutual responsibility" for the company's well-being. Workers freely enjoyed the cleaner and safer workplaces, new lunchrooms, pensions, and other benefits provided by their employers. Nevertheless, instead of paternalistic employers determining what they needed, workers preferred to earn higher wages that they could spend on what they wanted.

In *The Incorporation of America* (1982), Alan Trachtenberg claims that the "White City," the Chicago World's Columbian Exposition that opened in 1893, "seemed to have settled the question of the true meaning of America. It seemed the victory of elites in business, politics, and culture over dissident but divided voices of labor, farmers, immigrants, blacks, and women" (231). Looking back from the perspective of 1910, however, although corporate capitalism had accomplished much to reshape the political, economic, and social landscape of America in ways compatible with its needs, Trachtenberg's claims are nonetheless overstated. At the end of *Clockwork*, Eric Breibart's perceptive 1982 documentary on scientific management, the film's narrator recalls that Frederick Winslow Taylor suffered from recurrent nightmares throughout his life. Each night Taylor would dream that he was trapped in a giant machine from which he struggled in vain to free himself. Although Taylor saw himself creating a system in which "every human motion was regulated with clockwork precision," in his dreams there was, the narrator concludes, "still resistance." The same can be said for the incorporated society that large-scale capitalists had attempted to establish in the United States in the early 20th century.

BIOGRAPHIES

Nelson W. Aldrich, 1841–1915

Politician

After a short career as a banker in Rhode Island, Aldrich entered politics in 1869, initially at the local and state level. In 1871, he was elected to the U.S. House of Representatives and then, in 1881, he was sent to the Senate where he served until his retirement in 1910. Throughout his career, Aldrich aligned himself with business interests, becoming, as the historian Richard Hofstadter described him, "The watchdog of the corporations." He opposed the Interstate Commerce Act of 1887 and support protective tariffs. In 1906, Aldrich chaired the National Monetary Commission, whose recommendations led to the National Reserve Act of 1913.

Gertrude Beeks, 1867–1950

Welfare Worker

In the opening decade of the 20th century, Beeks defined the position of welfare worker. She served as the first "social agent" at McCormick Harvesting Machine Company in 1901 and, in 1903, became the first director of the Welfare Department of the National Civic Federation. She helped develop employer-initiated welfare work programs to improve employees' safety, health, and well-being in the workplace and in their homes. Throughout her career, she tried to professionalize the role of the corporate welfare worker.

Andrew Carnegie, 1835–1919

Iron and Steel Magnate, Philanthropist

Born in Dunfermline, Scotland, the son of a handloom weaver, Carnegie immigrated in 1848 to the United States with his family. Arriving in Pittsburgh, Andrew first worked as a bobbin boy in an area cotton textile mill. Later, working as a telegraph operator, Andrew caught the attention of Thomas A. Scott, superintendent of the Western Division of the Pennsylvania Railroad, who hired Carnegie to be his personal telegrapher and private secretary. In 1859, he replaced Scott as head of the rail line. Over the next three decades, Carnegie built an iron and steel empire. In 1892, a violent confrontation provoked by the Carnegie Company at its Homestead Works in Pennsylvania symbolized the growing confrontation between organized labor and the modern industrial corporation in the United States. In 1901, Carnegie sold his business to J. P. Morgan, which led to the formation of U.S. Steel. Carnegie spent the rest of his life as an active philanthropist, creating foundations that promoted education and peace.

Russell Conwell, 1843–1925

Lecturer and Minister

In 1882, Russell Conwell became pastor of Grace Church in Philadelphia. In 1888, Temple College was chartered and Conwell was chosen as the school's first president, a position he held for 38 years. Conwell is best known for his inspirational lecture "Acres of Diamonds," which he is said to have given more than 6,000 times between 1873 and 1924. Conwell celebrated the American dream of achieving success through one's own efforts.

Russell Conwell, U.S. educator, philanthropist, and religious leader. (Library of Congress)

Ralph Easley, 1856–1939

Editor and Reformer

Ralph Easley founded the Civic Federation of Chicago in 1893 to promote labor arbitration and conciliation, primary elections, and other reforms. In 1900, Easley organized the National Civic Federation (NCF) and was chair of its executive council. Here too he established departments devoted to reforms such as conciliation, pure food and drugs, and regulation of industrial corporations and utilities. Easley increasingly warned against the "evils of socialism" and opposed militant labor organizations like the Industrial Workers of the World. After World War I, the NCF became even more focused on antiradicalism, and in the 1930s, the organization attacked New Deal agencies like the Works Progress Administration for being wasteful and Communist dominated. By the mid-1920s the NCF had lost its influence.

Elbert H. Gary, 1846–1927

Lawyer and Steel Industry Leader

Elbert Gary served as president of the Chicago Bar Association (1893–1894) and was active in local politics in his hometown of Wheaton, Illinois. In the 1890s, his work as a lawyer led him to greater involvement with the consolidation movements in the iron and steel industry. In 1898, he became president of Federal Steel Company. Three years later, this company joined with seven other steel producers to form U.S. Steel, and in 1903, Gary became chair of its newly created board of directors. Known for the so-called "Gary Dinners," informal gatherings that brought together industry executives in the hope of stabilizing the steel industry, Gary promoted "healthy competition" based on trust and co-operation. A strong advocate of the "open shop" and a supporter of welfare capitalism, as chairman of U.S. Steel, Gary established stock-option, accident insurance, pension, and bonus plans at the company.

Cyrus Hall McCormick Jr., 1859–1936

Businessman and Founder of International Harvester

Son of the inventor of the reaper, Cyrus Hall Jr. joined his father in 1879 to manage the McCormick Harvesting Machine Company. In 1884, just after the death of his father, he became president of the company. After a decade of intense competition among harvester manufacturers in the 1890s, McCormick merged his company in 1902 with four other leading producers to become International Harvester. He became president of the new trust. Along with John D. Rockefeller (who was related to McCormick by marriage), McCormick owned a majority of the company's stock. At both McCormick Harvesting Machine Company and International Harvester, McCormick supported welfare capitalist programs such as the Employee Benefit Association, which, beginning in 1908, provided accident benefits and an employee pension plan.

John Pierpont (J. P.) Morgan, 1837–1913

Financier

After attending college in Switzerland and Germany, Morgan returned to New York City to work for the firm of Duncan, Sherman and Company, a job arranged for him by his father, Junius Morgan. In 1861, he started his own firm, J. P. Morgan and Company, a private wholesale bank that formed syndicates to jointly underwrite new issues of stocks and bonds. This bank and its successor, Drexel, Morgan and Company, helped reorganize many of the nation's leading railroads. Beginning in 1895, J. P. Morgan and Company played a major role in supplying capital to industry, especially the steel industry. In 1901, Morgan arranged a series of mergers that resulted in the formation of the United States Steel Corporation, the nation's first billion dollar company. The following year, Morgan underwrote the organization of International Harvester. Critics attacked Morgan as heading a "money trust" that accumulated enormous economic power through the use of interlocking directorates in major firms.

John H. Patterson, 1844–1922

Founder of the National Cash Register Company

After early failure in the family coal business, Patterson bought the rights to a mechanical "cash register" invented by a Dayton, Ohio, saloonkeeper. In

1884, Patterson established the National Cash Register Company to manufacture the machines. But first, he had to create a market for them. To promote the machines, he developed a system of "creative selling." Whereas salesmen traditionally worked as independent contractors, Patterson employed his all-male sales force to work in strict compliance with company directives. Each NCR salesman had a specified territory and had to meet quotas set by the company. Patterson also pioneered welfare programs to promote employment in NCR as a "way of life." Patterson employees received such benefits as profit-sharing, free medical care, and the opportunity to use the company's library and swimming pool.

George W. Perkins, 1862–1920

Insurance Executive, Financier, and Politician

An executive with New York Life Insurance Company, Perkins became a partner in J. P. Morgan and Company in March 1901. He helped manage the corporate reorganizations that the firm instituted. Morgan made Perkins chair of U.S. Steel's finance committee, and under Perkins, the steel corporation established a profit-sharing plan in 1902. Perkins also worked on the merger that created International Harvester and assisted Morgan in his successful efforts to end the Panic of 1907. In 1910, Perkins resigned from the Morgan company and devoted himself to politics. Perkins became chair of the newly organized Progressive Party that supported Theodore Roosevelt in his unsuccessful bid for the presidency in 1912. After Roosevelt's defeat, Perkins remained active in Progressive Party politics and, during World War I, headed a New York state committee on food distribution.

As chair of U.S. Steel's finance committee, George W. Perkins developed the company's profit-sharing plan in 1902. In 1907 he delivered an important series of public lectures on "The Modern Corporation." (Library of Congress)

John D. Rockefeller, 1839–1937

Oil Magnate

In 1863, Rockefeller, the co-owner of a successful produce commission house, entered the oil-refining business. By 1865, his company had the largest refinery in Cleveland, Ohio. Looking to expand by attracting new capital, the company reorganized in 1870 as the Standard Oil Company, and Rockefeller became its president. Rockefeller sought to develop a cooperative alliance with other oil producers to help stabilize their volatile industry. After these informal pooling arrangements failed, Standard Oil embarked on a series of acquisitions that ultimately gave it control of 90 percent of the nation's oil-refining capacity and dominion over both the transportation of refined oil, and the pipelines and storage facilities for crude oil in the Pennsylvania oil region. In 1882, to administer his growing empire, Rockefeller created the first modern trust in American business history, the Standard Oil Trust. Legal difficulties led to the formation of Standard Oil (New Jersey) as a holding company for all Standard Oil stock. Constantly challenged for pursuing unfair business practices, Rockefeller was the frequent target of press attacks, congressional hearings, and lawsuits. In 1897, Rockefeller retired from the daily management of Standard Oil and during the latter part of his life endowed a number of research and educational foundations.

The first president of U.S. Steel, Charles Schwab was forced to resign his position in 1903. He soon became president of Bethlehem Steel where he introduced a number of managerial innovations. (Library of Congress)

Charles Schwab, 1862–1939

First President of U.S. Steel

Andrew Carnegie hired Schwab in 1889 to be superintendent at his Edgar Thomson Steel Works, the largest steelworks in the nation. Schwab served Carnegie in other capacities through the 1890s, and then, in 1901, he became the first president of U.S. Steel. Schwab spent lavishly, building an ornate mansion in New York City that covered an entire block. Battles between the company's "steel" men and its "financial" men such as Elbert Gary led Schwab to resign from U.S. Steel in 1903; a year later, he took charge of the recently reorganized Bethlehem Steel Company. Schwab modernized steelmaking at Bethlehem, introduced a bonus system, and promoted younger men from within the company. Between 1904 and 1916, Bethlehem Steel's sales rose from $10 million to $230 million. After World War I Schwab semiretired from active management of Bethlehem Steel, and from 1927 to 1932 he served as president of the Iron and Steel Institute.

Frederick Winslow Taylor, 1856–1915

Engineer and Industrial Manager

Taylor is best known as the originator of the concept of scientific management. While working in the Philadelphia area at a number of iron and steel companies during the 1880s and 1890s, Taylor began experimenting with "time study," the use of the stopwatch to produce the most efficient organization of work. In 1898, Taylor went to work for the Bethlehem Iron Company, where he introduced cost accounting, production management, and other methods. At Bethlehem, Taylor also conducted his famous pig-iron "experiment" with Henry Noll, whom he would call "Schmidt" when he described the study in later lectures and in his book *The Principles of Scientific Management* (1911). Although industrial managers often opposed the full application of Taylor's system in their mills and factories, his concepts were part of the larger movement for more systematic management that began in the late 19th century.

REFERENCES AND FURTHER READINGS

American National Biography Online. http:www.anb.org/articles/15/15-00737-print.html.

Baritz, Loren. 1960. *The Servants of Power: A History of the Use of Social Science in American Industry.* New York: John Wiley and Sons.

Beckert, Sven. 1993. *The Monied Metropolis: New York City and the Consolidation of the American Bourgeoisie, 1850–1896.* New York: Cambridge University Press.

Bendix, Reinhard. 1956. *Work and Authority in Industry: Ideologies in the Course of Industrialization.* New York: Harper and Row.

Benson, Susan Porter. 1988. *Counter Cultures: Saleswomen, Managers, and Customers American Department Stores, 1890–1940.* Urbana: University of Illinois Press.

Bernstein, Irving. 1960. *The Lean Years: A History of the American Worker, 1920–1933.* Boston: Houghton Mifflin.

Brandes, Stuart D. 1976. *American Welfare Capitalism, 1880–1940.* Chicago: University of Chicago Press.

Braverman, Harry. 1974. *Labor and Monopoly Capital: The Degradation of Work in the Twentieth Century*. New York: Monthly Review Press.

Brody, David. 1969. *Steelworkers in America: The Non-Union Era*. New York: Harper and Row.

Calvert, Monte A. 1967. *The Mechanical Engineer in America, 1830–1910: Professional Cultures in Conflict*. Baltimore: Johns Hopkins Press.

Carnegie, Andrew. 1889. "Wealth." *North American Review* 148 (June): 653–664.

Carter, Joseph C. 1981. *The "Acres of Diamonds" Man: A Memorial Archive of Russell H. Conwell, A Truly Unique Institutional Creator*. Philadelphia: Privately printed by Temple University.

Chandler, Alfred D., Jr. 1959. "The Beginnings of 'Big Business' in American Industry." *Business History Review* 33 (Spring): 1–31.

Chandler, Alfred D., Jr. 1977. *The Visible Hand: The Managerial Revolution in American Business*. Cambridge: Harvard University Press.

Clockwork. 1982. Produced and directed by Eric Breitbart. San Francisco: California Newsreel. Videorecording.

Cochran, Thomas C. 1957. *The American Business System: A Historical Perspective, 1900–1955*. New York: Harper and Row.

Cochran, Thomas C. 1972. *Business in American Life: A History*. New York: McGraw Hill.

Cochran, Thomas C., and William Miller. 1961. *The Age of Enterprise: A Social History of Industrial America,* rev. ed. New York: Harper and Row.

Cohen, Lizabeth. 1990. *Making a New Deal: Industrial Chicago, 1919–1939*. New York: Cambridge University Press.

Commons, John R. 1935. *History of Labor in the United States, 1896–1932*. Vol. 3. New York: The Macmillan Company.

Comstock, Sarah. 1913. "A Woman of Achievement, Miss Gertrude Beeks." *The World's Work,* August.

Conference on Welfare Work. 1904. New York: Press of Andrew D. Kellogg Co.

Conwell, Russell H. 1975. *Acres of Diamonds*. Grand Rapids, Mich.: Fleming H. Revell.

Cronon, William. 1991. *Nature's Metropolis: Chicago and the Great West*. New York: W. W. Norton.

Dawley, Alan. 2005. "The Abortive Rule of Big Money." In *Ruling America: A History of Wealth and Power in a Democracy,* ed. Steven Fraser and Gary Gerstle, 149–180. Cambridge: Harvard University Press.

Edwards, Richard. 1979. *Contested Terrain: The Transformation of the Workplace in the Twentieth Century*. New York: Basic Books.

Fraser, Steve. 2005. *Every Man a Speculator: A History of Wall Street in American Life*. New York: Harper Collins.

Galambos, Louis, and Joseph Pratt. 1988. *The Rise of the Corporate Commonwealth: United States Business and Public Policy in the Twentieth Century*. New York: Basic Books.

Garraty, John. 1960. *Right-Hand Man: The Life of George W. Perkins*. New York: Harper.

Greenberg, Brian. 1985. *Worker and Community: Response to Industrialization in a Nineteenth-Century City, Albany, New York, 1850–1884*. Albany: SUNY Press.

Harris, Neil. 1990. *Cultural Excursions: Marketing Appetites and Cultural Tastes in Modern America*. Chicago: University of Chicago Press.

Harris, Neil. 1962. "The Gilded Age Revisited: Boston and the Museum Movement." *American Quarterly* 14 (4): 545–566.

Heilbroner, Robert, and Aaron Singer. 1999. *The Economic Transformation of America: 1600 to the Present,* 4th ed. Fort Worth, Tex.: Harcourt Brace.

Jacoby, Sanford. 1985. *Employing Bureaucracy: Managers, Unions, and the Transformation of Work in American Industry, 1900–1945*. New York: Columbia University Press.

Kanigel, Robert. 1999. *The One Best Way: Frederick Winslow Taylor and the Enigma of Efficiency*. New York: Penguin Books.

Korman, Gerd. 1967. *Industrialization, Immigrants, and Americanizers: The View from Milwaukee, 1866–1921*. Madison, Wisc.: State Historical Society of Wisconsin.

Kryder, Leeanne Giannone. 1985. "Humanizing the Industrial Workplace: The Role of the Early Personnel Manager, 1897–1920." *Henry Ford Museum & Greenfield Village Herald* 14 (1): 14–19.

Layton, Edwin T., Jr. 1971. *The Revolt of the Engineers: Social Responsibility and the American Engineering Profession*. Cleveland: Case Western Reserve University Press.

Lears, Jackson. 2005. "The Managerial Revitalization of the Rich." In *Ruling America: A History of Wealth and Power in a Democracy,* ed. Steve Fraser and Gary Gerstle, 181–214. Cambridge, Mass.: Harvard University Press.

Lescohier, Don D. 1935. *History of Labor in the United States, 1896–1932,* vol. 3. New York: The Macmillan Company.

Licht, Walter. 1995. *Industrializing America: The Nineteenth Century*. Baltimore: Johns Hopkins University Press.

Link, Arthur, and Richard L. McCormick. 1983. *Progressivism*. Arlington Heights, Ill.: Harlan Davidson.

Lynd, Robert S., and Helen Merrell Lynd. 1929. *Middletown: A Study in American Culture*. New York: Harcourt, Brace.

Mandell, Nikki. 2002. *The Corporation as Family: The Gendering of Corporate Welfare, 1890–1930*. Chapel Hill: University of North Carolina Press.

Marchand, Roland. 1998. *Creating the Corporate Soul: The Rise of Public Relations and Corporate Imagery in American Big Business*. Berkeley: University of California Press.

McCraw, Thomas K. 1987. "The Challenge of Alfred D. Chandler, Jr.: Retrospect and Prospect." *Reviews in American History* 15 (1): 160–178.

Meyer, Stephen. 1981. *The Five Dollar Day: Labor Management and Social Control in the Ford Company, 1908–1921*. Albany: State University of New York Press.

Miller, William, ed. 1952. *Men in Motion: Essays in the History of Entrepreneurship*. Cambridge, Mass.: Harvard University Press.

Montgomery, David. 1980. "Strikes in Nineteenth-Century America." *Social Science History*. 4 (February): 92.

Nelson, Daniel. 1975. *Managers and Workers: Origins of the New Factory System in the United States, 1880–1920*. Madison: University of Wisconsin Press.

New York Times. 1912. "Welfare Work May Conquer the Labor Problem," *New York Times*. November 17.

Noble, David. 1977. *American by Design: Science, Technology, and the Rise of Corporate Capitalism*. New York: Oxford University Press.

Ozanne, Robert. 1967. *A Century of Labor-Management Relations at McCormick and International Harvester*. Madison: University of Wisconsin Press.

Perkins, George. 1908. "The Modern Corporation." In *The Currency Problem and the Present Financial Situation*, 155–170. New York, Columbia University Press. http://www.sewanee.edu/amstudies/perkins.html.

Rodgers, Daniel T. 1978. *The Work Ethic in Industrial America, 1850–1920*. Chicago: University of Chicago Press.

Roosevelt, Theodore. 1899. "The Strenuous Life." Speech before the Hamilton Club, Chicago, April 10. www.bartleby.com/58/1.html.

Salvatore, Nick. 1982. *Eugene V. Debs: Citizen and Socialist*. Urbana: University of Illinois Press.

Serrin, William. 1993. *Homestead: The Glory and the Tragedy of an American Steel Town*. New York: Vintage Books.

Shifflett, Crandall. 1996. *Victorian America, 1876 to 1913*. New York: Facts on File.

Taylor, Frederick Winslow. 1947. *Scientific Management, Comprising Shop Management, the Principles of Scientific Management [and] Testimony before the Special House Committee*. New York: Harper.

Tone, Andrea. 1997. *The Business of Benevolence: Industrial Paternalism in Progressive America*. Ithaca: Cornell University Press.

Trachtenberg, Alan. 1982. *The Incorporation of America: Culture and Society in the Gilded Age*. New York: Hill and Wang.

Tucker, Barbara M. 1984. *Samuel Slater and the Origins of the American Textile Industry, 1790–1860*. Ithaca: Cornell University Press.

Usselman, Steven W. 2006. "Still Visible: Alfred D. Chandler's *The Visible Hand*." *Technology and Culture* 47 (3): 584–596.

Veblen, Thorstein. 1899. *The Theory of the Leisure Class*. New York: Macmillan Co. Reprinted New York: Modern Library, 2001. Page references are to the 2001 edition.

Wechsler, Harold S. 1977. *The Qualified Student: A History of Selective Admission in America*. New York: John Wiley and Sons.

Weinstein, James. 1968. *The Corporate Ideal in the Liberal State, 1900–1918*. Boston: Beacon Press.

Wiebe, Robert. 1967. *The Search for Order, 1877–1920*. New York: Hill and Wang.

Wrege, Charles D., and Amedio G. Perroni. 1974. "Taylor's Pig-Tale: A Historical Analysis of Frederick W. Taylor's Pig-Iron Experiments," *Academy of Management Journal* 17 (1): 6–27.

Zahavi, Gerald. 1988. *Workers, Managers, and Welfare Capitalism: The Shoe Workers and Tanners of Endicott Johnson, 1890–1950*. Urbana: University of Illinois Press.

Zunz, Olivier. 1990. *Making America Corporate, 1870–1920*. Chicago: University of Chicago Press.

Working-Class Life in Industrial America

OVERVIEW

In *Progress and Poverty,* one of the 19th century's most influential works of social and economic criticism, Henry George calls "the association of poverty with progress . . . the great enigma of our times." As long as "all the increased wealth which modern progress brings goes but to build up great fortunes, to increase luxury and make sharper the contrast between the House of Have and the House of Want, progress is not real and cannot be permanent. The reaction must come," he predicted (Fink 2001, 6–7). Many Americans in the late 19th and early 20th centuries shared the reformer George's fears that the nation faced a future rent by social conflict. Even *The New York Times,* although hardly sympathetic to George's radical theories, concurred, declaring that "the days are over" when "this country could rejoice in its freedom from the elements of social strife which have long abounded in the old countries" (Foner 1988, 585). From the early days of the republic, Americans confidently anticipated that they could have "capitalism without class conflict, industrialization without the 'dark and satanic mills' of Europe" (Foner 1988, 585). Those Americans living in the states that composed the Union during the Civil War had anticipated that the promise of America could be fulfilled under the prevailing free labor capitalist order. They thus responded to the concentration of economic and political power that paralleled the growth of giant corporations and factories in the United States in the late 19th century as a threat to their deepest aspirations for America.

At a campaign stop in New Haven, Connecticut, during the presidential campaign of 1860, Abraham Lincoln, the American most associated with free labor capitalism in the 19th century, rhetorically asked, "What is the true condition of the laborer?" Using himself as an example, Lincoln answered his own question: "When one starts poor, as most do in the race of life, free society is such that he knows he can better his condition; he knows that there is no fixed condition of labor for his whole life." Although "this year" a man may be, as Lincoln once had been, a hired laborer, in due course he could look forward to working for himself, and then, at last, to hiring "men to work for him." With its promise of social mobility and economic independence, the free labor system was for Lincoln, as it was for most of his audience that night and for many years beyond, the "true system" (Basler 1953, 24–25).

Through much of the 19th century, industry in America consisted mainly of the production of light consumer goods such as cloth, boots and shoes, and clocks. As industrialization concentrated in the nation's cities, a "metropolitan industrialization" emerged that rested on a diversity of manufactures (Wilentz 1984, 109–119). Manufacturing in cities ranged from artisan shops in which the craftsman still produced the entire good by hand to a mix of work settings that intensified the division of labor and often included outwork—women and children completing a specific task while working at home. Outside the cities, larger factories and mills employing water-powered machinery flourished, concentrating production along the nation's waterways. Nevertheless, at the turn of the century, the economy of the United States remained primarily agricultural. Even with the economic concentration that accompanied the Age of Morgan, 40 percent of Americans still worked on farms as late as 1901.

The concentration of ownership and the tremendous surge in industrial production during the late 19th and early 20th centuries transformed both the American workplace and the nature of work itself. Whereas the United States in 1860 had ranked behind Great Britain, France, and Germany in the value of its manufactures, by the turn of the century industrial production in America was greater than the combined total for the other three nations. By 1910, the U.S. industrial labor force (including manufacturing, construction, mining, and transportation) comprised just over 14 million people, roughly four times the number of workers so engaged 40 years earlier. Large-scale producers like steel grew even more. In 1870, only a few steel mills in the nation employed more than 500 workers; by the first decade of the 20th century, 1,000 American steel mills employed between 500 and 1,000 workers each (Licht 1995, 102).

Industry's demand for cheaper labor was insatiable. Looking to cut their labor costs, managers sought to undermine skilled workers' privileged position in the industrial workforce through increased mechanization and an intensive division of labor in the workplace. For example, after they defeated the Amalgamated Association of Iron and Steel Workers in the Homestead strike in 1892, Andrew Carnegie and Henry Frick eliminated union work rules and reorganized the job structures in their mills. As the size and scale of steel production increased in the wake of the strike, many operations were mechanized and the typical steel worker was transformed into a semiskilled operative adept at routine mechanical duties. As one English visitor commented on the greater worker productivity that he observed, "the various operations are so much simplified that an experienced man is not required. . . . The workingmen in America do not act upon their own judgment, but carry out the instructions given to them" (Brody 1969, 28–32). In the 20 years after 1890, significantly reduced labor costs lowered the cost of steel making by almost a third.

Steel is just one instance of what was actually a diverse pattern of change. Modern industry is often equated with mechanization and with mass, assembly-line production. The technological dimension was important, but change came even to industries relatively unaffected by mechanization. In the case of meat-packing—an outstanding example of the growth of monopoly capital in the early 20th century—new machinery affected packinghouse workers less than did than the intense subdivision of their jobs. Before the mid-1880s, nearly the entire slaughtering and cutting operation could be done by one man, the "all-around butcher." But during the next two decades assembly-line production was introduced in meatpacking, and the amount of skill required of packinghouse workers was vastly reduced.

Skill did not necessarily disappear, however. Looking at a broad range of occupations, the historian Andrew Dawson determined that the number of skilled workers in the United States dropped only slightly between 1870 and 1910 (Dawson 1979, 330–331). In a number of trades, skill remained essential. In fact, in the building trades and in fields like metalworking, despite the introduction of new machinery in the late 19th century, a range of new skills emerged that kept these trades as skilled crafts well into the 20th century. Also, these craft workers had more success than did the steelworkers in controlling access to the new machine-tending positions introduced in their industries.

The transformation of industry had relatively little impact on the work of "common" or unskilled laborers, the mainly young single men who loaded and unloaded ships, drilled tunnels, and constructed and repaired railway tracks. In manufacturing and in construction, laborers fetched, carried, loaded, or cleaned up, performing whatever task they were asked to do. In the early years of the 20th century, these unskilled workers were most likely to be immigrants from eastern and southern Europe. They often worked under the harsh direction of gang bosses, and their highly irregular employment was heavily dependent on both the weather and the business cycle. For example, although their wages improved in the early 20th century, unskilled laborers in steel were still paid only half what skilled men earned. Despite earning barely enough to subsist on, many of the immigrant workers endured their ill-paying and unpleasant jobs hoping to save enough money to eventually return home.

Not all industrial change in the late 19th and early 20th centuries involved large-scale, capital-intensive production. Through the 19th century, manufacturing, especially in major cities across the nation, meant the extensive production of diversified goods in small, frequently family-owned-and-operated firms. In the highly competitive production of inexpensive, ready-made clothes, for example, centered in Chicago, New York, and Philadelphia, small garment manufacturers rented space in lofts and tenement buildings. Italian and Jewish operatives, both men and women, sat at foot-pedaled sewing machines turning out a vast array of ready-to-wear garments. In a labor-intensive industry like the needle trades, contractors and bosses developed piece rate and task (work quota) systems that often pushed output per worker to the extreme. Worse still was the homework system in which immigrant women and children stitched clothing, rolled cigars, assembled artificial flowers, or engaged in many other occupations in their tenement apartments. Trade unions and social reformers like the journalist Jacob Riis led campaigns well into the 20th century to either abolish or severely regulate homework.

In the early 20th century, until state child-labor laws and advanced mechanization reduced their numbers, more than a quarter million children under the age of 15 worked in mines, mills, and factories in the United States. Especially harsh conditions prevailed among child laborers in the South's expanding textile industry. Unscrupulous mill owners encouraged poor white families to bind their children over at miserable wages. In the nation's cities, boys as young as 10, and some girls, sold newspapers, shined shoes, or scavenged in the streets.

In 1890, the U.S. Census Bureau began to distinguish between blue-collar manual laborers, who were paid either hourly wages or by piece rate, and white-collar workers, who earned a fixed salary. By the early 20th century, white-collar work was growing at a faster rate than industrial labor. Whereas in 1870 only 6 percent of the labor force held jobs as managers, salaried professionals, salespeople, and office workers, by 1910 white-collar work encompassed some 13.5 percent of the total workforce. A vast pool of clerks, typists, and bookkeepers materialized to collect and process the data and to keep the reports required by managers of corporate enterprise. In the 20 years after 1890, clerical work alone exploded by 400 percent. As in blue-collar work, technology often spurred specialization, but for the white-collar worker, skill remained an important consideration. The white-collar worker's steadier employment translated into greater economic security than could be achieved by most industrial workers, and some white-collar employees were even able to retain a degree of autonomy within the new bureaucratic structures of the modern corporation.

By the turn of the century, women had begun to fill white-collar jobs previously the exclusive province of male workers. Between 1890 and 1910, the number of women participating in the paid labor force rose by over a third. During these years, most immigrant and African American female wage earners still had to labor as domestic servants, but native-born white women began moving into teaching, nursing, clerical work, sales, and other service jobs. In offices, women usually performed the more routine tasks. By the turn of the century, young, unmarried, native-born women made up the vast majority of telephone operators. Not surprisingly, native-born parents preferred that their daughters work in "clean" jobs with higher earning potential than factory work, which was seen as more "dangerous" to girls both morally and physically (Diner 1998, 155–175).

After the Civil War, African American women also joined the labor force in large numbers. By the end of the first decade of the 20th century, of the approximately one million African American women working in nonagricultural jobs, nearly 90 percent toiled as domestics and laundresses (Foner and Lewis 1989, 355). African American men in the postbellum South found that most skilled industrial jobs were closed to them, except in the building trades and extractive industries. But by 1900, despite Jim Crow and union antipathy, the number of African American men in industrial jobs nationwide, though still small, began to increase steadily. Thus, in 1910 in Pittsburgh and in Allegheny City, Pennsylvania, employment of African American workers in the steel mills had risen to 3 percent of the total mill labor, more than double the number employed two decades earlier.

In the early 20th century, skilled and white-collar jobs remained largely the exclusive province of white men who were either native born or "old" immigrants from Great Britain and northern Europe, whereas jobs as semiskilled machine operatives and unskilled day laborers were increasingly filled by "new" immigrant workers from southern and eastern Europe. The crush of new immigrants after the turn of the century (which reached a high of one million per year in the decade after 1905) resulted in a working class in the United States divided by ethnic background and gender (and to a much lesser extent, by race). Within the American working class, an inequality based on widening wage differentials exacerbated cultural divisions. Between 1890 and 1914, the wages of skilled workers advanced at more than twice the rate of the wages of the unskilled (Dawson 1979, 332). Thus, a relatively privileged labor aristocracy of skilled men improved its economic position in these years.

Many skilled workers in the early 20th century achieved the "American standard" invoked by Samuel Gompers, president of the American Federation of Labor (AFL). While the earnings of skilled workers often provided them and their families not only a sufficiency of food but also a degree of personal comfort, especially in their ability to purchase a small home, the "paltry" wages earned by unskilled workers, as noted in a survey conducted in these years by the Pittsburgh Christian Social Service Union, barely enabled them to maintain "the lowest standard of living compatible with decency and comfort" (Shergold 1982, 506). In general, few industrial workers could support families on their individual earnings. Many working-class men supplemented their earnings with a "family income" generated by the labor of their wives and daughters, who provided the meals, washed the clothes, and kept up the rooms of boarders in their homes.

TIMELINE

1900	The National Civic Federation is formed.
	The International Ladies' Garment Workers Union is chartered by the American Federation of Labor.
1901	The Amalgamated Association of Iron, Steel, and Tin Workers strike against U.S. Steel.
	The AFL issues the "Scranton Declaration" upholding principle of craft unionism.
	The United Textile Workers of America (AFL) is organized.
1902	The United Mine Workers (UMW) of America strike against anthracite operators.
1903	The National Women's Trade Union League is founded.
	This year marks the beginning of the employers' open-shop drive.
	The U.S. Department of Commerce and Labor is created at the cabinet level.
1904	The Amalgamated Meat Cutters and Butcher Workmen of North America strike.
1905	The founding convention of the Industrial Workers of the World takes place.
1906	The AFL issues its "Bill of Grievances."
	The International Typographical Union conducts an eight-hour workday strike of book- and job-printing establishments.
1907	The Supreme Court of the District of Columbia issues an injunction against an AFL boycott of Buck's Stove and Range Company of St. Louis, Missouri.
1908	The AFL endorses the Democratic nominee, William Jennings Bryan, for president.
	The U.S. Supreme Court rules against the AFL in the Danbury Hatters case.
	U.S. v. Adair declares Section 10 of the Erdman Act, which outlawed "yellow-dog" contracts, unconstitutional.

1909	The IWW leads a strike against the Pressed Steel Car Company in McKees Rocks, Pennsylvania.
	The "uprising of the 20,000" general strike is led by the International Ladies' Garment Workers' Union in New York City.

"ALL THE LIVELONG DAY": THE CHANGING MEANING OF WORK

In his memoirs, John Brophy, a leader in the formation of the Congress of Industrial Organizations in the 1930s, described his father, who was a coal miner in the late 1800s, as a "good workman," a skilled worker who had "a pride in his calling." Each miner, Brophy continued, "was his own boss within his workplace." Yet by the end of the first decade of the 20th century, undercutting machines, first introduced into the mines in the 1880s, had taken over in soft coal production, transforming the skilled pit miner into a machine tender or conveyor loader. In mining, as it had in iron and steel, paper, glass, and so many other mass-production industries, deskilling through mechanization became common. Notwithstanding the training and traditions that had endowed them with collective autonomy, craft workers were forced to become machine operatives specialists whose work was subdivided and closely supervised (Diner 1998, 50–51; Brody 1969, 4–5; Montgomery 1987, 114–115).

Despite the magnitude of the changes wrought by mechanization and the subdivision of labor, many craftsmen proved capable of adapting. As existing skills disappeared or diminished, new occupations requiring expertise and training appeared. The introduction of a commercially viable linotype machine during the economically depressed 1890s displaced many skilled workers in the printing trade. Yet even as the linotype machine replaced the hand compositor, a skilled printer was still required to judge layout, to operate the linotype keyboard, and to maintain the equipment. More important, unlike in the steel industry, where consolidation into large companies broke the control of the union, the larger the size of the workplace in printing the more likely it was that the printer would belong to a union. Able to take a more flexible approach to technology and managerial initiatives, printers in the early 20th century retained some workplace autonomy and improved their wages and working conditions.

The corporate revolution at the turn of the century that transformed the blue-collar world of the industrial worker also created a new class of white-collar workers far more complex than had served the business sector 30 years before. The number of white-collar employees, although still under 5 percent of the total workforce in the United States, expanded at an even faster rate than industrial labor in the early 20th century. By 1910, large businesses were hiring salesmen to staff expanding corporate sales departments, as well as employing native-born

New York World-Telegram *print shop, ca. 1900–1920. (Library of Congress)*

women in greater numbers to fill positions as office and clerical workers, sales-clerks in department stores, and telephone operators. Although beset by many of the same conditions of intensified and specialized work that confronted their blue-collar brothers and sisters, white-collar workers were more likely to identify themselves as members of the middle class. Working at jobs that usually required greater refinement in dress, speech, and manner, and at least some formal schooling, they took pride in achieving a higher social standing than manual workers. White-collar work was usually steadier and better paid, as well as safer, cleaner, and, especially important for women, viewed as more respectable.

Immigrant men, especially those who were young and single, filled the ranks of the unskilled or of day laborers in the industrial cities of the early 20th century. Working as common laborers, building or repairing railroad tracks, loading and unloading freight in rail yards or on the docks, hauling building materials, digging ditches, paving streets and roads, shoveling coal into industrial furnaces, and moving goods, they performed tasks relatively unaffected by technology or mechanization. Despite constantly having to move from job to job and despite the very poor pay, some immigrants took these jobs as a matter of choice. The historian Virginia Yans McLaughlin found that Italian men in Buffalo preferred day labor jobs to the possibility of steadier and better-paying work in local steel mills because day labor left them free in the summer to work with their families

Table 2.1. Occupations of Male and Female Workers, 1910 (percent)

General Division of Occupations	Male	Female
All occupations	78.8	21.2
Agriculture, forestry, animal husbandry	85.7	14.3
Extraction of minerals	99.9	0.1
Manufacturing and mechanical industries	82.9	17.1
Transportation	96.0	4.0
Trade	87.1	12.9
Public service	97.0	3.0
Professional service	56.7	43.3
Domestic and personal service	32.9	67.1
Clerical occupations	65.8	34.2

Source: Adapted from Wolman 1924, 102.

in the fruit-and-vegetable–processing canneries located in rural areas surrounding the city (Yans McLaughlin 1982, 184–201).

Even though day labor jobs tended to be seasonal and heavily influenced by the health of the business cycle, the number of day laborers overall grew in the 50 years prior to World War I. A study of the steel industry in Allegheny County, Pennsylvania, estimates that in the first decade of the 20th century, almost half the workers in the region were common laborers or were paid at that rate. According to the 1910 census, about one-third of manual wage earners earned their living in manufacturing and transportation as common laborers. As the number of unskilled day laborers rose, so did their pay, but at a much slower rate than that of skilled workers and machine operatives. The historian Andrew Dawson concluded that between 1870 and 1910 the number of skilled workers held steady as their relative economic well-being increased. According to Dawson, during the quarter of a century before World War I, while wages for all manufacturing workers rose by 54 percent, wages paid skilled workers rose by 74 percent compared to an increase of only 31 percent for the unskilled. Dawson disputes the conventional wisdom that mechanization and the dilution of skill decimated the ranks of skilled workers. Based on the evidence of their wages, skilled workers proved to be highly adaptive in the face of advancing technology and the monopolization of industry (Dawson 1979, 325–351).

David Brody and the Making of New American Labor History

In 1960, Harvard University Press published *Steelworkers in America: The Nonunion Era* by David Brody. The prevailing approach to the study of labor history at the time, the "Wisconsin School" focused on the institutional structure of trade unions. Trained as economists, Richard T. Ely, Selig Perlman, and John R. Commons produced a vast literature in an effort to legitimize trade unionism in general and the "pure and simple" policies of the Samuel Gompers–led American Federation of Labor in particular (Greenberg 1993, 457–469). In the preface to *Steelworkers* Brody states, "This is a labor history . . . somewhat out of the ordinary. . . . My aim has been to study the process" by which the lives of workers in America's steel mills "were shaped in the nonunion era of the industry" (Brody 1969, ix). His claim that workers were impotent in the face of overwhelming managerial power marks *Steelworkers,* as Brody acknowledges, as "a transitional work" between the "old" and the "new" labor history. Since the early 1960s, much of new labor history has followed one of two paths: one, inspired by Herbert Gutman, concentrates on worker culture, on the rules and values that generated and guided workers' response to industrialism; the other, led by David Montgomery, argues that the workers' worldview was forged on the shop floor (Brody 1989, 11).

Assessing Gutman's contribution, Montgomery credits him with drawing the attention of scholars away from trade unions "to the communities where workers lived and fought" and, especially, "with teaching a generation of scholars to appreciate workers as makers of their own history" (Montgomery 1980, 501). In his studies of smaller cities and towns during the Gilded Age, Gutman challenged a number of the commonly held generalizations about labor: that workers received little sympathy from the rest of the community, that employers had a relatively free hand in imposing the new industrial discipline, and that the quest for wealth had obliterated nonpecuniary values (Montgomery 1978). Analyzing evolving class relations in American industry, primarily in the late 19th and early 20th centuries, Montgomery himself portrays as heroes the autonomous craftsmen who controlled production and resisted both the imposition of managerial authority and management's eagerness to transform the workmen into economic men (Montgomery 1980).

Yet the new labor history of American workers has also been deeply influenced by the work of the British labor historian E. P. Thompson, especially by his magisterial *The Making of the English Working Class* (1963). Indeed, the notion of agency, the idea "that the working class made itself as much as it was made" (to cite Thompson's classic definition), is the starting point for much of new labor history (Thompson 1963, 194). Brody's *Steelworkers,* if not a study of worker agency, is a significant portrait of managerial culture and managerial control. Comparing the experiences of organized steelworkers in Great Britain, where unions did not collapse, to those of steelworkers in the United States, where they did, the historian James Holt concludes that what stands out is the "sheer determination" with which American employers resisted trade unionism (Holt 1977). *Steelworkers* remains an important case study of how capital, using a combination of repression, welfarism, and, especially, at points of conflict, the power of the state, fought unions. The issues addressed by Brody in *Steelworkers in America* in 1960—the limitations of the institutional/trade union approach to labor history, the need to understand the experience of immigrant workers, management control and the labor process, steelmasters' vigorous antiunionism, welfare capitalism, worker protest, and the particular significance of World War I and the 1920s—continue to animate the writing of labor history.

Steelworkers and Skill

The decades bracketing the onset of the 20th century proved to be pivotal for basic changes in the conditions of work in the U.S. steel industry. Prior to the Homestead strike of 1892, steel work required training, experience, dexterity, and judgment. Work rules enforced by the Amalgamated Association of Iron, Steel, and Tin Workers controlled the pace of production. The union had also negotiated a sliding pay scale that enabled workers to share in the profits of their increased productivity. But the Homestead strike and the further defeats the union suffered at the hands of U.S. Steel in 1901 and 1909 broke the influence of the Amalgamated Association. By 1910, few steelworkers enjoyed union protection.

After 1892, steel masters succeeded in replacing skilled men with semiskilled machine tenders at every opportunity. Charles Schwab, the president of U.S. Steel, claimed in 1902 that he could "take a green hand—say a fairly intelligent agricultural labourer—and make a steel melter of him in six to eight weeks" (Stone 1974, 73). In the two decades after 1890, not only did the daily earnings of skilled workers fall by as much as 70 percent but steel companies also developed bonus systems that, like Frederick Winslow Taylor's differential piece rate, tied incentives to the enhanced productivity of the "first class workman." Moreover, even as mechanization made the work of semiskilled operatives more uniform, the steel companies introduced highly demarcated job ladders intended to create the illusion of vertical mobility. A panoply of welfare programs, including profit sharing and stock option plans, intended to encourage industriousness among the workers, reward discipline, and limit strikes and other collective actions by workers (Stone 1974, 69–78; Green 1980, 8–17).

Mass Production, Division of Labor, and the Meatpacking Industry

The rise of mass production in the United States usually resulted in the displacement of workers by machinery. In meatpacking, however, mechanization was not the key change. The transformation of the meatpacking industry was the result of an intensive division of labor. Before the end of the 19th century, the industry had already reached the limits of technological innovation. Almost

*Inspection of hogs at the Swift &
Company packinghouse in Chicago,
ca. 1900. In the early 20th century,
Chicago was the site of militant labor
struggles in the meatpacking industry.
(Library of Congress)*

unique to meatpacking, productivity, or output per man-hour, actually declined in the decade after 1909. Stagnation in the industry was a consequence of the limits imposed by the need to handle perishable and irregularly sized carcasses, which made packinghouse work highly labor intensive. Even though by the early 20th century the structure of the industry (the organization of the Big Five meatpackers) had been modernized and meatpacking had become the first assembly-line industry, production remained dependent on hand labor (Barrett 1990, 18–22).

By the first decade of the 20th century, each butcher performed the same minute operation a thousand times during the workday. Investigators from the federal Bureau of Corporations in these years remarked on the extensive division of labor: "In the largest slaughtering plants of today will be found hundreds, or even thousands, of workmen, each of whom performs a very small, narrowly defined task, in which by innumerable repetitions he becomes the expert" (Barrett 1990, 25–26). With "no room for individuality or artistry in beef butchering," a contemporary management text observed, workers could be easily "Taylorized," that is, made to cut "by the book" (Barrett 1990, 26). New conveyor systems introduced in 1908 for hog slaughtering and cattle killing further restricted the butcher's control of production and enabled more intensive supervision. The small group of remaining skilled butchers found themselves surrounded by an army of common laborers who made up two-thirds of the industry's labor force. Because managers employed butchers on an "as needed" basis, packinghouse work and pay became irregular for these skilled workers.

The Building Trades and Craft Traditions

Before 1910, carpenters successfully challenged employers' attempts to erode their skill through technology and the restructuring of the work process. Like the miners of John Brophy's father's generation at end of 19th century, journeymen carpenters took great pride in their craft. Yet their trade was also changing. Woodworking machinery introduced in the early 1870s cost many carpenters their jobs, as lumber mills employed poorly paid "green hands" to mass-produce

Women and Office Work

For working women, new machinery frequently meant greater opportunity for employment, particularly in jobs that had previously been held by men. After the 1880s, the typewriter became a familiar fixture in most offices, and women, who seemed to be more manually dexterous than men, began to be regularly hired as "type writers." The implementation of Taylorism, which increased the need for filing, correspondence, and record keeping and placed a premium on conscientious work habits, also created more opportunities for office work for women. Between 1890 and 1910 the number of Americans holding clerical positions jumped by 300 percent, from 381,000 to 1,524,000. Whereas in 1870 fewer than 2,000 women worked in offices, by 1910 more than a third of all clerical workers were female (Davies 1982, appendix table 1).

The women who became office workers in these years tended to be native-born, white, young (18 to 24 years old), and single (Schlereth 1991, 67). Although office work opened exciting new vistas for these women, the jobs did not necessarily pay well. For example, in 1892, Sears, Roebuck Company started typists at $208 a year even though the Illinois Bureau of Labor Statistics estimated the minimal living costs for a young woman in Chicago as $312 a year. However, women working in offices generally earned more than their sisters toiling in factories or as store clerks. Also, women office workers, unlike blue-collar operatives, worked a shorter day and usually had two-week paid vacations. Still, men doing comparable work earned 50 percent more than the women did (Diner 1998, 159).

In the latter decades of the 19th century, the telephone, like the typewriter, revolutionized communications and changed the conduct of business. Beginning in the 1880s, women and girls replaced teenage boys as the main workforce in the telephone companies. Companies hired women, known as the "hello girls," for their pleasing voices and nimble fingers. By the early 20th century the Bell Telephone System had become the largest employer of women in the United States. Telephone companies hired mostly second-generation, American-born single women between the ages of 17 and 26 who had had at least a grammar-school education. In the hope of attracting women of the middle class, the phone companies provided workplaces that were "wholesome and refined." Company cafeterias served nutritious meals, and matrons supervised "retiring rooms" for rest periods. The companies also sponsored reading rooms and libraries, and in some locations constructed dormitories so that women working at night did not have to return home in the dark.

In 1869, Francis Wayland Ayer formed N. W. Ayer and Son, one of the nation's first advertising agencies. In 1886, no longer capable of relying on direct communication to manage his business, Ayer hired its first stenographer. Ralph M. Hower, the company's historian, notes that by 1892, internal communication at Ayer and Son employed both a typewriter and a mimeographing machine. Telegraphy and then the telephone quickly became the necessary means by which field

Continued on next page

Women and Office Work, Continued

representatives contacted the home office. Early in the 20th century accounting records were also upgraded to provide more complete financial information (Hower 1939, 482–483). By 1900, Ayer and Son had a staff of 163 employees, a third more than a decade before. The firm continued to grow, and whereas Ayer hired its first female employee in 1876, by the first years of the new century about 40 percent of the firm's staff were women, mainly typists, stenographers, and other lower-level clerical workers (Davies 1982, 53).

More than a change in gender was involved in the reshaping of the office at the turn of the century. The male clerk who had been largely autonomous and had handled the whole of a business transaction was replaced by several office workers, each assigned to a specialized unit, such as the filing, accounting, purchasing, or marketing department. The introduction before 1910 of the time clock into the business office highlights the similarity between the changes in office work and the specialization process experienced by the factory worker. But although typists, stenographers, and adding-machine operators might work like assembly-line operatives, continuously repeating the same task, clerical work also required that they have a good command of English and often demanded that the employee show initiative, judgment, and precision. For working-class families, having a daughter who was a stenographer or typist demonstrated the family's well-being to friends and neighbors. To the single woman, office work, even with its limited opportunities for advancement, offered a safe and respectable opportunity to support herself and her family.

---

essential building materials such as doors and floorboards that could then be easily installed at the job site. Also, for carpenters more than for other building trades, the practice of "lumping"—using cheap labor recruited by subcontractors—threatened the integrity of their craft. But solidarity, especially in support of their union, strengthened the carpenters (Mendel 2003, 115). Between 1900 and 1904, the Brotherhood of Carpenters and Joiners of America signed up more than 100,000 members, especially among workers in local industries where small competitive firms predominated. Wage rates rose steadily, and the union was able to enforce craft standards (Green 1980, 40).

Other building tradesmen also effectively defended their craft. By the first decade of the 20th century, the building industry had been transformed by three factors: the successful introduction of the elevator, the replacement of structural steel for cast iron, and the use of reinforced concrete. The erection of larger buildings multiplied the number of skills needed in construction and revolutionized the older skills. Electricians, elevator riggers, metal lathers, and structural-iron and sheet-metal tradesmen now worked alongside carpenters, plasterers,

Department Store Clerks

Large department stores and major corporations established at the turn of the century transformed the job of retail selling. Throughout the 19th century, independent salesmen who worked as long-distance drummers, as door-to-door peddlers, or as clerks in mercantile houses and country stores sold the goods bought by most Americans. In his novel *Sister Carrie* (1900), Theodore Dreiser captures the opportunistic and entrepreneurial spirit of the "drummer" in the character of Drouet, whose flashy clothes and confident manner enable him to seduce the susceptible Carrie Meeber. In the early 20th century, as the large corporations sought to dominate an increasingly national market, they developed sales and advertising divisions staffed by loyal and professional male agents. Often well-paid—general sales agents for International Harvester earned between $2,500 and $3,600 a year in 1910, and assistant agents made between $2,000 and $2,500 (the annual wage for all manufacturing workers in 1910 was $558)—successful salesmen enjoyed unusual opportunities for autonomy and advancement. As representatives of prominent national corporations, the sales agents became respected members of their local communities (Diner 1998, 165–166).

By the turn of the century large department stores like R. H. Macy, Marshall Field, and John Wanamaker dominated retail selling in cities across the United States. Employment in these "palaces of consumption" stores and in smaller shops more than doubled in the first two decades of the 20th century. Women held most of these jobs. Edward Filene characterized his Boston Store as "an Adam-less Eden." On every floor of the department store, a journalist observed in 1910, "in every aisle, at every counter, women. . . . Behind most the counters on all the floors, . . . women. At every cashier's desk, at the wrappers' desks, running back and forth with parcels and change, short-skirted women" (Benson 1988, 76). Mostly native-born and well-spoken women with less formal education than office workers, salesclerks worked in stores for male department store managers, some of whom had begun as salesclerks. Not given the opportunity to rise to managerial positions, women benefited from the possibility of fairly steady employment, paid vacations, substantial discounts for merchandise, medical care, and other fringe benefits. Sales work was also appealing to women because they did not need as much formal education as clerical workers, and there was a certain glamour as well as respectability attached to these jobs (Diner 1998, 169). Complementing the full-timers was a corps of extras or contingents who worked part-time schedules or came in during holidays and other high sales periods. In Boston, for example, a regular saleswoman earned per week $8 or more while the extras earned less than $3 (Benson 1988, 184). Despite the stores' desires to impose elaborate rules upon them, salesclerks were able to exercise considerable autonomy.

Flowers and Feathers:
Immigrants and Homework

Performing only a very small part of the total labor needed to produce each finished item, homeworkers sewed pants and coats, made artificial flowers and feathers, sorted coffee beans or shelled nuts, embroidered, made human-hair wigs, rolled cigars, and made hats, among a vast number of jobs that historian Cynthia Daniels notes could be found in New York City's tenements. Homeworkers were paid by the piece at rates lower than factory workers received for doing the same work. One tenement labor investigator studied the Rapallo family, who made artificial flowers in their two-room apartment in New York, and found that in one week, 30-year-old Mrs. Rapallo and her seven children produced 18,000 violets, for which they were paid $4.50. With her husband out of work for the previous two years, Mrs. Rapallo's earnings barely covered the $11.00 per month rent for the family's tenement apartment. Nor were the Rapallos' circumstances unusual. One homeworker, asked why she did this work, replied, "The children need bread, shoes" (Daniels 1989, 18). Many immigrant families needed the pittance earned from homework just to survive.

Many young women at the turn of the century, both native born and immigrant, went to work as domestic servants. Rarely, however, would Italian or Eastern European women be among them; their husbands and fathers would not allow their wives and daughters to work in another man's house. Forced by circumstances to work long, hard hours, house servants objected to the subservience demanded of them and to the close supervision of their employers. In the early 20th century, the native-born daughters of immigrants left domestic service to take advantage of the greater opportunities in clerical and sales jobs, and African American women began to take their place in growing numbers. The sociologist W. E. B. Du Bois found that in Philadelphia in the 1890s, 60 percent of African American working men and 90 percent of African American working women earned their living as domestics. Nor did this pattern change much over the next 40 years. As one African American female domestic servant lamented, the conditions African Americans confronted working in northern households made them "literally slaves" (Green 1980, 25).

bricklayers, painters, and plumbers. Skilled building craftsmen still relied on hand tools and had to choose the appropriate materials and make accurate measurements. The demand for intricate ornamental features still required craftsmen capable of combining artistic talent with technical proficiency (Montgomery 1987, 293–294; Mendel 2003, 115–116). Unions in the building trades remained strong and proved themselves capable of defending their craft standards into the 20th century.

Table 2.2. Clerical Workers in the United States, 1900–1910

Job category	1900	1910
Bookkeepers, cashiers, and accountants	254,880	486,700
Male	180,727	299,545
Female	74,153	187,155
% Female	29.1	38.5
Office clerks	248,323	720,498
Male	229,991	597,833
Female	18,332	122,665
% Female	7.4	17.0
Messenger, errand, and office boys/girls	66,009	108,035
Male	59,392	96,748
Female	6,617	11,287
% Female	10.0	10.4
Stenographers and typists	112,364	316,693
Male	26,246	53,378
Female	86,118	263,315
% Female	76.6	83.1

Source: Based on Alba M. Edwards, *Comparative Occupation Statistics for the United States, 1870 to 1940* (1943), Tables 9 and 10. Adapted from Davies 1982, table 1.

Race and Ethnicity in the Workplace

The ranks of white-collar workers contained very few immigrants and virtually no African Americans. At the beginning of the 20th century, just over 90 percent of all female clerical workers were native-born whites. Even a native-born "greenhorn" like "Sister Carrie," who had migrated to Chicago from rural Wisconsin, found herself unwelcome when she applied for work in a downtown department store. In the industrial sector, the likelihood was much greater that the worker, whether male or female, would be foreign born and, in growing numbers, from eastern and southern Europe rather than from the British Isles or northwestern Europe. In 21 major industries in 1910, at least 58 percent of industrial workers were foreign born. This pattern persisted among young men employed as common laborers and among married women who did piecework at home. Thus, by 1901, only 10 percent of laborers in the northeastern United States were whites of native parentage and only 6 percent were African American; in New York City alone, according to one government survey, approximately 98 percent of all garments produced were finished by Italian women working at home.

Before World War I, few African Americans worked in factories. In the South, many African Americans worked as sharecroppers, unable to break free from a

Unknown location, ca. 1910. Among the few nonagricultural jobs open to African American men was work as longshoremen on the docks in such southern port cities as New Orleans. (National Archives)

perpetual state of credit dependency. Some African American men worked as bricklayers, blacksmiths, or carpenters, or as firemen or brakemen on the railroad, or held other skilled jobs, and about half of the laborers in Southern mines and forests were African American. But once they migrated north, African American men found few of the unskilled jobs as common laborers in industry open to them. In Philadelphia, for example, in the early 20th century, virtually none of the leading industrial firms employed African American workers. The Budd Company, Bendix, Cramps Shipyard, and Baldwin Locomotive, companies with a combined workforce of 35,000 people, hired not a single African American. The only firm that actively employed African American men before World War I, Midvale Steel (home to the scientific management schemes of Frederick Winslow Taylor), did so in the expectation that racism would promote disunity among the firm's workers (Licht 1995). Although African American men in the North sometimes could get jobs hauling and carting, they mainly found work as janitors, servants, and waiters.

The Standard-of-Living Debate and the Labor Aristocracy

It has long been assumed among historians and economists that a scarcity of labor in the United States resulted in the unprecedented affluence of American workers. One way to test the assumption that American workers enjoyed superior material conditions is to compare their standard of living with that of workers in another advanced industrial economy. Seeking to test this assumption, the historian Peter R. Shergold chose to compare Pittsburgh, "the Iron City," as a representative urban-industrial community in the United States, with Birmingham, England, a British city that in 1910 was of comparable size and economic structure. Both cities had, in addition to major iron and steel mills, a range of diversified manufactures.

During the first decade of the 20th century, money wages in both Pittsburgh and Birmingham increased. Yet in Pittsburgh, as in other American cities during the late 19th and early 20th centuries, skilled workers tended to experience much greater wage increases than did other manual workers. In contrast, in Birmingham there was less difference between the hourly rate paid to skilled workers and to unskilled workers in jobs in the city's building, engineering, and printing industries. The gap between skilled and unskilled workers' earnings was far more significant in the United States than in Great Britain, particularly following the 1890s depression.

Among all Pittsburgh workers, few had a family income that was more than 15 percent greater than that of their Birmingham counterparts; only skilled workers had a standard of living more than 20 percent greater than that of comparable groups in England. In fact, unskilled workers in Birmingham earned an income sufficient to sustain a standard of living almost as high as that of their colleagues in Pittsburgh. Despite assertions of greater affluence for American workers, real wage rates and real family incomes reveal that the lesser skilled laborers achieved similar levels of material welfare in Great Britain and the United States.

Only the skilled worker in Pittsburgh earned an income sufficient to achieve the "American standard" extolled by the American Federation of Labor's president Samuel Gompers. The Americans were more likely, Shergold found, to purchase their own homes, to enjoy indoor plumbing, "to buy hand-rolled stogies or the *National Labor Tribune,* or, occasionally watch the Pirates at Forbes Field or arrange an excursion to Kennywood Park" (Shergold 1982, 225). Unlike this increasingly privileged segment of the working population, lower-paid unskilled manual workers lived in Pittsburgh's overpopulated tenements and shared toilet facilities. Sleep was their main form of leisure, and what recreation they enjoyed was often spent in streets teeming with people, or briefly at a nickelodeon, or more likely, at a local saloon after work.

In Birmingham, by the end of the 19th century, working-class crowds enjoyed their "Saturday half-holiday" at football (soccer) games played at local stadiums. An American commentator observed that even at times of economic distress, "The attendance at games on Saturday is very large. . . . There is no lack of six-pences and shillings to gain entry to football games" (Shergold 1982, 61). Often the greater income of Pittsburgh workers came at the cost of longer hours at work. In addition to the Saturday half-holiday, Birmingham workers generally had more leisure time and worked under less pressure than their American peers. The standard of housing was probably lower, if also less expensive, in Birmingham than in Pittsburgh, but reformers won greater improvements for working-class housing in the English city than in the American one. Yet inadequate water and sewerage facilities plagued both cities. In sum, the evidence of the material conditions among manual workers in Pittsburgh and Birmingham around 1910 suggests the conventional wisdom that American workers experienced a much higher standard of living than their counterparts elsewhere in the world requires further examination.

THE AMERICAN FEDERATION OF LABOR AND CRAFT UNIONISM

Organized in 1886 as a federation of local and international trade unions, the American Federation of Labor (AFL) represented the interests of native-born skilled craft workers. Gompers, the federation's first president, insisted that unions belonging to the AFL be organized by craft and that membership be restricted to wage workers who shared similar work experiences. Under his leadership, which continued almost unbroken until 1924, the AFL espoused the idea of "pure and simple" unionism. Scorning social reform, especially that achieved by government intervention, Gompers saw trade unions as "voluntary associations of wage-earners" that could satisfy workers' "bread and butter" needs through collective bargaining with employers.

During the last decade of the 19th century, Gompers began a personal process of accommodation to the corporate reality of modern America by making a clean break with his socialist and radical past. At the AFL's annual convention in 1890, Gompers succeeded in excluding representatives of the Socialist Labor Party from federation membership, and four years later, he was able to defeat a resolution that would have committed the AFL to the organization of an independent labor party. But at the 1894 convention, Gompers lost the election for federation president to John McBride, the head of the United Mine Workers of America (UMW). In 1895, after what he referred to in his autobiography as "My Sabbatical Year," the AFL reelected Gompers as president. Gompers also fought the socialists at the AFL's 1903 convention. By then a vice president of

As head of the American Federation of Labor for almost 40 years, Samuel Gompers saw unions as "pure and simple" voluntary associations dedicated to achieving greater economic security for American workers. (Library of Congress)

the National Civic Federation, he had come to accept that the power of large-scale corporations was inescapable. Seeking to improve the standard of living of AFL members, Gompers committed the organization to compelling business to accept trade unions as a legitimate agency within modern industrial America.

Gompers's strategy bore fruit, and the AFL experienced a period of remarkable growth at the turn of the century. In the building trades, for example, membership grew from 67,000 members in 1897 to 391,600 in 1904. And the UMW advanced from 447,000 members to more than 2 million. Overall, membership in AFL unions increased by almost five times in these years. But in the wake of an employers' counteroffensive that began in 1903, the surge in union membership stalled. Moreover, even at its height, membership in AFL unions concentrated in smaller firms and represented only five percent of the national labor force. The AFL remained hesitant to organize among semiskilled machine operatives and common laborers—largely southern and eastern European immigrants—and among the growing force of women workers. Arguably, the federation's failure to grow after 1904 resulted as much from its own exclusionary practices as from employer opposition.

Three labor strikes during the first decade of the 20th century reveal how the diversity of the American workforce posed problems for the labor movement.

Table 2.3. Strikes in the Early 20th Century

Year	Number of strikes	Workers involved (in thousands)	Wage strikes (%)	Ordered by Unions (%)
1900	1,779	400	59.0	65.4
1901	2,924	396	46.6	75.9
1902	3,162	553	51.2	78.2
1903	3,494	532	51.5	78.8
1904	2,307	376	42.2	82.1
1905	2,077	176	44.5	74.7

Source: Adapted from Montgomery 1980, 92.

In 1901 U.S. Steel easily defeated a strike by the Amalgamated Association of Iron, Steel, and Tin Workers (in 1898 tin workers had joined the iron and steel workers' union)—a craft union that limited its membership to native-born skilled workers. In contrast, the following year the UMW, an industrial union that organized all miners regardless of skill or background, won a settlement despite the vehement opposition of Pennsylvania's anthracite coal operators. Although aided by President Theodore Roosevelt's intervention, this victory was largely the result of the extraordinary solidarity exhibited by the hard coal industry's ethnic groups. However, working-class solidarity and industrial organizations were no guarantee of success. In the first years of the 20th century, the Amalgamated Meat Cutters and Butchers Workmen of North America Union, which had been founded in 1897, also rejected the craft model of organizing. In 1904, after briefly recognizing the packinghouse workers' union, the Beef Trust fought back. A long strike ended in the defeat of the union's wage demands and the establishment of an open shop in the industry.

In *Middletown* (1929), the sociologists Helen and Robert Lynd selected Muncie, Indiana, as the community to represent the impact of modern industrialization in the United States. The Lynds contrasted workers' highly mechanized and routinized working conditions in the 1920s with those that had prevailed at the turn of the century, when Muncie's skilled machinists, glass blowers, and iron and steel workers exerted a degree of control over their work. The authority of Muncie's skilled workers in the workplace was, according to the Lynds, reinforced through some 30 organized AFL locals. During the 1890s in Muncie, one of "the best organized cities in the United States," unions brought tangible benefits to the city's native-born skilled craftworkers, including standardized wages scales, factory safety inspections, a four-year apprentice system that limited access to the skilled trades, and programs that assisted members in sickness or death. Moreover, by sponsoring a workingmen's library and reading room, balls, concerts, lectures, baseball games, and many other social activities, organized labor in Muncie formed "one of the most active coordinating centers" in the lives of the community's working-class families. Union members were well respected in Muncie. When Samuel Gompers traveled to Muncie to give a speech in 1897, he dined at the mayor's home before addressing a great crowd assembled at the opera house (Lynd and Lynd 1929, 76–79; Green, 1980, 33–34).

In his autobiography, *Seventy Years of Life and Labor* (1925), Gompers declared that, having successfully met the many challenges of the 1890s, the AFL "had developed discipline as an essential of trade unionism. With discipline the movement emerged from confusion of thinking and practice to a definite trade union philosophy" (Gompers, 1925, vol. 1, 375). In defining this philosophy Gompers observed, "I saw no reason why it was not just as practical for employes to mobilize and control their economic power as a counter-move" (Gompers, 1925, vol. 2, 1–2). To be effective, workers had to fashion trade unions as counterorganizations capable of dealing with capital on an equal footing. This would not happen, in his view, until unions, in addition to focusing on winning tangible—that is, "bread-and-butter"—benefits for members, centralized authority and developed a practical administrative system. Gompers renounced dependence on government action and radical change of the social order as means to achieve the federation's economic and social aims. Instead, he maintained, only when trade unions achieved a balance of power with capital could they, through collective bargaining, secure members' material needs: higher wages, shorter hours, and better working conditions. By the beginning of the new century, the AFL under Gompers embodied a pure-and-simple trade unionism that operated along business principles.

Steel: Craft Unionism Without Craft Workers

In industries such as steel manufacturing, a craft union's steadfast adherence to the principle of craft unionism produced harmful results. The introduction of open-hearth machinery into the steel mills in the late 1880s had reduced steelmakers' dependence on their workers' skill and, as transpired in the 1892 Homestead strike, enabled the owners to break the Amalgamated Association of Iron and Steel Workers Union. With the defeat of the union, steel managers replaced native-born and old-immigrant skilled craftsmen with lesser skilled new-immigrant machine operatives. Now, exulted a Carnegie associate, the managers could regulate "every detail of working the great plant," no longer "subject to the interference of some busybody representing the Amalgamated Association" (Montgomery 1987, 41). In 1901, J. P. Morgan forced a further confrontation with the remnants of the union. Having incorrectly assumed the indispensability of the experienced men, the Amalgamated called for a general strike against the U.S. Steel Corporation that was quickly broken due to a lack of unity among the workers and, because of improved machinery in the sheet and tin mills, the steel trust's ability to keep the mills running with strikebreakers. The Amalgamated never recovered from this bitter strike (Brody 1969, 63–68).

The continuous flow of new immigrant workers into the United States at the turn of the century supplied U.S. Steel and other steelmakers with a transient supply of cheap labor to meet the needs of reorganized production and an expanded market. By 1907, Slavic immigrants filled more than three-quarters of the common labor jobs in the Carnegie plants in Pittsburgh and its environs. Yet the skilled craft workers in the Amalgamated Association ignored the newer immigrants who came to labor in the steel mills. As a result, the union represented a declining portion of the workforce and could not unite all steelworkers against organized capital.

In 1909, U.S. Steel decided to sever all ties to the Amalgamated Association. On June 1, the Steel Corporation posted a notice that "after careful consideration of the interests of both the company and its employees" its mills would by the end of the month "be operated as 'open' [nonunion] plants" (Brody 1969, 71). Taken by surprise, a determined membership promised to mount "an aggressive fight" to save their union. Yet union organizers were successfully rebuffed in their effort to organize workers at one of the company's more modern mills, the large Vandergrift plant in Pennsylvania. Although the strike lasted through the summer, in September the company claimed that struck mills were operating at 70 percent capacity. After 14 months, the union was broken and U.S. Steel was an open-shop employer (Brody 1969, 70–73). Only after suffering yet another

Police arrest a striker during a 1909 strike at the Pressed Steel Car Company, a subsidiary of U.S. Steel, located in McKees Rocks, Pennsylvania. (Library of Congress)

crushing defeat would the Amalgamated Association open its ranks to workers "regardless of nationality or creed" (Green 1980, 9–18, 33; Brody 1969, 126–27).

The 1904 Packinghouse Workers' Strike in Chicago

At noon on July 12, 1904, in Chicago and other meatpacking centers throughout the nation, many thousands of packinghouse workers, members of the Amalgamated Meat Cutters and Butcher Workmen of North America, marched out of their plants in an organized and militant strike against Armour, Swift, and other members of the Beef Trust. The union, founded by four men only seven years earlier in the backroom of a Cincinnati, Ohio, Odd Fellows lodge hall, at first appealed to the skilled knife men among the industry's cattle, hog, and sheep butchers. Nevertheless, the union's first president, Michael Donnelly, a South Omaha, Nebraska, sheep butcher, insisted that there "must be no aristocracy in the labor movement. . . . It should be our purpose to make the injury of the common laborers the concern of the skilled workman." He continued, "Experience has taught us," however, that the unskilled "in their unorganized condition are a menace to those who are members of Union Labor." The only sensible action: "It is our duty to educate them in the labor movement" (Barrett 1990, 133).

Organized by department rather than plantwide, the Amalgamated Meat Cutters was not strictly an industrial union. Yet in each local the union did bring together production workers at all skill levels, and it organized without regard to ethnicity, race, or gender. The cattle butchers' local, for example, included not only the skilled splitters and floormen but also common laborers, who made up the majority of the local's membership. Moreover, although some butchers opposed women's employment, Donnelly openly supported the organizing of women, and he worked with the director of the University of Chicago Settlement House, Mary McDowell, to build Local 183, which organized all the women in the Chicago yards, and to develop the Chicago branch of the Women's Trade Union League.

The union also overcame traditional divisions based on ethnic background. Older immigrant groups in the union, particularly the Irish, built bridges to the new immigrant groups. Interpreters were used at local union meetings to encourage participation. One Lithuanian laborer described his experience with the union: "The night I joined the Cattle Butchers' Union I was led into a room by a negro member. With me were Bohemians, Germans, and Poles, and Mike Donnelly, the President, is an Irishman. He spoke to us in English and then three interpreters told us what he said" (Barrett 1990, 141). Although the skilled butchers led the movement to unionize the industry after 1900, they nevertheless ensured its spread among women and the younger immigrants who dominated the industry's unskilled occupations.

In the first years of the 20th century, the Amalgamated Meat Cutters exercised considerable authority in the packinghouses. As James R. Barrett has shown in his exhaustive study of Chicago's packinghouse workers, the union challenged management's control over work less by enforcing formal collective bargaining agreements than by asserting their informal bargaining power in the plants. Union locals established house committees consisting of three production workers elected semiannually in each department. Although the house committees' intended purpose was to hear grievances from both management and workers, they also successfully pushed for regular hours, restrictions on output, higher wages, layoffs and recall by seniority, and other controls over employment conditions. They often used unofficial spontaneous strikes around specific issues and limited to one department to enforce their demands. The number of such strikes was on the rise after 1902 and precipitated the bitter 1904 strike.

In the negotiations leading up to the national strike the union sought a uniform wage scale for all workers, skilled and unskilled. The packers countered with an offer that would have established a minimum wage for skilled meat cutters but provided nothing for the unskilled. The skilled butchers recognized that their acceptance of this offer would likely be quickly followed by a reclassification of their skilled jobs into the category of unskilled tradesmen. Thus, on July 12, some 50,000 packinghouse and 12,000 auxiliary workers in nine cities went out on strike. An initial agreement on July 20 soon fell apart, and the union settled in for a long strike. To maintain solidarity, the Amalgamated Meat Cutters held daily union meetings. Relief stations throughout Chicago and the other cities supplied strikers with meat, vegetables, and other necessities.

On August 7, in procession behind an American flag and chanting "We will win!" an estimated 20,000 men, women, and children marched through the streets of Chicago alongside skilled workers in auxiliary trades such as steamfitters and carpenters, and the leaders of Chicago's Federation of Labor. But despite this turnout and the active community support of churches, small businesses, the city's labor movement, and even the city's police court, the union failed to overcome the Beef Trust's resolve to break it. From the beginning of the strike, employers brought in scabs, and by September production levels had begun to return to normal output. The packers then offered, in return for the union's calling off the strike, to reemploy workers without discrimination against those who had gone out and to maintain wage levels for skilled workers. Although a members' referendum rejected the proposal, Donnelly, after securing further promises from the packers, called off the strike, and workers began to return to the slaughterhouses. The packers then violated their pledge and blacklisted Donnelly and the other activists, and the union soon split apart. The leaders of the Beef Trust quickly introduced an open shop in the packinghouse yards.

Women Workers, Collective Action, and the Cigar Makers' Union

The practical issue of female competition in the industry led the Cigar Makers' International Union (CMIU), Gompers's old union before he became AFL president, to become, in 1867, the first union to admit women to membership. To protect their trade and ensure themselves a decent standard of living, male cigar makers had built a stable union that offered numerous benefits to its members and was run on sound business practices. But as factory production and the division of the process of making cigars began to dominate the industry in the early 20th century, the proportion of female cigar workers increased and women became more than a majority of the total workforce in the trade. Nevertheless, even by the second decade of the 20th century women still made up only about 10 percent of the CMIU's membership. Hoping to maintain union standards in the trade, the CMIU confronted a fundamental strategic question: "Could they defend a craft without organizing an industry?" (Mendel 2003, 105). The simple answer was no. By 1900, union density in the cigar industry in such centers of cigar making as Brooklyn and New York was already in decline. Yet stubbornly adhering to traditional craft exclusiveness, the CMIU failed to aggressively organize women cigar makers.

The Printers: Craft Organization Defended

The American Federation of Labor claimed to speak for all of the nation's workers. Yet the federation's concentration on organizing skilled craft workers has led labor historians to question just how representative the AFL was of the American working class in the early 20th century. Gompers's commitment to the craft organization of skilled, native-born or first- and second-generation old stock (Irish and German) immigrant workers occurred at a time when mechanization and specialization were changing both the nature of work and the composition of the workforce. In 1901, the AFL issued the "Scranton Declaration," which made craft autonomy—the organizing of each group of skilled workers into a separate union—a principle of labor organization. In most instances, the AFL followed this policy. In printing, for example, technology had transformed the trade into a number of operations: compositors, pressmen, feeders, stereotypers, bookbinders, electrotypers, and photoengravers. Between 1889 and 1903, all but the compositors withdrew from the Typographical Union to form their own separate national unions.

Like other workers at the turn of the century, printers confronted employers who were resolved to reduce labor costs and increase productivity through mechanization. However, printers, as the historian Ronald Mendel has shown, were better positioned than most workers to meet this challenge. Mendel found, for example, that during the 1890s the durable craft unions built by the printers in Brooklyn and New York City not only withstood the impact of technological change and managerial initiatives to establish job control but also managed to upgrade members' wages and working conditions. Neither newspaper nor book publishers succeeded in producing assembly-line-like work processes in their plants. Distinct conditions such as the perishability of the product—newspapers had to be produced anew every day—and the high capital requirements to enter the industry strengthened printers' bargaining power and promoted unionization. International Typographical Union No. 6, in New York, and No. 98, in Brooklyn, spearheaded the formation of the Allied Printing Trades Council, which represented unions of pressmen, press feeders, photoengravers, mailers, stereotypers, bookbinders, and compositors. Under the Allied Council, printers established a union label and successfully defended union pay scales. Relying on informal bargaining rather than on strikes, printers used their pragmatic craft unionism to sustain a collective code of "manliness," or mutual respect, well into the beginning of the new century (Mendel 2003, 47–80).

THE HOUSE OF LABOR RESPONDS

In *American Workers, American Unions* (2002), labor historian Robert Zieger concluded that the American Federation of Labor under Gompers was something of a paradox. Self-proclaimed as the champion of all workers, the federation nevertheless effectively excluded many groups of working people from the House of Labor. Even when Gompers cautiously tried to broaden the federation's appeal, its trade union members resisted. Recognized by contemporaries as an agency of democratic rights, unions could also be corrupt or be administered by a narrow, self-interested bureaucracy. Nevertheless, as the largest organization of working people in the United States in the early 20th century, the AFL commanded the attention of even those progressives and labor activists critical of the federation's cautious approach to social change. Moreover, as the new century's first decade drew to a close, there was strong evidence that the AFL was moving beyond pure-and-simple craft unionism.

Between 1900 and 1910, the AFL began to reconsider the basic principles that governed the organization. At first, craft unions of machinists, printers, carpenters and other building trade workers, cigar makers, and iron molders formed the backbone of the federation. By 1910, however, unions in coal mining and garment manufacturing, whose members were increasingly drawn from eastern and southern European immigrants, organized on an industry-wide basis. Even the Amalgamated Association of Iron, Steel, and Tin Workers reconsidered its craft-exclusive practices. Long suspicious of the state, Gompers did not look to government to safeguard labor's interests. His prescription for trade unionism in America consisted of, in equal measure, a practical administrative system and an adherence to voluntary principles that would enable unions, still largely organized by craft, to bargain with employers on something of a level playing field. Capital was organized, and to be effective, so must labor be.

During the early 20th century, Gompers and the AFL faced not only a revolt by militants from within the ranks of labor but also opposition from a highly organized employer movement against unions. Numerous court decisions in the early 1900s that aided the employers' open-shop drive by severely proscribing union activities forced Gompers to reconsider his longtime opposition to partisan politics, or what he called "party slavery." In 1906, members of the AFL's Executive Council adopted a "Bill of Grievances" that itemized labor's political agenda. More than simply a plan to lobby for such reforms as an eight-hour law for government employees or elimination of the use of antilabor injunctions, the bill represented an agreement among the leaders of the AFL to move directly into electoral politics. That year, and then again in 1908, the AFL mobilized its rank-and-file membership on behalf of candidates friendly to labor.

The Open-Shop Drive

As the nation recovered from the economic depression of the 1890s, so too did trade union organization. A wave of strikes began at this point that surpassed previous periods of industrial strife in America. In 1896, some 184,000 workers were involved in just over 1,000 strikes; seven years later, almost three times the number of workers took part in more than triple the number of strikes. By 1904, as the number of strikes for wages declined slightly, walkouts by workers seeking union recognition and to enforce union rules reached their peak. Use of the strike became a tactic more likely to be ordered by unions. By the time the dust settled midway through the first decade of the 20th century and the employers mounted their counteroffensive, membership in AFL unions had risen to 1,675,000, or more than six times greater than it had been in 1896.

This 1903 Puck *cartoon depicts the sword of the coal strike hanging over the head of industry. Led by such organizations as the National Association of Manufacturers, business leaders sought to promote public opposition to the "tyranny" of strikes. (Library of Congress)*

Table 2.4. Union Membership, 1900–1910

Year	Total in labor force (thousands)	Total union membership (thousands)	%
1900	28,376	791	2.8
1910	36,709	2,116	5.8

Source: Bureau of Labor Statistics, records. Adapted from Shifflett 1996, 59.

The turn-of-the-century surge in union membership and strikes peaked in 1904 and then was severely undercut by an open-shop movement among employers. Smaller industrialists joined forces to oppose the "tyranny" of unions. The National Association of Manufacturers (NAM), which had been founded in Cincinnati in 1895, spearheaded the national antiunion drive beginning in 1903 under its newly elected president, David Parry. By 1908, NAM had 3,000 members across the country. In addition to establishing strike-breaking employment agencies in a number of major cities and hiring private guards from Pinkerton's and other detective agencies, NAM formed antiboycott associations to prevent unions in one trade from supporting strikers in others. Gompers himself nearly went to prison because of a suit brought in 1906 by the American Anti-Boycott Association against the AFL's "We Don't Patronize" list. The use of boycotts by unions was also at the heart of a dispute between D. H. Loewe and Company of Danbury, Connecticut, and the United Hatters of America that reached the U.S. Supreme Court in 1908 (Green 1980, 63).

Alleging that strikes and other labor practices violated the Sherman Act's prohibition against actions in "restraint of trade," courts during the first decade of the 20th century granted employers more than 10 times the number of injunctions they had issued during the previous 10 years. In 1902, the United Hatters led a strike for union recognition against Loewe and Company, a manufacturer of hats. The Anti-Boycott Association, which Dietrich Loewe had co-founded, took up the hat company's cause. Citing the Sherman Act, Loewe and Company sued 250 individual union hatters for a total of $240,000. In its 1908 decision, the Supreme Court affirmed that the hatters' boycott was a conspiracy in restraint of trade and that the members of the union were liable for damages.

Opposition to union boycotts also figured prominently in the battle between the AFL and James Van Cleave, a president of NAM. In 1906, the AFL placed Buck's Stove and Range, a company owned by Van Cleave, on its list of companies to be boycotted at the request of the Metal Polishers' Union, which was on strike against the company. Van Cleave obtained an injunction prohibiting the federation from conspiring to boycott. When Gompers defended the AFL's use of the boycott in editorials published in the *American Federationist,* Buck's company petitioned the Supreme Court of the District of Columbia to declare

Gompers, John Mitchell, and Frank Morrison in contempt of court for violating the injunction. The court ruled against the three AFL leaders, sentencing them to prison terms of 12, 9, and 6 months, respectively. The verdict was ultimately dismissed by the U.S. Supreme Court but only after seven years of costly appeals. American courts' willingness to grant injunctions against labor, as well as the tremendous expense of these cases, weakened the AFL's long-held antipathy to electoral politics (Greene 1998, 153–156).

Voluntarism Reconsidered

Reflecting in his autobiography on the AFL's founding, Gompers compared the organization to a "rope of sand and yet the strongest human force—a voluntary association united by common need and held together by mutual self-interest" (Gompers, 1925, vol. 2, 333). Gompers rejected state action and extolled the virtue of voluntarism—the notion that working people should defend their own interests through the agency of collective bargaining by their unions rather than seek redress through the government. He expressed the conviction that partisan politics would divide workers, advising unions to eschew what he referred to as "labor partyism." But the crippling effects of the antilabor judicial decisions compelled Gompers to reconsider his antipolitical and antistate convictions. Thus, beginning in 1906, Gompers and other AFL leaders urged union members to enter electoral politics and thereby engage in "a strike through the ballot box" (Greene 1998, 1).

In March 1906, the AFL's executive council prepared its "Bill of Grievances" identifying the federation's labor agenda for congressional action. Many of the issues it raised, including opposition to convict labor, advocacy of immigration restrictions, the demand for an eight-hour workday law for government employees, and a call for labor to be excluded from prosecution under the Sherman Anti-trust and Interstate Commerce laws, were long-standing goals of the AFL. Other objectives, such as its demand for the elimination of judicial discrimination through use of the labor injunction, an end to the alleged antilabor bias of the U.S. House Committee on Labor, and the right of petition for government employees, reflected more recent developments. The labor historian Julie Greene has observed that the AFL leaders hoped to free labor organizations from any state activity that limited the rights of trade unions, protect unions from what the leaders considered to be competition from cheap labor (usually immigrants, women, and African Americans), make American politics more democratic, and make the federal government a model employer (Greene 1998, 81–82). Labor's agenda in the early 20th century represented an equal mix of discriminatory caution and democratic enlightenment.

The AFL since the mid-1890s had regularly lobbied Congress for federal legislation. But in 1906, the federation went further and began to mobilize rank-and-file union members on behalf of electing politicians friendly to labor as well as to punish politicians who opposed labor's agenda. Seeking in particular to influence the choice of candidates, the AFL urged central labor unions, local unions, and state labor federations to hold conventions to nominate candidates for Congress and state legislatures. To assist in this political effort, the federation assembled a staff of 50 full-time salaried organizers, who were aided by some 1,300 volunteer organizers across the nation. Freed from their regular industrial work, these organizers became functionaries promoting the AFL's new political program. Based on correspondence between the AFL headquarters and local labor movements, union members appear to have been active in more than 400 congressional districts (30 percent of the total) in at least 27 states, especially in the more industrialized areas of the Northeast and Midwest. Despite Gompers's willingness to engage labor directly in the electoral process, the AFL leader still hoped to avoid partisan attachments, especially the formation of a labor party. Nevertheless, most of the trade unionists that ran for office did so as Democrats.

Having successfully mobilized the rank and file in 1906, the AFL prepared to step up its political campaign in the presidential election held two years later. The Supreme Court's decision in February 1908 in *Loewe v. Lawlor,* which confirmed the prosecution of labor organizations as trusts under the Sherman Act, only added to the federation's sense of urgency. The election of pro-labor candidates to Congress and the defeat of labor's political enemies appeared to offer the only solution to the deepening crisis. In the 1908 election, labor's agenda received a more positive reception from the presidential campaign of the Democratic Party's candidate, William Jennings Bryan, than from the Republican side. Bryan campaigned with the slogan "Shall the People Rule?" NAM, on the other hand, had close ties to the Republican Party and mobilized NAM members on behalf of the Republican candidate, William Howard Taft, known as the "injunction judge." During the election, the AFL and the Democratic Party cooperated in the areas of finance, campaign literature, and organizers (Greene 1998, 161; Green, 1980, 63). Taft prevailed in the election, but the AFL had forged ties to the Democrats during the campaign that would bear fruit in the next presidential election, that of Woodrow Wilson in 1912. Allied to reformers within the Democratic Party, the AFL began moving toward a more activist vision of the use of the state for progressive ends.

NEW WORKERS AND NEW UNIONS

During the first decade of the 20th century, the AFL experienced a revolt against craft unionism. In 1905, a small number of labor militants and radical unions came together to form an organization dedicated to class war. The founding convention of the Industrial Workers of the World (IWW), coming on the heels of violent strikes led by the Western Federation of Miners (WFM) in Cripple Creek, Colorado, was designated by WFM leader William "Big Bill" Haywood as the "continental congress of the working class." Yet it would not be until 1909, when the IWW led a strike among unskilled workers at the Pressed Steel Car Company at McKees Rocks, Pennsylvania, that the IWW became a credible challenger to the AFL.

Women's expanded labor force participation around the turn of the century produced a mostly negative response from the labor movement. Few unions admitted women into membership. In 1892, Gompers persuaded the AFL's executive council to appoint Mary Kenney, a bindery worker who been active in Chicago as an organizer of Women's Bookbinding Union No. 1, as the federation's first woman organizer. Yet after only six months, the federation let her position expire. By 1910, the number of women organized into trade unions had actually declined from the very modest 3 percent it had been 10 years earlier. The AFL never wavered from its basic goal of creating the conditions that would enable men to earn wages sufficient to provide a decent standard of living for their families. As proponents of the domestic ideal, most union officials, including Gompers, agreed with the views expressed in 1897 by a prominent Boston unionist who indicted the growing demand for female labor "as an insidious assault upon the home; it is the knife of the assassin, aimed at the family circle" (Boris and Lichtenstein 1991, 232–234). Until the 1909 "uprising of the 20,000" among female garment workers in New York City, unions mainly showed interest in organizing women workers only as it helped to protect the earning power of men.

Led by the International Ladies' Garment Workers' Union (ILGWU), the 1909 "uprising of the 20,000" among unskilled immigrant women shirtwaist makers in New York City's garment industry proved to be as much a victory for militant industrial unionism over the limited craft union principles of the AFL as against the organized employer opposition. The next year, industry-wide general strikes involving 50,000 cloakworkers in New York City and Chicago were resolved only after employers and the Amalgamated Clothing Workers accepted a mediated settlement arranged by the then attorney and later Supreme Court justice, Louis D. Brandeis. Each of these uprisings not only helped to revive the AFL but they also added momentum to the rise of militant industrial unionism within the federation.

Industrial Unionism in the Coal Mines

Not all unions within the AFL resisted organizing all the workers in their trades. By the early 20th century, the days when the skilled pit-face coal miner could exercise job control had largely faded. Moving beyond a craft union organizing strategy, skilled miners adopted a more inclusive, industrial union approach that reached out to all workers who labored underground. In 1897, the UMW struck the small- and medium-sized soft coal operators in western Pennsylvania, Ohio, Indiana, and Illinois, winning its first interstate contract agreement. After securing a closed shop in the Midwest, the UMW used skilled British, Irish, and African American organizers to move into the soft coal fields of the South. In 1902, almost two-thirds of Alabama's miners belonged to the UMW and, led by Richard Davis, an African American member of the union's executive board, more than half of these union members were African American. In Pennsylvania's anthracite fields, where native-born and English-speaking miners worked side by side with an almost equal number of Slavs and other eastern Europeans, immigrant associations rooted in the community, such as small businesses, loan societies, and newspapers, helped maintain solidarity through a long (165 days), and ultimately successful, strike in 1902.

Although the UMW's president, John Mitchell, embraced industrial union organization, he, like Gompers, advocated responsible business union practices and was conciliatory toward welfare capitalists. Both Gompers and Mitchell joined the National Civic Federation, a reform association dominated by big business, and promoted conservative trade unionism as an alternative to socialism. A more radical unionism arose in the early 1890s among the hard-rock metal miners in the West. Led by "Big Bill" Haywood, the Western Federation of Miners fought violent battles against Colorado's gold, silver, and copper barons in the Cripple Creek region in 1894 and then again in Leadville two years later. Committed to revolutionary social change in America, Haywood, in 1905, brought together militant industrial unionists and political radicals to found the Industrial Workers of the World. On behalf of the "emancipation of the working class," the IWW opposed "craft division," which, its manifesto proclaimed, "hinders the growth of class consciousness of the workers." The IWW's first real challenge to the AFL came in 1909, during the McKees Rocks steel strike in Pennsylvania.

The Amalgamated Confronts "One Big Union"

In 1909, the Amalgamated Association of Iron, Steel, and Tin Workers, facing a concerted open-shop drive by the Pressed Steel Car Company, a subsidiary of U.S. Steel, began organizing the company's largely immigrant workforce. But following violent clashes between striking immigrants from the Pressed Steel plant and the Pennsylvania police, the Amalgamated Association withdrew from the fray and the IWW took charge. Relying on multilingual organizers, foreign-language newspapers, and family and community solidarity, the IWW helped the strikers hold out for 45 days and win a victory against the Steel Trust. Although the Amalgamated Association had long dismissed the immigrant workers as poor union prospects, the McKees Rocks strike revealed on a very public

The Triangle Waist Company

By 1902 the Triangle Waist Company, which manufactured women's waists, or blouses, opened its doors at 27 Washington Place, on the east side of New York City's Washington Square Park. The firm occupied the ninth floor of the Asch Building, a new skyscraper built on the site. Popularized by the "Gibson Girl," an advertising symbol conceived by Charles Dana Gibson, the shirtwaist, or waist-and-skirt combination, symbolized the sexy and more practical style of dress favored by young women at the turn of the century. The company was owned by Max Blanck and Isaac Harris, two Russian immigrants in their early 30s who had arrived in New York some 30 years earlier. The owners constructed a large, modern "loft" factory, whose vast open rooms enabled the "Shirtwaist Kings" to employ more efficiently and productively a much greater number of sewing machines and workers than was possible in the sweatshops that had long characterized production in the garment industry in New York.

Over the next few years, the Triangle Waist Company expanded twice, taking over the floors above and below it in the Asch Building. By 1909, it was the largest blouse-making operation in New York; the Triangle Company employed each day more than 500 young Jewish and Italian immigrant women, who produced and shipped over a million shirtwaists a year. Blanck handled the financial end of the business, and Harris, who was married to a cousin of Blanck's wife, oversaw the manufacturing operations. "I laid out the factory and I put in the machines," Harris once noted, and "everything that was done about putting up the factory was done by me" (Von Drehle 2003, 44).

A major concern of the owners about centralizing production in one location rather than dispersing it across a large number of tenements was the increased possibility that workers might come together in an organized fashion to strike. Contractors had easily defeated wildcat strikes among sweatshop workers simply by closing the shop and relocating to another building. But owners of loft factories had considerable resources invested in their businesses and needed to keep them operating continuously during the busy season. As a means to distance themselves from the workers, Blanck and Harris employed "inside contractors," individuals who rented space in the workshops and then hired the workers to run the sewing machines. The contractor received a lump-sum payment from Blanck and Harris and in turn paid the workers. The Triangle Waist Company owners also established an in-house union, called the Triangle Employees Benevolent Association, which was run by members of their families. Those rabble-rousers who remained discontented with the owners' efforts to win workers' cooperation simply were fired. On September 27, 1909, Local 25 of the International Ladies' Garment Workers' Union declared a strike against the Triangle Company that was the result of Blanck and Harris's decision to fire any employee found organizing a union. As the strike dragged on through the fall, union leaders planned a mass meeting for November 22 at Cooper Union in New York City. That evening, the striker Clara Lemlich galvanized the audience into declaring a general strike, and the "uprising of the 20,000" was on.

Clara Lemlich and the Founding of the International Ladies' Garment Workers' Union

In the spring of 1905, the street-corner agitator Clara Lemlich joined with a dozen other young women and men to organize Local 25 of the International Ladies' Garment Workers' Union (ILGWU). Having immigrated only two years earlier at age 16 with her family from her native Ukraine, Lemlich swiftly immersed herself in the radical community of the Jewish immigrant "working girls" in New York's Lower East Side. In the early years of the 20th century, Jewish women in the Lower East Side organized kosher meat boycotts, rent strikes, and other community-based protests. As a reporter from *The New York Times* observed, "When East Siders don't like something they strike" (Orleck 1995, 28). The self-taught Lemlich—she read all the Russian classics available at her local library—also joined a free night school in her community and attended Marxist theory classes at the Socialist Party's Rand School. Not long after becoming a member of a lunchtime study group where she learned about trade unionism, she and other members of this group formed Local 25.

Lemlich knew from personal experience about the harsh conditions in New York's garment shops. Having worked as a seamstress starting at age 12, she soon found work as a dressmaker: "I went to work two weeks after landing in this country. We worked from sunrise to set seven days a week. . . . Those who worked on machines had to carry the machines on their back both to and from work. . . . The hissing of the machines, the yelling of the foreman, made life unbearable" (Orleck 1995, 33). Later, she wrote about the dehumanizing conditions: "And the bosses! They hire people to drive you!" (Orleck 1995, 33). The inside subcontractor system was especially oppressive. The subcontractor contracted with the manufacturer to complete a specified amount of work for an agreed-upon price. The lower the cost of producing each garment the greater the profit for the subcontractor. Subcontractors imposed fines on the workers for lateness or for sewing errors and made the women pay for the needles and thread that they used and for the electric power that ran their machines. The foreman or forelady rewarded more compliant workers with larger bundles of work, which enabled them to earn more money. The shop floor culture experienced by female garment workers and their growing community-based political consciousness crystallized in the development of an "industrial feminism" that, according to the historian Annelise Orleck, exploded in 1909 in the "uprising of the 20,000" (Orleck 1995, 6).

Lemlich was well known as a union activist who protested the oppressive conditions working women faced in New York's garment shops. Early on, the men leading the ILGWU had sought to organize mainly in the skilled trades dominated by men. For three years, Lemlich encouraged the union's officers to use women organizers to attract unskilled women shirtwaist workers. In 1907 and 1908 she took part in two strikes, and at the time of her dramatic Cooper Union appearance, Lemlich was recovering from a beating she had received for leading still another strike, at Leiserson's, the garment shop where she worked.

***Clara Lemlich and the Founding of the
International Ladies' Garment Workers' Union, Continued***

Responding to a call by the ILGWU for a mass meeting, thousands of shirtwaist workers converged on Cooper Union the evening of November 22, 1909, only to have to sit through speaker after speaker, each of whom urged caution. After American Federation of Labor president Samuel Gompers spoke and urged his audience not to act "hastily," Lemlich called out in Yiddish, "I want to say a few words!" The audience demanded that she "Get up on the platform!" Lemlich rose and announced, "I have no further patience for talk, as I am one of those who feels and suffers from the things pictured. I move that we go on general strike." There was an immediate uproar that was repeated after Benjamin Feigenbaum, the meeting's moderator, called for a second to Lemlich's motion. After quiet was restored, Feigenbaum raised his right hand and dramatically called out, "Will you take the Jewish oath?" And, as reported in the Yiddish newspaper the *Forward,* the audience then recited: "If I turn traitor to the cause I now pledge, may this hand wither from the arm I now raise" (Von Drehle 2003, 57–58). The "uprising of the 20,000" had begun.

stage that unskilled immigrant workers could be effectively organized. The IWW would again successfully organize across a number of nationalities in its famous "Bread and Roses" textile workers strike in Lawrence, Massachusetts, in 1912, and in other battles throughout the second decade of the 20th century (Dubofsky 1985, 106–111). After the McKees Rocks strike, the Amalgamated Association began to reconsider its opposition to industrial organization.

The Rising of Women and Industrial Feminism

The movement for organizing all workers in an industry into a single union without regard to skill was strengthened by the "uprising of the 20,000" in 1909 among the young, unskilled, mostly Jewish, female shirtwaist makers in New York City. A relatively new industry, the making of shirtwaists, or blouses, grew rapidly in the first decade of the 20th century; by 1909, the value of shirtwaists produced in New York City alone had reached $50 million. The three small garment industry unions already existing locally had made only sporadic efforts to organize the shirtwaist makers. Even though the thousands of workers who attended the public rally in 1909 at Cooper Union wholeheartedly endorsed Clara Lemlich's dramatic call for a general strike, when the strike began, Local 25 of the ILGWU had just more than 100 members and four dollars in its treasury.

Week after week, the strike went on, as an estimated 20,000 to 40,000 workers, mostly young women, stayed out. In her drive to organize shirtwaist workers,

Women strikers on the picket line during the 1909 "Uprising of the 20,000" garment workers' strike in New York City. The solidarity of the women strikers continued to infuse the labor movement long after the "uprising" ended. (Library of Congress)

Lemlich had, even before the strike, enlisted the support of Rose Schneiderman. Schneiderman, who had been a capmaker, was vice president of the New York branch of the Women's Trade Union League (WTUL). Already an active champion of organizing women workers, the WTUL, an organization of progressive middle- and upper-class women, took up the cause of the shirtwaist strikers. The New York WTUL joined the "uprising," putting its members and money at the service of the union. WTUL members joined mass marches as allies; they served as witnesses to the incidents of unlawful arrests. On behalf of the strikers, the organization's leaders went on fund-raising tours throughout New York and New England, down to Washington, D.C., and into the Pennsylvania coalfields. Although Schneiderman wondered if "women who were not wage workers themselves" could understand "the problems that workers faced," she became convinced of the need to build alliances among women regardless of their class backgrounds (Orleck 1995, 43).

"Industrial feminism," coined in 1915 by the scholar Mildred Moore, represented the commitment of Lemlich, Schneiderman, and many other progressive and socialist women to organizing trade unions that included women as part of a political and economic movement that bridged class, gender, and ethnic divides. Lemlich's passionate commitment to organizing working-class women reflected a socially conscious vision of trade unions as agencies of more sweeping change than that called for by the bread-and-butter trade unionism of the AFL and its president. Summing up what the strike achieved, Lemlich observed, "They used to say that you couldn't even organize women. They wouldn't come to union meetings. They were 'temporary' workers. Well, we showed them!" (Tax 1980, 240). The solidarity women achieved in 1909 would continue to infuse both the labor movement and the women's movement long after the "uprising" ended.

New Unionism and "More"

The strike by militant young women trade unionists with little money and limited union experience became a cause célébre sustained by a cross section of the nation's labor and progressive movements—reformers such as the WTUL, leading New York socialists, and settlement house workers, and such wealthy women as Mrs. Oliver Belmont and Anne Morgan, the sister of J. P. Morgan, who provided bail money. Students from Wellesley College donated $1,000 to the strike fund. Finally settled in mid-February 1910, the strike ended with some small improvements but without recognition for the ILGWU. Still, by end of the strike, the union had grown to 10,000 members and the ILGWU would successfully negotiate contracts with all but 19 of the 337 shirtwaist companies in New York and Philadelphia. Representing the potential for women and new immigrants to organize their own unions, the "uprising of the 20,000" would be a catchphrase forever imprinted on the history of the American labor movement. Energized by the shirtwaist makers' strike, cloakmakers went out five months later in a general strike. The cloakmakers' strike ended with the adoption of the famous Protocols of Peace, which provided for the establishment of a "union" shop, wage increases, shorter hours, and other improvements.

Gompers once asked rhetorically, "What does labor want?" and replied, "We want more school houses and less jails; more books and less arsenals; more learning and less vice; more constant work and less crime; more leisure and less greed; more justice and less revenge; in fact, more of the opportunities to cultivate our better natures, to make manhood more noble, womanhood more beautiful and childhood more happy and bright" (Kaufman et al. 1986–1998, vol. 3, 396). That trade unions continuously strove for "more," made them, in his view, the "natural" organization to improve the lives of workers in America. By 1910, the new workers that had joined the new unions had become a part of the struggle by organized labor for "more." Yet "new unionism" meant not merely securing greater material comforts. The rising militancy of industrial workers during the first decade of the 20th century was part of an ongoing clash over who was in charge at the workplace.

BIOGRAPHIES

Samuel Gompers, 1850–1924

Union Leader

The eldest child of Dutch-Jewish immigrant parents, Solomon and Sarah Rood Gompers, Samuel Gompers was born in Spitalfields, a poor silk-weaving district in East London. He and his family arrived in New York on July 29, 1863. The family settled into a squalid neighborhood in the notoriously overcrowded Lower East Side of Manhattan. Having learned to make cigars in London, Sam went to work rolling cigars in the shop his father set up in the front room of their first apartment. Both he and his father belonged to Cigarmakers' Local Union No. 15, which would eventually be headed by Sam's friend Adolph Strasser. In 1867, Gompers met and married Sophia Julian, who, like him, was a London immigrant and a cigar worker. In 1886, he joined with other skilled unionists to organize the American Federation of Labor (AFL), which, except for one year, he led until his death. Gompers dedicated the AFL to upholding the principle of unions as "pure and simple" voluntary agencies that avoided party politics while seeking to achieve the "bread-and-butter" goal of economic se-

curity for union members. By the end of the first decade of the 20th century, court victories won by antilabor employers led Gompers and the AFL to become more directly involved in politics and to begin to reach out to a wider spectrum of workers.

As a leader in the National Civic Federation, Marcus Alonzo Hanna believed that it was in the best interests of big business to work with organized labor to undermine what he saw as the threat of socialism in America. (Library of Congress)

Marcus Alonzo Hanna, 1837–1904

Businessman and Politician

The son of an Ohio grocer and a schoolteacher, "Mark" Hanna rose to become a prominent businessman, presidential campaign manager, and U.S. senator. In 1864, after his family settled in Cleveland, Hanna married Charlotte Augusta Rhodes, the daughter of a coal and iron magnate, and entered the oil refinery business. His company expanded into shipping, mining, railroads, and steel. Hanna then became interested in politics. A stalwart member of the Republican Party, his political career was closely associated with the rise of William F. McKinley, who became governor of Ohio in 1891 and whose successful presidential campaign Hanna ran in 1896. The following year, Hanna was appointed to fill a vacated Senate seat. In 1900, Hanna helped avert a major coal strike, and he then became active in the National Civic Federation. Although wary of government-led economic reform, Hanna believed that working with organized labor advanced the interests of business and weakened workers' interest in socialism. While possibly considering mounting a challenge for the Republican nomination for president in 1904, Hanna died of typhoid fever.

Clara Lemlich, 1886–1982

Garment Worker and Union Leader

Born in the Ukraine village of Gorodok, Clara Lemlich immigrated in 1903 to the Lower East Side of New York. Shortly after she arrived, she went to work making shirtwaists in New York City's garment factories, Lemlich got involved in efforts to organize women into the International Ladies' Garment Workers' Union. In 1907, she took part in her first strike against a speed-up of production. Still recovering from a brutal beating inflicted while she picketed the Leiserson shop where she worked, Lemlich ignited the mass rally at Cooper Union that resulted in the call for a general strike in 1909. After the strike, employers blacklisted her from further employment in the garment industry. In 1913, she married Joseph Shavelson, a printer who had emigrated from Russia after the failed revolution of 1905. She had met Shavelson when both took classes at the Socialist Rand School. The mother of three children, Lemlich remained politically active in the Communist Party and in social causes for the rest of her life.

Peter J. McGuire, 1852–1906

Woodworker and Union Leader

A native of New York City, Peter McGuire was the son of John J. McGuire, a porter, and Catherine Hand O'Riley. Having begun working after his father enlisted in the Union army in 1863, McGuire became an apprentice woodworker in 1869 in a piano shop. He quickly became an activist, leading demonstrations for the eight-hour workday in 1872 and a walkout at the piano factory the following year. In 1881, McGuire helped found the Brotherhood of Carpenters and Joiners and was elected its general secretary. That year he established the national office in Philadelphia and moved to Camden, New Jersey. The union grew after a slow start; by 1890, it had more than 50,000 members. McGuire warned against unions' becoming "mere" benevolent societies. Instead, labor organizations should be "primary schools" for political education and help build a "cooperative commonwealth." It is believed that Labor Day, first celebrated in 1882, originated in a suggestion by McGuire that a day should be set aside to honor those "who from rude nature have delved and carved all the grandeur we behold" (U.S. Dept. of Labor). At the 1900 national convention of the Carpenters and Joiners union, business agents—full-time local union officers—led an internal revolt against McGuire's leadership and his commitment to broad-based worker solidarity and insurgent politics. The campaign against McGuire continued, and in 1902, he resigned as president.

John Mitchell, 1870–1919

Union Leader

President of the United Mine Workers of America (UMWA) from 1898 to 1908, John Mitchell was the son of a coal miner, Robert Mitchell, and Martha Halley.

With John Mitchell as president, the United Mine Workers Union (UMW) experienced extensive growth during the first decade of the 20th century. Mitchell allied the UMW with Samuel Gompers's policy of cooperation with the big business leaders of the National Civic Federation. (Library of Congress)

He grew up in a small coal-mining village, Braidwood, Illinois, and began working in the mines before he was a teenager. In the late 1880s, Mitchell became active in the Knights of Labor. Believing that miners needed a union of their own, he became a founding member of the UMWA in 1890 and served as secretary-treasurer of the Illinois District 12 local from 1895 to 1897. The national union's executive board chose Mitchell as acting president in 1898, and he was elected president the following year. From 1900 to 1914, Mitchell served as second vice president of the American Federation of Labor and was also chair of the Trade Agreements Department of the National Civic Federation (NCF) from 1906 until 1911, when UMWA insurgents insisted that he resign from the NCF. Mitchell's cooperation during the 1902 anthracite miners' strike earned him plaudits as a "good" labor leader and model citizen from President Theodore Roosevelt. Under Mitchell's leadership, the UMWA membership increased by 34,000 miners to around 300,000 members.

Pauline Newman, c. 1893–1986

Labor Organizer and Director of the ILGWU

Pauline Newman was born in Lithuania and came to the United States in 1901 after her brother, who was living in the United States, sent for her and her family. She quickly found work in the Triangle Waist Company. In 1908, she became active in the Socialist Literary Society and campaigned for Eugene V. Debs for president, riding along with Debs on his "Red Special" campaign train. Having left the Triangle Company just before the 1909 "uprising of the 20,000," Newman traveled throughout New York State and New England raising money and support among women's groups for the shirtwaist workers' strike. After the strike, she became the first organizer for the ILGWU and, from 1912 to 1918, served as an inspector for the Joint Board of Sanitary Control, which had been established for the women's garment industry. In 1915, she was an unsuccessful Socialist candidate for Congress from New York's 18th congressional district. For the rest of her life, Newman remained active in the Women's Trade Union League and the ILGWU, especially in the union's health center that she had helped found in 1913 and, where, after 1923, she served as educational director.

Mary Kenney O'Sullivan, 1864–1943

Labor Organizer and Founder of the WTUL

Mary Kenney was born in Hannibal, Missouri, the daughter of Michael Kenney, a railroad machinist, and Mary Kelly. Going to work at age 14 in a book bindery, Kenney joined the Women's Federal Labor Union No. 2703 in the 1880s and was elected as a delegate to the Chicago Trades and Labor Assembly. The Women's Bindery Union No. 1, which she organized probably in 1890, met in Hull House, the Chicago settlement house run by Jane Addams. Kenney became a full-time resident of Hull House and in 1892 was asked by Samuel Gompers to become the first woman organizer for the American Federation of Labor. In 1894, after being fired when the AFL's executive committee failed to provide support for her position, she married John O'Sullivan, an AFL organizer and labor editor for the *Boston Globe*. Kenney O'Sullivan remained active in the labor movement and lobbied for protective labor legislation. A founder of the Women's Trade Union League (WTUL) in 1903, she served as secretary and vice president of the WTUL before breaking with it in 1912 when the organization failed to support the textile workers' strike in Lawrence, Massachusetts.

Rose Schneiderman, 1882–1972

Garment Worker and Union Leader

Born in Saven, Poland, the daughter of Adolph Samuel Schneiderman and Deborah (Rothman) Schneiderman, both of whom worked in the sewing trades, Schneiderman and her family immigrated to the United States in 1890, settling on the Lower East Side of New York. Two years later Rose's father died suddenly and she was placed briefly in an orphanage until her mother found work in a fur cape factory. In 1895, Schneiderman went to work in a local department store and then, three years later, found a better-paying job as a sewing machine operator in a cap factory. After a year in Montreal, Schneiderman returned to her old job in New York and soon became active in organizing a union, the first women's local to be chartered by the United Cloth Hat and Cap Makers' Union. In 1905, she led her local out in a bitter citywide strike for higher wages and better working conditions. The same year, Schneiderman joined the Socialist Party and the New York Women's Trade Union League (WTUL). In 1909, Schneiderman was active in the "uprising of the 20,000" as a member of the shirtwaist makers' union's executive board and helped found International Ladies Garment Workers' Union Local 62, a union of white-goods workers that she would serve as president. Except for a brief time as a member of the National Recovery Administration advisory board, Schneiderman was president of the New York WTUL from 1918 until 1949 and of the National WTUL from 1926 to 1950.

William Bauchop Wilson, 1862–1934

Miner, Leader of UMWA, Politician

Born in Scotland the son of Adam Wilson, a miner, and Helen Bauchop, William Wilson moved to Arnot, Pennsylvania, in 1870. He went to work at age nine as a breaker boy in the coal mines but would later also work as a farmer and railroad fireman. By age 14, Wilson was already secretary of his local miners' union. In 1890, he helped organize the United Mineworkers of America (UMW). In 1899, Wilson became president of District 2 in Pennsylvania, and in 1900, John Mitchell appointed him secretary-treasurer of the UMW. In 1906, he was elected to Congress as a Democrat from the 15th congressional district in Pennsylvania. As a member of Congress, Wilson introduced legislation to establish a committee to investigate mining disasters; this committee eventually developed into the U.S. Bureau of Mines and Mining. Wilson lost his bid for reelection in 1912. The following year, President Woodrow Wilson appointed him the first secretary of labor. In 1926, he was a candidate for senator from Pennsylvania, but he lost the election.

REFERENCES AND FURTHER READINGS

American National Biography Online. http:www.anb.org/articles/15/15-00737-print.html.

Barrett, James R. 1990. *Work and Community in the Jungle: Chicago's Packinghouse Workers, 1894–1922.* Urbana: University of Illinois Press.

Basler, Roy P., ed. 1953. *The Collected Works of Abraham Lincoln.* Vol. 4. New Brunswick, N.J.: Rutgers University Press.

Benson, Susan Porter. 1988. *Counter Cultures: Saleswomen, Managers, and Customers in American Department Stores, 1890–1940.* Urbana: University of Illinois Press.

Boris, Eileen, and Nelson Lichtenstein. 1991. *Major Problems in the History of American Workers, Documents and Essays.* Lexington, Mass.: D.C. Heath and Company.

Brody, David. 1989. "Labor History, Industrial Relations, and the Crisis of American Labor." *Industrial and Labor Relations Review* 43 (1): 7–18.

Brody, David. 1969. *Steelworkers in America: The Non-Union Era.* New York: Harper and Row.

Christie, Robert A. 1956. *Empire in Wood: A History of the Carpenters' Union.* Ithaca: New York State School of Industrial and Labor Relations.

Cooper, Patricia A. 1987. *Once a Cigar Maker: Men, Women, and Work Culture in American Cigar Factories, 1900–1919.* Urbana: University of Illinois Press.

Croly, Herbert. 1912. *Marcus Alonzo Hanna: His Life and Work.* New York: Macmillan Company.

Daniels, Cynthia R. 1989. "Between Home and Factory: Homeworkers and the State." In *Homework: Historical and Contemporary Perspectives on Paid Labor at Home,* ed. Eileen Boris and Cynthia R. Daniels, 13–32. Urbana: University of Illinois Press.

Davies, Margery W. 1982. *Woman's Place Is at the Typewriter: Office Work and Office Workers, 1870–1930.* Philadelphia: Temple University Press.

Dawson, Andrew. 1979. "The Paradox of Dynamic Technological Change and the Labor Aristocracy in the United States, 1990–1914." *Labor History* 20 (Summer): 325–351.

Diner, Steven J. 1998. *A Very Different Age: Americans of the Progressive Era.* New York: Hill and Wang.

Dubofsky, Melvyn. 1985. *Industrialism and the American Worker, 1865–1920.* New York: Harlan Davidson.

Fink, Leon, ed. 2001. *Major Problems in the Gilded Age and the Progressive Era: Documents and Essays,* 2nd ed. Boston: Houghton Mifflin Company.

Foner, Eric. 1988. *Reconstruction: America's Unfinished Revolution, 1863–1877.* New York: Harper and Row.

Foner, Philip S. 1979. *Women and the American Labor Movement: From Colonial Times to the Eve of World War I.* New York: Free Press.

Foner, Philip S., and Ronald L. Lewis. 1989. *Black Workers: A Documentary History from Colonial Times to the Present.* Philadelphia: Temple University Press.

Gompers, Samuel. 1925. *Seventy Years of Life and Labor: An Autobiography.* 2 vols., New York: Augustus M. Kelley. Page references are to the 1967 edition.

Green, James R. 1980. *The World of the Worker: Labor in Twentieth-Century America.* New York: Hill and Wang.

Greenberg, Brian. 1993. "What David Brody Wrought: The Impact of *Steelworkers in the Nonunion Era.*" *Labor History* 34:457–469.

Greene, Julie. 1998. *Pure and Simple Politics: The American Federation of Labor and Political Activism, 1881–1917.* New York: Cambridge University Press.

Holt, James. 1977. "Trade Unionism in the British and U.S. Steel Industries, 1880–1914: A Comparative Study." *Labor History* 18 (Winter): 5–35.

Howe, Irving. 1976. *World of Our Fathers: The Journey of the Eastern European Jews to America and the Life They Found and Made.* New York: Simon and Schuster.

Hower, Ralph M. 1939. *History of an Advertising Agency: N. W. Ayer & Son at Work, 1869–1939.* Cambridge: Harvard University Press.

Kaufman, Stuart, et al. 1986–1998. *The Samuel Gompers Papers.* 7 vols. Urbana: University of Illinois Press.

Kessler-Harris, Alice. 1983. *Out to Work: A History of Wage-Earning Women in the United States.* New York: Oxford University Press.

Licht, Walter. 1995. *Industrializing America: The Nineteenth Century.* Baltimore: Johns Hopkins University Press.

Lynd, Robert S., and Helen Merrell Lynd. 1929. *Middletown: A Study in American Culture.* New York: Harcourt, Brace and Company.

McClymer, John F. 1998. *The Triangle Strike and Fire.* Fort Worth, Tex.: Harcourt Brace College Publishers.

Mendel, Ronald. 2003. *"A Broad and Ennobling Spirit": Workers and Their Unions in Late Gilded Age New York and Brooklyn, 1886–1898.* Westport, Conn.: Praeger.

Montgomery, David. 1987. *The Fall of the House of Labor: The Workplace, the State, and American Labor Activism, 1865–1925*. New York: Cambridge University Press.

Montgomery, David. 1978. "Gutman's Nineteenth-Century America." *Labor History* 19:416–429.

Montgomery, David. 1980. "To Study the People: The American Working Class," *Labor History* 20 (Fall): 485–512.

Montgomery, David. 1980. "Strikes in Nineteenth-Century America." *Social Science History* 4 (February): 92.

Orleck, Annelise. 1995. *Common Sense and a Little Fire: Women and Working-Class Politics in the United States, 1900–1965*. Chapel Hill: University of North Carolina Press.

Ramirez, Bruno. 1978. *When Workers Fight: The Politics of Industrial Relations in the Progressive Era, 1898–1916*. Westport, Conn.: Greenwood Press.

Salvatore, Nick. 1982. *Eugene V. Debs: Citizen and Socialist*. Urbana: University of Illinois Press.

Schlereth, Thomas J. 1991. *Victorian America: Transformations in Everyday Life, 1876–1915*. New York: Harper Perennial.

Schnapper, M. B. 1975. *American Labor: A Pictorial Social History*. Washington, DC: Public Affairs Press.

Serrin, William. 1993. *Homestead: The Glory and the Tragedy of an American Steel Town*. New York: Random House.

Shergold, Peter R. 1982. *Working-Class Life: The "American Standard" in Comparative Perspective, 1899–1913*. Pittsburgh: University of Pittsburgh Press.

Shifflett, Crandall. 1996. *Victorian America, 1876–1913*. New York: Facts on File.

Stein, Leon, ed. 1977. *Out of the Sweatshop: The Struggle for Industrial Democracy*. New York: Quadrangle Books.

Stone, Katherine. 1974. "The Origins of Job Structures in the Steel Industry." *The Review of Radical Political Economics* 6:61–97.

Tax, Meredith. 1980. *The Rising of the Women: Feminist Solidarity and Class Conflict, 1880–1919*. New York: Monthly Review Press.

Thompson, E. P. 1963. *The Making of the English Working Class*. New York: Vintage Books.

U.S. Department of Labor. "The History of Labor Day." http://www.dol.gov/opa/aboutdol/laborday.htm.

Von Drehle, David. 2003. *Triangle: The Fire that Changed America*. New York: Atlantic Monthly Press.

Wertheimer, Barbara Mayer. 1977. *We Were There: The Story of Working Women in America*. New York: Pantheon Books.

Wilentz, Sean. 1984. *Chants Democratic: New York City and the Rise of the American Working Class, 1788–1850*. New York: Oxford University Press.

Wolman, Leo. 1975. *The Growth of American Trade Unions, 1880–1923*. New York: Arno Press.

Yans-McLaughlin, Virginia. 1982. *Family and Community: Italian Immigrants in Buffalo, 1880–1930*. Urbana: University of Illinois Press.

Zieger, Robert, and Gilbert J. Gall. 2002. *American Workers, American Unions: The Twentieth Century,* 3rd ed. Baltimore: Johns Hopkins University Press.

The Peopling of Modern America

OVERVIEW

Family and Community, Virginia Yans-McLaughlin's study of Italian immigrants in Buffalo, New York, from 1880 to 1930, describes the experience of the Barone family, who traveled to the United States from Valledolmo, a small Sicilian agricultural town in southern Italy. In 1887 at age 21, Francesco Barone was the first of his family to settle in Buffalo. A success story after years of hard work and saving, Francesco became a saloon keeper and his wife, Antoinetta, eventually joined him in Buffalo. By 1905, encouraged by Francesco's letters home, at least 14 of his relatives had followed his example and immigrated to Buffalo. Like most of the city's Italian immigrants, Francesco's brothers and cousins, many of whom had come with their families, settled in Buffalo's 1st and 19th wards.

Not all members of the Barone clan matched Francesco's success in America. Just before 1905, two single young men in their 20s, Anthony and Tony Barone, immigrated to Buffalo. Tony rented a room in a boardinghouse while Anthony lived with an Italian family in the city. Both men worked as unskilled laborers, and, like other immigrants who lacked the skills required by Buffalo's commercial and industrial enterprises, they struggled. Yet like all Italian immigrants to Buffalo, these young men also helped each other and benefited from their strong extended ties to the more fortunate and established members of the Barone family (Yans-McLaughlin 1982, 17, 55–56, 80).

In the United States, immigration took off in the 1880s and reached a crescendo during the first decade of the 20th century. Between 1901 and 1910, almost 9 million immigrants, more than double the number that had arrived during the decade before, entered the country. Among these immigrants were 2 million of the Barone family's compatriots, more than triple the number of immigrants from Italy who came between 1890 and 1900. Historians frequently distinguish between pre-1880, or "old immigration," which originated in the British Isles and in western Europe, primarily Germany and Sweden, and "new immigration," whose main sources were Italy, Greece, Russia, Lithuania, Latvia, and the smaller Balkan states. During the peak year of 1907, four out of five of the more than 1.25 million immigrants who reached the United States had journeyed from central, southern, and eastern Europe.

Not only Europeans made up the mix of new immigrants who came to the United States after 1880. Decades after the passage of the Chinese Exclusion Act in 1882, as economic and political conditions in China continued to worsen under the tightening control exercised by European imperialist powers, an annual average of almost two thousand Chinese migrants still entered the United States during the first decade of the 20th century. Well over 90 percent of these immigrants were men, including returning U.S. citizens and laborers as well as new and returning merchants and their sons. American employers, especially in the West, remained eager to hire Chinese labor whenever possible (Lee 2003, 110–119). Another wave of migrants came to the United States from Mexico. The modernization of the Mexican countryside conducted by President Porfirio Díaz displaced many Mexican peasants, who, ironically, left their homeland to find jobs in the expanding southwestern U.S. economy using the same railroads that had been built to enable the large haciendas to export their crops to the United States (Diner 1998, 79). These immigrants benefited from expansion of cultivated land made possible in part by the 1902 Newlands Federal Reclamation Act. By 1910, some 14 million acres of land in California, Nevada, Utah, and Arizona came under irrigation, almost 10 times the number of acres as in 1890. Mexican immigrants became the cheap labor source denied Southwestern farmers and mine owners by the exclusion of the Chinese. Between 1900 and 1910, the Mexican-born population in the United States more than doubled, reaching almost 222,000 (Gutiérrez 1995, 45).

TIMELINE

1899　　　　Scott Joplin publishes "Maple Leaf Rag."

1900　　　　The refurbished Ellis Island Immigration Station opens.
　　　　　　　The Labor Museum at Hull House in Chicago is founded.
　　　　　　　Booker T. Washington founds the Negro Business League.

1901	New York passes the Tenement House Reform Law.
	Booker T. Washington meets President Theodore Roosevelt at the White House.
1903	The Kishinev Massacre in Russia causes many Jews to flee to the United States.
	W. E. B. Du Bois publishes *The Souls of Black Folk*.
1905	The founding convention of the Niagara Movement takes place in Niagara Falls, Canada.
1906	Chinese cannery workers are driven from Astoria, Oregon.
	Abraham Cahan begins publishing the "Bintel Brief" column in the *Jewish Daily Forward*.
	Ed Johnson, an African American, is lynched in Chattanooga, Tennessee, which leads to the U.S. Supreme Court's jailing of Sherriff Joseph T. Shipp for contempt.
1907	This is a peak year for immigration to the United States.
	The U.S. Immigration Commission is created.
	A pro-immigration group, the North American Civic League, is founded.
	Scott Joplin begins writing his grand opera, *Treemonisha*.
1908	The U.S. Immigration Service begins to record immigrants who are leaving America.
	The African American boxer Jack Johnson wins the heavyweight title and a search begins for a "white hope" to dethrone him.
	The Hebrew Immigrant Aid Society begins publishing *The Jewish Immigrant*.
	The Melting Pot by Israel Zangwill opens in Washington, D.C.
1909	The NAACP is founded.
1910	*Twenty Years at Hull House* by Jane Addams is published.
	Boxer Jack Johnson defeats Jim Jeffries, the "Great White Hope."

Table 3.1. Immigration to the United States, 1890–1910

	1890–1899	1900–1909
Total in millions	3.7	8.2
Percent of Total	%	%
From:		
Ireland	11.0	4.2
Germany[1]	15.7	4.0
United Kingdom	8.9	5.7
Scandinavia	10.5	5.9
Canada[2]	0.1	1.3
Russia	12.2	18.3
Austria-Hungary	14.5	24.4
Italy	16.3	23.5

[1]Continental European boundaries prior to 1919 settlement.

[2]Canada includes Newfoundland; Canadian immigration was not recorded between 1886 and 1893.

Source: David Ward, *Cities and Immigrants: A Geography of Change in Nineteenth Century America* (1971), 53. Adapted from Shifflet 1996, 80.

COMING TO AMERICA

In seeking to understand the immigrant's decision to journey to the United States, historians of immigration attribute migration to either "push" or "pull" factors. Harsh and often declining economic conditions or discrimination in their home countries pushed persons to emigrate, whereas economic opportunity in America and the nation's reputation for political and religious liberty often pulled them in. For most immigrants a simple desire to improve their lot in life inspired them to leave their homelands. According to one observer in central Europe, "Whoever had in mind a goal that couldn't be fulfilled by lifelong work at home began deliberating at night about going overseas" (Diner 1998, 79). Ignazio Ottone recounted that he worked on his father's farm in Cicarro Mongerrato, Italy, earning only 10 to 15 cents per day, "That's why I left and come to this country. . . . It was too hard over there . . . too many hours for nothing" (Kraut 2001, 15).

The Push Factors

By the late 19th century, the modernization of the European countryside exacerbated rural impoverishment, wrenching the peasants from their traditional pursuits and motivating them to migrate to the United States. Mechanization in agriculture reduced the need for migrant labor even as the completion of railroad systems in southern and eastern Europe eliminated the need for construction labor. The expanded rail transportation made obsolete both the cottage industries such as the making of hats, lace, and rugs, and the local and long-distance carting services that had flourished in the rural countryside.

Beginning in the 1870s, modernization produced widespread economic hardship in Europe. At the same time, population growth soared throughout southern and eastern Europe. With a decline in epidemics and famine, mortality rates fell by a third, even as the birth rate in southern Italy and elsewhere rose to 11 per 1,000, a fourfold increase from previous decades (Taylor 1971, 21). With greater numbers of people came more intense pressure on limited economic resources. Family farms decreased in size as landlords divided estates into smaller plots of land and increased rental prices. In 1895, well over half the land holdings in Hungary, for example, had been reduced to less than seven acres (Taylor 1971, 52–53). Such small holdings could not sustain a basic standard of living for farm families.

Political constraints, especially discrimination motivated by ethnic and religious prejudice, also compelled many immigrants to leave their homelands. Under Magyar rule in Slovakia, Croatia, and Transylvania the use of local languages in public places was forbidden, newspapers were suppressed, intellectuals were imprisoned, and employment was restricted (Taylor 1971, 58). In Russia, Jews, who had experienced intense intolerance during the reign of Tsar Nicholas I (1825–1855), encountered even greater violence after the assassination in 1881 of his successor, Alexander II. Over the next two decades, Jews in Russia suffered severe restrictions on landownership, quotas in university admission, and expulsion from Moscow. An escalation of pogroms against Jews during these years, especially the bloody Kishinev Massacre in 1903 in which 49 persons were killed and more than 500 injured, convinced many Jews to immigrate to the United States. Similarly, the outbreak of the Russo-Japanese War in 1905 and the failed revolution that year contributed to a peak in Jewish emigration from Russia the following year (Kraut 2001, 15–29; Daniels 1990, 224).

The Pull Factors

Optimism rather than despair inspired most immigrants to come to the United States. Contrary to immigration lore, those who emigrated were not the poorest of the poor in their homelands but rather were persons filled with great expectations of improving their own and their family's standard of living (Daniels 1996, 68). With the U.S. industrial economy booming, skilled and unskilled jobs at comparatively high wages were more readily available in America than at home. In *World of Our Fathers,* Irving Howe cites the explanation offered by a

Jewish tailor who was 17 in 1905 when he immigrated to the United States: "Those days everybody's dream in the old country was to go to America. We heard people were free and we heard about better living" (Howe 1976, 60). Even if they did not encounter "streets paved with gold," they did, in the words of a former resident of County Komarom in Hungary, find that "here a man is paid for his labors and I am certainly not sorry that I am here." His wife, who worked in the same shop in America, earned as much as he had made in a month back in Hungary, "and people thought my job [there] was very good" (Kraut 2001, 50). Most Poles came to the United States *za chlebem* (for bread), which the historian Eva Morawska amended to "for bread, with butter" (Daniels 1990, 219).

Yet, as the tailor in Howe's book attested, Jews especially came because they had heard that in the United States people were free. Unlike the Orthodox Jews, who largely remained in Europe, perhaps fearful that too much freedom imperiled their religious faith, most Russian Jews who emigrated found themselves attracted by the absence of state-sanctioned restrictions on religious observance, as well as by the general absence of institutionalized anti-Semitic practices. Fleeing tyranny, a Russian Jew who migrated to Pittsburgh recalled that he had heard that "America was heaven for Jews. A free country where a Jew could even become president" (Kraut 2001, 17). Mary Antin, who had come to the United States from Russia in the early 1890s, later recalled her mother reading a letter from her father who had immigrated some years before. Although her father was simply describing his journey, Antin heard something else, "There was an elation, a hint of triumph. . . . My father was inspired by a vision. He saw something—he promised us something. It was this 'America.' And 'America' became my dream" (Gjerde 1998, 181).

Birds of Passage

Most immigrants to America during the late 19th and early 20th centuries were young adult males, except among the Irish immigrants, who, in 1900, were nearly 60 percent women. Immigration historian Alan Kraut cites official estimates that males made up 78 percent of the Italian and 95 percent of the Greek immigrants to the United States (Kraut 2001, 30). Beginning in 1900, however, the proportion of females among all immigrants began to rise, in particular among Poles, Slovaks, and southern Italians. For example, Yans-McLaughlin points out that in these years more and more Italian men immigrated to Buffalo with their families, and those already in the city sent for their wives and children. Although the percentage was unusually high among Italian migrants to the United States, she observes that the census categorized almost 90 percent of Italian-born residents in Buffalo living as members of a family rather than on their own (Yans-McLaughlin 1982, 69).

Many immigrants, especially the young men often in their late teens and early 20s, regularly traveled back and forth across the Atlantic. Hoping to improve their lives as outdoor day laborers in construction, agriculture, and mining, they arrived in America during the warm spring and summer months only to return to their native countries with the coming of cold weather. Although government officials did not begin to count returning migrants until 1908, according to Roger Daniels such "sojourners" might stay in the United States for only one season or for a few years, going back home once they had accumulated sufficient savings to improve their family's situation (Daniels 1996, 69). However, because of conditions at home, both Irish and Jewish immigrants were much less likely to repatriate than were other immigrants.

The "Uprooted"

Because immigrants came to America, for the most part, in search of work, economic conditions in the United States had a direct impact on immigration. Major economic downturns quickly reduced the flow of immigrants to America. The U.S. Immigration Commission reported in 1907–1908 that industrial activity the previous fiscal year had been strong, resulting in the largest immigration in the history of the country, but the tide reversed following the beginning of the industrial depression in October of 1907 (Kraut 2001, 32). The close connection between the state of the American economy and the flow of immigration highlights the significance of communication between the New World and the Old as well as the financial contributions that settled immigrants made to the migration of their relatives at home.

Almost all of the immigrants who passed through Ellis Island between 1908 and 1910 informed officials during the inspection process that they were joining family or friends. Immigrants often received the necessary transportation money to travel to the United States and carried with them letters from family members or friends already in America. After arriving in the United States, they usually located near or lived with these sponsors (Diner 1998, 80). Historians of immigration now believe that chain migration—the links forged between the more recent immigrants and the members of their family who had already settled—bound them together and made immigrants feel much less "uprooted," or displaced, than was claimed by Oscar Handlin, a founder of the field (Daniels 1996, 70). Moreover, as Kraut notes, although young men often left home alone, as Handlin reported, they rarely made the decision to relocate without first consulting kith and kin (Kraut 2001, 52). Ties to fellow immigrants who had left before them and their relocation to communities in which their compatriots resided lessened the trauma of uprooting.

As an example of the ties between immigrants leaving the Old World and their sponsors in the New, by the turn of the 20th century, one steamship ticket

Able to briefly escape the close confines below deck, steerage passengers "relax" on an ocean liner that was taking them to America, probably around 1905. (Library of Congress)

in three was prepaid, purchased in the United States either by an immigrant aid society, by a fraternal or other nationalist organization, or by an individual paying for the travel of a family member or friend from abroad. By 1900, almost all of those who crossed the Atlantic to the United States came by way of a steamship run by a European company. One of the leading steamship companies, the Hamburg-Amerika (HAPAG) line, employed more than 3,000 agents in the United States. In Liverpool, England, and other European port cities, HAPAG built an immigrant village for transients that included its own railway station, churches, and a synagogue. The cost of transporting an immigrant from Krakow, Poland, to Cleveland, for example, would be provided for in the United States. The ticket, purchased in Cleveland, would be picked up from a HAPAG agent in Krakow. It covered rail transportation to Hamburg, Germany, an overnight stay in the HAPAG facility, the trip across the Atlantic to New York, and then travel to Cleveland by rail (Daniels 1996, 70; Kraut 2001, 58). In Buffalo, Yans-McLaughlin found that in the early 1900s, some 1,200 to 1,500 Italians who entered the city annually had relatives there who had provided them with the means to emigrate (Yans-McLaughlin 1982, 58).

Becoming American: From *The Uprooted* to *The Transplanted*

Although the study of immigrants began in the 1920s, the inclusion of immigration as a distinct field of American history can be said to have started with the publication in 1941 of Oscar Handlin's *Boston's Immigrants, 1790–1860: A Study in Acculturation. Boston's Immigrants* focuses on the economic and cultural adjustment of Irish immigrants to life in Boston during the antebellum period. The Irish, who were forced by poverty and alienation to flee their homeland, found these conditions re-created in Boston. Criminal and generally dissolute behavior among them persisted until the Irish began to adjust to American life. Yet even as they ultimately organized new institutions, took advantage of job opportunities in industries being developed by the Yankee merchant elite, and eventually succeeded in establishing a political presence in Boston, the Irish,

Steerage

The trip across the Atlantic was not a holiday voyage. After 1891, American immigration law required steamship companies to disinfect, medically examine, and vaccinate their immigrant passengers prior to sailing. By 1900, immigrant passengers generally traveled in steerage, that is, in one of the below-deck holds located fore and aft on the ship. These former cargo holds were six to eight feet high and had no portholes. Crammed into these spaces would be two or more tiers of narrow metal bunks. Travelers had to bring their own straw mattresses, which would be thrown overboard on the last day of the journey. Often men and women were separated by nothing more than a few blankets draped over a line in the center of the compartment. Children stayed with their mothers. Some of the larger ships squeezed as many as 2,000 men, women, and children into compartments barely fit to live in (Kraut 2001, 55–59).

according to Handlin, maintained a "group consciousness" that resisted assimilation (Gerstle 1997, 532). Writing ten years later in *The Uprooted: The Epic Story of the Great Migrations That Made the American People,* Handlin clarifies his approach to the immigrant experience as one based more in uprootedness and alienation than in adjustment. Emphasizing immigrants' break with their past Handlin announces, "Emigration was the end of peasant life in Europe; it was also the beginning of life in America" (Handlin 1951, 37). Even more than in *Boston's Immigrants,* Handlin portrays the immigrant, as the historian Gary Gerstle notes, "forever alien and alienated in their new home" (Gerstle 1997, 532). In each of these volumes, Handlin characterizes the immigrants' past as one of wrenching displacement in which they made a life for themselves as individuals who would never really belong to American society.

New social historians—in particular, Herbert Gutman, especially in his 1973 essay "Work, Culture, and Society in Industrializing America, 1815–1919," and John Bodnar, in *The Transplanted: A History of Immigrants in Urban America* (1985)—challenge the central premises of Handlin's work. For this group of historians, the key variable is agency, the idea that immigrants, workers, and other subordinate groups are not powerless, that what these groups do is more an expression of their beliefs and desires than of what is determined for them by those in power. Focusing on the first generation of factory workers both before 1843 and after 1893, Gutman observes the way in which these workers used the pre-modern work habits and collective rituals and practices they brought with them into the workplace to confront their employers. In contrast to Handlin, Gutman denies cultural breakdown and insists that immigrant workers did not want to become Americans, by which he means incipient capitalists (Gerstle 1997,

537). Bodnar also emphasizes the ways in which immigrants relied on familiar transplanted institutions, such as the family and the community, to gain a degree of control (Kazal 1995, 455). Their ethnic traditions enabled immigrants to resist Americanization and fashion a way of life that was as much a product of the old ways as an adjustment to the new. Few historians now believe that, in becoming Americans, immigrants either had no past or completely gave up their past.

Arrival and Settling In

Once the ship reached New York, first- and second-class passengers were processed on board while steerage-class passengers were ferried to Ellis Island, an island in New York Bay that had once been owned by Samuel Ellis, on which were located federal facilities constructed in 1892. After an inspection that could take three to five hours, and if their papers were in good order, and if the immigrants had no obvious ailments, the new arrivals would be ferried to Manhattan or to Hoboken, New Jersey, where they might board a train for travel to other cities within the United States (Daniels 1997, 41). An improved Ellis Island facility opened in December 1900, replacing the wooden structures destroyed in a fire three years earlier. Given the language difficulties, fear of being rejected (immigrants referred to Ellis Island as the "Isle of Tears"), and even the often unfamiliar food (one Slavic immigrant recalled that she had "never [seen] a banana in my life"), the processing experience, although not especially long, could still be very traumatic (Kraut 2001, 65). During one spring day in 1907, Ellis Island, which had been intended to handle about 1,500 immigrants a day, processed more than 10 times that number. Fiorello La Guardia, who was mayor of New York from 1933 to 1945, had worked in his youth as an inspector at Ellis Island. He recalled, "I never managed during the years I worked there to become callous to the mental anguish, the disappointment and the despair I witnessed almost daily" (Howe 1976, 45–46).

Private religious and charitable organizations helped lessen the arriving immigrants' anxieties and difficulties. The Hebrew Immigrant Aid Society (HIAS), for example, met arriving Jewish immigrants and distributed information sheets printed in Yiddish that explained the inspection procedures. Once inspection was completed, the HIAS agents, who were wearing blue caps embroidered with the society's initials in Yiddish, then steered the immigrants past the many swindlers gathered to take advantage of the new arrivals and helped their charges find family members who were waiting for them. The HIAS also ran an employment bureau that stayed open every night but Friday. In 1908, the HIAS began publishing a bilingual monthly, *The Jewish Immigrant,* which was distributed in Russia to provide reliable information on who could and could not be admitted to the United States (Howe 1976, 46–48). Religious missionaries from

The immigrant landing station of Ellis Island opened in 1892 and was rebuilt eight years later after being destroyed by a fire. During the first decade of the 20th century an average of 5,000 immigrants were processed at Ellis Island each day. (Library of Congress)

the Industrial Committee of the YMCA, as well as from such nationalist organizations as the St. Raphael's Society, the Society for the Protection of Italian Immigrants, and the Polish Catholic Union, also developed comprehensive programs that protected and actively assisted newly arriving immigrants (Kraut 2001, 71–72).

After being processed at New York's Ellis Island, or at inspection depots in other ports of entry in Massachusetts, Maryland, or Pennsylvania, most immigrants moved on to cities throughout the United States. According to the 1910 census, about 75 percent of new immigrants settled in 17 cities concentrated, with the exception of San Francisco, in the Northeast and North Central states. Urban areas that were either ports of arrival, supply and export entrepôts, or specialized manufacturing or mining centers that required unusually large amounts of cheap labor had the largest concentrations of immigrants. The 17 cities included the metropolitan centers of Boston, New York City, and Chicago and the industrial centers of Pittsburgh, Detroit, Cleveland, Fall River, Lowell, Providence, Bridgeport, Paterson, Newark, and Jersey City; each had a population of between 30 and 45 percent foreign-born residents (Ward 1971, 75–81).

Ellis Island

Early in the 19th century, New York City's Board of Commissioners processed arriving immigrants through Castle Garden at the tip of Manhattan, built originally
as a fort to protect New York harbor. By the late 1880s, the surge of immigrants
coming to the United States overwhelmed this facility and federal officials built a
new center just off the New Jersey shore on Ellis Island, which opened on January 1, 1892. Five years later, fire engulfed this facility's wooden buildings and a
new Ellis Island Immigration Station, constructed at a cost of $1.5 million, opened
on December 17, 1900.

Immigrants arrived at the new Ellis Island by ferry from their ships and entered the Main Building, a massive redbrick structure notable for its four cupola-
like towers and the enormous open second-floor Registry Room in which newly
arrivals were processed. Located on two islands (a third island had additional
hospital facilities constructed in 1910 to isolate immigrants who had contagious
diseases), the Immigration Station consisted of buildings containing dormitories,
records and administrative offices, a baggage and receiving room, and a railroad
ticket office (Kraut 2001, 64–65). In planning the new facility, immigration officials
had mistakenly calculated that they would be processing no more than 500,000
immigrants a year at Ellis Island. But on April 17, 1907, Ellis Island processed a
record 11,745 immigrants in one day; through the station's first decade, on average 5,000 immigrants would be examined, interviewed, and sent on their way
each day.

A journalist visiting Ellis Island compared an immigrant's day of arrival there
"to the final Day of Judgment, when we have to prove our fitness to enter Heaven"
(Howe 1976, 42). Inspections of the immigrants took place in the Registry Room
(or Great Hall). Doctors soon became adept at conducting "six second physicals"
in which they checked, in particular, for infectious diseases. As the immigrants
passed through the examination area, the doctors made chalk marks on their garments indicating the various problems revealed by the medical exam: L for lame-
ness, K for hernia, G for goiter, H for possible heart ailments, X for mental defects,
and so on; such problems could be cause for the detention or rejection of an immigrant. Immigrants could also be rejected if, during the interview process, a legal inspector thought that they were "likely to become a public charge" or were
"contract laborers," immigrants whose passage had been paid for by an American
employer in return for a promise to perform future labor. Some immigrants were
detained, but as Allen Kraut notes, after a few days' rest and some nourishing
food most of them were sent on their way. Although being rejected was the great
fear of newly arriving immigrants, during the peak years only 2 to 3 percent of
those being processed at Ellis Island were sent back (Kraut 2001, 67–70).

Out to Work

Many of the new immigrants, especially young men in search of economic opportunity, had already left the countryside and moved into the cities of eastern and southern Europe before to coming to the United States. Through the late 19th century, economic hardship in the rural areas of Eastern Europe as well as the tremendous expansion of railroad transportation led Austrians to move to Vienna, Hungarians to Budapest, and Poles to Warsaw. By 1900, these cities had almost quadrupled in population over the previous half century as migrants from the provinces came to work in their mills, iron works, machine shops, and other industries (Kraut 2001, 20). Whether they came from a farm or a city in the old country, however, by the beginning of the 20th century, more than half of the immigrants to the United Sates who reported having an occupation (and those who did not were likely to be women or children) identified themselves as servants and laborers. Fewer than a quarter considered themselves to be skilled laborers, just over 10 percent identified themselves as farmers, and about 5 percent claimed to be commercial tradesmen or professionals. New immigrants increasingly filled up the proletarian ranks of the cities they settled in.

According to a study conducted in 1910, immigrants, the vast majority of whom were from southern and Eastern Europe, accounted for more than half of the labor force in 21 leading industries in the United States. The percentage, Alan Kraut points out, was even higher in industries like textiles, clothing manufacture, ore mining, meatpacking, slaughtering, and cigar manufacture. With the exception of Jewish newcomers, two-thirds of whom were skilled or semi-skilled workers, skilled craftsmen in the United States tended to be either native-born or immigrant males from western Europe (Kraut 2001, 8). New immigrants filled the ranks of America's industrial operatives and unskilled labor force. By the 20th century, Slav and Italian immigrants had largely replaced the Irish as the usual workers on railroads and in construction (Kraut 8, 45–46). In the 1890s, as newer technology in textile manufacturing replaced older machinery, thereby speeding up and intensifying production, skilled Irish and British workers were replaced by French Canadian immigrants. Roger Daniels refers to the early-20th-century emigration of French Canadians as the "third colonization of New England." By 1900, they had begun settling in immigrant enclaves in cities like Fall River, Massachusetts, hoping to earn enough from their "meager earnings—adults could earning as much as $1.22, children as little as 28 cents, per day for a six-day, sixty-hour week—to buy a good farm back home in Canada" (Daniels 1996, 79).

About three-quarters of those immigrants who reported their occupations in 1907, a year of an especially large inflow, were recorded as unskilled (Daniels 1996, 74). In the steel industry, the recent arrivals dominated the bottom ranks. A survey of common laborers in the Carnegie iron and steel mills of Allegheny County, Pennsylvania, found that as of March 1907, 11,694 of the 14,359 workers, or 81 percent, came from Eastern Europe. One-third of the steelworkers surveyed by the Immigration Commission were single, and roughly three-quarters of the married men who had been in the country for less than five years reported that their wives were still abroad. Like the French Canadians, many of these immigrants hoped to earn a stake in a few years and then return to their homelands. Between 1908 and 1910, 44 southern and Eastern Europeans departed for every 100 that arrived; altogether, 590,000 immigrants left the United States in that short span.

But more remained, and those who stayed rose in the ranks and saw their earnings grow. In 1910, as the labor historian David Brody has shown, among those immigrants with less than two years' experience in the Carnegie mills, none had skilled jobs, 56 had semiskilled, and 314 had unskilled. But among those who had been working in the mills for more than 10 years, 184 were skilled, 398 were semiskilled, and 439 were unskilled. And although only one-tenth of those who had worked less than five years earned $15 per week, one-fifth to one-third of those with more than 10 years' experience did earn that much (Brody 1969, 96–111).

In 1890, the Baron de Hirsh Fund surveyed Jews living on the East Side of Manhattan and found that almost half of the more than 25,000 Jews gainfully employed were garment workers in the men's clothing and women's wear industries. In the decades that followed, as the garment industry grew in the United States so did the number of Jewish workers (Howe 1976, 154). Working in the multitude of small factories and sweatshops owned by German Jews who had come to the United States during the mid-19th century, Eastern European Jews, listed in the census as "Russian-born," predominated, but they were soon joined by Italian *contadini,* or peasants. Italian men with experience in the garment trades tended to work in custom-tailoring shops in New York City while the "green hands" worked as sewing machine operators and clothes pressers. By 1900, a sufficient number of Italian women immigrants with experience in home manufacturers had arrived in New York to monopolize the city's home garment-finishing industry (Jackson 1995, 451–452).

Many Italian immigrants toiled as manual laborers. By the early 20th century, Italian rather than Irish immigrants were building America's railroads, paving its streets, and working as laborers in the building trades. As one Italian immigrant put it: "We thought that the streets were paved with gold. When we got here we saw that they weren't paved at all. Then they told us that we were expected to pave them" (Daniels 1996, 77). Manual laborers relied on their hands and backs to do jobs such as digging ditches or loading freight in railroad yards. The vast majority of Polish immigrants settled in cities in the North Central region of the United States and usually held the lowest or the next-to-lowest jobs. Manual laborers frequently changed jobs in search of better pay or to break free of oppressive gang bosses. An observer for the Immigration Commission noted that a gang of laborers on New York City's new aqueduct "may work in the stone

Woman carrying a heavy bundle of clothing to work on at home. During the early 20th century, Italian immigrant women dominated the home garment finishing industry in New York. (Library of Congress)

quarry one day, on concrete work the next, or in moving the track for the dirt tracks the following day" (Diner 1998, 59–60). Yet in Buffalo, a city with expanding heavy industries, Italian husbands and fathers chose the familiar and traditional, but irregular, outdoor manual labor jobs over steadier and better-paying factory work. These jobs left the men free to work during the summer alongside their families in the fruit- and vegetable-processing canneries that surrounding the western New York City.

The vast majority of new immigrants migrated to America from the rural countryside of their homelands. Yet some of these immigrants brought with them experience in other areas as well. In Italy, as elsewhere in southern and Eastern Europe, peasants sometimes could supplement farm work with employment as village artisans in small-scale enterprises or as itinerant provision merchants. Others found work as railroad laborers or in public utility construction. Some new immigrants had experience in industrial pursuits. Eastern European Jews were the most likely to have been skilled workers, especially in the needle trades. The historian Arthur Goren claims that two-thirds of the Russian Jewish immigrants who had occupations were skilled workers (Daniels 1990, 225).

Immigrant Entrepreneurs

Immigrants who harbored entrepreneurial ambitions found success in serving members of their own community. Pushcarts owned by Italian and Jewish immigrants crowded the streets in many of America's cities. Much less common, apparently, despite the stereotype, was the Italian organ grinder and his monkey. Besides the Italians, Greeks, Irish, Armenians, and Eastern European Jews dominated peddling. Peddling required little capital; usually a fellow countryman supplied the newcomer with the necessary goods, and after he sold them he paid the supplier back. Because peddlers usually sold in their own neighborhoods to fellow immigrants, knowledge of English was not a job requirement (Diner 1998, 82–83). Among Italians and Greeks, shoe shining was also a popular entry-level job that also required little English. For this job, all that was necessary were strong arms and backs and a willingness to work long hours every day. Virtually all the bootblacks in New York City in the mid-1890s were Italian (Kraut 2001, 112). Also in New York, almost everything the Jewish community needed was supplied by one of their fellow immigrants. Jewish pushcart vendors packed the streets of their neighborhoods. Jews owned a variety of retail establishments on the East Side. Some Jewish entrepreneurs also rented cheap stores in their neighborhood and, charging a nickel a head, operated nickelodeons that showed the first movies (Howe 1976, 163–165).

The successful Francesco Barone, who immigrated to Buffalo in 1887, became a saloon keeper in his adopted country. A flourishing soda-water business developed among Jews in the early 1900s that "was attributed to the nonalcoholic drinking habits" of these immigrants (Bodnar 1985, 134). Also during these years, Italians opened "two-bit eateries" in Coney Island as well as barbershops in New York City. Other immigrant groups, such as the Greeks, also operated restaurants. They served inexpensive everyday meals, much like a "greasy spoon" does today. In addition to operating restaurants wherever they settled, Greeks established themselves as ice-cream manufacturers, candy makers, florists, and wholesale distributors of fruits and vegetables (Daniels 1990, 203–204). In much the same fashion, after 1880, Chinese immigrants living in large cities operated restaurants and laundries. Successful Chinese entrepreneurs hired their compatriots to work at minimal wages and often under appalling working conditions in San Francisco, Portland, Seattle, and New York (Daniels 1996, 78). Few of the immigrants who operated these businesses in the United States had ever run a comparable enterprise in their homelands (Daniels 1990, 203). Nor should these businesses be thought of only as individual enterprises. Often the shared resources of members of the immigrant community and the labor of family members were necessary to sustain immigrant businesses (Bodnar 1985, 134).

Ethnic Food and Ethnic Identity

The German sociologist Werner Sombart's insight into American character—that material abundance explains *Why There Is No Socialism in the United States* (1906)—has particular salience when applied to the immigrant experience with food. Immigrants generally left behind conditions of scarcity and a limited diet in their home countries and found in the United States relative plenty and a more varied diet. Recent research by social historians focuses on the role that food played in shaping ethnic identity and in the formation of community among immigrant groups in the United States. In *Hungering for America: Italian, Irish, and Jewish Foodways in the Age of Migration,* Hasia Diner contrasts the experiences of different immigrant groups in the United States with both hunger in the Old World and abundance in the New.

A bustling Hester Street in New York City, ca. 1903. Hester Street was a center of immigrant life and commerce on the Lower East Side. (National Archives)

In Italy the *contadini,* or landless poor who made up most of the Italians, who migrated to the United States had a limited diet based on the staple (corn, wheat, or rice) grown in the region in which they lived. Except for Christmas, Easter, and the local saint's day, when the landowner distributed special foods, the poor ate no meat. In America, however, Italian immigrants could afford foodstuffs such as olive oil (they preferred the more expensive imported oil), "Italian" cheese, meat, and macaroni that, in their homeland, was consumed only by the wealthy. Parish associations sponsored "spaghetti dinners," and macaroni shops abounded in Italian neighborhoods. "Meatballs and spaghetti" became a standard "Italian" dinner first in America and only later was transferred back to the Old World. Diner concludes that Italian immigrants in America fashioned an identity around foods that "had become sacred to them, and Italian foods in particular symbolized their communities' lifeblood" (Diner 2001, 70).

For the Irish-Catholic poor who immigrated to America after the "Great Famine" of the 1840s, food, other than the potato, never had a special significance either in Ireland or in the United States. An elaborate diet was the preserve of the Irish Protestant landed class and of the despised English market to which the crops produced in Ireland were exported. Rather than food, it was drink, enjoyed in

Immigrants and Education

Especially among Eastern European Jews, education ranked high as a way for immigrants to achieve success in their new homeland. A 1908 survey of high school graduates in New York City found that among the new immigrants, Jewish children were much more likely to stay in school and receive diplomas than were Italians. Researchers for the U.S. Immigration Commission admired the willingness of Jewish parents to sacrifice to keep their children in school and lauded the academic achievements of Jewish students (Kessner 1977, 97). Furthermore, a Jewish child's education did not necessarily end with high school graduation. In 1890, a few Eastern European Jewish boys joined the German Jews already attending City College, which offered free tuition. By the early 20th century, more than 75 percent of City's student body was Jewish; in 1910, at least 90 students of the 112 in the college's graduating class were Jewish, mainly from Eastern European families (Howe 1976, 281). Immigration historians have concluded that the attendance of Eastern European Jewish immigrants in college was less a matter of financial sacrifice and reverence for learning than it was a measure of the economic success that some members of this community had already achieved (Bodnar 1985, 196; Kraut 2001, 163). Even so, early in the century, because of anti-Semitism, few Jewish college graduates were able to follow their native-born American peers into the professions; they would later on.

the *shabeen* (a hidden public house), and later in the legal public house, that was integral to Irish folkways. Once in the United States, the Irish did not give food the special significance that it had for Italian immigrants. Drink, however, remained at the center of Irish American ethnic culture. Diner cites a 1907 *Boston Globe* sketch featuring "Mr. Dooley," written by the Irish American satirist Finley Peter Dunne, on the meaning of alcohol: "Dhrink never made a man betther, but it has made many a man think he was betther. A little iv it lifts ye out iv th' mud where chance has thrown ye; a little more makes ye' think the stains on ye'er coat are apllylets" (Diner 2001, 136).

Food had always been at the center of the culture of Eastern European Jews. In the Old World, special religious laws, or *kashrut,* regulated the consumption of food. The celebration of the Sabbath and of religious holidays was associated with special foods. In the United States food cost relatively little, and it remained at the heart of Eastern European Jewish culture. Diner points out that the poverty experienced by Eastern European Jews in the Old World came as much from religious and political persecution as it did from physical deprivation. Eastern European Jews found the greater material abundance of the United States liberating and readily adopted new forms of consumption. In America, Jews could partake more often of such traditional foods as herring, dark bread, gefilte fish, and borscht, and they encountered and embraced a diversity of new foods, such as sandwiches made with bologna or corned beef. Chinese food and other ethnic dishes also appealed to them. For Eastern European Jews, food became one more issue over which their ties to the Old World contended with their embrace of the new.

Kinship Ties

The economic success achieved by new immigrants was as much a matter of family cooperation as of individual achievement. Rather than immigrants' undergoing a family breakdown in their confrontation with modern urban-industrial society, which had been the assumption of early interpretations of the immigrant experience, their kin connections enabled them to better negotiate their new lives in America (Bodnar 1985, 71). In fact, as Virginia Yans-McLaughlin reveals, notions of kinship that in the Old World might have extended only to protecting family honor assumed new roles in Buffalo that included arranging housing, travel, and employment, and utilized social ties to relatives, friends, and neighbors beyond the immediate family. She mentions the owner of a soda-

A mill worker family at Amoskeag Mills in Manchester, New Hampshire. Many of the workers at textile mills like Amoskeag were immigrants. Usually the father, mother, and at least one child all worked in the mills. (Library of Congress)

Paying the Rent: Taking in Boarders

In the years before their children were old enough to work, immigrant families took in boarders, usually young men of their own nationality, as a supplement to meager wages. The going rate for most immigrants working as common laborers in the steel mills in Pittsburgh in 1910 was, according to the Pittsburgh Associated Charities, far below what was needed to support a family of five. Under the "boarding boss system," boarders paid $2.50 a month for food and lodging. Rose Popovich, the daughter of a Croatian immigrant steelworker, recalled that her family had "a room just for boarders" in their house in Pennsylvania: "They would pay ten dollars just to have their clothes washed and for their rooms" (Diner 1998, 70). Such arrangements enabled working-class mothers to care for their young children at home while contributing to the economic security of their families. Although many immigrants relied on the family economy to help sustain them, they also made use of more sophisticated forms of organization—economic, religious, and communal. Trade unions, churches, synagogues, and ethnic mutual aid societies functioned in complex ways to help immigrants adjust to the many demands of their new environment. As they adjusted to life in America, immigrants availed themselves of the traditions they brought with them through these institutions.

bottling business who employed his own relatives. "'We were all friends,' he said, 'and helped each other in business'" (Yans-McLaughlin 1982, 63–67). Immigrant children understood, the historian John Bodnar observes, that family goals superseded individual aspirations. He notes the truism expressed by one immigrant child: "You never left your mother and father." And according to another, "I turned most of (my earnings) over to my mother. That's what I was working for" (Bodnar 1985, 72–73). The economic value of family reciprocity was recognized by most immigrant communities. Historian Tamara Hareven found that the most economically secure families in the Amoskeag textile mills in New Hampshire in the early 1900s were generally those in which a husband, wife, and at least one child worked. Similarly, almost half of the family income among unskilled Poles in eastern Pennsylvania was generated by the earnings of children, although less so where the father was a skilled worker (Bodnar 1985, 76–77).

BUILDING A COMMUNITY

Italian immigrants celebrated patron saints to maintain a strong sense of group identity as well as to preserve religious rituals that they brought with them. Among Italians in Buffalo, kin connections, or *paesani*, often served the same purposes that mutual aid or religious associations fulfilled in other immigrant communities. Yans-McLaughlin notes that in America this concept referred to a more intense emotional bond than simply being born in the same village in Italy. Although community associations did develop among Italians, as did ties to the Catholic Church, especially among women, *paesani* fulfilled the basic needs for economic security and mutual support for Italian families in Buffalo. Such family-centered behavior, Yans-McLaughlin maintains, was not just a cultural pattern rooted in the past but was also shaped by the conditions Italians found in America, especially a sense of exclusion from the prevailing social and political life. Like the Italians in Buffalo, each immigrant group would adjust their traditional practices to fit the circumstances that confronted them in America (Yans-McLaughlin 1982, 55–81).

Immigrants and Religion

Even among secularist Jews, the synagogue remained the central institution of immigrant Jewish life in the United States. Most of the synagogues, or shuls, on the Lower East Side—one survey found 326 in 1907—basically served *landsleit,* persons from the same town, and some were so small that they had difficulty maintaining a minyan, the minimum of 10 adults necessary for formal services (Daniels 1990, 228). Eastern European Jewish immigrants followed familiar rituals and rejected American Reform Judaism's more liberal innovations, such as holding services in English or eliminating religious laws that governed daily life such as kashrut, the maintaining of a home and food as kosher. Jews in America appreciated their newfound autonomy. Unlike in eastern Europe, Jews in the United States did not have to pay heed to a state-sanctioned authority, the *kehillar.* The rabbi became an employee of the shul, hired by a lay board of trustees. Nor could the rabbi enforce religious observance. Without a governing body, anyone could advertise meat as "kosher," and because most immigrant Jews worked on Saturday, few could attend Sabbath services (Diner 1998, 90).

If lacking the official sanction of their Eastern European counterparts, shuls in America nevertheless provided a range of activities for Jewish immigrants that matched the activities of secular associations. Irving Howe describes a prominent Forsyth Street synagogue on the Lower East Side that, in 1900, had a *"khevra kadisha* consisting of over twenty members who perform all the rites connected with the burial of members: the *khevra* is social, for it gives banquets very often" (Howe 1976, 191). The same synagogue had organized another religious society whose members studied the Talmud, a basic religious text, every evening. Most synagogues were not nearly as impressive, some having been established in storefronts or in tenements, yet they still provided a consecrated place to carry on centuries-long traditions.

Roman Catholics, who made up the majority of immigrants to America in the early 20th century, found an already established church in the United States. Unlike Judaism, Catholicism had a recognized, hierarchical structure. In every city that had substantial numbers of Catholic immigrants, there was a diocese headed by a bishop and numerous Catholic churches. Newer immigrants who arrived after 1890 encountered a Catholic Church that was an Irish American institution. Yet, these newcomers wanted priests who spoke their language and churches whose practices honored their patron saints and distinctive rituals. Most of the new immigrant groups quickly organized their own nationality-based parishes and built formidable churches that followed traditional religious practices (Diner 1998, 86–87).

Polish Catholics bitterly fought the church hierarchy in America. "Is it that the Irish want to dominate the Catholic world?" a leading Polish journal asked in 1900. "Can't Polish Catholics have as much freedom as the other nationalities?" (Dinnerstein and Reimers 1975, 65). Nationalists who had struggled with the hierarchy in the Old World over their efforts to establish a Polish nation found themselves confronting priests in America who had been sent over by the same Resurrectionist order to staff the Polish parishes in their new homeland. In Chicago, Polish nationalists formed a new parish and battled with the bishop to find a like-minded priest. Eventually, in 1911, they founded the Polish National Church, whose membership encompassed about 5 percent of Polish Catholics in the United States (Diner 1998, 88). The formation of this separate national church also reflected Polish Catholics' protest against what they believed was the insensitivity of the Irish American Catholic Church to their customs. Polish leaders and laymen took the initiative in establishing parishes in which they replaced the use of Latin in religious services with the Polish language (Bodnar 1885, 153). In her study of Polish Americans, Helen Znaniecki Lopata observes that during the years of their heaviest migration to the United States, Polish peasants "combined a Polish version of Catholicism with pagan and magical beliefs in animated natural objects and spirits" (Kraut 2001, 139). Like the founders of the Polish National Church, peasant immigrants rejected the more formal practices of the Irish-dominated American Catholic Church and continued to follow rituals transplanted from their home villages in Poland.

Italian immigrants also saw the Catholic Church in the United States as an Irish American institution. Yet rather than protest or attempt to set up their own distinctive parishes, many Italians continued to be only nominally Roman Catholic. In Italy, where the Catholic Church had been seen as ally of the wealthy landowners, a deeply ingrained anticlericalism had been practiced. In Buffalo, according to Yans-McLaughlin, although the Church of Saint Anthony of Padua, founded in 1890, had been the first community-wide institution of any consequence, Italians rarely led or controlled their local parishes. Even when the diocese did appoint Italian-speaking priests, they tended to be from the better-educated classes of northern Italy, a background different from that of the local immigrant community, which came from the poorer regions of the south (Yans-McLaughlin 1982, 119–120). Like the peasant immigrants from Poland, Italian immigrants carried with them religious practices that they had followed in their homeland. In Italy, they often prayed to special local patron saints, such as Santa Lucia, San Gennaro, or San Michele. Much like in the Old World, then, in the Little Italys of America, immigrants frequently celebrated a *festa* that honored a patron saint with a parade, bands, and special foods (Kraut 2001, 140).

Abraham Cahan and the "Bintel Brief"

Born in 1860 in Lithuania, Abraham Cahan immigrated to the United States at age 22. In 1897, already a major figure among New York's socialists and labor radicals, Cahan helped launch a Yiddish newspaper, the *Jewish Daily Forward*. Hoping to attract new readers, women as well as men, to the *Forward,* he introduced in January 1906, the *"Bintel briv"* (literally, bundle of letters), a personal advice column. At least in the column's early years, Cahan himself responded to the letters from readers that described their personal problems with such issues as intermarriage, apartment house life, sexual mores, and religious ritual. The letters were often semiliterate but could also be very poignant. Cahan sometimes used professional writers to "improve" the letters. The column immediately became very popular.

In *World of Our Fathers,* Irving Howe describes the first letter that appeared in the "Bintel Brief." A mother wrote that a watch, "which he adores and needs for work," that belonged to her "boy, who's now the breadwinner in the family, [and who] is as deaf as the wall" had been stolen by a neighbor and was at the pawnbroker's. "Please," she begged her neighbor through the column, "mail back the pawn ticket to me" and nothing more would be said. Not surprisingly, love and marriage was a popular letter theme. A female correspondent wrote about living with a man outside of marriage, "We're living together now for the eighth month and I feel as if I'm losing my mind, I can't stand his bass voice—it's a saw rasping my bones." Manners and morals were also issues of common interest. For example, one writer, "a socialist and freethinker" asked if it was appropriate for him to observe *yortsayt* (prayers for the dead). Another correspondent confessed that he had been a scab during the 1910 cloakmakers' strike. A detective asked if he was violating his duty because he could not bring himself to arrest a poor restaurant owner who was selling liquor without a license. Cahan's responses were often pragmatic, and he generally advised his correspondents not to be too rigid. Howe observes that whenever Cahan was confronted by problems beyond solution he "[fell] back on his own deep fatalism: *vos vet zany,* what will be, will be" (Howe 1976, 533–537).

Immigrants and the Labor Movement

Many of the skilled workers among the older immigrant groups who came to America before 1890 had previous experience with trade unions in their homelands. Based on this experience, they often became active in the labor movement after immigrating to the United States. But most of the southern and Eastern Europeans who immigrated after 1890 in ever-greater numbers were more likely drawn from rural areas of their homelands and, once in America, commonly worked as unskilled or day laborers. The labor movement, and the American Federation of Labor (AFL) in particular, scorned the new immigrants as unorganizable and as a competitive threat—an abundant source of cheap labor that enabled employers to cut costs by lowering wages and to replace skilled labor by introducing more modern machinery. AFL affiliates discriminated against the foreign born by enforcing special requirements for union membership; as one immigrant recalled, "It was difficult for an immigrant to get into the building trades. . . . The smallest initiation fee was $25.00; in some cases it was as high as $100." Even the immigrant who could pay such high fees might fail the required examination (Green 1980, 47). Yet their exclusionary practices came at a high cost to AFL unions. In the early 20th century, the AFL represented only a small minority of the workforce, mainly in unions concentrated outside the mass-production sectors of the industrial economy (Dubofsky 1975, 64).

As an exception to the AFL's restrictive practices, the United Mine Workers (UMW) readily organized new immigrant workers. By 1900, English-speaking groups made up just more than 50 percent of the workforce in the anthracite mining region of Pennsylvania; non-English-speaking Slavic immigrants from Poland and Lithuania made up about 40 percent. Earlier efforts to unionize miners had failed, primarily because of the united opposition of employers to a union and a lack of solidarity among the men, including an initial reluctance to reach out to the Slavic miners. Also, the Slavic miners initially saw themselves as transients and resisted unions. Once they accepted that they were staying permanently in the United States, however, Slavic miners became more open to organizing (Kraut 2001, 91). In May 1902, after efforts to mediate a settlement with the mine owners had failed, the UMW called a strike. Five months later, the strike ended with a union victory. The victory, as Victor Greene shows in *The Slavic Community on Strike,* was in large measure the result of the efforts of a united Slavic community. The tightly knit institutions of Slavic communal life—Catholic parish associations, the boarding house, and mutual aid societies—sustained the workers while they were on strike and enforced discipline. Even Slavic musical groups supported the strikers. Music and dancing were an important part of Old World folkways, and parishes maintained these traditions in America. Two local touring bands educated the public at large about the main issues in the dispute and collected funds for the strikers. In addition to financial support, "Many of the foreign societies . . . adopted resolutions expelling

---

The International Ladies' Garment Workers' Union (ILGWU)

During the first decade of the 20th century, rank-and-file militancy among immigrant workers in the garment trades in New York City helped establish the International Ladies' Garment Workers' Union (ILGWU). Located on the Lower East Side of Manhattan, the garment industry employed over 200,000 persons in 1910, more than double the number three decades earlier. On each block of these East Side streets one could hear, according to Jacob Riis in *How the Other Half Lives* (1890), the "whir of a thousand sewing machines, worked at high pressure from the earliest dawn till mind and muscle give out all together" (Green 1980, 21). In 1909, the area resonated with the "Uprising of the 20,000," a strike led by young Russian and Italian women who made shirtwaists. Allied with Local 25 of the ILGWU and supported by prominent middle-class allies, these immigrant women won this strike after a three-month battle fought in the depth of winter against their employers and the police. Before the strike, the ILGWU had 500 members and only four dollars in its treasury; afterward, Local 25 had 10,000 members and the ILGWU was able to negotiate contracts in all but 19 of the 337 shirtwaist companies in New York and Philadelphia (Green 1980, 71–72). The next year, the mostly male Italian and Jewish cloakmakers followed their sisters into the streets, giving birth to a militant, more radical, and more inclusive labor movement that drew on the strength of the immigrant community in the United States.

---

those members who have refused to strike," and other ethnic fraternal groups fined transgressors (Greene 1968, 197). Such worker solidarity ultimately impressed even President Theodore Roosevelt. Fearful that coal operator obstinacy was promoting a spirit of socialism among the miners, Roosevelt intervened in the dispute, appointing an arbitration commission that included representatives of labor and that eventually settled the strike (Green 1980, 56).

Immigrants and Radicals

Radicals and socialists challenged the AFL's craft union conservatism in the early 20th century. In 1905, a small group founded the Industrial Workers of the World (IWW), dedicated to "industrial solidarity"—that is, the organization of all workers to secure and defend their rights through direct action. Openly appealing to the new immigrant workers, the IWW led a series of industrial battles throughout the Northeast over the next few years. In 1909, at McKees Rocks, Pennsylvania, and in other steel towns in the Midwest, the IWW organized mass strikes that challenged the power of U.S. Steel. Moreover, by 1909, the Slavic workers in these towns had settled in, and through a display of community solidarity, they organized effectively against the introduction of a piece-rate system that tied workers' pay to output (Green 1980, 67–69). Throughout its history, the IWW reached out to new immigrants and other oppressed groups across the United States.

Founded in 1901, the Socialist Party of America (SPA) grew steadily until World War I, drawing support from working-class voters and socialist trade unions. Strong socialist movements developed among certain immigrant groups in particular locations, such as among Germans in Milwaukee or Jews on the Lower East Side of Manhattan (Diner 1998, 68). In *Labor and the Left,* John Laslett studied six national unions—the United Mine Workers, the Boot and Shoe Workers, the International Association of Machinists, the United Brewery Workers, the Western Federation of Miners, and the International Ladies' Garment Workers— to show how socialism's appeal to the working class transcended regional, craft, and ethnic lines. The unions that Laslett looked at varied in the ethnic and religious backgrounds of the membership, their location in the United States, and their union structure. Yet to a greater or lesser degree, each of these unions supported the socialist movement (Dubofsky 1975, 97–100). But beyond those organizations formally affiliated with the SPA, socialism's appeal was evanescent, an ideal, a hoped for alternative that underscored the dignity of labor and held out the possibility of a more cooperative future. Opposition to the immigrant community's ties to socialism came not just from employers but also from religious and ethnic leaders (especially the Catholic Church) who rejected socialism's opposition to capitalism as anti-American.

Mutual Aid Societies

Immigrants of every nationality formed a broad range of communal associations that provided them with a certain degree of economic security and a measure of self-respect. By 1910, two-thirds of the Poles in America belonged to at least one of approximately 7,000 Polish associations; the National Slovak Society boasted almost 37,000 members; Eastern European Jews had created more than 3,000 societies, known in Yiddish as *landsmanshaftn;* and Hungarians had formed 800 Hungarian associations (Diner 1998, 90–92). In the Bohemian section of Chicago in 1902 there were more than 30 savings and loans and 259 benefit societies as well as 35 gymnastic clubs, 18 singing societies, 5 bicycling clubs, and 4 drama groups. Investigators from the Hull House settlement believed that every Bohemian man and woman belonged to a least one order or beneficial society; some appeared to belong to several (Barrett 1990, 75). For many immigrants, such associations had been a part of their lives in their homelands. By 1893, southern Italians, for example, had established more than 6,000 associations (Diner 1998, 91). Limiting their membership mostly to men, mutual aid societies in the United States provided modest illness, death, and other insurance benefits to their members' families, and they served as social clubs. Men who might not even speak English could run lodge meetings and become respected members of their local community. Ethnic associations also sponsored picnics, dances, and other forms of social interaction.

Immigrant Jews, who rarely felt loyalty to Russia or Poland, the nations they had willingly left behind, formed deep attachments, Irving Howe has noted, to their town or village in the old country. Such local identities provided the basis for the *landsmanshaftn,* or lodges, that they organized in the United States. These groups could function simply as places where the immigrant Jews could gather to play cards, or they could offer financial assistance for a *landsman* who was ill, or build a cemetery and provide a proper burial for a fellow lodge member. In its constitution, one such association, the Ershte Turower, stated, "This organization exists to help sick and needy brothers, also to pay expenses of death cases and endowments." Another group set its goal as maintaining "the spirit of fraternity. . . . That ideal has to be kept alive among the younger generation born in this land and an attempt must be made to plant in them an awareness of their origins" (Howe 1976, 185). Sometimes several societies came together to form federations, or *farband.* Howe cites a Galician federation formed in 1904, a Polish federation in 1908, and a Russian federation in 1909. Pooling their resources, federations established hospitals, convalescent centers, and old-age homes (Howe 1976, 183–189).

When scorned by the AFL, immigrants turned to mutual aid and fraternal societies for help and protection. In the steel industry, the Amalgamated Association of Iron, Tin, and Steelworkers represented largely the English-speaking workmen who, until the late 19th century, had dominated the industry. After U.S. Steel defeated the Amalgamated Association in a 1901 strike, the corporation moved to take greater control over the labor process by introducing new technology into its now nonunion plants and, in the years that followed, replacing skilled workers with new immigrant semiskilled machine tenders and unskilled laborers. Mainly single young men, these Poles, Slovaks, Croats, Serbs, and Hungarians earlier had been transient workers who sought merely to earn money and return home. However, once enough of their fellow countrymen had gathered in a mill town, James Green points out, they would form mutual aid associations, usually affiliated with national ethnic organizations, to provide insurance and death benefits at cheap rates. Thus, the Polish National Alliance claimed to have 30 locals in Pittsburgh by 1908. Just outside Pittsburgh, in Homestead, the Greek Catholic Union, the National Slavonic Society, the First Catholic Slovak Union, and the National Croatian Society each had more than 100 members. For these immigrants and many of their compatriots elsewhere, such religious and ethnic societies were the foundation of a permanent community and mediated their experience with industrial capitalism (Green 1980, 14).

Members of the Russian Labor Association marching in a May 1909 labor parade in New York City. (Library of Congress)

RESTRICTION AND AMERICANIZATION

As more and more new immigrants settled into their adopted country in the first decade of the 20th century, they sought to become Americans but on their own terms. New immigrants responded to the challenges posed by urban, industrial America based on the norms, values, and worldviews that they brought with them. The immigrant transition to America, as Yans-McLaughlin has observed, must be understood as "a dynamic process of give and take between new conditions and old social forms" (Yans-McLaughlin 1982, 20). The reaction of American natives (many of whom were themselves recent immigrants) took two forms: a restrictive nativism that looked to exclude new immigrants from the United States, and "Americanization," a coercive process that attempted to "melt" the new immigrant "into a single race, culture or nation, unvarying across space and time" (Gerstle 1997, 525). In either case, by 1900, many Americans had come to regard the new immigrant as an "alien menace" who posed a threat to the well-being and stability of the nation's institutions. The basic difference lay in whether the nativist ascribed these differences to race, that is, viewed them as inherent and therefore incapable of adjustment, or to culture, which presupposed that the newcomers wanted to shed their Old World traditions and adopt the language and customs of their new homeland. The first view culminated with legislation in 1921 to restrict immigration; the second was represented by a profusion of Americanization schemes that sought to enforce cultural conformity, often through public institutions such as schools, which were given responsibility for inculcating American values and beliefs into the young, and other, more informal, mechanisms tied to the workplace and home.

From the moment of their arrival at Ellis Island and at the other U.S. ports of entry, immigrants felt the pressure to Americanize, to abandon their traditions and adopt the language and customs of their new home. As best they could, inspectors recorded the names of the immigrants, who usually could not speak English. The story is told, for example, about a Russian Jew who, frustrated by questions he did not understand, said "Shoyn fargesn" (I forget already) and thus became Sean Ferguson in America. In 1908, attending an opening night performance in Washington, D.C., of *The Melting Pot,* by Israel Zangwill, President Theodore Roosevelt celebrated "the man who becomes completely Americanized—who celebrates . . . the Fourth of July rather than St. Patrick's Day and who talks 'United States' instead of the dialect of the country which he has of his own free will abandoned—is not only doing his plain duty by his adopted land, but is also rendering himself a service of immeasurable value" (Kraut 2001, 170–171). Unlike restrictionists, Roosevelt had confidence that the melting pot would work as a force to unify and strengthen America.

Unionization and involvement with insurgent groups like the IWW and the SPA were also part of the process of Americanization. Even though during the first decade of the 20th century the AFL came out in support of immigration restriction, individual unions remained open to organizing immigrant workers. For their part, many immigrants brought with them prior experience with unions in the old country. In the packinghouse districts of Chicago, skilled butchers reached out to the Eastern and southern European newcomers. The immigrant John Kikulski, who had been active in the Polish Alliance and the Polish Falcons, became a paid organizer for the AFL. Prior to the 1904 packinghouse workers' strike, Kikulski started a newspaper that drew thousands of Poles and Lithuanians into the union (Bodnar 1985, 101–102).

The IWW was especially active in working-class immigrant communities. Immigrants began the 1909 McKees Rocks strike in Pennsylvania to protest working conditions at the Pressed Steel Company. After an AFL organizer blamed "foreign labor" for the violence that resulted from the strike, the IWW joined the conflict, sending in multilingual organizers and helping the workers hold out for 45 days. Immigrant militancy led to a victory over the company (Green 1980, 67–69). Socialists too were active in the immigrant working-class communities. Italian cigar makers in Tampa, Florida, formed radical clubs, and in

Race Thinking and Immigration

According to John Higham, the dean of historians of nativism in the United States, two "streams" of race thinking existed in 19th-century America, a self-congratulatory romantic nationalism that celebrated the nation's Anglo-Saxon traditions and, beginning in the 1890s, a second type that translated physical and cultural differences into racial feelings of white superiority. By the early 20th century, Higham concludes, "racial science increasingly intermingled with racial nationalism" converting a "vague Anglo-Saxon tradition into a sharp-cutting nativist weapon and ultimately, into a completely racist philosophy" based on the emerging "science" of eugenics, "which certified that the betterment of society depended largely on the improvement of the 'inborn qualities' of 'the human breed'" (Higham 1968, 150). Viewing the immigration question as at heart a matter of biology, advocates of eugenics apprehended that native Americans, by permitting "degenerate breeding stock" to freely enter the United States, were committing race suicide. Previous restrictive immigration movements culminated in 1897 in the formation of the Immigration Restriction League (IRL). Led by members of the Boston and Harvard elite, the IRL called for the imposition of a literacy test intended to cut Eastern and southern European immigration in half by banning all adult males who were unable to read and write in their own language (Higham 1968, 101). However, as the depression of the 1890s ended, national self-confidence revived and interest in restricting immigration quickly waned (Higham 1952, 87).

Xenophobia and the movement for imposing a literacy test did not end, however. Under the leadership of Massachusetts senator Henry Cabot Lodge, prominent New England families, the veterans of immigration restriction, pressed again in 1905 and 1906 for literacy test legislation. At this point organized labor entered the fray. Through the 1890s, the AFL had resisted immigration restriction, asserting the international solidarity of the working class. But when organized labor found itself significantly challenged by an employer-led antilabor open shop drive during the first decade of the 20th century, the AFL turned to immigration restriction and the literacy test as main legislative objectives, resulting in a strange alliance between the patrician Lodge and the union labor leader, Samuel Gompers (Higham 1968, 163–164). Once again, however, the restrictionists failed to achieve their objectives. But in 1907, Congress did establish the U.S. Immigration Commission under the chairmanship of Vermont's senator William P. Dillingham. The Dillingham Commission, as it was known, labored for three years and in 1910 produced a multivolume report that, as Alan Kraut observes, denounced the new immigrants as less fit physically, intellectually, economically, and culturally than earlier American settlers and recommended the adoption of effective restrictive legislation based on nationality to "protect" the country from southern and Eastern Europeans. Nevertheless, it was not until 1921, after the heightened nationalism unleashed by World War I and the renewed immigration to prewar levels that followed the conflict, that Dillingham succeeded in gaining legislation that established restrictive quotas (Kraut 2001, 209).

> ### Race Thinking and Immigration, Continued
>
> Through the late 19th and into the early 20th centuries, views held by native-born Americans toward the new immigrants blended freely with their ideas about race. The concept of "ethnic" as it is currently applied to immigrant groups was alien to both foreign- and native-born Americans in these years. The historian David Roediger has represented the status of the new immigrant as one of "in-betweenness," as not yet white (i.e., accepted as equal to the native-born American) but as still not the racial equivalent of African Americans and other peoples of color. Immigrants in America did not confront the "hard, exclusionary and often color-based racism of Jim Crow segregation, Asian exclusion, and Indian removal" (Roediger 2005, 12). At the dawn of the new century, the assumption of white supremacy both hardened and extended the barriers that African Americans had to overcome.

1902, an Italian Socialist Federation was organized in Hoboken, New Jersey, which published its own newspaper, *Il Proletario.* Early in the century, the Workmen's Circle, a fraternal society founded by Jewish socialists in New York City, doubled its membership from 5,000 to 10,000. Even though electoral victory eluded socialists on New York's East Side, passionate soapbox orators, enthusiastic street meetings, and torchlight campaigns enlivened the community's social life.

Immigrants neither completely rejected nor completely surrendered to Americanization. Historians of immigration have come to represent the relationship of the foreign born to Americanization as a process of negotiation between the old and the new, between the hold of traditional values and the appeal of the American way. The collusion of Italian parents in Buffalo with cannery owners to avoid child labor laws and truancy regulations derived not from deference to their employers' wishes but from economic need, a desire to resist state meddling in family life, and a preference for having mothers and children work together. Alexander Harkavy, a Polish Jew who wrote the *English Teacher,* a text used by many Jewish immigrants to learn English, wrote in 1907, "The Russian Jew is expected to adapt himself to American conditions of freedom and democracy . . . but America does not demand of him that he forget the ties that bind him to his mother country, no matter how cruel she may have been, or that he forget his race, no matter how prosperous or how wretched that race may have become" (Diner 1998, 99). Harkavy expressed a pluralist vision embraced by many immigrants in which, even as the immigrants adjusted to a very different life in America, they remained loyal to the values of their countries of origin.

Mexican Immigrants Confront Race Thinking Among the Anglos

Racialization is the process that best explains the abduction of 40 Irish orphan foundlings over 10 days in October 1904 in the area around the copper mining towns of Clifton and Morenci, Arizona. The Sisters of Charity had transported the children from a Catholic orphanage in New York City to the Arizona towns where they were to be placed with area Mexican Catholic families who had been selected by a local priest. Offended that the "white" Irish orphans, who, ironically, in New York City would have been labeled "Irish" and treated not unlike African Americans, were being placed in "Mexican" homes, white Protestant Anglo women in the Arizona towns goaded their husbands and other local white men to "take *back* the foundlings" (Gordon 1999, 76, 115). The Anglo men, believing that they were acting nobly "to protect the welfare of the children and to preserve peace and order in the community," formed vigilante groups and "rescued" the children, who were then placed in the homes of the well-to-do Anglo women (Gordon 1999, 159). The Catholic Church in New York sued to get the orphans back, but the U.S. Supreme Court ruled in favor of the vigilantes, agreeing that it was in the "best interests" of the children to be left in the homes of "Americans" rather that removed to live with "half-breed Mexican Indians" (Gordon 1999, 294).

In many ways, the events that transpired in the fall of 1904 in Clifton and Morenci represented the latest episode in a labor strike the previous year by the largely Mexican workforce against the Anglo owners of the local copper mines. Because by 1910 three-quarters of all active mines in Mexico were U.S.-owned, coming to work in the Arizona mines was simply a move across the border for Mexican miners attracted by the higher wages (Gordon 1999, 51). Although better paid than in their home country, the miners from the south confronted extremely dangerous and harsh working conditions (the biggest killer among miners was silicosis contracted in the mines) and a "Mexican" wage that paid them at best 40 percent less than white miners received for doing the same work (Gordon 1999, 214, 218). Proud of their work and of the improvements that they had been able to make in the lives of their families, the Mexican workers went out on strike in 1903. Shutting down the mines, they sought an equalization of wages and better working conditions, including locker rooms where they could shower and change their dirty clothes, company-paid hospitalization costs, and other benefits (Gordon 1999, 222). The owners considered the demands impossible and viewed the strike as an "uprising, a massive threat to 'American' arrangements of power" (Gordon 1999, 220). After a massive flood killed 39 local people, the Mexican strikers, demoralized and now living under martial law, ended the strike on June 12. Among the negative consequences for the Mexican miners was a greater division between them and their white coworkers as well as a growing conviction in the white community in general that the Mexicans were radical, dangerous, and not "American." Similar racial views and a desire for revenge against the Mexican community caused by the strike animated the Anglo response to the arrival of the Irish orphans in Clifton and Morenci 16 months later.

The Dillingham Commission

In 1907, a bill "to regulate the immigration of aliens into the United States" passed both houses of Congress. To reduce the number of undesirable applicants for admission, the new immigration act's provisions called for an increase in the head tax from two dollars to four dollars; added certain persons to the excluded class, including women imported for immoral purposes, feeble-minded persons, and persons afflicted with tuberculosis; restricted contract labor and the padrone system, an arrangement in which hiring agents controlled the earnings of young male immigrants until the young men were of age; instituted improvements in conditions for steerage passengers; and created a bureau of information to

Immigrants held for deportation at Ellis Island, 1902. Immigrants could be refused entry into the United States for reasons of health or if they were seen as likely to become a "public charge." (Library of Congress)

facilitate the distribution of immigrants throughout the United States ("The New Immigration Law," 1907, 453–454).

Intense congressional debate over inclusion of a literacy test in the immigration act led to a compromise agreement to form a commission to produce a comprehensive statistical and demographic study of immigration in the United States. Composed of three senators, three representatives, and three persons chosen by president, the Immigration Commission was given a million-dollar appropriation; William P. Dillingham (Vt.), chair of the Senate Immigration Committee and a supporter of the literacy test, headed the commission. Between 1907 and 1910, the Dillingham Commission, as it came to be called, produced 41 volumes containing data on 3.2 million individuals. The commission surveyed the European countries from which the immigrants came. It also studied the conditions of immigrants in U.S. industries, the lives of immigrants in the major metropolitan and agricultural areas, the schooling of immigrant children, and the number of times that immigrants sought charity or were convicted for crimes.

Historian Desmond King notes that one innovation of the Dillingham Commission was the idea of a dichotomy between Northern and Western European, or "old," immigration, and southern and Eastern European, or "new," immigration. More than a shift in the countries of origin had taken place since 1890. The commission distinguished old immigration as "largely a movement of settlers who came from the most progressive sections of Europe for the purpose of making themselves homes in the New World." These immigrants "mingled freely with the native Americans and were quickly assimilated," even those, in later years, who came from non-English-speaking "races." In contrast, the new immigrants were largely unskilled laboring men "who have come, in large part temporarily, from the less progressive and advanced countries of Europe" and who concentrated in "'colonies' of their own race" in large cities. For the commission, both the temporary character of new immigration and the living arrangements of the new immigrants reflected resistance to assimilation: "Racially [the new immigrants] are for the most part essentially unlike the British, German and other peoples who came during the period prior to 1880, and generally speaking they are actuated in coming for different ideals, for the old immigration came to be a part of the country, while the new, in large measure, comes with the intention of profiting, in a pecuniary way, by the superior advantages of the new world and then returning to the old country" (King 2000, 59–61).

The Dillingham Commission used three measures to assess assimilation: learning English, acquiring U.S. citizenship, and abandoning native customs. Yet, according the commission, the new arrivals' most "debilitating characteristic" was that "'the new immigration as a class is far less intelligent than the old'" (King 2000, 61). Curiously, the commission relied on studies conducted by Franz Boas, the nation's premier anthropologist, that rejected the idea of static "racial types" and argued instead, according to the historian Robert Zeidel, "that members of

The 1906 Humboldt County, Oregon, Chinese Roundup

In the United States, the restrictionists' first victory against immigration was passage of the Chinese Exclusion Act of 1882. Centered in the American West, anti-Chinese prejudice stigmatized these immigrants as the "Yellow Peril." Brought to the United States as unfree laborers, initially through the so-called Coolie trade, Chinese immigrants worked in mines, on farms, in factories making shoes and clothing, in laundries, and on the railroads throughout the 19th century. Chinese immigrants were already ineligible for citizenship under the Naturalization Act of 1870, which limited naturalization to "white persons and persons of African descent." Further Chinese immigration was suspended for 10 years under the Chinese Exclusion Act, which was regularly renewed until 1943. By 1910, from a high in 1890 of just over 100,000, the Chinese population in the United States decreased by one-third (Daniels 1990, 239–247).

In *Driven Out: The Forgotten War Against Chinese Americans,* historian Jean Pfaelzer recounts numerous episodes beginning in the mid-19th century and extending into the 20th of the many ways, often violent, in which towns in California and the Pacific Northwest sought to "cleanse" themselves of Chinese immigrants. On September 30, 1906, 23 Chinese men disembarked in Astoria, in Humboldt County, Oregon, from the steamer *Roanoke.* These men, along with 4 Japanese men and 6 Russian women, had been smuggled aboard the steamer by a labor contractor to work in a salmon cannery 20 miles south of Astoria, in Port Kenyon at the mouth of the Eel River. Immediately upon their landing, the cannery workers were surrounded by a hostile gang chanting anti-Chinese slogans. They quickly returned to the ship to await the train that would take them to their destination. The crowd grew more and more threatening. When the afternoon train for Port Kenyon finally arrived at the wharf, the cannery workers left the *Roanoke* and boarded the train. That day the headline in the local newspaper, *The Daily Humboldt Times,* pronounced "TWENTY-SEVEN CELESTIALS BROUGHT TO EUREKA ON ROANOKE FOR CANNERY AT PORT KENYON." The next day the newspaper declared, "THE CHINESE MUST GO," citing the "unwritten law of [the] county" that 20 years earlier had driven the Chinese from the area in violent roundups (Pfaelzer 2007, 337).

During the 1906 incident, public meetings led by local labor unions demanded that the cannery, Starbuck, Tallant and Grant, fire the men. As the threats against the Chinese escalated, including the promise made by a men's drinking club to "exterminate" the cannery workers, the Chamber of Commerce met and called on local public officials to ask the governor to send in the state militia to protect the workers. Claiming that the Chinese workers were skilled and not cheap labor, the cannery promised that it would send the workers away in two months, at the end of the fall salmon run. The lumberjacks and timbermen in the region would have

Continued on next page

The 1906 Humboldt County, Oregon, Chinese Roundup, Continued

none of this, and they resolved that the cannery had "contaminated the air of the county with the filthy Chinese whom the fathers of the present generation were forced to resort to strenuous means to eject" (Pfaelzer 2007, 338). Conscious of the local pride at play in the earlier roundups, and fearful of what might come out of the current protest, the company decided to abandon the season. However, the Chinese workers refused to quit, and the cannery paid off the contract. Four days after they had arrived, the Chinese workers again boarded the *Roanoke* and left Humboldt County. Within a year, the Smith Cannery Machine Company advertised "The Iron Chink," a mechanical fish cleaner, in the newspapers. Reprinting articles on the recent labor problems, the ads admonished the canners, "Don't Fool with the Question any Longer" (Pfaelzer 2007, 339).

---

ethnic groups could change over time under the influence of both heredity and environment" (Zeidel 2004, 87). Boas used data from the physical measurements of 120,000 immigrants and their children, in particular from their "changes in bodily form," as a means of settling "once and for all the question [of] whether the immigrants from southern Europe and from eastern Europe are and can be assimilated by our people" (Zeidel 2004, 86). Based on studies of cranium length, Boas concluded that immigrants' children quickly assumed the characteristics associated with native-born Americans. For Boas, the American environment was capable of having a positive influence on immigrants and their children. *The New York Times* remained unconvinced. The newspaper dismissed Boas's discovery of an "American physical type" among immigrant children and that they had become "more physically American" (Zeidel 2004, 98). Similarly, eugenicists like Prescott Hall, secretary of the Immigration Restriction League, expressed a lack of confidence in Boas, rejecting him as a potential member of a eugenic study committee.

Dillingham, who had introduced the 1907 immigration law, insisted that the United States "permit only those to enter who are sound in mind, sound in body, sound in morals, and fit to become fathers and mothers of American children" ("The New Immigration Law," 1907, 453). The commission recommended restrictions that, had they been enacted, would have established Dillingham's standard. Taking for granted the unassimilable character of recent immigrants, the commission unanimously recommended a tougher assessment of immigrants' criminal records and mental aptitudes and sought to limit the entry of single, unskilled males from southern and Eastern Europe through a literacy test, a fixed quota by race based on a percentage of the average of that race who had arrived during a designated period of years, the exclusion of unskilled workers unaccompanied by dependents, annual limits on the number of immigrants admitted at each port, and an increased but leniently applied head tax (King 2000, 76). President William Howard Taft vetoed the literacy test, as would President Woodrow Wilson, but the momentum for immigration restriction built after World War I, resulting in eventual passage of both the literacy test and quotas based on national origin.

The Melting Pot

In 1782, even before the American Revolutionary War had ended, the French immigrant Hector St. John de Crèvecoeur asked rhetorically, "What then is the American, this new man?" Crèvecoeur responded that the American is one who has left "behind him all ancient prejudices and manners, receives new ones from the new mode of life he has embraced. . . . Here individuals of all nations are melted into a new race of men" (Gerstle 1997, 524). Crèvecoeur's invocation of the United States as a special place in which the cultures of the world are "melted" into one has had a very long history. During the first five months of 2007, *The New York Times* carried 12 stories that employed the melting pot as a primary image for describing the immigrant experience in America.

Popular acknowledgment of the melting pot as the symbol of the American experience became more commonplace with the production of Israel Zangwill's play *The Melting Pot*. The play opened in October 1908 in Washington D.C., and then, almost a year later, in New York City, where it ran for 136 performances. Although praised as an important and powerful play by notable Americans ranging from President Theodore Roosevelt to Jane Addams, *The Melting Pot* was dismissed as "cheap and tawdry" by *The New York Times* critic in his September 1909 review. One respondent to the *Times* review strongly protested, citing the play as "one of the greatest we have seen in recent years, a true exposition of the intense Americanism which characterizes the intelligent alien" (*New York Times,* September 10, 1909). Oddly, as immigration historian Philip Gleason has pointed out about the playwright, it was an English Jew who captured the American spirit and gave to Americans this enduring symbol of the United States as a "nation of nations" (Gleason 1964, 22–25).

In his study of the melting pot as a symbol of American society, Gleason summarizes the plot of *The Melting Pot*. Zangwill's protagonist is David Quixano, a young Jewish immigrant who has fled Russia after his family was murdered in the Kishinev Massacre. Quixano is an idealistic composer working on a "great American symphony" that he hopes will capture in music his understanding of his adopted nation as "God's Crucible, the great Melting-Pot where all the races of Europe are melting and reforming!" David has fallen in love with Vera, a fellow Russian immigrant in New York, who is a Christian. David's love for Vera is an expression of America as a New World unbound by the inherited prejudices and antagonisms of the Old. But when David learns that Vera is the daughter of the Tsarist officer who had led the pogrom in Russia, he breaks off with her. After the triumphant performance of his symphony, in the last scene of the play, the lovers are reconciled. Standing on the roof of the settlement house and looking out at the Statute of Liberty, David delivers his paean to the glory of the American nation:

> David   There she lies, the great Melting Pot. Listen! Can't you hear the roaring and the bubbling? There gapes her mouth—the harbour where a thousand mammoth feeders come from the ends of the world to pour in their human freight. Ah, what a stirring and a seething! Celt and Latin, Slav and Teuton, Greek and Syrian—black and yellow.
>
> Vera   Jew and Gentile—
>
> David   Yes, East and West, and North and South. . . . Ah, Vera what is the glory of Rome and Jerusalem where all nations and races come to worship and look back, compared with the glory of America, where all races and nations come to labour and look forward! (Gleason 1974, 26–27).

The response among his contemporaries to Zangwill's vision of America as a melting pot for assimilation encapsulates the core concerns about Americanization. Restrictionists, those who did not hold out much hope that the melting pot would be an effective crucible, condemned the play. Speaking for "traditional Americans," one reviewer in 1909 in *The Forum* worried about "the indiscriminate commingling of alien races on our soil" and derided the notion that "the scum and dregs of Europe" could enrich America (Gleason 1974, 28). In contrast, Zangwill's embrace of assimilation offended those immigrants who were unwilling to renounce their traditional values. Gleason cites a German American who dismissed *The Melting Pot* as "simply a mixture of insipid phrases and unhistorical thinking" that represented "just the contrary of that toward which we strive," the preservation of the cultural values of the old country (Gleason 1974, 28). Yet although Zangwill intended *The Melting Pot* as a tribute to assimilation, how the melting pot should work in reality is unclear. Was America, to use Zangwill's phrase, "a purging flame" that purified immigrants of their cultural heritage, as those who embraced "100 percent Americanism" hoped? Or, did the melting pot actually reflect a process through which becoming an American positively combined the Old World with the New? The 21st-century debate over immigration indicates that this question remains very much unsettled.

The "Americanizers"

Once they were settled in their new home, immigrants continuously encountered American associations and institutions in their community and at their workplace intent on coercing them to embrace a new American identity. Pro-immigration forces like the North American Civic League, an organization founded in 1907 on the principle of "Not Restriction, but Americanization," promoted education as a means of transmitting and preserving American ideals. Established in the mid-19th century as a missionary agency dedicated to the moral and intellectual development of young men, the YMCA had by 1900 turned into an organization that provided a range of social services for the urban immigrant poor. In 1907, sympathetic to Roosevelt's positive view of Americanization, the YMCA began organizing classes in English and civics for foreigners. Two years later the YMCA, aroused by what they thought to be the negative influence of foreign-born students on the moral climate in the nation's high schools, founded Hi-Y clubs. Designed to promote "Christian Citizenship," Hi-Y clubs focused on the "four C's": clean speech, clean athletics, clean scholarship, and clean living. From a start of 150 clubs in 1910, student membership grew over the next two decades and by 1930, about 30 percent of American public high schools had Hi-Y clubs. The YMCA is just one community-based organization that relied on education as a primary means of protecting the national character from the presumed dangers posed by the flood of new immigrants after the turn of the century (Setran 2005, 207–216).

Public schools came to be seen as the most efficient agency for Americanizing the masses of new immigrants threatening to "foreignize" the nation's cities. For such education to work, immigrant children not only had to learn new skills but they also had to shed their traditional culture. As David Tyack, a historian of urban education, indicates, many educators believed that "Anglo-conformity" demanded that they foster in their immigrant students a sense of shame in being "foreign." Textbooks aimed at immigrants prescribed cleanliness, a proper diet, health precautions, proper clothes, and well-ordered recreation. According to Julia Richmond, a teacher, principal, and school superintendent on New York's Lower East Side during these years, immigrant parents "must be made to understand" that "in forsaking the land of their birth, they are also forsaking the customs and traditions of that land; and they must be made to realize an obligation, in adopting a new country, to adopt the language and customs of that country" (Tyack 1974, 237). Both children and parents were continuously subjected to heavy doses of socialization in what it meant to be an American.

Immigrants both spurned and embraced Americanization. The massive immigration that occurred at the turn of the century reinforced native-born Americans' confidence in the public school as an instrument for Americanization. By 1900, the vast majority of states had passed compulsory education laws, which usually required school attendance by children aged 8 to 14. Not surprisingly, even though such laws were rarely enforced, by 1910, the cost of public education was twice as high as it had been 10 years earlier. On average, between 1890 and 1918, one high school was built every year and school attendance increased by 711 percent, almost seven times the population growth rate for the same period (Tyack 1974, 183). Yet a concern for protecting their children led both Catholic and Jewish parents in America to look to alternative, religion-based educational systems. In New York, the University Settlement and the Educational Alliance ran Hebrew schools free of charge, usually after public school classes were over. Among Orthodox Jews, yeshivah education replaced the public school altogether. So too, did the Catholic Church, which had operated parochial schools since the mid-1850s to provide religious education for young members of the faith. The church also succeeded in winning release time from public schools for Catholic children to attend religious instruction one afternoon per week (Kraut 2001, 159–160).

Even as immigrants resisted its pull, the public school became a highly valued institution among immigrants. Outside the South, which provided only minimal public schooling even for white children, public school attendance among immigrant children was equal to or better than that of the native born. Immigrants also varied in their enthusiasm for education. In 1909, the U.S. Senate Immigration Commission surveyed the progress rates of different ethnic groups in 12 cities in the East (not including New York) and the Midwest. The commission found differences in the "retardation" rates (pupils who were two or more years older than the norm for their grade) among the native born and the various ethnic groups. Children of Russian Jewish fathers who had lived in the United States for 20 years had lower retardation rate (29.7 percent) than comparable southern Italian children (55.4 percent). The commission found similar differences in attendance, truancy, and IQ. Although immigrant parents often feared the impact of Americanization on their children, for some immigrant groups, public schools represented a doorway to opportunity (Tyack 1974, 241–244).

Americanization through education also took place behind factory gates. Here too the YMCA proved active. In 1907, Peter Roberts, a Welshman who had spent years in Pennsylvania's coalfields, became the head of the industrial department of the YMCA's national council. Focusing on what Roberts called the "immigrant zone," the industrial area bounded on the west by the Mississippi River and on the south by the Potomac and Ohio rivers, the YMCA launched language and citizenship programs for working immigrants. In less than a decade, the YMCA had 500 branches operating in this area. In 1910, the International Harvester Company adopted Roberts's methods. Company superintendents supported English-language classes as a way to reduce accidents and increase productivity. As Gerd Korman details in his history of Americanization and International Harvester, English classes stressed discipline (e.g., "I hear the whistle, I must hurry," "I work until the whistle blows to quit," and "I leave my place nice and clean") and practical lessons to familiarize immigrant workers with Harvester's operations ("The Employee Benefit Association is composed of the employees of the International Harvester Company," "When you are sick or hurt report to your time-keeper and doctor at once," and "No benefits will be paid if you are hurt or get sick as a result of having been drinking") (Korman 1967, 144–146). Although Americanization was not the specific reason for Harvester's safety education program, the teaching of English to immigrants appears to have encompassed that objective.

Americanization was not always coercive. Settlement house workers offered a more humanitarian and culturally pluralist variant of the melting pot, one that acknowledged immigrant traditions and customs. Among the many programs of Chicago's Hull House that demonstrated the valuable contribution that immigrants made to America, Jane Addams, in her memoir *Twenty Years at Hull-House,* singled out its Labor Museum. This educational enterprise had been created to keep alive such traditional crafts as pottery, textiles, basketry, and metalwork. Hoping that "our American citizenship might be built without disturbing these foundations which were laid of old time," Hull House also helped its Italian neighbors commemorate such Old World national events as the birthdays of the Italian patriots Giuseppe Mazzini and Giuseppe Garibaldi (Addams

A photo by the social investigator Lewis Hine of tenement buildings on New York's Upper East Side. The rent sign states that these are "Eleganti Apartmenti." (Library of Congress)

The Tenement Law of 1901

Tenements were first built in the mid-19th century to provide compact, inexpensive rental housing for the growing immigrant population in New York City. These multiple-unit residential buildings were often dark, unventilated, and overcrowded. In one Italian neighborhood, the typical apartment had only two rooms and almost all of the families shared a backyard privy or primitive toilet. In the immediate aftermath of the Civil War and again 10 years later, reform efforts to improve the sanitary and moral conditions in tenement dwellings resulted in some physical improvements. Yet by the end of the 19th century, only 306 of 253,033 persons living in Manhattan's Lower East Side had bathrooms in their apartments. The privy waste was supposed to be removed each day and flushed in what were known as "school sinks." Following investigations into the deteriorating conditions and overcrowding by the Tenement House Committee of the Charity Organization Society (COS), a private relief association, and with support from such prominent reformers as Jacob A. Riis, Lillian Wald, and Alfred E. Smith, the New York State legislature passed the Tenement Law of 1901 (Jackson 1995, 1162–1163).

A July 1901 story in *The New York Times* on the new law emphasized the provisions intended to "purify the moral conditions of houses." The law imposed fines if tenement apartments were used as houses of prostitution; any woman found guilty of soliciting a man or a boy would be deemed a vagrant and committed to the county jail for up to six months time (*New York Times* July 2, 1901). However, the main objective of the new law was to improve living conditions for tenement residents. New buildings were required to have a greater area set aside on the sides and in the back, changes that limited tenements to only three-quarters of the standard-sized lot. One room in each apartment had to be at least 120 square feet, and no room could be smaller than 70 square feet. Other changes were devised to increase the amount of light and air in the public halls of new tenements, as well as in the often dark interior rooms of older buildings. The COS's Tenement House Survey had discovered that there were "over 350,000 dark interior [windowless] rooms" in existing tenements (Dolkart 2006). The new law mandated that in every apartment a window be cut into the partition between the interior room and the room with windows looking out over the street. Unlike the public hall changes, these modifications were costly and led to a loss of rentable space, triggering organized opposition from real estate and taxpayer groups. But the most important and controversial change mandated by the Tenement Law was the removal of all the backyard privies, which were replaced with water closets that had flush tanks connected to proper sewers instead of school sinks to remove the waste. Implementation of this provision was resisted by the tenement owners until a lawsuit brought by the COS in 1903 forced them to install the required toilet facilities. By 1906, almost all tenements had indoor water closets in hallway compartments, one facility for every two families. The new law also created the Tenement House Department, which administered improvements in roughly 83,000 "old law" structures and enforced the new standards on buildings under construction (Dolkart 2006).

The Tenement Law of 1901, Continued

Even though conditions improved because of the tenement law of 1901, living in tenements remained difficult. A survey conducted in 1903 by the Tenement House Department of the City of New York found that the population of the Tenth Ward on New York's Lower East Side to be just under 70,000, or 665 people per acre, making it the most densely populated neighborhood in the city (Dolkart 2006).

1910, 147). Addams recalls one visitor to another Hull House initiative, a coffeehouse, observing that "this would be a nice place to sit in all day, if one could only have beer." She concludes that their experience with the coffeehouse taught Hull House residents "not to have preconceived ideas of what the neighborhood ought to have, but to keep ourselves in readiness to modify and adapt our undertakings as we discovered those things which the neighborhood was ready to accept" (Addams 1910, 97–98). According to Addams, Hull House looked to build a bridge between the Old and the New World experiences of its immigrant community.

Immigrants and Reformers

Settlement workers had to walk a fine line between sensitivity to immigrant traditions and enabling immigrants to adapt to their new lives in America. Addams recounts the death of an abandoned infant in the Cook County hospital to reveal the unintended consequences of being an outsider. The decision by the settlement workers to let the child be buried by the county was quickly overturned by an outraged community, which took up a collection to defray the cost of the funeral. Addams concludes from this incident that "no one born and reared in the community could possibly have made a mistake like that" (Addams 1910, 150). Citing the reflections of two immigrants on their experiences with the Educational Alliance, a New York City settlement house, Irving Howe captures the ambivalence immigrants expressed toward these agencies of Americanization. The memories of Eugene Lyons, a journalist and writer, were bitter: "We were 'Americanized' [at the Educational Alliance] about as gently as horses are broken in. In the whole crude process, we sensed a disrespect for the alien traditions in our homes" (Howe 1976, 234). On the other hand, the philosopher Morris Raphael Cohen recalled, "It was there that I drew books from the Aguilar Free Library and began to read English. . . . A window of my life opening on the soul-strengthening vista of humanity will always be dedicated to the Educational Alliance" (Howe 1976, 234–235).

Virginia Yans-McLaughlin recounts the deep suspicion in which southern Italian immigrants in Buffalo held public or organized private agencies. To them, any form of assistance offered by these outsiders represented an unwonted interference in family life. Even the Catholic Church concerned itself chiefly with individual salvation and not with philanthropy. Despite social workers' efforts to influence their leisure-time activities, family-based leisure and popular customs remained central to the social life of the Italian immigrant community in Buffalo (Yans-McLaughlin 1982, 134). Folk culture was important among other immigrant groups as well. Each nationality organized societies that held celebrations and festivals that kept alive traditional practices. Finns working in America's mines, lumber camps, and mills organized the Finnish National Temperance Brotherhood, which held festivals. In Worcester, Massachusetts, Swedish immigrants celebrated the Fourth of July by holding church picnics. Polish polka bands played folk songs in small saloons and at special events. In New York City, cafes, which contemporaries referred to as the "universities of the ghetto," and Yiddish theater enabled the eastern European Jewish community to keep alive their Old World customs even as they tried to make a new life for themselves in America.

AFRICAN AMERICAN MIGRATION NORTH

In 1900, African Americans made up just over 11 percent of the total American population. Nearly 90 percent resided in the South and at least half this population worked in agriculture. In Mississippi and South Carolina, African Americans made up nearly 60 percent of the population, and in these and the other so-called Black Belt Southern states, the number of African Americans engaged in agriculture reached almost 70 percent. The plantation proved to be a highly resilient institution. The vast majority of former slaves, although legally free, found themselves working as tenants on their erstwhile owners' plantations. In Mississippi in 1910, for example, about 85 percent of African Americans in agriculture worked as tenants rather than owned their own farms (McMillen 1990, 113). By contrast, in the North, farmers owned their work animals and agricultural machinery and commonly rented land only for a few years before purchasing it. Because the end of slavery had left them without land and with few resources, African Americans in the South had to rely on planters to supply them with seed, fertilizer, work animals, even the houses they lived in, through a system known as sharecropping. Sharecroppers had to cede from one-half to two-thirds of the cotton that the landowners demanded they produce. Most Southern states made it a crime for tenant farmers or sharecroppers who owed money to landowners to leave the land. In 1907, it was estimated that as many as one-third of African American farmers in Alabama, Georgia, and Mississippi were

Before the Great Migration

The harsh conditions and limited prospects that African Americans faced in the post–Civil War South led them to move frequently. First they left the countryside for Southern cities but then abandoned the South altogether. Between 1900 and 1910, the urban African American population in the South increased by almost 900,000. Nearly every Southern town or city had a segregated section that whites designated "Bucktown," "Niggertown," or "Coon Town." Although the Great Migration of African Americans north began in 1915 and continued into the 1920s, between 1890 and 1910 almost 380,000 departed the South, about 2.5 percent of the South's total African American population in these years. In 1900, Washington, D.C., had the largest African American population of any city outside the South, and Baltimore, Philadelphia, and New York City each had 50,000 African American residents. As the African American population arriving in the North grew, so too did northern segregation (Southern 2005, 81–82).

As more African Americans moved north, they faced a growing hostility that included housing segregation and being denied access to restaurants, hotels, and theaters. YMCAs in the North had either African American or white members, but each location could not have both African American and white members. Whereas African Americans had played professional baseball in the late 19th century, that opportunity closed for them in the early 20th. In 1910, after an African American Arthur "Jack" Johnson defeated Tommy Burns for the world's heavyweight championship, "white hopes" settled on Jim Jefferies, a retired champion who nevertheless assured the white race that he was fit to "defend its athletic superiority" (Southern 2005, 68–69). During the first decade of the 20th century, hostility to African American migration produced race riots in northern cities such as New York (1900), Evansville, Indiana (1903), Springfield, Ohio (1904), Greensburg, Indiana (1906), and Springfield, Illinois (1908). Such events were marked by unrestrained violence by whites against the African American community and few, if any, convictions of the vigilantes.

forced to work the land involuntarily. By the beginning of the 20th century, African American sharecroppers had become further indebted to local merchants who provided necessary farm supplies after taking a lien against their crops; each year the African Americans fell deeper and deeper into a state of debt peonage.

Similar to the new immigrants' response to Americanization, African Americans resisted but could not ignore white supremacy. The African American scholar Cornel West insists that "while black people have never been simply victims, wallowing in self-pity and begging for white giveaways, they have been—and are—*victimized*" (Southern 2005, 4; emphasis in original). In citing the experiences of the Barone clan in adapting to life in Buffalo, Yans-McLaughlin points out that the key issue was not so much their typicality or the statistical recurrence

Table 3.2. Black Population in Cities, 1910

City	Black population	Total population (%)
Chicago	44,000	2
New York (Manhattan)	61,000	2
Philadelphia	84,000	5
Baltimore	85,000	15
Washington, D.C.	94,000	28
New Orleans	89,000	26
Detroit	6,000	1
Atlanta	52,000	33
Los Angeles	15,500	2.6
Denver	6,000	2
San Francisco	2,400	4.7
Seattle	2,894	9

Source: Based on Carson, Lapsansky-Werner, Nash, 2007, 354.

of each incident as it was "the adaptive process it illustrates" (Yans-McLaughlin, 1982, 80-81). Life in the United States during the first decade of the 20th century also presented African Americans with many challenges. Yet even as they adapted to oppressive conditions they were able to forge an identity of their own.

Ragtime

In August 1899, John Stark, a sheet music publisher in Sedalia, Missouri, signed a contract with Scott Joplin, a young African American pianist and composer, for the right to publish Joplin's "Maple Leaf Rag." Instead of the usual small fixed fee, Stark agreed to pay Joplin one cent for every copy of the sheet music that was sold. Over the next 20 years, "The Maple Leaf Rag" sold more than half a million copies. Before his death in 1917, Joplin published more than 64 songs or piano rags, including "The Entertainer" (1902), "Breeze From Alabama" (1902), and Sugar Cane" (1908), earning him the sobriquet the "King of Ragtime Writers."

Joplin and Stark were the first persons in the music business to self-consciously call their music "ragtime." Using syncopated or "ragged" melodies, and complex harmonies, ragtime was the music played by African American musicians in the saloons and brothels of the South and Midwest beginning in the 1880s. At the 1893 World's Columbian Exposition, ragtime was played at the popular, but unofficial, Midway Plaisance "honky-tonk" dance halls, but it was banned from the much grander Court of Honor of the fabled "White City." By the early 20th century, ragtime had become widely popular among the working classes, black and white, even as Victorian middle-class and highbrow commentators contemptuously dismissed the music for its sensuality and lack of restraint. When "Maple Leaf Rag" appeared in print, the editor of *The Etude* deplored the popularity of ragtime as "a term applied to the peculiar, broken rhythmic features of the popular 'coon song'" (Curtis 1994, 112). Other High Art critics used "disease" metaphors for ragtime, referring to such music as an "an epidemic," "a rapidly increasing mania," musical "pimples," and the source of "mental aliments" (Curtis 1994, 112).

Joplin's efforts to produce *Treemonisha,* a grand opera about plantation life in southwestern Arkansas, which he began writing in 1907 (it was published four years later), were frustrated by the unwillingness of the managers of legitimate theaters to stage serious work by an African American. Written in the tradition of Booker T. Washington, an acknowledged leader of African American people in these years and an outspoken

Sheet music cover for the song "Maple Leaf Rag," composed by Scott Joplin. Ragtime was a widely popular music form that challenged Victorian cultural standards. (Hulton Archive/ Getty Images)

advocate of self-help, the libretto of *Treemonisha,* celebrated rural African American culture and expressed the composer's conviction, like Washington's, that African Americans were victimized by their own ignorance and superstition but could improve their lives through industrial education. Joplin's ragtime music as well as his ambition to be accepted as a writer of serious work, is a good illustration of what the historian and activist W. E. B. Du Bois meant by African Americans' "double consciousness"—the sense of always looking at one's self through the eyes of others. Joplin, Curtis concludes, remained conscious of the standards of the dominant society on which his livelihood depended as he sought to convey through his music the values and experiences of his people (Curtis 1994, 12).

African Americans at Work

Not all African Americans worked in agriculture. Although after the Civil War many African Americans lost the skilled jobs as bricklayers, coopers, carpenters, and tailors that they had performed under slavery, African Americans did work in some of the emerging industries of the New South, especially timber, shipping, steel, and mining. By 1900, half of the more than one-quarter million timber workers in the South were African American. Usually working at the least desirable jobs, like gathering turpentine, they nevertheless made relatively good wages. Many African Americans found work on the docks in Southern ports. Yet around the turn of the century, their numbers were in decline relative to white teamsters and draymen. In Birmingham, Alabama, the center of the Southern steel industry, African Americans made up almost 40 percent of the steel mill labor force, working mainly in the unskilled and dangerous jobs that paid the least. In addition, large numbers of African Americans were employed as miners in the coal and iron fields of the South. Working long hours under primitive conditions, miners often received script redeemable at the company's store, which charged exorbitant prices. Not uncommonly, through the use of convict leasing, Southern mining companies put prisoners to work in the mines as a way of undercutting unions and keeping wages low.

African American women in the South had even fewer job prospects than African American men had. Up to 90 percent of African American working women not laboring in the fields found employment as cooks, maids, and laundresses. In Mississippi in 1910, African American women accounted for 82 percent of gainfully employed women. More likely to be single than married, African American servants usually went home after a long day of cleaning, child care, and domestic jobs. One constant fear was the ever-present threat of sexual assault. As one domestic servant recalled about her experience in South Carolina, "Nobody was sent out before you was told to be careful of the white man or his sons. They'd tell you the stories of rape" (Diner 1998, 129).

Employer opposition to labor unions led the owners to recruit African Americans as strikebreakers. In his study of African American steelworkers in western Pennsylvania, Dennis Dickerson identifies a number of examples in which Carnegie steel managers recruited African American steelworkers in the South to work in their northern plants. Dickerson reports that between 1880 and 1910 almost a quarter of a million African Americans from the South migrated to the industrial communities along the Allegheny, Monongahela, and Ohio rivers. In these years, Pittsburgh's African American population quadrupled (Dickerson 1986, 17).

Yet what drew African Americans north had less to do with greater economic opportunity and more with escape from the claustrophobic conditions created by Jim Crow segregation. Noting the limited job prospects open to African Americans in the North, Oswald Garrison Villard, the grandson of the great abolitionist leader William Lloyd Garrison and an influential publisher, observed in 1907 that "it is our northern disgrace that a negro finds it harder to get work here that in the South" (Southern 2005 78). Industrial employers hired the newly arriving European immigrants to work in their factories in greater numbers than they employed African Americans. By 1910, 33 percent of new immigrants held skilled industrial jobs compared with only 8 percent for African Americans.

During the early years of the new century, African Americans began to lose even the service jobs they had previously held as fancy hotels started hiring Greek waiters and the wealthy replaced their African American cooks with French chefs (Southern 2005, 78–79). But even if economic discrimination was not restricted to the South, African Americans still began moving north to liberate themselves from a caste system defined by Jim Crow segregation and second-class citizenship.

Jim Crow

During the later decades of the 19th century, after the federal government had abandoned Reconstruction and Southern whites had regained political power, Southern state and local governments passed laws to impose segregation on public and semipublic facilities such as schools, libraries, streetcars, railroads, bathrooms, and even drinking fountains. Some parks placed signs at their entrances that announced "NEGROES AND DOGS NOT ALLOWED" (Southern, 2005, 101). But it was custom as much as law that transformed the Jim Crow system into an immutable "Southern way of life." When African Americans visited a white home, they knew to go to the back door with hat in hand. African Americans were expected to give way to whites when walking on the street and to yield to any white when waiting on a line. All African Americans had to refer to whites as "Mr." or "Mrs." In contrast, whites would use "boy" or "auntie" or "uncle" or "girl" for an African American. An African American who painted or fixed up his or her house faced the prospect of being reviled for acting "uppity" by the white community. The historian Neil R. McMillen refers to these and other demanded forms of deference as the "etiquette of race" (McMillen 1990, 23–28). Perhaps a better frame of reference would be the "etiquette of place," of the apparent need among white Southerners to surround African Americans with reminders of their presumed inferior status.

To ensure the permanence of the caste system that was being put into place, white Southerners began in the 1890s to formally exclude Africans American from the political process. After years of using force and fraud to constrain African American political participation, Mississippi convened a new constitutional convention in 1890 that, in the words of Mississippi's future governor James K. Vardaman, "was held for no other purpose than to eliminate the nigger from politics" (McMillen 1990, 43). Although presumably the 15th Amendment of the U.S. Constitution guaranteed adult African American males suffrage rights, Mississippi's new constitution imposed registration requirements, such as a two-dollar poll tax and the mandate that voters "be able to understand" or give a "reasonable" interpretation of any section of the state constitution, that, in practice, served to fulfill Vardaman's exclusionary objective. Between 1895 and 1919, seven Southern states added a "Grandfather clause" to their constitutions that

Lynching

The most direct and forceful mechanism for keeping the African American population "in place" was lynching. In the decades after 1890, the pace of lynching rapidly increased, a phenomenon that the historian Joel Williamson observes, "stands out like some gigantic volcanic eruption on the landscape of Southern race relations" (Southern 2005, 29). Whereas in the 1880s mobs lynched more whites than African Americans, by the 1890s, 8 out of 10 lynchings occurred in the South and three-quarters of them were of African Americans. Lynching could include a further desecration of African American victims through torture, mutilation, and burning of the body. Members of the lynch mob often claimed parts of the body as souvenirs. The gory details covered in newspaper accounts created what has been called a "folk pornography" of lynching. Pictures, often available in postcards intended to commemorate the event, reveal crowds of well-dressed whites, including children, who appear to be enjoying a community outing or picnic (Southern 2005, 29–30). What stands out about the story of lynching in these years was the lack of opposition to it. Lynch mobs knew that they would not be held accountable for their acts.

allowed men to register to vote only if they could have voted in 1867 (before African Americans were allowed to vote in the South) or were descended from an 1867 voter.

ACCOMMODATION AND RESISTANCE

Booker T. Washington stands out among African American leaders at the start of the 20th century for discouraging African American migration north. In his famous Atlanta Exposition address in 1895, in which he acquiesced to segregation, Washington advised those among his race who looked to leave the South to "cast down your bucket where you are" and to pursue farming, manual labor, small business, and domestic service in the South (Washington 1895). Washington had been born a slave in Virginia in 1856. His prominence as an African American leader was validated when President Theodore Roosevelt invited him to the White House in 1901 to discuss political patronage. Roosevelt, who in a Lincoln Day speech in 1905 spoke of the need for the "backward race" to move forward in such a way that "the forward race" could "preserve its civilization unharmed," was sympathetic to Washington's message of accommodation and gradualism (Southern 2005, 116). Emphasizing self-reliant economic development, Washington urged the African American community "to put brains and skill into the common occupations of life" and advance through industrial education, hard work at menial jobs, and strict moral behavior (Washington 1895). Taking charge of Tuskegee Institute in 1881 and running the Alabama school until his death in 1915, Washington built up Tuskegee as a model for African American education that gained the support of industrialists like Andrew Carnegie, who in 1903 donated $600,000 to the school.

At first reluctantly but then with increasing fervor, African American opposition to Washington was led by W. E. B. Du Bois, the first African American to earn a Ph.D., which he received in 1895 from Harvard University. After publishing his dissertation, *The Suppression of the African Slave Trade to the United States of America, 1638–1870* (1896), and a landmark sociological study, *The Philadelphia Negro* (1899), Du Bois began teaching history and economics at Atlanta University, where he remained until 1910. During this time he wrote the essays collected together in *The Souls of Black Folk* (1903), which Du Bois called a prolonged reflection on "the strange meaning of being black" in a society that looked on African Americans "with amused contempt and pity." In the third chapter, "Of Mr. Booker T. Washington and Others," Du Bois attacked "the Tuskegee Machine" for suppressing opposition and indicted Washington for practically accepting "the alleged inferiority of the Negro Race." Insisting that African Americans needed all their constitutional rights, including the right to vote, Du Bois emphasized the development of a "Talented Tenth" through higher education and attacked Washington as "the leader not of one race but of two,—a compromiser between the South, the North, and the Negro" (Du Bois 1903, 16–17). In 1905, Du Bois joined with William Monroe Trotter, the owner of the *Boston Guardian,* to organize the Niagara Movement, a collaboration of Talented Tenth leaders on behalf of an aggressive campaign for African American political and economic rights. Lasting only five years, the Niagara Movement nevertheless presaged the coming of a stronger and more permanent organization, the founding in 1909 of the NAACP as an interracial organization opposed to racism.

The Souls of Black Folk

Published originally by A. C. McClurg and Company in April 1903, *The Souls of Black Folk* is a collection of 14 essays in which the author, W. E. B. Du Bois, explores the "strange meaning of being black" in a society that looked on African Americans with "contempt and pity." In *Souls* Du Bois, having already established himself as an accomplished historian and social scientist, fuses history, sociology, and religion with a deeply personal testament on racism, politics, economics, and African American culture. "The problem of the Twentieth Century," Du Bois asserted, "is the problem of the color line." Each vivid essay examines just how Du Bois believed this to be so.

In the first essay, "Of Our Spiritual Strivings," Du Bois poses for the reader the questions that African Americans constantly faced: "How does it feel to be a problem?" and "Why did God make me an outcast and a stranger in mine own house?" The historian David Southern notes that these questions reflect Du Bois's interest in "double-consciousness," his idea that African Americans "look at themselves through the eyes of unfriendly whites." As a result, Du Bois concludes, "One ever feels his two-ness,—an American, a Negro: two souls, two thoughts, two unreconciled strivings; two warring ideals in one dark body, whose dogged strength alone keeps it from being torn asunder." At the core of every African American's life is the perpetual struggle to overcome this conflict and "attain self-conscious manhood, to merge his double self into a better and truer self" (Du Bois 1903, 38–39). Yet even so, as David Blight contends in his introduction to a modern edition of the *Souls,* the book "should be read as a testament against the American system of racial apartheid that developed from approximately 1890–1910" (Du Bois 1903, 3). In the essay "Of Mr. Booker T. Washington and Others," Du Bois criticizes "Mr.Washington" for enabling whites, North and South, to "shift the burden of the Negro Problem to the Negro's shoulders . . . when in fact it belongs to the nation, and the hands of none of us are clean if we bend not our energies to righting these great wrongs" (Du Bois 1903, 72). To this end, all persons of "conscience" must "ask [of] the nation three things": civic equality, the education of youth according to ability, and the right to vote (Du Bois 1903, 69). Acting on this mandate, Du Bois and others founded the NAACP in 1909. The formation of the NAACP represented a growing cooperation between white activists and African American leaders to fight for black civil rights.

The Niagara Movement

Led by W. E. B. Du Bois and William Monroe Trotter, the editor of the African American newspaper *The Guardian,* which was published in Boston, 29 prominent African American intellectuals met in July 1905 at Niagara Falls, Ontario, Canada, to launch an aggressive campaign for African American equality. The initial call had been for the meeting to be held in Buffalo, New York, but the leaders moved the location after hotels in that city refused service to the African American delegates. Opposed to Booker T. Washington's expression of Negro accommodation to racial subordination in the Atlanta Compromise of 1895, the delegates to the Niagara conference issued a Declaration of Principles that called for full civil liberties for African Americans, abolition of racial discrimination, and recognition of human brotherhood. Among the enumerated rights was that of protest: "We refuse to allow the impression to remain that the Negro-American assents to inferiority, is submissive under oppression and apologetic before insults" (Frazier 1988, 211). The "color-line" was singled out for elimination: "Any discrimination based simply on race or color is barbarous, we care not how hallowed it be by custom, expediency, or prejudice" (Frazier 1988, 211). The declaration recognized that with demands came also "corresponding duties upon our people: The duty to vote. The duty to respect the rights of others. The duty to work. The duty to obey the laws. The duty to be clean and orderly. The duty to send our children to school. The duty to respect ourselves, even as we respect others" (Frazier 1988, 212).

Despite Washington's attempts to suppress the Niagara Movement, including a generally successful effort to compel African American newspapers to ignore it, membership grew to about 400 and eventually included women and a few sympathetic whites. A second meeting was convened in 1906 at Harpers Ferry, Virginia, to commemorate the 100th anniversary of John Brown's raid against the armory in that city. Following this meeting, the Niagara Movement issued an "Address to the Country" that declared that they "will not be satisfied to take one jot or tittle less than our full manhood rights. We claim for ourselves every single right that belongs to a freeborn American, political, civil and social; and until we get those rights we will never cease to protest and to assail the ears of America with the stories of its shameful deeds towards us" ("The Niagara Movement"). Although the members of the Niagara Movement continued to meet for the next three years, internal conflicts, a lack of funds, and the unrelenting opposition from Washington and his supporters led to its demise by 1910. At this time, many of the Niagara activists responded to the call for "all believers in democracy" to meet in the national conference that led to formation of the NAACP.

The Formation of the NAACP

Almost a year after the bloody race riot in Springfield, Illinois, in August 1908, a multiracial group of activists met in New York City and dedicated the NAACP to the abolition of segregation and discrimination in housing, education, employment, voting, and transportation. Du Bois joined the staff of the NAACP as director of publicity and research and, most importantly, as editor of the group's magazine, *The Crisis*. In the first year of its publication, 10,000 readers each month read Du Bois's denunciations of race prejudice, forced segregation, lynching, disenfranchisement, and the denial of equal opportunity for African Americans (Southern 2005, 166–167).

During its first decade, the NAACP could do little more than publicize racial injustice. African Americans during these years had to devise ways to cope with oppression. Although they had few resources and were constrained by white supremacy, African Americans still sought to make their lives better and to secure their civil and political rights. Migration, of course, was one way of trying

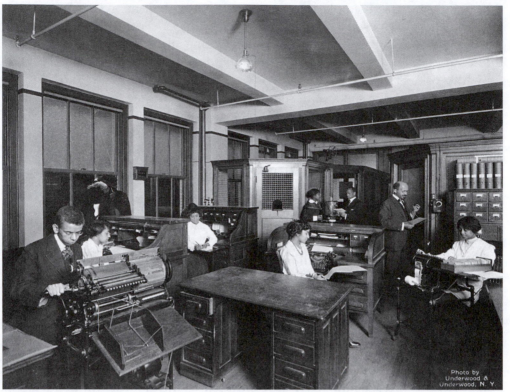

A founder of the NAACP, W. E. B. Du Bois (standing top right) served as editor of the association's magazine, Crisis. *(Underwood & Underwood/Corbis)*

to make a change in their lives. Economic opportunities in the North, while limited by discrimination, were still greater than those that the South offered. Also, in the North, African American males could vote and African American children could attend public school. A South that was convinced that educating African Americans would undermine their subservience provided negligible resources for African American education. Beginning in the late 19th century, religious groups supported denominational private institutions that provided elementary education for African American children. The historian Stephen Diner refers to an African American woman from South Carolina who recalled that because there was no local school for African Americans, her father built "a small log house" on his property to serve as one: "my father said he wanted every one of his children to learn to be able to read and write" (Diner 1998, 139). "Little Tuskegees," private institutions, were opened by the African American community throughout the South. The Piney Woods Country Life School is one example, begun when African American farmers in Jefferson Davis County, Mississippi, who wanted their children to go to school secured a $600 loan from a local white banker.

The Talented Tenth

By the first decade of the 20th century, a small African American middle class consisting of teachers, ministers, physicians, lawyers, and other professionals had emerged. In 1910, no more than two to three percent of African Americans held white-collar jobs. African American professionals usually served only members of their own community. Like most African American lawyers, Noah Walter Parden, who in 1906 successfully engaged the Supreme Court to conduct a criminal trial against white officials in Chattanooga, Tennessee, for their failure to prevent a mob from lynching an African American prisoner, never represented a white man and was often paid for his services with an invitation by his client for a home-cooked dinner. Much like new immigrants, African Americans also operated numerous mutual aid, burial, and social organizations. In Georgia, for example, Stephen Diner calculates that before World War I there were 10,000 African American Masons, 15,000 Colored Knights of Pythias, and 30,000 African American members of the Grand United Order of Odd Fellows. Between 1870 and 1920, African American fraternal orders in Mississippi paid $16 million in burial and sickness benefits to their members. African American YMCAs and YWCAs offered the African American community the same kind of support services and recreational programs as did white YMCAs and YWCAs. So too did African American business, such as insurance companies and funeral homes (Diner 1998, 143–144). Historian Judith E. K. Walker refers to the period between 1900 and the Great Depression as "the golden age of black business activity" in the United States (Southern 2005, 85).

The Supreme Court Acts against Lynching

Near midnight on March 19, 1906, a mob forcibly removed Ed Johnson, an African American inmate, from his cell in the Chattanooga, Tennessee, jail, marched him through town, spit at him, kicked him, and struck him with rifles, and then hanged him from a nearby bridge spanning the Tennessee River. When one bullet severed the rope and Johnson fell to the deck of the bridge, several shots were fired into his head and one member of the mob, a Chattanooga police officer, cut off one of the victim's ears as a souvenir. Johnson had been wrongly convicted at a sham trial of raping a white woman and then sentenced to die (Curriden and Phillips 1999, 199–214). To this point, there is nothing unusual about this scenario. In the early 20th century, an African American man could be lynched for simply trying to talk to a white woman without a white man present. Johnson's lynching was only one of a reportedly 65 incidents that occurred in the United States in 1906 alone. But what followed Johnson's conviction was unprecedented in legal annals (Curriden and Phillips 1999, 216).

Around the turn of the 20th century, lynch mobs increasingly took "justice" into their own hands. Most of the mobs' victims were African Americans. (Library of Congress)

Following Johnson's trial, Noah Parden, an African American attorney in Chattanooga who had assisted in Johnson's defense, decided to file a writ of habeas corpus in the federal circuit court challenging the trial's fairness. The circuit court denied the writ but stayed Johnson's execution while Parden appealed its decision in the U.S. Supreme Court. Based on the original trial record, Parden convinced Justice John Marshall Harlan to approve the appeal. This further delayed Johnson's execution and created the possibility that his conviction would be overturned. In response, the trial judge, Samuel D. McReynolds, publicly blamed the Supreme Court for any violence that might ensue. The Chattanooga sheriff, Joseph F. Shipp, already under attack for having prevented an earlier mob attempt to lynch Johnson, remained conspicuously absent as the crowd gathered outside the jail on the fateful evening when Johnson was killed. With Johnson's death, his conviction could no longer be appealed. Moreover, a local grand jury found no one responsible for his lynching.

Furious at Chattanooga's defiance of its order, the Supreme Court sent two Secret Service agents to the city to gather evidence. The court then issued contempt citations against Shipp and other members of the jail staff and participants in the lynch mob. In 1909, the justices decided by a vote of five to three to convict Shipp, two members of his staff, and three lynch mob members of contempt, and ordered them jailed for terms of 60 to 90 days. Although an outstanding victory for the rule of law, the Court's decision in 1909 did nothing to change the fact that Johnson had been unfairly tried and then murdered. When Shipp returned to Chattanooga from Washington, after receiving early release for good behavior, he was given "a hero's welcome," according to the local newspaper, by a crowd of 10,000 local citizens, as a band played "Dixie" and "Home, Sweet Home" (Curriden and Phillips 1999, 338).

BIOGRAPHIES

Abraham Cahan, 1860–1951

Jewish Immigrant, Writer, Lecturer

The son of Shakhne Cahan and Sheyne Sarah Goldarbeter, both teachers, Cahan was born in Podberezy, Lithuania. The family moved to nearby Vilna, and Cahan graduated from the Vilna Teachers' Institute for Jewish Students in June 1881. Fearing political persecution for his socialist activities, he fled to the United States, arriving in June 1882. Cahan settled on New York's Lower East Side. He soon became fluent in English and began writing articles for the New York newspapers, as well as for the Yiddish press. Cahan became well known as a writer and lecturer for the socialist and labor movements. He also wrote fiction, including *Yekl, a Tale of the New York Ghetto* (1896) and *The Imported Bridegroom and Other Stories of the New York Ghetto* (1898). After editing a number of Yiddish publications, Cahan, in 1897, helped found the Yiddish *Jewish Daily Forward*. In 1903, Cahan became editor of the *Forward,* a position he held for 50 years. By 1923, the *Forward* was published nationally in 11 cities. Cahan's most important contribution to immigrant fiction was the novel *The Rise of David Levinsky* (1917), a story about the personal costs of success and assimilation experienced by a successful Jewish businessman.

William Paul Dillingham, 1843–1923

Lawyer, Politician, Chair of the U.S. Immigration Commission

Born in Waterbury, Vermont, the son of Paul Dillingham, a lawyer and political leader, and Julia Carpenter, Dillingham was active in state politics. After studying law in the Milwaukee, Wisconsin, office of his brother-in-law, Matthew H. Carpenter, he returned to Vermont and completed his study of the law under his father, who was then the state's governor. Dillingham was admitted to the Vermont bar in 1867 and became a prosecuting attorney in Washington County in 1872. A lifelong Republican, he then held a number of positions in state government and served in the state house of representatives and state senate before being elected and serving one term as governor in 1888. In the 1890s

A Republican senator from Vermont and an outspoken advocate for immigration restriction, William Paul Dillingham chaired the Senate's Committee on Immigration. (Library of Congress)

Dillingham briefly left public service to become president of the Waterbury National Bank until, in 1900, he was elected to the U.S. Senate, where he served until his death more than two decades later. Dillingham was a member of the Senate Committee on Immigration, which he chaired from 1903 to 1911. An outspoken advocate of immigration restriction, he became chair of the United States Immigration Commission in 1907. In 1921, Congress passed legislation introduced by Dillingham that established quotas on immigration.

W. E. B. Du Bois, 1868–1963

Author, Educator, and Civil Rights Activist

Born in Great Barrington, Massachusetts, William Edward Burghardt Du Bois was the son of Mary Silvina Burghardt, a domestic worker, and Alfred Du Bois, an itinerant laborer. The first African American graduate of Great Barrington high school, he earned a B.A., an M.A., and, in 1895, a Ph.D. in history from Harvard University. In 1896, Du Bois married Nina Gomer, a student he met while teaching languages and literature at Wilberforce University in Ohio. That year, with the support of the University of Pennsylvania, he conducted interviews in 2,500 households in Philadelphia's Seventh Ward as part of a study that was published in 1899 as *The Philadelphia Negro*. In his 1903 essay "The Talented Tenth," Du Bois chastised Booker T. Washington, an acknowledged African American leader, for denigrating institutions of higher learning and classical education in favor of industrial training. Du Bois proposed that an educated African American elite (10 percent) should lead the African American community by example. That same year, Du Bois published a collection of essays, *The Souls of Black Folk*. In these and later works focusing on the problem of race in America, Du Bois articulated his opposition to Washington's accommodationist policies. By 1910, Du Bois had left Georgia's Atlanta University, where he had been working for more than a decade, to become an officer in the newly established NAACP and the editor of its monthly magazine, the *Crisis*. Later in life Du Bois became an active proponent of Pan-Africanism, a movement that advocated the unity of all African people and opposed colonialism. He was also a peace activist and a supporter of the Soviet Union. For the last two years of his life, Du Bois lived in Accra, Ghana.

Scott Joplin, 1868–1917

Songwriter, Playwright

The son of a former slave, Jiles Joplin, and of Florence Givens, a free-born African American woman, Joplin grew up in Texarkana, in the pine forests of northeastern Texas. As a boy, Joplin began playing the piano in the home of the white family for whom his mother worked as a domestic, and he later received formal lessons from a German music teacher. He apparently left Texarkana at some point in the 1880s, and in 1894, he settled in Sedalia, Missouri. After studying music at Sedalia's George R. Smith College in the mid-1890s, Joplin developed a local reputation as a pianist and composer, performing regularly at the Maple Leaf Club. In 1899, Joplin composed one of his most famous works, "The Maple Leaf Rag," which sold over half a million copies and helped earn him his reputation as the "King of Ragtime Writers." In 1901, Joplin moved to St. Louis, where he continued composing, including a ragtime opera, *A Guest of Honor*. Neither this work nor his second opera, *Treemonisha*, was successfully produced in his lifetime. By the time of his death, Joplin had published 64 works, mostly rags and other syncopated piano pieces.

William Monroe Trotter, 1872–1934

Publisher and Civil Rights Activist

Born in Chillicothe, Ohio, the son of James Monroe Trotter, a politician, and Virginia Isaacs, a former slave, William Trotter became a newspaper publisher and civil rights activist. He was the first African American to be elected to Phi Beta Kappa at Harvard University. After graduating, he established himself in real estate. Trotter's increasing opposition to segregation led him to launch the *Boston Guardian*, making him a force in the African American press. Throughout his life, he was a ceaseless opponent of Booker T. Washington. In 1905, Trotter allied with W. E. B. Du Bois to found the Niagara Movement, a civil rights organization and the precursor of the NAACP. Believing that the crusade for civil rights should be led and financed by African Americans exclusively, Trotter organized the National Equal Rights League in 1908 as an all-black association for racial equality. His outspoken militancy isolated Trotter in his later years. After his newspaper failed during the Great Depression, he apparently committed suicide in 1934.

Booker T. Washington, ca. 1856–1915

African American Leader and Founder of the Tuskegee Institute

Born on a plantation in Virginia, the son of an unknown white father and Jane, a slave cook, Washington became the most recognized leader among both whites and African Americans on race relations during the decades bracketing the start of the 20th century. In 1872, he entered Virginia's Hampton Institute, where he was introduced to a practical education based on physical labor—the ideal that would animate his understanding of what was best for African Americans for the rest of his life. Having rejected a career in the ministry, Washington eventually helped found Tuskegee Institute in Alabama. The school opened with few resources but under his direction grew to include 100 buildings on 2,000 acres, a faculty of nearly 200, and an endowment of close to $2 million. In September 1895, Washington gave an address, dubbed the "Atlanta Compromise" by his critics, in which he articulated the basic

Born a slave, Booker T. Washington founded the Tuskegee Institute as a school to provide industrial education for African Americans. Washington urged patience, hard work, and morality as the best means for the advancement of African Americans in the United States. (Library of Congress)

components of his philosophy on race in America. Urging African Americans to "stay in the South," he admonished that the "wisest among my race" understood that progress would come only through hard work and the respect of their white neighbors. Believing it to be "extreme folly" to agitate on "questions of social equality," Washington pronounced, to the acclaim of his white audience, "in all things that are purely social we can be as separate as the fingers, yet one as the hand in all things essential to mutual progress" (*American National Biography Online*). Although challenged by W. E. B. Du Bois and other emerging African American leaders, Washington continued to emphasize industrial education and to urge patience, high morals, and thrift as the basis for African American advancement in America.

Ida Wells-Barnett, 1862–1931

Newspaper Writer and Anti-Lynching Activist

The child of former slaves James Wells and Elizabeth Warrenton, Wells-Barnett was born in Holly Springs, Mississippi. After her parents and a sibling died of yellow fever while she was attending Rust College in her hometown, she started teaching to provide for her remaining siblings. In 1881, she moved with her younger siblings to Memphis, Tennessee, where she continued teaching. After writing an article about an incident in which she challenged Jim Crow seating on a train, she also became a journalist, contributing to African American publications under the pen name "Iola." In the 1890s, after three friends were lynched by a mob, Wells began her lifelong crusade against lynching. In 1895, she married Ferdinand L. Barnett, a Chicago lawyer, and became active in Chicago affairs, writing articles on lynching for the *Chicago Conservator*. She took part in the Niagara Movement and in 1909 helped in the founding of the NAACP. In 1913, she started the Alpha Suffrage Club, which may have been the first African American women's suffrage organization. Throughout her career, she remained outspoken on the evils of lynching.

REFERENCES AND FURTHER READINGS

Addams, Jane. 1910. *Twenty Years at Hull-House with Autobiographical Notes*. Reprint edition, edited with an introduction by Victoria Bissell Brown. Bedford Series in History and Culture. Boston: Bedford/St. Martin's, 1999. Page references are to the 1999 edition.

American National Biography Online. http://www.anb.org/articles/15/15-00737-print.html

Barrett, James R. 1990. *Work and Community in the Jungle: Chicago's Packinghouse Workers, 1894–1922*. Urbana: University of Illinois Press.

Bodnar, John. 1985. *The Transplanted: A History of Immigrants in Urban America*. Bloomington: Indiana University Press.

Carlson, Robert A. 1970. "Americanization as an Early Twentieth-Century Adult Education Movement." *History of Education Quarterly* 10 (Winter): 440–464.

Carson, Clayborne, Emma J. Lapsansky-Werner, and Gary B. Nash. 2007. *The Struggle for Freedom: A History of African Americans*. New York: Person Longman.

Curriden, Mark, and Leroy Phillips Jr. 1999. *Contempt of Court: The Turn-of-the-Century Lynching that Launched a Hundred Years of Federalism*. New York: Faber and Faber.

Curtis, Susan. 1994. *Dancing to a Black Man's Tune: A Life of Scott Joplin*. Columbia: University of Missouri Press.

Daniels, Roger. 1990. *Coming to America: A History of Immigration and Ethnicity in American Life*. New York: Harper Collins.

Daniels, Roger. 1996. "The Immigrant Experience in the Gilded Age." In *The Gilded Age: Essays on the Origins of Modern America,* ed. Charles C. Calhoun, 63–89. Wilmington, Del.: Scholarly Resources Books.

Dickerson, Denis C. 1986. *Out of the Crucible: Black Steelworkers in Western Pennsylvania, 1875–1980*. Albany: State University of New York Press.

Diner, Hasia. 2001. *Hungering for America: Italian, Irish, and Jewish Foodways in the Age of Migration*. Cambridge, Mass.: Harvard University Press.

Diner, Stephen J. 1998. *A Very Different Place: Americans of the Progressive Era*. New York: Hill and Wang.

Dinnerstein, Leonard, and David M. Reimers. 1975. *Ethnic Americans: A History of Immigration and Assimilation*. New York: Harper and Row.

Dolkart, Andrew. 2006. "The 1901 Tenement House Act" http://www.tenement.org/features_dolkart.html.

Dubofsky, Melvyn. 1975. *Industrialism and the American Worker, 1865–1920*. New York: Harlan Davidson.

Du Bois, W. E. B. 1903. *The Souls of Black Folk*. Reprint edition edited and with an introduction by David W. Blight and Robert Gooding-Williams. Boston: Bedford Books, 1997. Page references are to the 1997 edition.

Frazier, Thomas R. 1988. *Afro-American History: Primary Sources*. Chicago: The Dorsey Press.

Gerstle, Gary. 1997. "Liberty, Coercion, and the Making of Americans." *Journal of American History* 84 (September): 524–558.

Gjerde, Jon, ed. 1998. *Major Problems in American Immigration and Ethnic History: Documents and Essays*. Boston: Houghton Mifflin Company.

Gleason, Philip. 1964. "The Melting Pot: Symbol of Fusion or Confusion?" *American Quarterly* 16 (Spring): 20–46.

Gordon, Linda. 1999. *The Great Arizona Orphan Abduction*. Cambridge: Harvard University Press.

Green, James R. 1980. *The World of the Worker: Labor in Twentieth-Century America*. New York: Hill and Wang.

Gutiérrez, David G. 1995. *Wall and Mirrors: Mexican Americans, Mexican Immigrants, and the Politics of Ethnicity*. Berkeley: University of California Press.

Handlin, Oscar. 1941. *Boston's Immigrants: A Study in Acculturation*. Cambridge: Harvard University Press.

Handlin, Oscar. 1951. *The Uprooted: The Epic Story of the Great Migration that Made the American People*. New York: Grosset and Dunlap.

Higham, John. 1952. "Origins of Immigration Restriction, 1882–1897: A Social Analysis." *Mississippi Valley Historical Review* 39 (June): 77–88.

Higham, John. 1968. *Strangers in the Land: Patterns of American Nativism, 1860–1925*. New York: Atheneum.

Howe, Irving. 1976. *World of Our Fathers: The Journey of the East European Jews to America and the Life They Found and Made*. New York: Simon and Schuster.

Jackson, Kenneth T., ed. 1995. *The Encyclopedia of New York City*. New Haven, Conn.: Yale University Press.

Kazal, Russell A. 1995. "Revisiting Assimilation: The Rise, Fall, and Reappraisal of a Concept in American Ethnic History." *American Historical Review* 100 (April): 437–471.

Kessner, Thomas. 1977. *The Golden Door: Italian and Jewish Immigrant Mobility in New York City, 1880–1915*. New York: Oxford University Press.

King, Desmond. 2000. *Making Americans: Immigration, Race, and the Origins of the Diverse Democracy*. Cambridge, Mass.: Harvard University Press.

Korman, Gerd. 1967. *Industrialization, Immigrants, and Americanizers: The View from Milwaukee, 1866–1921*. Madison: The State Historical Society of Wisconsin.

Kraut, Alan M. 2001. *The Huddled Masses: The Immigrant in American Society, 1880–1921*, 2nd Ed. Wheeling, Ill.: Harlan Davidson.

Lee, Erika. 2003. *At America's Gates: Chinese Immigration During the Exclusion Era, 1882–1943*. Chapel Hill: University of North Carolina Press.

McMillen, Neil R. 1990. *Dark Journey: Black Mississippians in the Age of Jim Crow*. Urbana: University of Illinois Press.

The National Park Service. http://www.nps.gov/sth/serv02.htm.

"The New Immigration Law," *The American Journal of International Law,* 1 (April 1907): 452–458. http://www.jstor.org/.

"The Niagara Movement," "Address to the Country." African American History of Western New York. http://www.math.buffalo.edu/~sww/0history/hwny-niagara-movement.html.

Pfaelzer, Jean. 2007. *Driven Out: The Forgotten War against Chinese Americans*. New York: Random House.

Roediger, David R. 2005. *Working toward Whiteness: How America's Immigrants Became White*. New York: Basic Books.

Setran, David P. 2005. "'From Moral Aristocracy to Christian Social Democracy': The Transformation of Character Education in the Hi-Y, 1910–1940." *History of Education Quarterly* 45 (Summer): 207–246.

Shifflett, Crandall. 1996. *Victorian America, 1876 to 1913*. New York: Facts on File.

Southern, David W. 2005. *The Progressive Era and Race: Reaction and Reform, 1900–1917*. Wheeling, Ill.: Harlan Davidson.

Taylor, Philip. 1971. *The Distant Magnet: European Emigration to the U.S.A.* New York: Harper Torchbooks.

Tyack, David B. 1974. *The One Best System: A History of American Urban Education*. Cambridge, Mass.: Harvard University Press.

Washington, Booker T. 1895. "'Cast Down Your Bucket Where You Are': Booker T. Washington's Atlanta Compromise Speech." History Matters, the U.S. Survey Course on the Web. http://www.historymatters.gmu.edu/d/39.

Yans-McLaughlin, Virginia. 1982. *Family and Community: Italian Immigrants in Buffalo, 1880–1930*. Urbana: University of Illinois Press.

Zeidel, Robert F. 2004. *Immigrants, Progressives, and Exclusion Politics: The Dillingham Commission, 1900–1927*. DeKalb: Northern Illinois Press.

Urban Life

OVERVIEW

During the years between 1900 and 1909, the United States experienced tremendous changes in areas such as technology, transportation, housing, and education. These changes often led to precipitous shifts in the quality and scale of urban life in America. The process of urbanization increased both the size and number of major cities in the nation. Industrialization, a process under way simultaneously with urbanization in the United States, changed the national economy from an agricultural and artisanal society to one characterized by manufacture and mass production. New industries drew people to cities with the promise of employment, prosperity, and the advantages of a cosmopolitan environment. Countless migrants from rural and small-town America moved to cities to improve their station in life. During this period in the nation's history, immigrants from other countries also flooded America's cities, seeking their share of prosperity, freedom, and security.

Accompanying these changes in material life were social and cultural shifts. The population of the United States grew sharply during this era, and the influx of population to the nation's cities made urban centers more diverse in terms of race and ethnicity than ever before. Population growth led to crowding in the cities, which caused urban structures and services to near, reach, and sometimes exceed their breaking points. Aspects of public life were also undergoing corresponding transformations. Chief among these changes were Progressive era reforms in housing design, educational practice, and city planning, all of which contributed to a renewal of American urban life during the early 20th century.

TIMELINE

1900   L. Frank Baum publishes *The Wonderful Wizard of Oz*.

On October 16, the first meeting of the Automobile Club of America is conducted at New York's Madison Square Garden; electric and steam cars are featured.

More than 100,000 stenographers are employed within the United States.

The first juvenile court begins operation in Chicago.

The first American-made, gasoline-powered truck appears.

Great Americans are profiled in a Hall of Fame opened in New York City on March 5.

On March 14, Congress establishes the gold standard, ending the free-silver controversy.

Congress establishes the Hawaiian territory on April 30.

Engineer John Luther "Casey" Jones dies in railroad collision on April 30.

From September 7 to 8, Galveston, Texas, is struck by a hurricane; between 6,000 and 7,000 perish.

Thirty-one states have compulsory school attendance laws in place.

Excavation for New York's subway system commences.

1901   Booker T. Washington publishes *Up from Slavery*, thereby sharing his life story with the American reading public.

On September 6, President McKinley is shot by Leon Czolgosz while at the Temple of Music at the Pan-American Exposition in Buffalo, New York.

On October 25, Yale University marks its bicentennial.

Andrew Carnegie's gift of $5.2 million launches the nation's first public library system.

New York's Fuller Building (better known as the Flatiron Building), the nation's first real skyscraper, is under construction.

Starting on June 15, the New York Central Railroad offers travel from New York to Chicago in 20 hours.

Theodore Roosevelt causes a commotion by inviting Booker T. Washington to dine with him on October 16 at the White House.

1902   Motorized tractors appear for the first time.

Fifteen thousand anthracite miners walk out in a Pennsylvania strike by the United Mine Workers of America (UMWA).

1903   Labor organizers found the National Women's Trade Union League of America.

Milton Hershey acquires the Pennsylvania land that will later be renamed Hershey, Pennsylvania.

The Office of the United States Bureau of the Census is established on March 6.

On March 29, radio service begins to convey news regularly between New York and London.

The Ford Company sells its first automobile on July 23.

The first cross-country automobile trip is taken from one coast to the other, completed between May 23 and July 26.

Williamsburg Bridge, spanning New York City's East River, opens to motorists.

On December 17, Orville and Wilbur Wright achieve a 59-second flight of a heavier-than-air craft, traveling 852 feet at Kitty Hawk.

The National Afro-American Council protests discrimination, disenfranchisement, and racial violence.

1904   The state of New York specifies automotive maximum speed limits: 20 mph in the country, 15 mph in small towns, and 10 mph in cities; it is the first state to so legislate.

The United States hosts the 1904 Olympic Games, but competitors from only six other countries participate.

Offset printing commences.

The first automobile road maps are published.

An initial segment of New York City's subway system opens for business on October 27.

New York City slums have a population density of 1,000 residents per acre.

1905   The chemical fire extinguisher is developed.

The Niagara Movement, so named because of the location of its first meeting (Niagara Falls), unites African Americans for the cause of racial equality.

On February 20, the Supreme Court upholds compulsory vaccination laws at the state level.

On June 18, the Twentieth Century Limited begins travel between New York and Chicago, completing the trip in 18 hours each way.

Between July and October, a yellow fever outbreak hits New Orleans, Louisiana.

On November 8, the Overland Limited of the Chicago and North Western Railroad, specifically its run between Illinois and California, becomes the first to feature electric lamps.

1906   In July, New Jersey sets in place the first law requiring automobile drivers to be licensed.

San Francisco, California, becomes the site of an April 18 earthquake; some 25,000 buildings are destroyed and approximately 500 die in the quake and its aftermath.

The New York Police Department begins use of fingerprints to investigate criminal cases.

1907   On August 24, New York's Singer Tower becomes the tallest building in the world at 612 feet or 41 stories.

Oklahoma becomes a state on November 16.

The first "taxicabs" begin to operate in New York City during May.

New York's Plaza Hotel opens for the first time.

Annette Kellerman is arrested for swimming barelegged at Revere Beach in Boston, Massachusetts.

Waves of immigration to the United States crest as more than 1.2 million immigrants arrive this year.

William Graham Sumner's *Folkways* appears in print for the first time.

1908   Henry Ford debuts the Model T, quipping that customers may purchase it in any color so long as they choose black.

The so-called "Ash Can School," a group of American painters, becomes notorious for painting realistic scenes of urban life.

Philadelphia's subway opens on August 3.

The first fatality due to air travel occurs on September 17.

1909   With W. E. B. Du Bois at the helm, a group of civil rights activists forms the NAACP.

The Queensboro Bridge, linking Manhattan and Queens, becomes available for use by travelers on March 30.

The Manhattan Bridge opens on December 31.

The *Pittsburgh Survey* is published.

The National Conference on City Planning takes place.

On March 7, California first establishes Arbor Day as a state holiday paying tribute to Luther Burbank.

AMERICAN CITIES IN THE SPOTLIGHT: WORLD EVENT, WORLD POWER

The period from 1900 to 1909 witnessed numerous world's fairs and expositions in the United States. With a new century dawning, many Americans felt inclined to reflect on the accomplishments of the nation's past and the prospects for its future. From social commentators to journalists, scholars to public figures, there was a renewed interest in assessing historical progress and channeling current collective efforts toward greatest result.

During the first decade of the 20th century, the American people had the opportunity to visit at least four major public displays of this kind: the Pan-American Exposition (Buffalo, New York, 1901), the Louisiana Purchase Exposition (St. Louis, Missouri, 1903), the Lewis and Clark Centennial Exposition and American Pacific Exposition and Oriental Fair (Portland, Oregon, 1905), and the Alaska Yukon Pacific Exposition (Seattle, Washington, 1909). Each was a showcase for human endeavor, offering displays of technological innovations, cultural achievements, agricultural practices, and the like.

While some of these celebratory public events were more successful than the others were from a financial point of view, each of these world's fairs and expositions succeeded in capturing the popular imagination. An estimated 100 million visitors found their way to world's fairs during the period from 1876 to 1920 (Rydell, Findling, and Pelle 2000, 3). Clearly, the spectacles proved attractive to the public, and those who could afford the time and money to attend made a point to do so.

The nation's fairs and expositions during this era furnished pageants of progress and, at least for some, stories of prosperity. These fairs and expositions were elaborate affairs, often several years in the making. Consequently, they typically remained open to visitors for durations of six months or more. The visitor experience was not entirely an educational one. While some halls were filled with displays and demonstrations intended to edify and uplift visitors, there were also plenty of sources of entertainment of other kinds at these events. The midway, for example, which usually consisted of a clustering of popular amusements and concessions, proved magnetic for visitors to these fairs and expositions.

Echoes of Chicago: The 1893 World's Columbian Exposition

The theme for Chicago's 1893 exposition was the 400th anniversary of Christopher Columbus's voyage to the New World. Numerous major American cities vied for the right to host the event, including New York, St. Louis, and the District of Columbia. Chicago's campaign for the honor prevailed, and 633 acres of the city's Jackson Park became the site of the Columbian Exposition.

Architecture on the grounds was completed in the *Beaux Arts* style, and together the ivory-colored classical structures comprised the "White City," a layout intended to suggest an ideal urban environment. An entertainment district of 80 acres, designated as the Midway Plaisance, helped cover the costs of constructing the exposition. Visitors to the World's Columbian Exposition saw the first elevated electric railway, a moveable walkway, and a variety of other marvels. New products such as Pabst Beer and Aunt Jemima syrup made their debut at the Chicago event, and guests at the fair could snack for the first time on Cracker Jack, a confection combining savory and sweet elements: peanuts, popcorn, and caramel.

Just as Chicago's World's Fair bore the influence of Philadelphia's 1876 Centennial Exhibition, there is little question that the World's Columbian Exposition served as a powerful precedent for subsequent fairs and expositions. Some of the influences were direct. For example, the beloved Ferris wheel that debuted at Chicago was reprised at Buffalo's 1901 Exposition. Entire amusement park designs, such as George Tilyou's Steeplechase Park, were inspired by the Chicago event. Other impacts of the Columbian Exposition were indirect. For instance, later American fairs and expositions would attempt to extract lessons from the experience with Chicago's Columbian Exposition regarding the optimal means to draw in visitors, cover design and construction costs, and perhaps even turn a profit.

The Pan-American Exposition (Buffalo, New York)

From May 1 to November 2, 1901, Buffalo, New York, occupied a prominent place on the world stage. As the site of the Pan-American Exposition, the city of

View of the Pan-American Exposition in Buffalo, New York, 1901. (Library of Congress)

Buffalo received 8,120,000 visitors. The original plan for the event called for Cayuga Falls (near the natural spectacle of Niagara Falls) to host the event in 1899, but planning was suspended due to the Spanish-American War. When work on the exposition resumed, Buffalo waged a successful challenge, securing the event for their city. To avoid a conflict with the Paris Exposition of 1900, the decision was made to hold the Buffalo event in 1901 ("The World's Fair").

In keeping with the tenor of the times, the theme chosen for the 1901 exposition was the relationship of the Americas. The ultimate goal of the exposition was to promote Pan-American trade, with special emphasis on the region of Latin America. Accordingly, Spanish Renaissance was selected as the featured architectural style for the exposition's buildings. The site boasted 100 structures, 20 of which were major buildings. As distinct from many previous fairs and expositions, at which the buildings were all rendered in white, the Buffalo exposition included building exteriors of many hues, with the darkest ones at the perimeter and the lightest at the center of the site's layout. Hundreds of thousands of lights adorned the outside of the halls, dazzling visitors after dark. At the center of the exposition's layout was John Galen Howard's Electric Tower, a 375-foot monument to electrification culminating in the figure of a Goddess of Light.

Was the Buffalo Exposition Indicative of Trends in the New Century's Social History?

The central design message at the Pan-American Exposition was one of national progress, highlighting the emergence of the United States as a world power. Especially in terms of the ethnological displays presented to exposition visitors, the event's emphasis was on providing a rationale for American imperialism in such areas as Hawaii and the Philippines. For instance, an 11-acre Filipino Village was fashioned for the exposition from photographs. As the exposition neared its opening date, natives of the Philippines were brought to Buffalo to appear for the benefit of exposition visitors. With displays of this kind, the exposition's designers and sponsors hoped to convey that American power had been exercised judiciously abroad and that the nation's leaders were acting in the best interest of all concerned. The implicit attitudes toward imperialism abroad mirrored some of the interactions among racial and ethnic groups within the United States. Immigrants and people of color, including those born in America, remained subject to discriminatory attitudes and practices. In some situations, particularly in major cities, they were regarded as inferior or demonized as sources of illness and moral contagion. Therefore, while the Pan-American Exposition sought to portray the triumphant pageant of American progress, old prejudices persisted and shaped the experiences and opportunities of many persons during the years from 1900 to 1909, both at home and abroad.

The whole experience of the "Pan-Am" could be had for the price of daily admission, 50 cents for adults and 25 cents for youth. As with previous expositions, visitors to the Pan-American could witness the latest developments in a variety of fields, including agriculture, machinery, ethnology, fine arts, forestry, and transportation. They could ride camels at the Streets of Cairo exhibit, visit a haunted house created especially for the occasion, or participate in a simulation of space travel with the popular Trip to the Moon attraction. Other memorable displays at the Pan-American Exposition included an X-ray machine, baby incubators, and submarines. New consumer products also found their showcase at Buffalo. Instant coffee, hearing aids, and electric typewriters were among the innovations shown to the American public for the first time at the exposition.

As impressive as the sightseeing might have been, something unexpected overshadowed all the exposition displays and demonstrations. The Pan-American Exposition became notorious as the site of Leon Czolgosz's assassination of President William McKinley. On September 5, 1901, after returning from a rail trip to Niagara Falls, President McKinley returned to Buffalo to make an appearance at the exposition. While the President greeted fairgoers assembled in a receiving line at the Temple of Music, Czolgosz managed to fire off the shots that would result in McKinley's death on September 14. While the Pan-American Exposition continued after this incident, it was difficult for the exposition to recover its previous energy and air of excitement. Thereafter, in the popular imagination, the Pan-American Exhibition would remain linked to national tragedy.

CHANGES IN THE AMERICAN LIFE SPAN AND URBAN LIFESTYLE

At the turn of the 20th century, the United States was experiencing brisk population growth. As the country's population grew, cities also developed rapidly. For instance, the population of Los Angeles tripled in the period from 1900 to 1910 (Batchelor 2002, 261). It was hardly the only city to experience such population growth. According to the United States Census, during the period from 1860 to 1910, the number of cities with more than 50,000 residents increased from 16 to 109. Westward expansion had begun to scatter those cities from one coast of the country to the other. Over the hundred-year period from 1800 to 1900, the geographical center of the population of the United States shifted 475 miles west. When the results of the 1900 census report were complete, Columbus, Indiana, was identified as the new center of the nation's population.

The 1900 Census and the Urban Family

The 1900, or 12th, census tallied an American population totaling 76,094,000 (Time-Life 1998, 35). By 1909, the figure would rise to 90,490,000. Cities were growing in size and number, and the United States approached the point at which it would have more urban residents than rural ones. The material conditions for most Americans, however, were not keeping pace with population or city growth. As J. W. Keenan remarked in the June 7, 1900 issue of the *Saturday*

A scene in the ghetto, New York, ca. 1902. (Library of Congress)

Two Views on Working-Class Community

Margaret Byington on Homestead, Pennsylvania Mill Families

As an observer of the everyday life of members of the American working class in Homestead, Pennsylvania, social worker Margaret Frances Byington helped call attention to the social and material circumstances of mill workers and their families. Byington's full-length study, *Homestead: The Households of a Mill Town,* appeared in book form in 1910. It formed part of the Pittsburgh Survey, an attempt to document daily life for ordinary Americans. In particular, she considered the impact of industrialization on family life. "It is through the households themselves," concluded Byington, "that the industrial situation impresses itself indelibly upon the life of the people" (Edwards 2006, 132). Her findings were presented in narrative form, along with relevant illustrations and tables. Through her on-site fieldwork, Byington witnessed the lifestyles of the nation's working people. Distinguishing her efforts is an attention not only to the economic privations but also to the social implications of those conditions. While her writing is poignant, Byington readily acknowledges that her perspective must remain that of an interested observer rather than a participant in these events. Nonetheless, Byington's account of everyday life in Homestead provides a detailed and sobering look at the adversities encountered by the country's hard-working men and women.

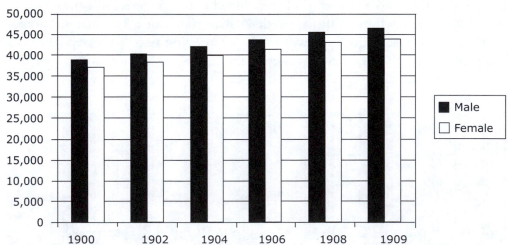

Figure 4.1 *Annual Estimates of United States Population, 1900–1909 (in thousands).*
Source: *Adapted from Kurian 2001, 7, 9.*

Milton Hershey's Chocolate Town Reinvents the Company Town

Milton Hershey had already embarked on a career as a candy maker in Philadelphia and Lancaster, Pennsylvania, at the point when he took time out to visit the 1893 Columbian Exposition. A chocolate-making exhibit there convinced Hershey to turn from his caramel business to become a chocolatier. For a time, he produced chocolates in Lancaster, meanwhile dreaming of building one of the nation's largest chocolate factories. With this purpose in mind, Hershey acquired property in Derry Church, near the farm where he had grown up in Pennsylvania. Building began on the site, and Hershey's chocolate town would be the result.

In June 1905, the facility was ready to begin candy production. Candy was not Hershey's only concern, and he hoped to position himself not only as an entrepreneur but also as a model employer. As part of his business venture, Milton Hershey wanted to construct an ideal factory town in which his workers could live. His goal was to devise an alternative to the grim row houses that typified company town developments near mills and factories. To make it feel like a hometown to its new residents, he invested heavily in buildings, services, and facilities. Brick homes, good schools, affordable public transit, and recreational facilities were among the improvements Hershey furnished. Hershey aspired to create a total environment for his employees, not merely a place to sleep between shifts. He wanted to set in place settings that would support healthy families and a wholesome community with parks, gardens, and leisure activities such as boating available. Through this process of innovation, the town's transformation became official with a 1906 renaming, in which the location once known as Derry Church was reborn as Hershey, Pennsylvania.

The distinctive features of Hershey, Pennsylvania, drew attention to the town. In fact, one of the parks Milton Hershey established for workers and their families in April 1907 attracted so many visitors that it eventually became an amusement park. Even the factory itself quickly began to draw tourists. In 1909, Hershey chocolate bar wrappers enclosed postcards depicting the town. Hershey also devoted a portion of his proceeds to charitable activities, including the Hershey Industrial School for Orphan Boys, which he and his wife, Catharine, opened on November 15, 1909. In this way, Hershey bridged his interests in commerce and philanthropy.

Evening Post, "So far as the production of wealth is concerned, the present age is a phenomenal success. It is in the distribution of wealth produced where a failure is made" (National Geographic 1998, 78). Only 1 percent of the American population owned as much as the remaining 99 percent combined (Katz and Lehman 2001, 19). Maureen Flanagan states the case even more starkly by contending that the top 1 percent of the nation's population controlled 87 percent of the nation's wealth (Flanagan 2007, 7). In either case, the bounty of American progress was unequally enjoyed.

In 1905, the U.S. Bureau of the Census estimated an average worker's annual earnings at $523.12. Meanwhile, sociologists reckoned the minimum income necessary to sustain an American family at $800 (Andrist 1972, 106). Nine in ten workers commanded less than $1,200 in earnings each year, and many of those fell below the $800 mark (National Geographic 1998, 79). While there were conflicting estimates of the era's poverty line, at least one in five Americans was poor (Hunter 1912).

Industrial work changed the American family as profoundly as it changed the landscape. Clock time began to structure everyday life in a way it had not before industrialization, when people instead followed the patterns of sunlight, season, and weather. Factory shifts or work hours governed family mealtime. The cost of living in industrial cities often made it necessary to make one's children a part of the workforce. Because some factories would not take children younger than eight, youths or their parents lied about a child's age to secure work. Children who worked full-time could seldom stay in school. Workplaces were subject to few safety or health restrictions, and so at any moment an injury or accidental death on the job could change a family's fortunes and their destiny. In 1900, for instance, 2,675 railroad workers lost their lives at work, and another 41,142 sustained on-the-job injuries (Katz and Lehman 2001, 12). Few if any programs were in place to sustain the families of those injured at work or, for those who perished, their survivors.

America's Households Become Ever More Urban

Writers during the period from 1900 to 1909 saw the American city as the source of both hope and dread. Many took the view that if the cities of the United States could thrive, so would the rest of the nation. If they could not flourish, what would become of modern American democracy? Frederick C. Howe, author of *The City: The Hope of Democracy* (1905), was one such thinker. In that work, Howe claimed that, "Man has entered on an urban age. He has become a communal being . . . and society has developed into an organism, like the human body, of which the city is the head, heart, and centre of the nervous system" (quoted in Flanagan 2007, 13). Cities and their success appeared to be pivotal to the nation's future.

In 1900, the majority of Americans still resided on farms or in communities with fewer than 2,400 inhabitants. Nonetheless, the size and number of American cities were growing in a manner that was unprecedented in the nation's history. The urban population of the United States rose from 5 million to 54 million in the years from 1870 to 1920 (Nasaw 1993, 3). With steep increase in the number of cities with more than 50,000 residents, America was fast becoming an urban society. The largest of the nation's cities—Chicago, Philadelphia, and New York—all exceeded one million residents by 1900 (Time-Life 1998, 28). Other cities, including Cleveland, Los Angeles, and St. Louis, were not far behind in population size and growth.

James Weldon Johnson and the NAACP Anthem, "Lift Every Voice and Sing"

As a writer, teacher, and civil rights advocate, James Weldon Johnson (1871–1938) helped build a legacy for African Americans. The child of two free black parents, James William Johnson was born in Jacksonville, Florida, on June 17, 1871. He changed his middle name to Weldon in 1913.

Johnson was accomplished at writing poetry, lyrics, essays, and fiction. The book-length Johnson work that is still read today is *Autobiography of an Ex-Colored Man* (1912). This text tells the fictional story of an African American who is so light-skinned that he can pass as a white person. The novel explores the protagonist's experiences across and between racial worlds. Johnson's other works include *Black Manhattan* (1930) and an autobiography, *Along This Way* (1933). In something of the manner of earlier African American authors such as Paul Laurence Dunbar, Johnson wrote dialect verse reminiscent of 19th-century folk speech. He aimed to portray a more accurate and dignified version of African American speech than the era's minstrel shows, still quite popular in the nation's cities, ever provided.

For a 1900 commemoration of Abraham Lincoln's birthday, Johnson composed the verse for which he may be most widely known, "Lift Every Voice and Sing." Set to music, these lyrics became first an anthem for the NAACP. Formed in 1909, the NAACP battled racial discrimination and lynching. The group's members campaigned for enforceable legislation for racial equality. Johnson's tune proved a fitting one for the organization, and his lyrics are uplifting and motivating to singers and listeners:

> Lift every voice and sing,
> Till earth and heaven ring,
> Ring with harmonies of liberty.
> Let our rejoicing rise

Writer, teacher, and civil rights activist James Weldon Johnson (1871–1938). (Library of Congress)

High as the listening skies,
Let it resound loud as the rolling sea.
Sing a song full of the faith that the dark past has taught us,
Sing a song full of the hope that the present has brought us.
Facing the rising sun of our new day begun,
Let us march on till victory is won.

James Weldon Johnson devoted his writing to conveying to his readership the creative richness of African American culture. With "Lift Every Voice and Sing," Johnson inspired not only the members of NAACP but also African Americans more generally. The song became an informal national anthem for African Americans.

Key Shifts in Other 20th-Century Social Demographics

The years from 1900 to 1909 represented a time of social changes that could, at least in part, be measured numerically. At this time, the average American family had 3.56 children (Shiftlett 1996, 309). The nation's infant mortality rate was still fairly high. Historian Edward Wagenknect suggests that during the years from 1900 to 1909, more than 108 out of every 100,000 babies would not live to see a second birthday (Wagenknecht 1982, 2). Children who survived infancy often entered the workforce even before they entered school. This was particularly the case for city children. At least 4 in 10 nonfarm workers were children 15 or younger (Andrist 1972, 106). Life expectancy for those reaching adulthood were increasing, although not as quickly for people of color as for white Americans. According to historian Noel Kent, "The average man in 1900 was living a decade longer than his grandfather had" (Kent 2000, 33). The life span varied by race and gender. As the decade opened, the gap between life expectancy for whites and nonwhites in the United States was approximately 14.6 years, favoring longevity for whites. At the same time that life expectancy was increasing, suicide was on the rise in America. The divorce rate in the United States was also climbing.

These developments commanded the attention of theorists and practitioners across the social sciences. The years from 1900 to 1909 represented a period of professionalization in fields such as sociology and social work. Figures associated with each discipline had an interest in understanding changes in American family life. The increase in divorce in the United States offers a case in point. After an 1889 study of marriage and divorce statistics appeared as a report, debates about the issue of divorce escalated. Sociologists of the era tended to view this phenomenon as the result of economic hardships and shifts in gender roles favoring women's independence. Meanwhile, social workers, although also interested in the reasons behind such trends, faced the more immediate challenge of helping address the needs of America's families.

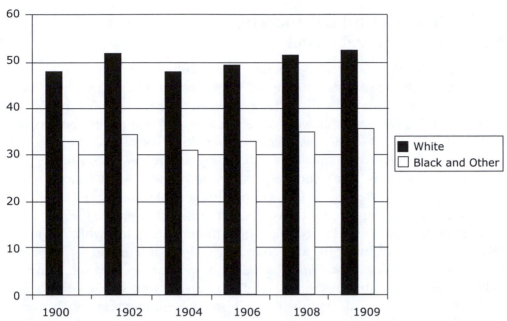

Figure 4.2 *Life Expectancy for Residents of the United States, by Race and Sex, 1900–1909 (in years).* Source: *Adapted from Kurian 2001, 47.*

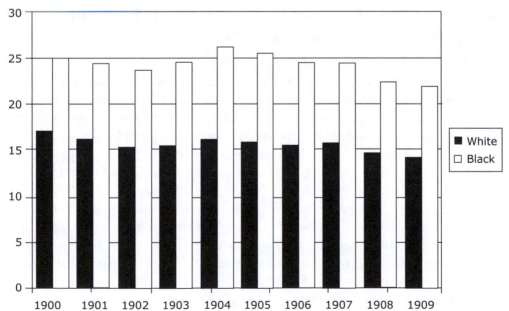

Figure 4.3 *U.S. Death Rate, 1900–1909, by Race (number of deaths per 1,000 of population; does not include fetal deaths).* Source: *Adapted from Kurian 2001, 50.*

With Changes Come Concerns: Maintaining Moral Order

The Progressive Era's far-reaching attempts at combating social ills often targeted the nation's urban residents. During the years from 1900 to 1909, there were countless programs for uplift and self-improvement. For reformers of this period in American history, major cities became prime sites for applying the theories of the emerging social science disciplines—psychology, sociology, anthropology, and the like—to real-world situations. Urban programs represented a test of progressive philosophies and principles. At this time, there were concerns that America's growing cities would fail to uphold the moral standards civic-minded leaders deemed essential to social welfare. Progressives regarded the city as an emblem of the nation's health, as well as of its moral order. Meanwhile, for many urban Americans life went on with considerably less fanfare and fewer ready-made solutions to social problems including premarital sex, divorce, and infidelity. While some urban residents had direct contact with social workers and reformers, others instead took their cues from success literature. Such stories and books urged readers to improve their lives by means of upward social mobility. Through these rags-to-riches plots, Americans became immersed in the rhetoric of upward mobility, and embraced tales of individual success accomplished through will alone.

Bachelor Girls and Moral Hazards: Edith Wharton's Lily Bart and *The House of Mirth*

Edith Wharton's novel *The House of Mirth* tells the story of Lily Bart, a woman who grapples with city life, finances, and a moral order in which marriage is compulsory for women. Within the society Lily inhabits and the station to which she is born, a woman's vocation is to marry well, furnish heirs, preside over a household, and uphold the womanly attributes associated with the female ideal residual to the Victorian era's cult of domesticity: ornamental beauty, self-effacement, and moral purity. For that matter, the chief appeal of *The House of Mirth*'s fictional genre, the novel of manners, consists of the central female character's quest for domestic mastery, a narrative typically constructed as the struggle to conduct herself according to gendered protocol, marry a man of suitable socio-economic status, and culminate her quest by setting up housekeeping for her family. Within these terms, a proper woman shall rule the domestic realm or die trying. As a consequence, novels of manners typically conclude in one of two ways for the central female protagonist: marital triumph or merciful death.

For Lily Bart, the options by which to achieve respectable womanhood remain few. To enjoy the legal and moral privileges of a widow, she must first marry and outlive a husband. To enjoy the social liberty of a divorcée, she must endure marriage and withstand the stigma of a failed union. To enjoy the shielded life of a spinster, she must have relatives or friends well heeled enough to provide the means to survive untainted. Unwilling to marry and unable to secure sponsorship, Lily finds her reputation compromised because she has crossed the boundaries of acceptable conduct for women. Lily's death by overdose conveys the futility of an existence attempted outside the protections of marriage.

CITY LANDSCAPES

The city was becoming more attractive to new residents and so more crowded; more productive and so more magnetic for the nation's unemployed and underemployed; more racially and ethnically diverse and so more fraught with tensions of cultural difference; more networked to the nation's other cities and so more complex in terms of its interdependence. Taken together, these changes were transforming America's urban landscape in profound ways. Between the increase in population density and the crowding of city streets, cities such as New York employed new methods of construction to establish underground travel via subways. Not all the signs of modernization were buried underground. Overhead, recent technological advances permitted erection of taller structures; skyscrapers started to appear in the central business districts of the nation's cities. Such changes made skylines more imposing, and travelers approaching a city for the first time were greeted by architectural spectacle. Once there, new arrivals to the city learned to navigate the complicated and often intimidating streets of cities like New York and Chicago. Along with them, these migrants, immigrants, and visitors brought their hopes for a magical experience in the city.

An Emerald City Ahead?

L. Frank Baum's *The Wonderful Wizard of Oz,* the well-known children's tale, saw its first edition in 1900. This beloved story of the adventures of Dorothy Gale, an American farm girl, has been retold countless times and has been adapted for stage and screen. Within the fantasy framework of the book, the force

Completed in 1902, the Flatiron Building is one of New York City's earliest skyscrapers. (Library of Congress)

of a Kansas tornado transports Dorothy to another place populated by strange beings. Once there, she embarks on a quest to return home to her family. Joined by creatures she meets along the way, Dorothy travels to an Emerald City, where she hopes to enlist the help of the Wizard of Oz. Each figure making this pilgrimage seeks the Wizard's assistance in some way. A scarecrow wants a brain, a tin woodsman a heart, a lion courage, and Dorothy the means to travel home once more.

As a work of children's literature, Baum's *Wonderful Wizard of Oz* taps into familiar childhood fears that inform many fairy tales. Through the violence of a twister, a youth finds herself suddenly displaced from all the people and places she knows. She must then contend with an entirely new environment filled with bizarre characters and customs. Upon her arrival, she finds herself unexpectedly implicated in the death of a witch. Once she gets back on her feet after this set of shocks, the girl realizes that she now stands at the center of an intrigue she scarcely understands. That is, Dorothy's possession of a magical pair of ruby slippers places her at conflict with one of the remaining witches of the land. The emotional palette of Baum's tale resembles that of the story of Hansel and Gretel, in which two innocents must grapple with powerlessness, becoming lost, and falling subject to the will of evil others.

Beyond noting its resemblance to a traditional fairy tale, however, readers of *The Wonderful Wizard of Oz* have interpreted the text as a message operating on other levels. Some regard it as a playful account of the cultural shifts accompanying such processes as urbanization and industrialization in America. Others find it a story about a clash between the haves and have-nots. Still others consider it a parable of populism and a political allegory addressing the free-silver controversy. Whatever inferences one draws from the tale, however, the story of Dorothy's trip to Oz features a theme of homecoming and of return as renewal. Although the characters who brave the city believe themselves deficient and so look to the Emerald City's wizard for guidance, they need only look within themselves and their solid heartland upbringing for the strengths to which they aspire. Therefore, while Dorothy and her friends suppose the city will solve their dilemmas, these matters find resolution through self-knowledge and, for Dorothy, return to her rural home and family. On these terms, *The Wonderful Wizard of Oz* functions as a therapeutic tale about the importance of looking within, finding in one's own convictions rather than in other's claims, the wisdom to inform life's journeys.

The Social Impact of Electrification

In the world of American nonfiction, cities gleamed with electric lights rather than with the emeralds suggested by Baum's novel. At the turn of the 20th century, electricity was not a new invention, but it was slowly revolutionizing everyday life in the United States. Household operations, workplace functions, leisure opportunities, and transportation all underwent significant alterations with the introduction of electrification. These technological innovations in turn changed the social history of the nation during the years from 1900 to 1909.

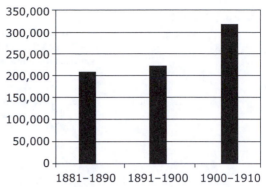

Figure 4.4 *U.S. Patents for Inventions, 1881–1910.* Source: *(Shifflett, 1996)*

Electrical service during this period rose precipitously. In Muncie, Indiana, for example—the community later made famous in the 1920s studies of "Middletown" conducted by Helen and Robert Lynd—the number of residential customers grew from 22 in 1899 to 1,056 in 1907 (Nye 1991, 16). In America's homes, electrical service became increasingly more common. As this happened, inventors began to develop devices to make the tasks of ordinary life easier and more efficient. It was during the years from 1900 to 1909 that such innovations as the electric iron, electric toaster, electric razor, electric washing machine, electric hairdryer, and electric typewriter became part of American life.

As light bulbs replaced gaslights, for example, it became easier to inhabit the night. Mills and factories welcomed electricity as an alternative to water and steam power. With electric rail and trolley travel, distances became easier to bridge in the era before automobiles became common. Electricity made it possible, for instance, for New York's Times Square to become the "Great White Way." At amusement parks and fairs, lights adorned the midways and dazzled patrons.

By no means did the arrival of electrical service in the homes and businesses cause Americans, especially those residing in remote locations or those of modest means, to discontinue their use of kerosene and coal as fuels. In fact, in 1907, a mere 8 percent of American homes were wired for electricity (Schlereth 1992, 115). Still, it was becoming clear that the nation's days of oil lamps and pot-bellied stoves were numbered.

Aviation: From Avocation to Transportation

The Wright Brothers enjoy the distinction of being the first Americans to achieve air flight. While at the turn of the 20th century onlookers might have had reason to regard the fascination with flight as more of a hobby than an innovation, all that changed when it became possible to control travel of a heavier-than-air craft.

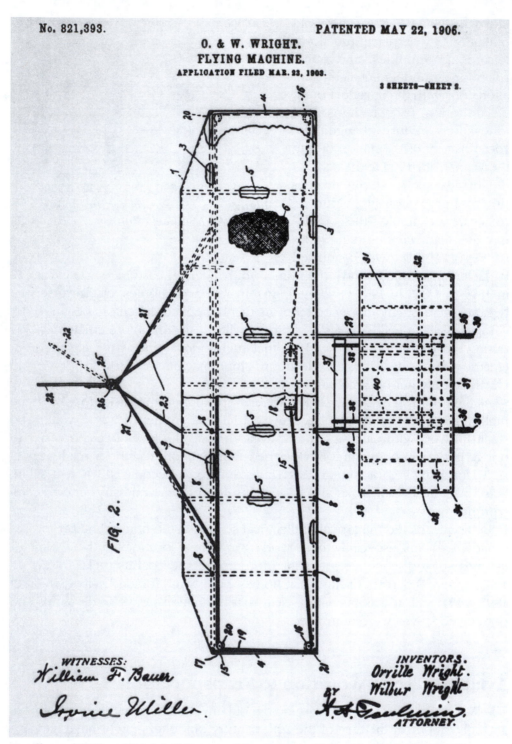

No. 821,393.

PATENTED MAY 22, 1906.

O. & W. WRIGHT.
FLYING MACHINE.
APPLICATION FILED MAR. 23, 1903.

3 SHEETS—SHEET 2.

FIG. 2.

WITNESSES:
William F. Bauer
Irvine Miller

INVENTORS.
Orville Wright.
Wilbur Wright
BY
H. A. Toulmin.
ATTORNEY.

Orville and Wilbur Wright's flying machine, patented May 22, 1906. (National Archives)

Avid inventors and aviators, Orville Wright and Wilbur Wright secured their places in the histories of both technology and transportation when they successfully manned a controlled flight on a powered glider the called the "Flyer." This historic event in aviation took place at Kitty Hawk, North Carolina, on December 17, 1903.

The story of the Wright Brothers began, however, with their births in Dayton, Ohio. They became part of a progressive family that lent active support to progressive causes from women's rights to abolition. Their parents also encouraged the life of the mind, and while the Wright Brothers would not become scholars, they would achieve great ideas. Because of the Wright Brothers' prominent role as inventors, Dayton is considered by many to be the birthplace of flight. Wright Field, a site where subsequent test flights have taken place, stands as a tribute to their ingenuity.

Orville and Wilbur Wright worked together in several other endeavors before venturing into aviation. In 1890, they launched a printing business. Three years later, they added a bicycle business that would lend technological inspiration to their later experiments in flight. Fascinated as both men were by vehicles, and enticed by the prospect of human flight, they fashioned a wind tunnel and began to research the idea. By 1900, their flight experiments began in earnest. They devised several versions of their aircraft before arriving at the one that made that memorable 1903 journey. Although that first flight lasted only 12 seconds and spanned only 120 feet, its implications were far greater than the time or distance traveled.

Because the Wright Brothers triumphed in this effort without benefit of high school diplomas, training in engineering, or subsidies of any kind, their story has taken on symbolic importance within American history. They are hailed as heroes reminiscent of the protagonists in Horatio Alger stories, by prevailing chiefly through persistence and conviction. Observances of Wright Brothers' Day on December 17 each year serve as reminders of the role the Wrights played both in American technology and the popular imagination. Even for those who never boarded a plane, the Wright Brothers still had an impact through the way flight transformed transport of mail and goods.

Traversing the 20th-Century City

An American living during the first decade of the 20th century, particularly one working or residing in the nation's cities, could attest to the rapidity with which transportation patterns were changing. The nation's hubs ceased to be walking cities with centralized downtowns or cores. Consequently, urban residents needed to find ways to get around the city, both for business and pleasure. The city streets were also undergoing a transformation. No longer were

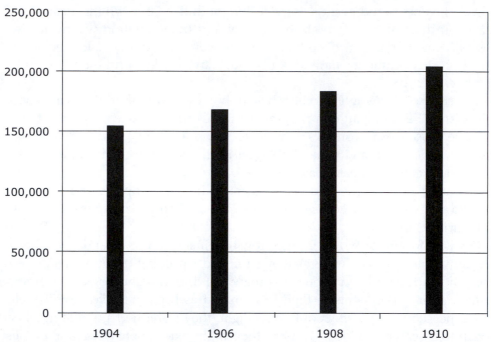

Figure 4.5 *Surfaced Roads, 1904–1910 (in miles).* Source: *U.S. Department of Commerce, 1989, 710.*

these streets dominated just by handcarts, buggies, surreys, and delivery wagons. An influx of vehicles, including electric and steam-powered ones, took place. It was the age of electric trolleys, streetcars, elevated railroads, subways, and interurban electric lines.

Automobiles were still something of a novelty; they were primitive instruments and not yet a practical and reliable form of transportation. Few autos were available in 1900, when approximately 4,192 horseless carriages were owned in America. Even for those in possession of one of these vehicles, there were significant obstacles to auto travel. Surfaced roads suitable for motorists were rare. In 1900, America could claim less than 150 miles of paved road (Time-Life 1998, 34). At this point in history, cars were extremely costly and were reserved for the wealthiest members of society, at least until Ford's Model T brought the price down to the still-steep cost of $850. Furthermore, the operation and maintenance of these early models demanded considerable mechanical aptitude and more than a little patience. Automobiles were started with a crank, proved temperamental on the roads, and often got stuck on pathways not designed with such vehicles in mind. As the decade unfolded, motor vehicle registrations rose and barriers to motorists fell. In 1910, 1,870,000 automobiles were produced in the United States (Andrist 1972, 107).

Table 4.1. United States Motor Vehicle Sales and Registration (thousands)

Year	Passenger cars	Total motor vehicles	Auto registrations
1900	4.1	8.0	8.0
1901	7.0	14.8	14.8
1902	9.0	23.0	23.0
1903	11.2	32.9	32.9
1904	22.1	55.2	54.5
1905	24.2	78.8	77.4
1906	33.2	108.1	105.9
1907	43.0	143.2	140.3
1908	63.5	198.4	194.4
1909	123.9	312.0	305.9

Source: Kurian 2001, 312.

Trolley Neighborhoods and Streetcar Suburbs

At the time of the 1893 World's Columbian Exposition, a variety of individuals were asked to make predictions about the pivotal changes ahead in the next hundred years in the United States. One of these forecasters, an electrical engineer named John Joseph Carty, focused on the trolley railways as one of the most change-making developments for the years ahead. He was particularly concerned with the impact of public transportation innovations capable of linking rural and urban communities. Carty wrote of trolleys, "They are simply going to annihilate distance and to make the man who lives in the country, to all intents and purposes, an inhabitant of the nearest city" (Walter 1992, 170). In a sense, Carty's vision of the future in America was accurate. As early as the turn of the 20th century, public transportation began to make it more possible for some individuals to work in the city and reside outside the city.

In 1887, electrical engineer Frank Julian Sprague developed an electric streetcar for use in Richmond, Virginia. This rapid and inexpensive form of transit quickly gained in popularity in America's cities. By 1895, there were 850 trolley lines operating in the United States. Interurban trolleys and streetcars began to facilitate Americans' leisure as well as their commutes to work. In fact, in 1904, a newly married couple, Louise and Clinton Lucas, spent their honeymoon riding such conveyances. They published their account of this experience in a book, *A Trolley Honeymoon* (Schlereth 1992, 24–25).

Streetcars were common at this point in the life of America's cities. By 1902, the vast majority of them, estimated at 94 percent by social historian David Nasaw, operated on electric power. Riders were assessed a flat rate of five cents, which included a free transfer to another trolley line (Nasaw 1993, 9). These routes moved passengers between urban neighborhoods and residential community

Young boy selling newspapers via trolley, St. Louis, Missouri, May 1910. Lewis Hine photo. (Library of Congress)

positions as railroad suburbs. These developments in transportation helped render the United States a nation of commuters, shuttling daily between home and work.

Henry Ford Salutes Small-Town America

As someone closely associated with industrialization and technological progress, Henry Ford (1863–1947) might seem an unlikely person to express nostalgia for a simpler time in American life. After all, with his pioneering efforts in the automobile industry, Henry Ford embodied the American ideal of the self-made capitalist. Nonetheless, Ford cherished memories of bygone chapters in American history and lent his support to efforts to preserve that history and share it with future generations.

Ford was born July 30, 1863. Although he had an enjoyable childhood on the family farm, Ford felt called to pursuits that would take him away from agriculture and toward industrial technology. In 1879, he apprenticed as a machinist in Detroit and proved adept at repairing, retooling, and running machinery and instrumentation. These talents helped him land a position as an engineer with Detroit's Edison Illuminating Company, where he became chief engineer in 1893. This work served as a platform for Ford's own pursuits as an entrepreneur.

The Ford Motor Company had its beginnings in Detroit and Highland Park. Ford introduced his now-legendary Model T in 1908. His Model T became so popular that by 1918, this vehicle accounted for nearly a 50 percent share of the American auto market. This was the kind of success Ford had envisioned for his industry. He wanted to achieve an efficient production of a solid means of transportation for the average American consumer.

Henry Ford's hometown of Dearborn, Michigan became the site for the Ford Company's industrial complex in the 1920s. At this plant on the edge of the Rouge River, Ford realized his mass production concepts, such as the moving assembly line. His success as a manufacturer helped transform American culture into a car culture, bringing with it a national network of highways, dotted with roadside attractions, and amenities such as fuel stations and diners.

Dearborn also served as the location for Ford's Greenfield Village. With something of the reverence Walt Disney would later express for small-town America in his design of such attractions as "Main Street USA" at Disneyland, Ford sought to make of Greenfield Village "America's Hometown." The building for what is now the Ford Museum, but then the Edison Institute, was dedicated in 1928. Ford collected an unusual array of Americana, including both plainspoken objects and such items as a Revolutionary War camp bed used by George Washington and the Ford Theater balcony chair in which Abraham Lincoln was seated at the time of his assassination.

The 13-acre property around the Ford Museum first opened in 1933, featuring reproductions and 80 historical structures. In something of the visual arrangement of a New England village, Ford had arranged a suite of historic districts for visitors to experience. Perhaps predictably, there was a version of Ford's first assembly plant. Because Ford so admired another American inventor, also available were versions of both Thomas Alva Edison's residence and his Menlo Park, New Jersey labs. Along with these areas were sites designed to recall the homes of the Wright Brothers, George Washington Carver, Noah Webster, and Robert Frost. Visitors could also see Ford's take on a William Holmes McGuffey School, paying tribute to the man behind the popular readers used with American schoolchildren since 1836. With Greenfield Village, Ford expressed his admiration for his country and its success stories.

Ford did not invent the automobile, but he did help establish it as the dominant form of transportation in the United States. His own rise to wealth and success as an industrialist, along with his reverence for the nation's patriotic heroes, helped establish Henry Ford as someone capable of being forward-looking and nostalgic at the same time.

Casey Jones as Folk Hero

American folklore boasts tales about a number of figures whose careers evoked the romance of the nation's railroad history. One such individual is rail engineer Casey Jones. Although he was known to the public as Casey Jones, this individual began life as John Luther Jones in 1863 and fondly took the name "Casey" from the town in which he was raised, Cayce, Kentucky.

Jones had a fine reputation as a deft railroad engineer, celebrated in story and song. He worked the Cannonball Express, which ran between Chicago and New Orleans. One day in 1900, the train crashed and Casey Jones died in service to the occupation at which he excelled. As the story has it, the man's body was found with one hand on the whistle and the other on the brake.

A 1909 popular song, entitled "Casey Jones (The Brave Engineer)," eulogized the railroad man who would in time become a well-known figure in occupational lore. Like most such heroes, Jones was not without detractors. For instance, in 1912, the labor movement songwriter, Joe Hill, penned and sang a parody of the 1909 homage to Jones. He called his version, "Casey Jones the Union Scab," evidently to suggest that Jones was no friend to organized labor. In the lyrics of the Joe Hill tune, Casey Jones arrives in heaven only to take up as a scab during an angel strike, a decision that ultimately delivers him to hell. For others, however, John Luther "Casey" Jones takes his place among many American folk figures, both historical and imagined, who prove memorable through their close association with their specific occupations and fields of endeavor, from John "Johnny Appleseed" Chapman to Paul Bunyan.

The Twentieth Century Limited

During the years from 1900 to 1909 in the United States, the nation's rail system expanded dramatically, making passenger and freight movement possible to more places and rendering more timely movement of people or goods to once inaccessible or remote locations. In 1900, 193,368 miles of track were already in place (Time-Life 1998, 27).

There was a price paid for such infrastructure improvements. During the year 1900 alone, 2,675 railroad workers lost their lives and 41,142 sustained injuries (Katz and Lehman 2001, 12). Even before that, the United States had laid claim to quantities of land occupied by the Plains Indians, making transcontinental railways possible through land seizure.

The Twentieth Century Limited passenger line of the New York Central Railroad got its start on June 15, 1902. This route linked Chicago's LaSalle Street Station with New York's Grand Central Terminal. By keeping stops to a minimum, this train completed a one-way trip in less than 16 hours. This particular rail service was famous for its pace and its luxury. The idea of "red carpet service" is associated with the rail line's theatrical boarding rituals used to welcome passengers at the express line's select station stops. With its reputation for time efficiency and service luxury, the Twentieth Century Limited symbolized modern transportation in the United States. As the nation developed its rail system, Americans the nation's residents gained greater access to consumer goods, to once remote locations, and to one another.

City Lives

During the years from 1900 to 1909, the urban design of America's cities continued to move away from walking cities and toward locations structured around travel via mass transportation. Business and leisure establishments alike positioned themselves to prove accessible and convenient to potential customers. Such arrangements of city street plans and available services together constituted a journey that cultural geographer J. B. Jackson once described as "the stranger's path." Although a native of a particular American city might have deeper knowledge than a newcomer, even short-term visitors could use the stranger's path to find their way to the necessities of life: lodging, food, drink, and the like. Ease in wayfinding became especially crucial as cities became more populous and expansive. While new arrivals might not have the financial means to meet all their needs or the savvy to shield themselves from the city's criminals, they would nonetheless find a path ready to lead them on their journeys. Once in America's cities, residents faced the challenges of dense urban areas and all the problems that accompany concentrated population and social inequality. Consequently, Progressive era reformers turned a great deal of their attention to improving living and working conditions in the nation's cities.

Iconography of American Opportunity

"Miss Liberty" is the name sometimes used to refer to the figural sculpture known as the Statue of Liberty. Along with Uncle Sam, Miss Liberty is the personification of the United States, and her image is prevalent in American folk culture, from Independence Day trinkets to patriotic-themed quilts.

This monument and national icon has a rich history. The Statue of Liberty originated as a gift to the United States from France. It was offered as a symbol of friendship between the two nations, a particular kinship that dates back to the Revolutionary War. The statue was formally accepted as a gift by President Grover Cleveland, acting on behalf of the United States.

Frederic Auguste Bartholdi was the sculptor who developed the design for this enormous piece. The figure itself is just more than 150 feet tall from head to foot, not including the platform on which it stands. As most Americans and

Emma Lazarus 1883 Poem, "The New Colossus," Emblazoned on Base of Statue of Liberty in 1903

Not like the brazen giant of Greek fame,
With conquering limbs astride from land to land;
Here at our sea-washed, sunset gates shall stand
A mighty woman with a torch, whose flame
Is the imprisoned lightning, and her name
Mother of Exiles. From her beacon-hand
Glows world-wide welcome; her mild eyes command
The air-bridged harbor that twin cities frame.
"Keep, ancient lands, your storied pomp!" cries she
With silent lips. "Give me your tired, your poor,
Your huddled masses yearning to breathe free,
The wretched refuse of your teeming shore.
Send these, the homeless, tempest-tost to me,
I lift my lamp beside the golden door!"

Source: Library of Congress exhibit, "From Haven to Home: 350 Years of Jewish Life in America," Manuscript poem, bound in journal. Courtesy of the American Jewish Historical Society, New York and Newton Centre, Massachusetts.

countless people the world over know, the statue depicts a classically draped woman wearing a crown. In one hand, she grips a tablet, inscribed with the date July 4, 1776. In the other, she lifts above her head a lit torch. It is presumably for this reason that the sculpture bore the title "Liberty Enlightening the World." In its immediate reference to 1776, the statue pays tribute to the United States' independence. The suggestion of this title for the piece, however, was that the American Revolution carried a message with worldwide implications for the cause of freedom.

The gift of the Statue of Liberty was intended to arrive in time for America's centennial celebration in 1876. Circumstances both in France and the United States required a delay, however, and only a portion of the monument, the arm with its torch, appeared at the Centennial Exhibition. The full statue would not be open to visitors until its dedication on October 28, 1886. From the time that it first welcomed the public up to the present, the statue has held many meanings for beholders.

Although the earliest documentation about the initial gift of the statue suggests that international friendship, along with a commemoration of the Revolutionary War, were the purposes for the gift, alternative symbolisms have been posited for the monument. For example, the timing of the gift, coming as it did during the years following America's Civil War, put many in mind of the issue of liberty granted to U.S. slaves by the Emancipation Proclamation. This impression of the statue is underscored by the visual effect of broken shackles at the figure's feet. Rumors have also circulated, including some urban legends, that the model for the statue was an African American woman and that the subtext of abolition was intentional on the part of designers. Therefore, instead of conjuring images of the Revolutionary War, the statue reminds some viewers of the Civil War and the institution of slavery.

In the years since its dedication, the Statue of Liberty has also assumed an iconic importance for immigrants to the United States. This effect is due in part to the 1903 addition of an Emma Lazarus poem to the monument's base, opening with the familiar line of welcome to new arrivals, "Give me your tired, your poor . . . ." This inscription, along with the placement of the statue at Ellis Island, historically an entry point for immigrants to the United States, lead many to regard the statue's message of liberty as equally relevant to those who come to America seeing refuge and freedom from persecution. Accordingly, the United Nations designated the Statue of Liberty as a World Heritage Site. The site of the Statue of Liberty is maintained as a landmark by the U.S. Department of the Interior's National Park Service.

Regardless of which forms of freedom a viewer most associates with the Statue of Liberty, this monument—widely recognized the world over—and her image and nickname, Miss Liberty, have come to function as both an emblem for the United States and a symbol of hope for newcomers.

Rhetoric Versus Reality:
The Problems with America's Cities

Despite the ideology of American opportunity, it did not take new arrivals to America's cities long to realize that the streets were not paved in gold. In fact, urban living conditions were anything but glamorous. Regardless of one's station in life, there were some realities of city living no urban dweller could escape entirely. In the years between 1900 and 1909, urban residents contended with streets strewn with horse manure and other debris. Garbage removal systems could not keep up with the refuse that accumulated near or in the city streets. Consequently, anyone venturing onto urban roadways breathed in air heavy with fumes of ammonia, sulfur, and other gases. If a disease, such as yellow fever, reached a city, it could decimate the public health, afflicting rich and poor alike. Urban streets were crowded, traffic was scarcely regulated, and the pace of movement through the city streets was only increasing with the advent of mechanized vehicles.

Urban streets became dangerous for other reasons, as well. Among the city crowds were criminals, such as pickpockets, who threatened others' safety and possessions. Violence, unrest, and moral temptation were also features of city life, no matter what an individual social standing. Particularly in the sections of town that observer Robert Hunter called "districts of vice" in American cities, such as New York's Bowery and Tenderloin District, gambling and prostitution were daily realities and lures to lower impulses (Hunter 1912, 106).

In addition to those challenges facing all of those working in or residing in American cities, there were difficulties and dangers disproportionately affecting the disadvantaged and dispossessed. In fact, in the poorest neighborhoods of America's cities, living conditions were deplorable. In apartment houses and tenements, ventilation could not be achieved, and so fresh air could not circulate and the smell of kerosene stoves would hang in the air. Coupled with crowding of residents, these circumstances aided the spread of diseases such as diphtheria, malaria, tuberculosis, typhoid, and typhus. Light and heat were scant or absent. Sanitation was minimal, and most residences located in these slums lacked hot water—or water of any kind. Pests such as mice, rats, roaches, and bedbugs were pervasive. Due to cost and crowding, privacy was nonexistent. Furthermore, because housing conditions were not subject to many legal standards of fitness at the turn of the 20th century, urban structures were seldom adequately constructed or maintained for minimum features of health and safety. For example, some buildings had no fire escapes at all while others had malfunctioning ones in place. During the years from 1902 to 1909, approximately 250 people died in Manhattan apartment fires (Nasaw 1993, 25). Deaths from other causes, such as homicide and disease, were also more frequent among the poor.

The Housing System Strained: America's Urban Slums and Ghettoes

Residential conditions and building patterns in America's cities during the first decade of the 20th century provided ample evidence that the current housing system could not withstand the growth of the nation's cities. American authors such as Anzia Yezierska, Abraham Cahan, and Michael Gold wrote accounts, both autobiographical and fictional, that detailed the immigrant experience of life in urban slums and ghettoes. Virtually every large city in the United States had its slums, including Clabber Alley in St. Louis, the Lower East Side in New York City, the North End in Boston, the Stockyard district in Chicago, and the Flats in Cleveland. According to historian David Ward, slums were closely associated with immigrant poor, whereas a "ghetto" described an area where racial minorities or unassimilated immigrants lived in segregation (Ward 1989, 95). By the modest standard of the times, an apartment consisting of three rooms plus a kitchen was considered spacious. Rental rates were on the rise, and the high rent required for such accommodations might well require a family to take in borders, a common

Gertrude Stein's *The Making of Americans* as a Narrative of Cultural Assimilation

Although Gertrude Stein's *The Making of Americans: Being a History of Family's Progress* corresponds closely on many points to events in Stein's family history, this novel does more than chronicle the author's family history, for it also tells the more general story of "old people in a new world." Issues of race, class, ethnicity, gender, and religion all play a part. Stein not only represents the experience of the transplanted business-class family, as suggested by her own origin but also depicts the lives of the working class and service professions. Therefore, while the lived perspective of the author is that of one accustomed to privilege, Stein makes an effort to include (albeit through elite eyes) the lives of seamstresses, governesses, servants, and their families. As a result, *The Making of Americans* is rich with the social relations of class.

In some ways, it seems only natural that Stein's Martha Hersland, the character most closely corresponding to Gertrude Stein in this somewhat autobiographical fiction, should see issues of ethnicity in terms of her family's servants. Like her character, Stein probably got her first exposure to class and ethnic differences through servants in the Steins' employ (including her Czech tutor and Hungarian governess). With the character of Martha Hersland, Stein points out that children raised in a middle- or upper-class home often know the household staff better than they know their relations. The children may spend most of their time and receive most of their care from servants whose backgrounds are likely to be different from the children's. Stein's gestures toward depicting a cross-section of society leads the author to sketch out (literally, diagrams in her notebooks) men and women in an effort to render each character complete, regardless of social standing.

The Making of Americans explores typologies of human character. What types of people could be said to populate the United States? Is there such a thing as a national character? How do people's personalities shape their interactions and relationships? How do the structures of the traditional family help create character? How do people encounter those socially different from themselves? These are the issues underlying Stein's text. Within her effort to write what she calls "a history of every one," Stein offers explanations for the human differences she observes. Given its focus on immigrant life, *The Making of Americans* has to do with issues of ethnicity as well as class, and, as the novel's subtitle indicates, the process of cultural assimilation.

Stein's *The Making of Americans* resists literary classification. While some critics regard it as a novel, it may be better characterized as a daybook, containing literary sketches, reflections, and, frequently, a running commentary on the text's own writing. *The Making of Americans* is the volume that Gertrude Stein claimed had begun modern writing. This piece, some 550,000 words and 925 pages in its unabridged form, represents nearly eight years of work by Stein (1902–1911).

A family sits in their New York City tenement. Photo by photographer and social reformer Jacob Riis. (Library of Congress)

phenomenon among the urban poor. Such living conditions helped inspire specific progressive reforms, such as the playground movement, which attempted to provide places for wholesome recreation for urban youth.

THE SETTLEMENT HOUSE MOVEMENT

Conditions for the urban poor were so worrisome that progressive reformers initiated the settlement house movement. Settlement houses provided resources for the nation's displaced, disenfranchised, and impoverished. Forces such as modernization, urbanization, and industrialization altered the way Americans lived. In the face of the growing challenges facing America's cities, such as poverty, crime, and illness, settlement houses offered an alternative to crowded tenements and dangerous streets. At landmark settlement houses, such as New York's Henry House and Chicago's Hull House, the nation's have-nots could find solace and help. Typically, the initial inspiration for settlement workers was direct observation of others' suffering. The opening line of Lillian Wald's *The House on Henry Street,* her own account of the origins of Henry Street Settlement, briskly explains the specific and personal reason why she took up residence among tenement dwellers. Wald writes, "A sick woman in a squalid rear tenement, so wretched and so pitiful that, in all the years since, I have not seen anything more appealing, determined me, within half an hour, to live on the East Side" (Wald 1915, 1). Reformers associated with settlement houses found America's industrial cities ripe for social justice work. Settlement workers provided direct services to the people of the nation's cities while simultaneously working for systemic changes that could bring more lasting improvements in their standard of living. Such efforts hinged on the belief that it was the poor influences of environment, rather than deficiencies of character, that kept the urban poor from enjoying a higher quality of life.

Why Settlement Houses?

The original concept behind America's settlement houses came from a precedent observed in London. While traveling in England, reformer Jane Addams and her friend and colleague, Ellen Gates Starr, had occasion to visit the first settlement house established in the United Kingdom, Canon Samuel Barnett's Toynbee Hall, and to see the facility at work. With the involvement of Oxford University, the staff at Toynbee Hall aided London's industrial poor. In Toynbee Hall, Addams and Starr discovered a model for the reform they resolved to bring to the United States: settlement houses.

Addams and Starr established Chicago's Hull House, one of the most widely recognized examples of American settlement houses. Hull House itself became an influential model for settlement houses created in other major cities in the nation, such as Boston and New York. Settlement house founders acquired property, usually located right in the neighborhoods where their target populations resided. Members of the settlement movement often lived among the poor at or near the settlement houses they established, both to be accessible to clients and to be sensitized to the conditions in which those clients lived and worked.

By occupying a position within the urban communities where Americans needed help, settlement houses attempted to reach people where they lived. Rather than expecting the disadvantaged to venture outside the portions of the city they considered their own, settlement workers went to them.

How Settlement Houses Conducted Their Work

The contributions of settlement houses varied somewhat depending upon their administration, clientele, and locations. For the most part, however, settlements functioned as community centers for people who would otherwise have no place to go for medical care, union meetings, instruction, or referrals. Settlement houses also became sites of wholesome sociability, free from the temptations surrounding commercial places of leisure such as dance halls or saloons.

Reformers situated at settlement houses wanted to improve the public health, but that was not the only goal to which they aspired. One key objective of settlement houses was to provide opportunities for immigrants and the poor to increase their prospect for social mobility. Education played an important role within this uplift philosophy. Visitors to settlement houses could take a range of classes, such as literacy instruction or courses in domestic science. Quite a few urban residents turned to settlement houses for the express purpose of gaining education, hoping to take classes and acquire practical skills. In fact, musician Benny Goodman was once a member of the Hull House Boys' Band (Ashby 2006, 154). Settlement workers acted on the premise that disadvantaged urban residents, if given opportunities for betterment, would become able to improve their own circumstances in lasting ways.

The Way to His Heart: *"The Settlement"* Cook Book (1903)

The first edition of *"The Settlement" Cook Book* arrived in 1903. It was released under the name of Lizzie Black Kander, an affluent woman and reformer who had been instrumental in the first settlement house in Milwaukee, Wisconsin. Kander was an advocate of social services, vocational training, and other progressive causes. While a cookbook might not on first glance appear to be a very telling historical artifact, this one has an underlying message for its readers. Its author, sometimes described as the "Jane Addams of Milwaukee," believed that she should express her gratitude for her own good fortune by increasing the prospects available to others. The content of the book reflects the time's concern with domestic management, efficiency, and healthful housekeeping. Settlement houses across America offered alternatives to charity for the underprivileged by providing the public with classes on these subjects, and Kander's cookbook was intended to support instruction, particularly of young women, and to raise funds for the settlement house movement. The cookbook's language is plainspoken and its directions systematic. Readers of this work can find within its pages practical advice on such topics as constructive uses for stale bread. The book was extremely successful, and its strong sales enabled Kander to establish the Settlement Cook Book Company. Since its first edition in 1903, *"The Settlement" Cook Book* underwent countless revisions, updates, and reprintings. The book's subtitle, "The Way to a Man's Heart," reflects the aphorism that "the way to a man's heart is through his stomach." If viewed as a document of social history, this cookbook informs the study of foodways, women's education, and the emerging field of domestic science.

Settlement Workers and Those They Served

Workers at America's settlement houses were not entirely different from other Progressive era reformers. Most, though not all, had their origins in the middle and upper classes and had sufficient financial security to pursue such projects. The majority of settlement house founders were college educated, and some regarded their work in America's cities as the logical extension of their academic pursuits in emerging fields such as sociology, psychology, and social work. They did not merely wish to examine social conditions; they also wanted to intervene in them.

During the Progressive era, reform movements tended to identify target populations for their work. In the case of settlement houses, for instance, the chief beneficiaries were urban residents. Within this context, immigrants and the poor derived the greatest benefits. Perhaps because many settlement house founders and staff members were women, or perhaps because of the gender-coded nature of the specific programs offered at settlement houses, women were frequently the best-served clients of the settlement movement.

As with any other reform, some groups appear to have been underserved by American settlement houses. For example, migrants to the nation's cities did not seem to be the chief focus of programs and services made available through the settlement movement. Therefore, while urban emigrants may have been in the same poverty as immigrants to the nation's cities, they did not receive as much support from settlement houses located there. Similarly, the racial segregation and bias of this era in the United States created obstacles to settlement houses providing help to African Americans that would be comparable to that afforded European Americans.

The Rise of Home Economics

At the turn of the 20th century, home economics was still a relatively new academic discipline. The movement owed its beginnings to the 19th century, during which time a program at Kansas State University helped fledge the field at their campus and establish similar programs at other land grant universities in the United States.

The term itself was coined in 1899 and figured prominently in a series of conferences held between 1899 and 1909 at New York's Lake Placid. During these meetings, home economists arrived at a plan for the development of their field. Their chief goal was to develop a curriculum that would educate youth, from primary grades to college, about the domestic arts. They also hoped that this move would help increase the career opportunities for young women in America.

The study of home economics represented an attempt to dignify and professionalize household management. The field included multiple areas, such as cooking, nutrition, consumer science, human development, parenting, health,

Hull House Becomes an Exemplar of the American Settlement House

Jane Addams' Hull House was an oasis from urban ills, situated in the very same city that had inspired both Upton Sinclair's *The Jungle* and Theodore Dreiser's *Sister Carrie.* Along with her colleague, Ellen Gates Starr, Addams acquired land on Chicago's South Halsted Street. The private residence standing on that property, Hull Mansion, was repurposed to serve as a settlement house. Community members arriving at Hull House could enjoy the benefits of such facilities as a nursery, kitchen, and gym.

Jane Addams, founder of Hull House, also helped establish social work as a profession. Addams had a lengthy career as a leader of reforms, including terms as president of the National Conference on Charities and Correction, head of the National Federation of Settlements, vice president of the National American Women Suffrage Association, and president of the Women's International League for Peace and Freedom.

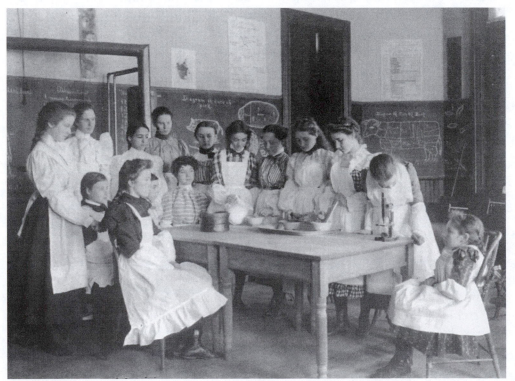

Girls posed in home economics class in Washington, D.C., ca. 1899. Photo by Francis Benjamin Johnston. (Library of Congress)

interior design, sewing, and budgeting. America's home economics curriculum was the product of a time during which components of public schooling remained highly differentiated by gender. It was customary at this time for girls to take home economics while boys were expected to engage in other applied arts, such as carpentry. The rise of home economics as a profession was a clear signal that the country valued the knowledge required to nourish and nurture American families.

THE CITY RETHOUGHT AND REBUILT

Back in 1893, orator John James Ingalls had predicted that an impulse for reform would help define the next hundred years in the United States. Taking a cynical view of such efforts, he asserted his opinion that "the attempt to abolish poverty, pay debts, and cure the ills of society by statute will be the favorite prescription of ignorance, incapacity, and credulity for the next hundred years— as it has been from the beginning of civilization" (Walter 1992, 144). Despite such warnings as his, the era's intellectuals persisted in their pursuit of changes in law and public policy that might address the issues of slums, corruption, and crime in the nation's cities.

By 1901, there was growing attention to the problems facing America's major cities. As historian Maureen Flanagan observed, "Words such as evil, ignorant, lawless, and vicious were freely used by many Americans to describe cities at the turn of the twentieth century. Another word was corruption" (Flanagan 2007, 25). Along with this attention to urban problems came an increased awareness of the risks these challenges posed to public health and safety in the United States. During the years from 1900 to 1909, architects, reformers, and city planners turned their energies to rethinking their concepts of the American city. Together, they hoped to create more humane, appealing, and wholesome urban communities for the nation.

Housing Reform

By the turn of the 20th century, the need for housing reform in American cities was great. In volumes such as Robert W. DeForest and Lawrence T. Veiller's *The Tenement House Problem* (1903), observers called for changes in the way Americans approached urban architecture, particularly in terms of residential buildings.

One of the more problematic urban designs was the dumbbell tenement, which was prevalent in United States building from 1879 to 1900. These structures were typically five-story walk-up residences. They crowded occupants into small rooms with minimal light or ventilation although some incorporated air shafts between the buildings. Inhabitants of these old-style tenements suffered

The Making of an American:
Urban Photojournalist Jacob Riis

There is a saying in the United States applied to the process of looking beyond one's own circumstances to learn about the lives of other people; whether finding out that their lives are better or worse than one's own, a common way of referring to this inquiry is seeing "how the other half lives." That phrase came to national prominence through the work of a documentary photographer, Jacob Riis.

Jacob August Riis arrived in America from his native Denmark in 1870. Three years later, he was working as a police reporter for the *New York Evening Sun.* He served in this same capacity for several newspapers in the area. In so doing, Riis made an unusual acquaintance with the city. As Riis followed the crime stories that his job required him to monitor, Jacob Riis simultaneously witnessed the wretched conditions in which many New Yorkers of the time lived. He began to photograph the city's slums and their residents, documenting the levels of adversity facing the nation's underclass. His early use of flash powder, combined with the unsafe conditions of the interiors he documented, occasionally resulted in fiery explosions in the homes of the very New Yorkers he wished to help.

While working for *Scribner's Magazine* during the 1880s, Riis launched the project that would later become a book-length study of urban poverty: *How the Other Half Lives* (1890). Although the content of Riis' image captions and essays betrayed the man's stereotypical perceptions of the people he photographed, particularly in terms of race and ethnicity, Riis revealed to his viewers and readers the squalor of the tenements in a way words alone might not. By 1900, Riis spent his time writing and lecturing rather than taking photographs. Nonetheless, his reform-minded photojournalism changed attitudes and, in time, policies and codes regarding housing standards in America's cities. As his 1901 autobiography, *The Making of an American,* suggested, Riis helped call attention to the consequences of social and economic inequality. Collections of his images are compiled in *The Battle of the Slum* (1902) and *Children of the Tenements* (1903). His efforts helped define "muckraking" journalism, a brand of Progressive era reporting that aspired to change the unjust conditions it exposed. Americans have since named various urban schools and parks in his honor.

from features of the built environments in which they were forced to live because they could not afford to rent more suitable accommodations.

Tenements were profitable for landlords, who received 33 percent higher rent than they would for more spacious and affluent accommodations (Katz and Lehman 2001, 8). This high profit margin proved a disincentive for building owners to change the system voluntarily.

In 1901, however, New York passed the Tenement House Law, putting an end to the construction of dumbbell tenements. The law called for more healthful and habitable buildings. Features such as courtyards, water closets in apartments, ventilation, and fireproofing became more standard in new construction.

Beyond the efforts to improve architectural standards, American cities tried to provide green space for urban youth. Urban children had no room to play at home, no time or place to play when they left home. There were relatively few recreational spaces like playgrounds and a limited number of parks. New York had Central Park, Boston had its Commons, and Chicago had Lincoln, Jackson, and Washington parks.

At the turn of the century, 11 of the largest 100 cities in the nation had public playgrounds in place (Flanagan 2007, 66). By 1909, however, 77 of those 100 cities had funded playground construction (Flanagan 2007, 67).

To address the limited sanitation in the nation's cities at this time, proponents of the municipal bath movement hoped to improve the lives of urban dwellers across the United States. By raising the cleanliness standard of urban life, municipal baths also aspired to reduce the transmission of germs and diseases among urban residents. During the years from 1890 to 1915, for example, 31 American cities established public baths (Batchelor 2002, 300). Through these reforms to housing and neighborhood design in American cities, the standard of living rose at least somewhat for urban residents. Housing became better regulated, parks more plentiful, and bathing facilities more accessible.

The City Beautiful Movement

The City Beautiful Movement represented an effort to soften the appearance of America's industrial cities. The nation's cities had grown so quickly that they sometimes lacked a coherent plan, feel, and look. In treatises such as Charles Mulford Robinson's *The Improvement of Towns and Cities* (1901), advocates of urban planning argued that cities in America could be both beautiful and efficient. City Beautiful designers tried to restore visual order and appeal to urban centers.

The movement had its beginnings in the 1890s and found a public platform through the "White City" at the 1893 World's Columbian Exposition in Chicago. Because the exposition was a temporary installation, of course, beauty was an easier goal to achieve and maintain. Furthermore, because no one lived in this ideal city, there was no poverty or hunger with which to contend, no schools to fund, and no criminal or delinquents to reform.

Designers hoping to apply City Beautiful principles to actual American cities faced a tougher challenge. Working in the public interest, they envisioned modern cities that could meet the needs of those who resided and worked there while still proving aesthetically pleasing. Architect Daniel Burnham (1846–1912), master planner for the 1893 World Columbian Exposition in Chicago, typified the City Beautiful Movement. Working in what was sometimes referred to as

Bird's-eye view of proposed city plan model for Washington, D.C., 1902. (Library of Congress)

"the Chicago Style," Burnham conducted several other high-profile projects. He prepared city plans for San Francisco (1905) and Chicago (1909) as well as designing Union Station in Washington, D.C. (1902). While the premise of the movement may have been idealistic, its optimistic approach to the future of America's cities was encouraging to all those who sought to close the gap between the rhetoric and the reality of the city as a place to pursue the American dream.

L'Enfant's Revitalized Design for a National Showcase

In 1899, as the 19th century drew to a close, optimistic Americans had forecast that in another 100 years, urban problems from grime to crime would be largely resolved. Meanwhile, Americans would have to satisfy themselves with incremental improvements to the quality of life in American cities.

The success of the temporary ideal of the "White City" on view at Chicago's World Columbian Exposition helped inspire similar plans for actual cities across America during the first decade of the 20th century. A case in point was the nation's capital, the District of Columbia. In a sense, the 1901 plan for Washington, D.C., was simply an attempt to realize more fully the original intent of the city plan developed by Pierre L'Enfant.

As the 20th century began, the hope was to revitalize the city by deepening its symbolic function, increasing its role as a heritage center, and enhancing its core of public buildings, gardens, and monuments. To accomplish this goal, a commission of celebrated architects and city planners were convened. Many of their efforts were directed toward the National Mall, a corridor of civic structures housing the nation's bounty of cultural, scientific, and artistic achievements. Classical architecture alluded to the Grecian and Roman antecedents of American democracy. The redesign aspired to provide a clear message of the nation's legitimacy and the leadership's legitimacy. Washington, D.C.'s revitalized city plan sought to convey a powerful message about both the nation's past and its future. Its point was to awe visitors as a symbolic landscape rather than to function as a model for other metropolitan cities. It did, however, fuel the City Beautiful Movement, a trend in urban planning that aimed to produce more visually pleasing and livable cities.

BIOGRAPHIES

Leon Franz Czolgosz, 1873–1901

Leon Czolgosz was born one of seven children to immigrant parents residing in Detroit, Michigan. He grew up amidst poverty and began work as a laborer at the age of 10. Czolgosz's mother died when he was just 12. The remaining family members relocated to Cleveland, where Czolgosz found work in a wire mill. When the wire workers participated in a strike to advocate for a living wage, they were fired. By some accounts, Czolgosz experienced some form of breakdown in 1898. Corporate mistreatment of employees coupled with what Czolgosz regarded as the government's failure to intervene on behalf of the workers, left him enraged. In his search for remedies, Czolgosz sought to befriend anarchists in the Cleveland area. Czolgosz was quite taken with the speeches of anarchist Emma Goldman and the deeds of anarchist Gaetano Breschi, who was implicated in the 1901 assassination of Italy's King Humbert I. Later that same year, Czolgosz implemented a similar plan in the United States. He went to Buffalo, New York, site of the Pan American Exposition. Once there, he purchased a revolver, which he used to shoot President McKinley during a visit to the exposition. Czolgosz viewed the assassination as a public expression of his commitment to the cause of everyday Americans. He was found competent to be tried, determined to be guilty of the shooting, and executed on October 29, 1901.

Sadie Frowne, ca. 1885–?

Sadie Frowne was only 13 when she immigrated to the United States from her native Poland. Since her father's death three years prior, Frowne had grown accustomed to the hard work vital to help the remaining families earn a living. She had worked as a domestic servant while still quite young. Not long after arriving in America, however, Frowne's mother succumbed to tuberculosis. Frowne began work in a sweatshop associated with the garment industry, sewing women's skirts. She vowed to continue her education when she could, in hopes of becoming more Americanized and advancing her employment options. Her obligations at the sweatshop left the teenager little time to herself, but when Frowne had sufficient energy, she would go on picnics or visit Coney Island. At night school she learned the "3R's": reading, writing, and arithmetic. With these skills, she became an avid reader. Frowne especially enjoyed escapist fiction, such as Charlotte Braeme's *A Mad Marriage*. Of this work, Frowne remarked, "You feel as if you were the poor girl yourself going to get married to a rich duke" (Katzman 1982, 56). As time passed, Frowne became a union member and sought improvements in her rights and protections as a laborer.

Herman Hollerith, 1866–1929

Born in 1866 to German immigrant parents residing in Buffalo, New York, Herman Hollerith took a circuitous route to financial success. Trained as a bookkeeper and mining engineer, Herman Hollerith also fancied himself an inventor. Of these efforts, only one—but an important one—received notice. While employed with the United States Bureau of the Census, Hollerith discovered that both population growth and the increased complexity of the census forms used had rendered analysis and report of the U.S. Census a ponderously slow process. He sought to devise a rapid but accurate way of automatically tabulating the findings of collected census data. To that end, he developed an apparatus that read and sorted cards on which hole punches encoded information. The content of census forms, once transcribed onto these keypunched cards, fed automatically into the tabulator for reading and processing. Various versions of this technology were used to calculate census findings commencing with the 1890 and 1900 collections. His statistical innovation found many applications of data processing throughout the business world, and Hollerith eventually left the Census Bureau to work a corporation later known as International Business Machines (IBM). With his contributions to the early phase of automated compu-

Herman Hollerith, pioneer in automated computation (1866–1929). (Library of Congress)

tation, Hollerith shaped and sped the methods by which Americans learned about their nation's population. He also initiated the process of computer programming.

Mary "Typhoid Mary" Mallon, 1869–1938

Mary Mallon was an Irish immigrant who arrived in the United States in 1883, while still in her teens. She began residing in Manhattan in 1901. Once there, Mallon earned her living as a cook, working within family homes in the immediate vicinity of New York City. It was in this capacity that Mary Mallon became a notorious figure. Although Mallon was not afflicted with the symptoms of typhoid, she was a healthy carrier of the illness. As she performed her kitchen duties, Mallon infected many of the household members where she was employed. As she moved from one job to the next, those eating the food she had handled fell sick. Although accounts vary, there was at least one fatality. With time, suspicions about the cook's role in their plight grew. When a health worker searching for the source of the outbreak attempted to interview Mary Mallon, she was uncooperative. Nonetheless, Mallon was quarantined for three years. When released, she used another name in order to resume her work as a cook. This time, she secured employment at a hospital, where numerous unsuspecting diners became infected, and more people succumbed to typhoid. Once again, Mallon was placed in quarantine, where she passed the rest of her natural life.

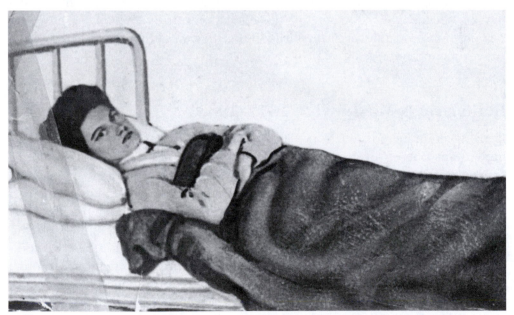

Mary Mallon, or "Typhoid Mary," the first known carrier of typhoid bacilli in the United States in New York, ca. 1900. (Bettmann/Corbis)

Although she never became ill with typhoid, an autopsy proved conclusively that she carried the bacteria associated with the disorder. Because of her reckless disregard for public health, Mallon was dubbed "Typhoid Mary." Her behavior and its consequences served to heighten urban fears about contagion as well as anxieties about immigrants.

Victoria Earle Matthews, 1861–1907

Born into slavery, Victoria Earle Matthews was the child of a union between a Georgia slave woman, Caroline Smith, and her slave master. Although her mother became a fugitive from slavery at the time of the Civil War, in time she returned to retrieve her children. They relocated to New York City in 1873, where Victoria attended public school until it became necessary for her to secure paid employment as a domestic servant. During the late 19th century, Matthews launched her career as a writer of essays and short stories. Her work appeared in various newspapers. Best known among her works was "Aunt Lindy: A Story Founded on Real Life," first published in 1893. The story was a fictional account of a slave who takes the life of her master. In addition to her publishing activities, Matthews also became active in racial uplift. She helped found the National Federation of Afro-American Women, which got its start in 1895. Under Matthews' leadership, this organization combined with the National Colored Women's League. She also helped launch the National Association of Colored Women and the White Rose Industrial Association, a group dedicated to supporting African American youth in their search for employment. During the first decade of the 20th century, this educational program evolved into a settlement house. Matthews distinguished herself as an author, lecturer, advocate for youth, and reformer.

Belle Israels Moskowitz, 1877–1933

Born Belle Lindner in New York City, this daughter of East Prussian immigrants grew up as one of seven children in the household. After attending Columbia University's Teachers college for just a year, Lindner left and became a social worker in 1900. She married an artist and bore four children. Under her married name, Belle Israels, the young reformer set out to address the moral hazard posed by the new century's dance halls. With the influx of both migrant and immigrant populations to the major cities of the United States, young people working and residing there availed themselves of new forms of recreation. Although dancing itself might not be objectionable, at such establishments as dance halls, alcohol consumption and prostitution were fairly common practices. In hopes of elevating the moral standard of the urban environment, especially for young women in America's growing cities, Israels promoted legislation for better regulation of dance halls. She went on to work on other social and economic causes, including occupational safety. In an era of widespread progressive efforts to raise the living and working conditions of Americans, Belle Israels Moskowitz proved an effective reformer of leisure for women in the nation's cities.

Hilda Satt Polacheck, 1882–1967

Arriving as an immigrant to Chicago from Poland in 1892, Hilda Satt found it necessary to leave school at age 12. Her reason for doing so was a common one during this era; she needed to find paid employment to help the family make ends meet. She entered the garment industry, which frequently employed children and youths. Satt found solace at Hull House, one of the best known of the Progressive era's settlement houses. While there, she was able to continue her education through the programs Jane Addams' facility provided to young people in her situation. Satt maintained an association with Hull House, including teaching classes there when she became an adult. Her autobiographical narrative, *I Came a Stranger: The Story of a Hull-House Girl,* provides a firsthand account of the experience of those clients served through the settlement movement. As a rare document of this kind, Polacheck's memoir provides another perspective on settlement houses than texts written by the reformers themselves, such as Jane Addams' *Twenty Years at Hull House.*

Flora Rose, 1874–1959

Flora Rose was a native of Denver, Colorado, where she grew up as a person of privilege. Longing for an experience she would find more personally gratifying than the role of a socialite, Rose decided to pursue an education in the household arts. She attended Framingham Normal School, Kansas State University, and Columbia University. Rose developed particular expertise in the field of nutrition and became an instructor in this subject. Rose emerged as an early proponent of the new discipline of home economics, approaching leaders at both Stanford University and Cornell University in 1905 about establishing programs for its study. In 1907, Rose joined the agriculture faculty at Cornell. In 1908, she partnered with Cornell colleague Martha Van Rensselaer to found a department of home economics on campus. In 1919, this program achieved autonomy as the School of Home Economics, which later became the New York State College of Home Economics. Through her career as an educator, Rose applied her knowledge of food and nutrition to a variety of reform activities, including efforts to reduce the incidence of infant mortality and to combat diseases such as tuberculosis.

Rose Schneiderman, 1882–1972

Rose Schneiderman arrived in the United States in 1890, when her family emigrated from Poland. After her father's death two years later, Schneiderman spent more than a year in an orphanage while her mother struggled to stabilize the family's financial situation. By 1895, Schneiderman had entered the paid workforce, performing the kinds of jobs many young women in New York found. These occupations included department store cashier and lining stitcher in a factory that produced caps. While so engaged, she became active in organized labor, playing a role in New York's 1905 cap-making strike. By 1908, she was elected vice president of the local branch of the New York Women's Trade Union League and later served as national president of the International Ladies' Garment Workers' Union. Schneiderman had a lengthy career as an activist, working on behalf of such issues as workplace safety and women's suffrage. She is credited with the memorable term "bread and roses," a phrase that reminded listeners that disenfranchised women need more than the means for physical survival to thrive. Her 1967 memoir, *All for One,* recounts the many chapters of her life, as immigrant, department store worker, garment worker, socialist, labor organizer, and feminist.

Anna Louise Strong, 1885–1970

Anna Louise Strong was born in Nebraska but grew up in the vicinity of Oak Park, Illinois. While residing there, Strong participated in the settlement house movement by teaching sewing classes for immigrants. In her 1931 memoir, *I Change Worlds,* Strong recalled her experience teaching classes at a Chicago settlement house:

> I was still in my early teens when I discovered the poverty of Chicago's west side: I went there to teach sewing in settlement classes. I was told that this poverty was due to ignorance; these people were not yet developed. I never thought of them as a different "class." They were just immigrants from a more backward world who had not yet attained the polished prosperity which America gave. They would go to schools (my sewing classes were such schools) and play in the city playgrounds which Chicago so magnificently built. Then they or at least their children, would be American like us. (Katz and Lehman 2001, 115)

Strong's account typifies many of the prevailing perceptions of the time. Education would conquer poverty. Americanization was the best pathway for immigrants wishing to begin a new life in the United States. Her direct experiences working with immigrants and the urban poor shifted some of her thinking in this regard. By the time she penned her autobiography, if not before, Strong found occasion to contest these assumptions. Strong went on to become a journalist in Seattle, Washington.

Anzia Yezierska, 1880–1970

Born as 1 of 10 children in a family residing near the border between Poland and Russia in 1880, Anzia Yezierska began life in poverty. When Yezierska was 15, her family relocated to New York City in hopes of finding a better life there. Yezierska's family resided in a tenement in the Lower East Side. Once in New York, Anzia Yezierska secured work in a sweatshop, in laundries, and as a maid. She attended night classes to learn English. Yezierska benefited from the settlement house movement, and for a time she lived at a residential trade school, New York's Clara de Hirsch Home for Working Girls. In a few years time, Yezierska earned a scholarship to Columbia's Teachers College. While there, she prepared for a career as a domestic science instructor. Yezierska taught elementary school from 1908 to 1913. Along the way, however, Yezierska discovered her love of creative writing. Although she married twice and bore a daughter in 1912, Yezierska made her writing the priority of her life. Many of her works, both fiction and nonfiction, depict the experience of Jewish immigrants in America's cities during the first decades of the 20th century. After a brief foray in Hollywood as a screenwriter, after one of her films was to be adapted as a silent film, Yezierska returned to New York to continue her writing. Yezierska's published works include *All I Could Never Be, Bread Givers, Red Ribbon on a White Horse, Hungry Hearts, Children of Loneliness, Salome of the Tenements,* and *The Open Cage: An Anzia Yezierska Collection.* Yezierska also wrote many book reviews, articles, essays, and short stories. Her literary efforts help represent the experience of poverty and marginality in the United States.

REFERENCES AND FURTHER READINGS

ABC-CLIO. 2002. *Teaching with Documents: Using Primary Sources from the National Archive, 1880–1929.* Santa Barbara, Calif.: ABC-CLIO.

Addams, Jane. 1909. *Spirit of Youth and the City Streets.* New York: Macmillan.

Alterman, Hyman. 1969. *Counting People: The Census in History.* New York: Harcourt, Brace and World.

American Memory Collection, Library of Congress. http://www.memory.loc.gov .ammem/browse/

Andrist, Ralph K. 1972. *American Century: One Hundred Years of Changing Life Styles in America.* New York: American Heritage Press.

Ashby, LeRoy. 2006. *With Amusement for All: A History of American Popular Culture since 1830*. Lexington: University Press of Kentucky.

Barbuto, Domenica M. 1999. *American Settlement Houses and Progressive Social Reform: An Encyclopedia of the American Social Movement*. Phoenix: Oryx Press.

Batchelor, Bob. 2002. *The 1900s: Amrican Popular Culture through History*. Westport, Conn.: Greenwood Press.

Bauman, John F., Roger Biles, and Kristin M. Szylvian, eds. 2000. *From Tenements to the Taylor Homes: In Search of an Urban Housing Policy in Twentieth-Century America*. University Park: Pennsylvania State University Press.

Beauregard, Robert A. 2006. *When America Became Suburban*. Minneapolis: University of Minnesota Press.

Bettmann, Otto L. 1974. *The Good Old Days—They Were Terrible!* New York: Random House.

Bowen, Louise DeKoven. 2002. *Growing Up with a City*. Urbana: University of Illinois Press.

Bowne, Ezra, ed. 1969. *This Fabulous Century, 1900–1910*. Alexandria, Va.: Time-Life Books.

Boyer, Paul. 1978. *Urban Masses and Moral Order in America, 1820–1920*. Cambridge, Mass.: Harvard University Press.

Byington, Margaret. 1974. *Homestead: The Households of a Mill Town*. Pittsburgh: University of Pittsburgh Press.

Carrier, Esther Jane. 1985. *Fiction in Public Libraries, 1900–1950*. Littleton, Colo.: Libraries Unlimited.

"Doing the Pan": Pan-American Exposition. http://panam1901.bfn.org/.

"Early Motion Pictures of World's Fairs and Expositions." 1997. Corrales, N.M.: New Deal Films. http://www.newdealfilms.com/compilations.html.

Edwards, Rebecca. 2006. *New Spirits: Americans in the Gilded Age, 1865–1905*. New York: Oxford University Press.

Engs, Ruth Clifford. 2000. *Clean Living Movements: American Cycles of Health Reform*. Westport, Conn.: Praeger.

Eyewitness to History. http://www.eyewitnesstohistory.com/20frm.htm.

Flanagan, Maureen A. 2007. *America Reformed: Progressives and Progressivisms, 1890s–1920*. New York: Oxford University Press.

Gauthier, Jason G. 2002. *Measuring America: The Decannial Censuses from 1790 to 2000*. Washington, DC: U.S. Census Bureau.

Gregory, Ross. 1995. *Modern America, 1914 to 1945*. New York: Facts on File.

Hayden, Dolores. 2003. *Building Suburbia: Green Fields and Urban Growth, 1820–2000*. New York: Pantheon Books.

Hayden, Dolores. 1981. *The Grand Domestic Revolution: A History of Feminist Designs for American Homes, Neighborhoods, and Cities*. Cambridge, Mass.: Harvard University Press.

Historical Census Browser (population information), University of Virginia Library. http://fisher.lib.virginia.edu/collections/stats/histcensus/.

Howard, Ronald L. 1981. *A Social History of American Family Sociology, 1865–1940*. Westport, Conn.: Greenwood Press.

Howe, Frederic Clemson. 1967. *The City: The Hope of Democracy*. Seattle: University of Washington Press.

Hoyt, Edwin Palmer. 1974. *Horatio's Boys: The Life and Works of Horatio Alger, Jr.* Radnor: Chilton Books.

Hungerford, Edward. 1913. *The Personality of American Cities*. New York: McBride, Nast and Co.

Hunter, Robert. 1912. *Poverty*. New York: Macmillan.

Husband, Julie, and Jim O'Loughlin. 2004. *Daily Life in the Industrial United States, 1870–1900*. Westport, Conn.: Greenwood Press.

Isenberg, Alison. 2004. *Downtown America: A History of the Place and the People Who Made It*. Chicago: University of Chicago Press.

Jackson, Kenneth T. 1985. *Crabgrass Frontier: The Suburbanization of the United States*. New York: Oxford University Press.

Katz, William Loren, and Laurie R. Lehman, eds. 2001. *The Cruel Years: American Voices at the Dawn of the Twentieth Century*. Boston: Beacon Press.

Katzman, David M., and William M. Tuttle Jr., eds. 1982. *Plain Folk: The Life Stories of Undistinguished Americans*. Urbana: University of Illinois Press.

Kent, Noel Jacob. 2000. *America in 1900*. Armonk, N.Y.: M. E. Sharpe.

Klein, Herbert S. 2004. *A Population History of the United States*. New York: Cambridge University Press.

Kurian, George Thomas. 2001. *Datapedia of the United States, 1790–2005: America Year by Year*. Lanham, Md.: Bernan Press.

Lane, James B. 1974. *Jacob A. Riis and the American City*. Port Washington, N.Y.: Kennikat Press.

Littman, Mark S., ed. 1998. *A Statistical Portrait of the United States: Social Conditions and Trends*. Lanham, Md.: Bernan Press.

Macleod, David. 1998. *The Age of the Child: Children in America, 1898–1920*. New York: Twayne.

Maddow, Ben. 1979. *A Sunday between Wars: The Course of American Life from 1865 to 1917.* New York: Norton.

Martin, Lowell Arthur. 1998. *Enrichment: A History of the Public Library in the United States in the Twentieth Century.* Lanham, Md.: Scarecrow Press.

Martin, Robert Sidney, ed. 1993. *Carnegie Denied: Communities Rejecting Carnegie Library Construction Grants, 1898–1925.* Westport, Conn.: Greenwood Press.

McKelvey, Blake. 1963. *Urbanization of America.* New Brunswick, N.J.: Rutgers University Press.

Mechel, Richard A. 1990. *"Save the Babies": American Public Health Reform and the Prevention of Infant Mortality, 1850–1929.* Baltimore: Johns Hopkins University Press.

Melosi, Martin, ed. 1980. *Pollution and Reform in American Cities, 1870–1930.* Austin: University of Texas Press.

Melosi, Martin. 2000. *The Sanitary City: Urban Infrastructure in America from Colonial Times to the Present.* Baltimore: Johns Hopkins University Press.

Mohl, Raymond A. 1985. *The New City: Urban America in the Industrial Age, 1860–1920.* Arlington Heights, Ill.: H. Davidson.

Nasaw, David. 1993. *Going Out: The Rise and Fall of Public Amusements.* New York: Basic Books.

National Digital Newspaper Program, National Endowment for the Humanities. www.neh.gov/projects/ndnp.html.

National Geographic, ed. 1998. *National Geographic: Eyewitness to the Twentieth Century.* Washington, DC: National Geographic Society.

Nye David E. 1990. *Electrifying America: Social Meanings of a New Technology, 1880–1940.* Cambridge, Mass.: MIT Press.

Peterson, Jon A. 2003. *The Birth of City Planning in the United States, 1840–1917.* Baltimore: Johns Hopkins University Press.

Rose, Cynthia, ed. 2004. *1900–1909.* Vol. 1 of *American Decades: Primary Sources.* Detroit: Gale.

Rosenzweig, Roy, and Elizabeth Blackmar. 1992. *The Park and the People: A History of Central Park.* Ithaca: Cornell University Press.

Rydell, Robert W. 1984. *All the World's a Fair: Visions of Empire at American International Expositions, 1876–1916.* Chicago: University of Chicago Press.

Rydell, Robert W., John E. Findling, and Kimberly D. Pelle. 2000. *Fair America: World's Fairs in the United States.* Washington, DC: Smithsonian Institution Press.

Schlereth, Thomas J. 1992. *Victorian America: Transformations in Everyday Life, 1876–1915*. New York: HarperPerennial.

Schultz, Stanley K. 1989. *Constructing Urban Culture: American Cities and City Planning, 1800–1920*. Philadelphia: Temple University Press.

Shifftlet, Crandall. 1996. *Victorian America: 1876 to 1913*. New York: Facts on File.

Shumsky, Neil Larry, eds. 1998. *Encyclopedia of Urban America: The Cities and the Suburbs*. Santa Barbara, Calif.: ABC-CLIO.

Spain, Daphne. 2001. *How Women Saved the City*. Minneapolis: University of Minnesota Press.

Stolley, Richard B., and Tony Chiu, eds. 1999. *Life: Our Centuries in Pictures*. New York: Bulfinch Press.

Thernstrom, Stephan. 1989. *A History of the American People: Since 1865*. New York: Harcourt Brace.

Time-Life Books, ed. 1998. *Dawn of the Century, 1900–1910*. Vol. I of *Our American Century*. Alexandria, Va.: Time-Life Books.

Tompkins, Vincent, ed. 1996. *American Decades: 1900–1909*. Detroit: Gale Research.

Trattner, Walter I., ed. 1986. *Biographical Dictionary of Social Welfare in America*. Westport, Conn.: Greenwood Press.

U.S. Department of Commerce, Bureau of the Census. 1989. *Historical Statistics of the United States, Colonial Times to 1970*. White Plains, N.Y.: Kraus International Publications.

Wagenknecht, Edward. 1982. *American Profile, 1900–1909*. Amherst: University of Massachusetts Press.

Wald, Lillian. 1915. *The House on Henry Street*. New York: Henry Holt and Company.

Walter, Dave. 1992. *Today Then: America's Best Minds Look 100 Years into the Future on the Occasion of the 1893 World's Columbian Exposition*. Helena, Mont.: American and World Geographic Publishing.

Ward, David. 1989. *Poverty, Ethnicity, and the American City, 1840–1925: Changing Conceptions of the Slum and the Ghetto*. New York: Cambridge University Press.

Warner, Sam Bass. 1978. *Streetcar Suburbs: The Process of Growth in Boston, 1870–1900*. Cambridge, Mass.: Harvard University Press.

Warner, Sam Bass. 1995. *The Urban Wilderness: A History of the American City*. Berkeley: University of California Press.

Wattenberg, Ben J. 1976. *Statistical History of the United States: From Colonial Times to the Present*. New York: Basic Books.

Weinberg, Arthur, and Lila Weinberg, eds. 1961. *The Muckrakers: The Era in Journalism that Moved America to Reform, the Most Significant Magazine Articles of 1902–1912*. New York: Simon and Schuster.

West, Elliott. 1996. *Growing Up in Twentieth-Century America: A History and Reference Guide*. Westport, Conn.: Greenwood Press.

Wiegand, Wayne A. 1989. *An Active Instrument for Propaganda: The American Public Library during World War I*. New York: Greenwood Press.

Wilson, Chris, and Paul Groth, ed. 2003. *Everyday America: Cultural Landscape Studies after J. B. Jackson*. Berkeley: University of California Press.

Working Women, 1800–1930 (advice literature), Harvard University Library Open Collections Program. http://ocp.hul.harvard.edu/ww/.

World's Columbian Exposition of 1893, Illinois Institute of Technology Library. http://columbus.gl.iit.edu/.

"The World's Fair and Exposition Information and Reference Guide." Earth Station 9. www.earthstation9.com/worlds_2.htm.

Wright, Russell O. 1996. *A Twentieth-Century History of United States Population*. Lanham, Md.: Scarecrow Press.

Progressivism and Social Reform

OVERVIEW

The years from 1890 to 1920 represented the height of the Progressive era, particularly in terms of social reform. The time was marked by considerable idealism in the face of the nation's problems. Rapid social and cultural changes had accompanied urbanization and industrialism, and now the country's major cities grappled with poverty, crime, disease, and inequality. In fact, according to historian Maureen Flanagan, "By 1900, a dangerous gap existed between the rich and the rest of the population. That year, 1 percent of the U.S. population owned 87 percent of the wealth, while at the other extreme ten million people (one-eighth the population) lived in abject poverty" (Flanagan 2007, 7). Such disparities of condition made for a volatile situation in the United States, and so reformers may have seen their work as simultaneously an investment in the human condition and as a means of shielding Americans from the natural consequences of a nation so deeply divided in material ways.

Progressive reformers made urban centers, as concentrations of population, a major focus of their energies. Rather than pursuing more radical solutions, such as revolution, such reformers typically sought only to repair or improve the systems in place to meet human needs in the United States. Although they recognized the plight of many Americans, particularly those of women, children, immigrants, and the urban poor, progressive reformers rarely challenged the fundamental tenets of American capitalism or democracy. Instead, they worked to promote a more humane form of capitalism and a more participatory model of democracy. They seldom if ever questioned the fundamental notion of American history as a triumphant narrative, in which social progress is the inevitable result.

TIMELINE

1900   The United States has approximately 100,000 saloons, but four states—Maine, New Hampshire, Kansas, and North Dakota— are dry.

Women in five states may vote: Idaho, Wyoming, Colorado, Utah, and Montana.

Good Housekeeping magazine launches its research lab, in which products depicted within the magazine undergo testing.

Cocaine ceases to be an ingredient in Coca-Cola.

More than 1.3 million telephones are in use in the United States.

Army surgeon Dr. Walter Reed determines that yellow fever can be linked to a mosquito-borne virus.

More than 4 billion cigarettes were produced during this year.

Lincoln Steffens becomes managing editor for *McClure's*.

Carry Nation launches her raids on America's saloons.

1901   Precursors to the 4-H clubs, the Boys' Corn Club and Girls' Home Club, begin meeting in Iowa.

Instant coffee is first developed.

Lizzie Black Kander publishes *The Settlement Cook Book*.

The National Bureau of Standards begins regulating measures and weights of consumer goods.

New York's Bedford Hills Reformatory for Women opens.

The Scholastic Aptitude Test (SAT) is administered for the first time.

Upton Sinclair establishes his own press, Sinclair Press.

The New York Times observes its 50th anniversary as a newspaper.

1902   The first soda fountain opens for business in Philadelphia, Pennsylvania.

McClure's magazine runs a series of articles on Standard Oil Company written by Ida Tarbell.

More than 200 lynchings take place in the United States during this year.

Polygraph machines are first used to detect lies.

1903   Lester Frank Ward publishes *Pure Sociology.*

Sanka, a decaffeinated coffee, debuts.

Through a donation from Joseph Pulitzer, Columbia University establishes a school of journalism.

Construction starts on the Hershey candy factory sited at Derry Church, Pennsylvania (the location is later renamed Hershey, Pennsylvania).

Dentists begin to use porcelain fillings to treat tooth decay.

New Hampshire ends 48 years of prohibition by legalizing liquor sales.

The *Ladies' Home Journal* achieves over one million paid subscriptions, becoming the first American publication to do so.

On July 4, Mother Jones heads a children's march, designed to bring attention to the industrial injuries sustained by the nation's youngest workers.

1904   Helen Keller completes her degree at Radcliffe College.

Tea packaged in steeping bags makes its first appearance on the market.

Americans consume $400 million worth of chocolate.

The banana split makes it first appearance at Strickler's Drug Store in Latrobe, Pennsylvania.

Campbell's sells 16 million cans of its condensed soups.

Lincoln Steffens' *Shame of the Cities* appears in print.

Reformers found the National Child Labor Committee.

The *Ladies' Home Journal* challenges the patent medicine industry.

1905   The nation's first pizzeria opens in New York City.

Scientist Albert Einstein arrives at the theory of relativity.

On July 9, Niagara Falls becomes the site of a meeting of civil rights activists including W. E. B. DuBois and Ida B. Wells Barnett.

A yellow fever outbreak strikes New Orleans.

1906   The Playground Association of America and the American
                     Sociological Association are founded.

                     Upton Sinclair's *The Jungle* is published.

                     Freeze-dried foodstuffs become possible through a newly
                     developed process.

                     Kellogg's Corn Flakes first become available for sale, quickly
                     becoming a popular prepared breakfast food.

                     Jell-O gelatin, which secured its trademark in 1903, enjoys
                     more than $1 million in sales.

                     President Theodore Roosevelt employs the term "muckraker"
                     to describe the era's aggressive journalists in a March 17
                     address at Washington, D.C.'s Gridiron Club.

                     The Meat Inspection Act and the Pure Food and Drug Act
                     become law (June 30).

1907   Canned tuna is introduced to the market.

                     Philanthropists establish the Russell Sage Foundation to
                     improve the nation's social and living conditions through the
                     study of the social sciences.

                     Bernarr Macfadden is arrested on obscenity charges for
                     distributing magazines that explain the means by which
                     venereal diseases are transmitted.

1908   Gen. Robert Baden-Powell founds the Girl Guides and Boy
                     Scouts.

1909   Herbert Croly's *The Promise of American Life,* a cornerstone
                     writing of the progressive movement, appears in print.

                     Sigmund Freud visits the United States to deliver lectures.

                     The FBI launches.

                     Bans in 15 states prohibit cigarette sales.

                     The Senate passes a bill on February 21 calling for truthful
                     labels on all food products.

                     The first spoken-word radio broadcast, delivered by
                     Harriot Stanton Blanch, addresses the subject of women's
                     suffrage.

                     The NAACP founded on February 12.

                     The Indian head penny is replaced by the Lincoln penny on
                     August 2.

Congress approves the imposition of a federal income tax, a ruling that resulted in the 16th Amendment in 1913.

Twenty of America's cities are committed to maintaining parks or recreational spaces for urban youth.

VICTORIANISM AND THE POLITICS OF HEALTH

During the Progressive era in the United States, various clean-living movements endeavored to improve individual health and increase the level of public health. Clean-living advocates addressed themselves to a range of reforms, including campaigns against smoking and drinking. In general, such reformers called for either abstinence or restraint in the habits that were believed injurious to human health. They also invited Americans to explore ways to enhance the general experience of health through nutrition, exercise, sexual purity, and maintenance of a wholesome living environment.

Most of all, however, through their efforts, clean-living proponents sought to educate Americans about the hazards of substance use. Some even sought to restrict the nation's legal access to items such as alcohol and tobacco. From regulation of trade to legislative bans, clean-living advocates tried to combat known medical risks. In some cases, they also attempted, through prohibition of potentially harmful substances, to combat the moral dangers they regarded as closely associated with intemperance. It was in this sense that abstinence, or at least moderation, came to represent a virtue rather than just a value in terms of both physical and spiritual health.

Smoking Habits in the United States Compromise Public Health

During the first decade of the 20th century, sales of tobacco products in the United States rose sharply. From 1900 to 1910, cigarette sales alone soared from 3,870,000,00 to 9,782,000,000 (U.S. Department of Commerce 1989, 690). Tobacco was a big business, and it was not until 1911 that the monopoly in the American cigarette industry came to an end with a Supreme Court decision declaring Dukes' American Tobacco Company in violation of the 1890 Sherman Anti-Trust Act. In these days, cigarettes could commonly be purchased by the piece rather than the pack, making Americans of all ages and incomes susceptible to the lure of tobacco.

At this point in American history, there was at least a tacit association in the public mind between smoking and immorality. The pleasure sought through smoking somehow became sexualized in the popular imagination. In that regard,

African Americans, mostly women, sorting tobacco at the T. B. Williams Tobacco Co., Richmond, Virginia, ca. 1899. (Library of Congress)

cigarettes became known as "white slavers," establishing a parallel on some level between one's enslavement to a smoking habit and the sexual slavery reputed to hold captive abducted Caucasian girls in forced prostitution. For this and other reasons, many Americans regarded smoking as an unseemly habit, particularly for the nation's females.

Although smoking was a widespread habit in the United States at the turn of the 20th century, it was still primarily one formed by the nation's men. While some American women may have smoked in private at this time, women smoking in public risked arrest. This gender imbalance in consumption makes the overall increase in the nation's tobacco consumption at the turn of the 20th century all the more remarkable.

The Antismoking Cause

In an age concerned with improving both the quantity and the quality of human life, it seemed inevitable that progressive reformers would take up the cause of exposing the harmful effects of tobacco use. Indeed, there were entire organizations dedicated to ending or reducing Americans' use of tobacco products. In

Table 5.1. U.S. Sales of Tobacco Products, 1900–1910 (in millions)

Year	Tobacco and snuff (pounds)	Cigars	Cigarettes
1900	301	5,566	3,870
1901	314	6,139	3,503
1902	348	6,232	3,647
1903	351	6,806	3,959
1904	354	6,640	4,170
1905	368	6,748	4,477
1906	391	7,148	5,502
1907	388	7,302	6,345
1908	408	6,489	6,833
1909	431	6,668	7,880
1910	447	6,810	9,782

Source: U.S. Department of Commerce, 1989, 690.

a few cases, umbrella organizations emerged that addressed a whole range of unhealthy habits, such as the Clean Life Army and the Life Extension Institute. Some groups concerned with a different substance collaborated in fighting other forms of indulgence. For instance, the Women's Christian Temperance Union with its campaign against strong drink partnered in the effort to educate the nation about the dangers of smoking. Such opponents to smoking perceived tobacco not only as a health risk in itself but also a pathway to other bad habits such as drinking and drug use. In addition, there were a few dedicated groups specifically targeting tobacco. Examples include the No-Tobacco Army, the Non-Smokers Protective League, and the Anti-Cigarette League. Members of these groups worked to reduce the nation's total use of cigars, cigarettes, pipe tobacco, and snuff. Joining them in these efforts were numerous public figures, such as Thomas Edison and Henry Ford. This support was, to some degree, merely lip service, because Ford donated little or no money to the cause and Edison himself is reputed to have smoked cigars. Corporate donors to the Anti-Cigarette League included Andrew Carnegie and the presidents of Montgomery Ward and Sears, Roebuck and Company.

At the turn of the century, smoking was increasingly regarded as an impure appetite. Tobacco's addictive qualities caused many to regard it as similar to other narcotics, a category of substances that remained largely unrestricted in the United States until the 1914 Harrison Act. There were even rumors at this time that commercially sold cigarettes were laced with opium or other drugs to increase both consumer appeal and dependency. Even those who set aside such rumors wondered whether the vice of smoking might lead to other forms of dissipation.

Since one of the particular concerns in the United States was tobacco use by youth, antismoking reformers received support from agencies such as the Parent Teacher Association (PTA), National Education Association (NEA), Salvation Army, YMCA, Boy Scouts of America, and Girl Scouts of America. Progressive reformers such as David Starr, Francis Willard, and Lucy Page Gaston spearheaded the efforts to break the nation's smoking habit.

The Struggle against the Saloon

The economic pressures of family life, combined with the physical demands of daily work life, made ordinary Americans susceptible to the allure of the barroom or saloon. Particularly in the nation's towns and cities, bars were not difficult to find. In fact, in 1900, there were some 100,000 saloons in the United States.

Especially for persons working outside the home, it was both easy and tempting on the way home from a work shift to stop in at a nearby drinking establishment. Consequently, there was always a danger that hard-earned wages originally intended to cover household expenses might instead be spent on drink.

Family bonds and budgets both struggled against the deleterious impact of drinking. Women often took extraordinary measures to ensure that their husbands stayed away from saloons or limited their time there. In part, this was an expression of concern about overindulgence in strong drink. Stops at saloons usually also meant more time spent away from the family. Furthermore, drinking at bars might be accompanied by other suspect—and costly—behaviors, such as gambling. In 1900, for example, more than 16.5 million decks of playing cards were purchased in the United States (Giordano 2003, 15). For many Americans, alcohol proved a costly, unhealthy, and unwholesome activity. An increasing number of Progressive era reformers came to perceive strong drink as a threat not only to the individual but also to the households in which they resided.

Anti-Saloon League of America

In the face of the perils posed by excessive consumption of alcohol, reformers banded together to champion the cause of temperance. This was especially the case for reformers who had witnessed the negative effects of alcohol on American families. In groups such as the Anti-Saloon League of America and the Women's Christian Temperance Union, opponents of drinking battled the bottle's harmful implications for individuals, families, and communities.

The Anti-Saloon League got its start in 1893, and the group went national in 1895. A large part of the organization's effort consisted of public education through printed information made available to American consumers. In addition, the league worked to promote legislation that would ban alcohol production.

Rather than expecting Americans to exercise restraint, League members believed it better for the organization to intervene decisively in the situation, acting in what they believed to be the public's best interest by eliminating the alcohol industry. Of course, drinkers, saloon owners and operators, and purveyors of alcoholic beverages opposed such attempts at ending or restricting trade. Nonetheless, efforts by such groups eventually led to the nation's experiment with Prohibition during the 1920s.

Carry Nation and her Saloon-Smashing Campaign

During the first decade of the 20th century in the United States, some temperance advocates, not satisfied with the slow process of changing and enforcing the nation's laws regarding the pro-

Anti-Saloon League of America poster showing a menacing hand over a little girl. (Library of Congress)

duction and sale of alcohol, decided to take the law into their own hands. Perhaps the best known of these figures was Carry A. Nation. She earned a wide reputation not only for her leadership and oratory on behalf of the temperance movement but also for her unconventional ways of expressing her conviction.

Her state of residence, Kansas, was among the first to amend the state constitution to prohibit the sale of alcoholic beverages, making that change in 1880. Because that amendment was not always fully enforced, temperance proponents sometimes felt it necessary to intervene in the operation of drinking establishments. Nation was discouraged that, 20 years after the sale and service of alcohol had been made illegal in Kansas, some saloons still defied the law.

Because she believed that saloons were immoral influences in the community, tempting patrons with strong drink, gambling, and prostitution, Nation employed a tactic that had been used by previous reformers during the 19th century: saloon smashing. From 1900 to 1910, Nation was arrested some 30 times for destroying the stock and fixtures of saloons.

Nation's hatchet became a symbol for her crusade, and she was frequently photographed with her hatchet and her Bible, both invoked as weapons in her movement. In order to fund the reform efforts, Nation sold "home defender"

What Propelled the Progressive Era Reformers?

Although American historians have devoted a great deal of attention to studying Progressivism, there is still no simple way of explaining what motivated the era's reformers. While progressive reformers shared a conviction that they could be effective in improving the human condition, their reasons for believing and doing so differed widely. These were hardly the first Americans to attempt national re-forms. Others, such as abolitionists, had joined forces to shape earlier chapters of the nation's history. Still, at the turn of the 20th century, there was a renewed energy for social and political reforms. Some American reformers saw their efforts as the logical extension of their religious convictions. Others felt that the fortunate in a society had an obligation to help those for whom life was more difficult.

While it is difficult to generalize about progressive reformers as a group, most believed that the nation's emphasis on individual rights, however important, needed to be counterbalanced with collective responsibility for social welfare and civic order. With their programs and policies, these reformers contested the no-tion that America was a place where any individual, if only willing to persist, could thrive. Although many reformers emphasized the difference between a "handout" and a "hand up," they considered federal programs and public resources neces-sary to improve the lot of disadvantaged groups such as immigrants, dependent children, the sick, and the poor.

Progressive reformers were not without their faults. It would seem easy to argue that such reformers were not merely idealistic in outlook; they were also paternalistic in practice. There is some level of arrogance inherent in the notion that a reformer can intervene in complex human problems, helping people solve prob-lems they cannot. Neither were progressive reformers free of the time's biases about race, class, gender, and ethnicity. To help their clients or constituents, pro-gressive reformers had to arrive at hypotheses about the sources of their problems. In some cases, these hypotheses were founded on the premise that social differ-ences might be construed as defects or deficiencies. However benevolent their intentions, then, progressive reformers might nonetheless reinforce stereotypes about people different from themselves.

In fact, some of these biases even divided America's progressive reformers from one another. For instance, because women in the United States still did not have the legal right to vote, they tended not to receive the recognition they were due as social reformers from their male counterparts. Similarly, among women reformers, there were fairly deep divides among white women's clubs and benevolent associations and those of African American women. Therefore, while reformers at work in the United States from 1900 to 1909 had many common methods and causes, they did not always find ways to work in concert toward those objectives.

Most of the matters receiving central attention from progressive reformers were either direct or indirect results of industrial capitalism. As historian Glenda Elizabeth Gilmore indicated in her own characterization of the Progressive era

What Propelled the Progressive Era Reformers?, Continued

reformers, "They doubted their ability to harness technology and deplored the lack of meaning in industrial work. They tried to create livable spaces, to control diseases for which they knew no cures, and to tame a sexual revolution. They worried about the breakdown of kinship networks, and the nuclear, male-headed family. . . . They did not completely solve the problems they tackled, but they began their tasks full of faith in the ability of people to remake their world. In the end, that faith in human action may be a more valuable lesson for us than any of the solutions they enacted" (Gilmore 2002, 17–18). Progressive reformers might have sought to exercise social control, yet through those efforts, they also developed services and programs that benefited a great number of Americans. Most importantly, they were steadfast in the belief that they could, and must, make a difference in the face of human inequality and suffering.

buttons, photographs of herself, and souvenir hatchet pins. Nation also published "The Smasher's Mail," a periodical issued in support of the temperance cause.

THE MEN (AND WOMEN) WITH THE MUCKRAKES: PROGRESSIVE ERA INVESTIGATIVE JOURNALISM

The muckrakers of the Progressive era were journalists and other writers who used language as their chief medium of reform. With their articles, essays, and books, America's muckrakers advocated for social and political change. Not content to report the news of the day as those in power would wish it to be communicated, muckraking journalists became known for their doggedness in research and their candor of account. Without regard to the displeasure their findings would inspire in the nation's civic and corporate leaders, such writers spoke and wrote the truth as they saw it. They worked in the public interest and were unafraid to criticize impropriety wherever they found it. They also pointed out alternatives to the problems their writings exposed and, in some cases, posited necessary steps in redressing such problems.

President Theodore Roosevelt was the first to apply the term "muckraker" to American writers in a March 17, 1906, speech delivered at the Gridiron Club in the District of Columbia. Roosevelt's use of the term was an allusion to John Bunyan's *Pilgrim's Progress* (1678). The specific reference is to a man who uses a rake to collect dirt. Roosevelt's analogy was intended to be unflattering to writers, suggesting that they are purveyors of filth for its own sake. The language of the speech suggested that muckraking writers always ran the risk of seeking out the most negative features of the national life rather than glorifying the country's strengths. Although Roosevelt's speech expressed misgivings about writers who sought only to cast the United States in an unfavorable light, he defended those who did so truthfully and responsibly. Roosevelt explained, "The men with the muckrakes are often indispensable to the well being of society; but only if they know when to stop raking the muck, and to look upward to the celestial crown above them, to the crown of worthy endeavor."

Of course, despite Roosevelt's phrase, not all these journalists were men. Prominent muckrakers at work during the years from 1900 to 1909 included Ida Tarbell, Ray Stannard Baker, Frank Norris, Jacob Riis, Frances Kellor, Samuel Hopkins Adams, and Upton Sinclair. As their writings revealed the society's imperfections and, in some cases, outright corruption, to the American reading public, the muckrakers performed a valuable service, employing the free press in order to promote an aware citizenry.

The Photography of Lewis Wickes Hine

A key figure in the history of photography in the United States, Lewis Hine helped define the documentary tradition in America. Hine did not begin taking photographs until 1903. Among his best-known images are the exterior shots of the nation's youth at work on city streets. He traveled extensively, recording the photographs and life stories of child laborers in a wide range of low-paying occupations. Although reformers sought to restrict child labor in the United States, Hine's work attested to the pervasiveness of the problem. In 1900, one in every five American children was a worker, and that figure remained fairly constant throughout the decade (West 1996, 31). Conducting his research in cities from New Haven, Connecticut, to St. Louis, Missouri, Hine brought to light a pattern of injustice that was not limited to a state or region. His journeys through the streets of America's cities revealed the heartbreaking stories of the young but thwarted lives he chronicled. Hine photographed such children and gathered their stories through interviews, which became the captions and accompanying text for his published images of American children at work. His archive provides iconic photographs of the many kinds of work even the youngest and smallest children were expected to perform. Bootblacks, newsboys, messengers, peddlers, trash pickers, breaker boys from coal mines, glass factory workers, spinners and doffers from textile mills, and other forms of juvenile laborers stare out from Hine's prints. His work dramatized the plight of child labor and inspired legislative reform. Hine went on to serve as a photographer for the National Child Labor Committee from 1907 to 1914, the American Red Cross, the Works Progress Administration, the Tennessee Valley Authority, and the National Research Project. In one especially memorable commissioned project, Hine documented the construction of the Empire State Building. Lewis Hine's memorable images, especially his iconic images of Americans at work, show both the rate and the cost of the nation's progress.

Ida Tarbell, *The History of the Standard Oil Company* (1900–1902), and *McClure*'s Magazine

Along with her male counterparts among America's muckrakers, Ida Tarbell conducted groundbreaking investigative journalism in the public interest. As she would later recount in her 1939 autobiography, *All in a Day's Work,* Tarbell's story was one of an undying commitment to educating the American people and an unusual gift for unmasking the ways power asymmetries undermined the nation's well-being.

Tarbell grew up in Pennsylvania, where her father supported the family by building oil storage tanks. He went on to a career as an oil producer. Consequently, as a girl, Tarbell witnessed the struggles of hard-working people in the oil industry. During the 19th century, for instance, the South Improvement Company had threatened the livelihoods of smaller oil concerns. The experience sensitized Tarbell to the problems of inequality and corporate greed.

Ida Tarbell pursued an education in biology and after a short stint as a science teacher embarked on a career as a writer. At first, she prepared instructional materials for home study. Tarbell subsequently became a staff writer with *McClure*'s magazine. Her most recognized work for this publication was a series of articles that began in 1902 and were collected in a 1904 book, *The History of the Standard Oil Company.* The project originated with interviews Tarbell conducted with an employee of Standard Oil, Henry Huttleson Rogers. These interviews launched a full-scale investigation into the company's practices and their implications for everyday Americans. Tarbell used plain language to make the public aware of John D. Rockefeller Sr.'s oil trust. In this way, she

Ida Tarbell's condemnation of the Standard Oil monopoly at the beginning of the 20th century placed her among the leading American muckrakers and brought her international fame as a journalist. (Library of Congress)

appealed to the American people's sense of fair play and in so doing helped change public sentiment toward both Rockefeller and Standard Oil. A few years later, a 1911 Supreme Court decision broke up the companies organized with Standard Oil, ending their near-monopoly over the industry. Through Tarbell's work, Americans learned how the power of words could topple a corporate titan.

Upton Sinclair, *The Jungle,* and the Federal Meat Inspection Act

Although a novel does not always represent with total accuracy the lived world that it portrays, if the depiction is convincing enough, it can still transform the way people understand that world. Just as Harriet Beecher Stowe's *Uncle Tom's Cabin* altered the way readers thought about slavery, Upton Sinclair's *The Jungle* shaped the way Americans understood the need for federal regulation of food processing. The novel relates the story of Lithuanian immigrants employed in the stockyards of Chicago during the late 19th century. These laborers, engaged in what Sinclair depicted as a form of wage slavery, lived grim lives of dangerous work, poverty, and deprivation.

Sinclair's central purpose in writing the book, first published in 1906, had not been to promote legislative reform. Instead, he hoped to inspire readers to rethink the human costs associated with industrial capitalism. The author, supported by a stipend provided by a socialist newspaper, set out to Chicago to write a novel that could advance the cause of the labor movement. Sinclair rented a residence near the stockyards and spent time observing the realities of the meat-packing industry. Before *The Jungle* appeared as a book, it was published in serial form by the sponsoring newspaper, *The Appeal to Reason*.

For many of the nation's readers, however, the disturbing images of unsanitary and unwholesome food processing commanded more attention than the challenges faced by the meat industry's workers. Several copies of the book found their way to President Theodore Roosevelt, including one sent by Sinclair himself. Roosevelt eventually dispatched investigators to look into the level of accuracy within Sinclair's representations of the stockyards. When the results of the investigation into the meat industry confirmed rather than contradicted the novelist's findings, pressure to improve safety and strengthen inspection requirements grew.

Because of the public reaction to *The Jungle,* new laws were developed to protect both workers and the buying public. In particular, the effort to address the unhygienic conditions suggested by Sinclair's novel culminated in passage of the Federal Meat Inspection Act in 1906. This measure authorized the Department of Agriculture to ensure that meat sold in the United States was properly handled and free of anything "unsound, unhealthful, unwholesome, or otherwise

Government Corruption and Lincoln Steffens' Shame of the Cities

Among the most politically influential American muckrakers of this era was journalist Lincoln Steffens. Born into privilege, Steffens had the opportunity to attend college, where he encountered a wide range of social and political views. As he launched his career as a writer, Steffens formed an affiliation with *McClure's* magazine, one of the periodicals most active in publishing the muckrakers. While with *McClure's*, he worked closely with other activist journalists including Ray Stannard Baker and Ida Tarbell.

Lincoln Steffens' chief area of responsibility in his magazine coverage was politics. He quickly became known for his investigations of corruption and misconduct in American government. Steffens worked with *McClure's* until 1906, publishing many articles over the years. Several collections of his pieces were released as books, including *The Shame of the Cities* and *The Struggle for Self-Government.*

As did other muckrakers, Lincoln Steffens approached his writing as a vehicle for change, and he was frequently an advocate for political reform. In *The Shame of the Cities,* Steffens took aim at the incidence of corruption in the government of the nation's urban centers. In exposing these issues to the public, Steffens placed the responsibility for addressing corruption squarely with the citizenry, asserting that "the misgovernment of the American people is misgovernment by the American people" (quoted in Stave 1972, 16). Although later in his life Steffens explored more radical solutions to such ills, during the years from 1900 to 1909, Steffens remained very much a part of the Progressive era spirit of reform.

unfit for human food." It was at approximately the same time that the nation took the initiative to promote broadly based legislation to protect the integrity of the nation's food supply, both in its production and distribution phases.

In an important sense, these outcomes only served to distress Upton Sinclair. He wanted to make people question capitalism, not merely make it a more orderly system. Sinclair had never been interested in measures that would simply increase federal spending to keep meatpacking concerns from evading laws regarding safety and cleanliness. Nonetheless, Sinclair's *The Jungle* was most influential as fuel for progressive reformers who found in it an opportunity to clean up the meat industry.

SOCIAL WELFARE AND MUNICIPAL HOUSEKEEPING

Given the rate at which the American population grew at the turn of the 20th century, it became necessary to build a network of institutions to benefit the social welfare. New and expanded facilities were needed to house populations of people in need of new or better services. In fact, total spending on social welfare through civilian public programs soared from $18 million in 1890 to $150 million in 1913 (Wattenberg 1976, 193).

The corrections system, for instance, needed to accommodate the rise in the number of incarcerated persons. While the rate of inmates within the general population grew only slightly from 1880 to 1910—from 116.9 per 100,000 to 121.2 per 100,000—the growth in the nation's total population meant that the corresponding growth size of the prison population would require, at minimum, the provision of more cells.

Even more dramatic was the growth in those social welfare institutions dedicated to the care of vulnerable populations. For example, the number of persons housed in mental hospitals and residential facilities nearly tripled during the years from 1880 to 1910. Populations served by homes and schools for mentally handicapped individuals grew even more sharply, from 4.8 per 100,000 in 1880 to 22.5 per 100,000 in 1910 (Cahalan 1987, 208–210).

Similar levels of growth occurred in a variety of benevolent institutions during the years from 1900 to 1909. As progressive reformers such as Jane Addams and Florence Kelley identified persons in need, they established settlement and other sites of reform suited to address those needs.

Prison Houses and America's Public Safety

Although American prisons had largely functioned as places of punishment for criminal acts, during the Progressive era this approach to prison management received considerable scrutiny. As with many aspects of national life and, in particular, social institutions in place during the years 1900 to 1909, prisons became an object of remark and potential site for reform.

The proposed reforms took several forms. One strand of prison reform essentially sought to apply scientific principles to prison management, rendering it more consistent and efficient as a mechanism of law's enforcement. Another element of prison reform, sometimes characterized as the medical model, approached criminal behaviors as the symptom of health defects in the perpetrators. Often, this argument became tied to the eugenics movement and its notions of the superiority of some social groups over others. Still other Progressive era reformers, while they did not share the convictions of eugenics advocates about the inherent deficiencies of certain populations of people, nonetheless viewed prisons as sites where perpetrators could be productively rehabilitated rather than simply contained for the duration of their sentences. For such reformers, the goal was not merely the maintenance of civic order but lasting behavior modification through education, therapy, or retraining for prisoners.

During the first decade of the 20th century, a corrections reform movement sought to establish separate courts and detention centers for juvenile offenders.

In this way, youth who had violated laws would not be placed in prison along-side adults where they might be victimized by adult offenders or apprenticed to them in criminal conduct. The establishment of a separately administered criminal system for juveniles also signaled a shift in the way Americans viewed youth, as a separate phase in the lifespan requiring distinctly different attention and, in the event of misconduct, redress.

Children in the Metropolis: Canaries in the Mine?

Child-Saving, the name sometimes given to the nation's children's rights movement, flourished during the years from 1900 to 1909. There was ample cause for concern about the nation's children, especially those living in cities. Observer Robert Hunter may have summed it up best when he writes of children in America's cities: "Their health is imperiled and not seldom destroyed by unsanitary homes; they are injured morally and otherwise by a *necessary* street life; their food is in many cases so poor that it will not feed their brain, and they are consequently unable to learn; they are early pressed to do a man's labor and are often ruined physically and blighted in other ways by the early and unnatural toil" (Hunter 1912, 329). Urban youth faced a toxic environment at home, in the streets, and in exploitative work settings. Often, these children lacked nutrition, supervision, or opportunities for education that might help them better their lot in life. Instead, they fended for themselves as best they could, sometimes working long days and nights or, failing that, wandering the streets while their parents worked their shifts. Even so, such youths were not assured of the nourishment needed for their growth and development. Children in American's cities seemed to suffer most from the problem of hunger. In 1908, a representative for Chicago's Board of Education deemed 5,000 youth "habitually hungry," 10,000 lacking "sufficiently nourishing food," and still others markedly "underfed" (Katz and Lehman 2001, 9). Poverty affected entire families, but it seemed to take its greatest toll on the health and prospects of children.

Child Labor

In a 1951 letter, immigrant Pauline Newman recalled the working conditions she experienced as a newcomer to the United States. She was a Lithuanian youth who came to America in 1901 at the age of 11. While still a teenager, Newman commenced paid employment. She worked in a variety of paid occupations, including hand-rolling cigarettes and making hairbrushes. In time, she landed a job at the Triangle Shirtwaist Company, where women's shirtwaists were produced. Newman worked as a "cleaner," trimming threads left behind on garments during the assembly process. With a starting weekly wage of $1.50 a week, she found herself working exceptionally long hours. She was required to report seven days a week, and was often required to work until 9 p.m. to complete her duties.

Breaker boys in Hughestown Borough, Pennsylvania, coal mine, 1911. Photo by Lewis Hine. (Library of Congress)

To evade penalties for these child labor practices, the factory operators concealed young workers in clothing cases when an inspector arrived. As Newman's story suggests, child labor in America was pervasive and likely more common than even the era's statistics would indicate. In fact, it seems probable that agricultural child labor went largely unreported because they worked in an unpaid status on family farms.

Long hours were not the only hardship facing the nations' child laborers, but exhaustion made other difficulties worse. For example, workplace injuries were common during the industrial era. Children, often posed precariously near or atop machinery, became susceptible to even greater risks of harm. As they grew weary in their work, some fell asleep on the job. In this way, many lost digits or limbs. Even those who escaped such deformities displayed the physical signs of their exploitation: fatigue, pallor, malnourishment, and stooped posture.

Match Boys, Bootblacks, and Horatio Alger Jr.

Horatio Alger Jr.'s name summons images of rags-to-riches stories in which poor boys rise to financial and social success through pluck, responsibility, and persistence. Even though Alger died at the end of the 19th century, his stories retained their popularity well into the 20th century.

As the author of more than 100 popular juvenile novels, Alger was a bestselling writer of his day. Although most of his titles remain out of print today, the message of his "strive and succeed" stories endures, and it continues to inform, however indirectly, the aspirations of many born to humble beginnings.

Alger was born in 1832 and, contrary to the heroes of his pages, enjoyed sufficient privileges in youth to enable him to attend Harvard, where he cultivated his talents as a writer. He went on to Harvard Divinity School and emerged from that study to combine his work as a preacher with freelance efforts as a fledgling writer, establishing himself as the pastor of a Unitarian church in Cape Cod.

Amidst allegations of undue familiarity with young men in his charge, Alger was forced out of the clergy but nonetheless sought a way to promote the religious ideals that first drew him to the spiritual life. Resituating himself for this purpose in New York City, Alger looked for a way to atone for his misconduct and exert a more positive influence on others.

Nineteenth-century New York afforded Alger a host of social ills to address through such good works. At that time, city children had to contend with poverty, child labor, crime, squalor, homelessness, and, in many cases, insufficient adult influence on their moral maturation. Many children were mistreated or abandoned by their parents. It was in this context that reformers established philanthropic ventures such as the Children's Aid Society, dedicated to securing the safety and affirming the worth of urban youth.

Alger traversed the streets of New York's slums, conversing with such waifs and reflecting on their future prospects. Convinced that one's outlook could do much to counteract worldly misfortune, Alger resolved to devote his work as a writer to promoting the values he felt most salutary to the salvation of these unfortunates. For adult readers, Alger hoped to expose the nature and magnitude of the problem. For young readers, he hoped to point toward its solution.

Hence, Alger's young male protagonists—newsboys, bootblacks, match boys, and the like—combine luck with industry to escape their unfortunate station as street urchins. In a sense, Alger's stories popularized the moral and ethical messages of earlier American writers such as Benjamin Franklin, whose autobiography espoused the practices of hard work and thrift. Through Alger's novels, new generations of readers watched characters resist temptation and vice and prevail through the consequences of sound values and prudent choices.

Alger's life ended in 1899, as the century that his fiction characterized drew to a close. His writing's impact, however, would extend well beyond the 19th century. In recognition of the values his works represent, enthusiasts founded the Horatio Alger Association of Distinguished Heroes in 1947 and Horatio Alger Society in 1961. These organizations celebrate the messages of Alger's fiction and applaud their realization in the lives of readers. In 1982, a commemorative

The National Child Labor Committee

Founded in 1904, the National Child Labor Committee (NCLC) was established as a private, nonprofit organization. Its mission was "promoting the rights, awareness, dignity, well-being, and education of children and youth as they relate to work and working." Members of the committee conducted this work through advocacy at the local, state, and national levels. At the very least, the NCLC hoped to help establish minimum standards for the conditions under which children labored as part of the nation's workforce. Ultimately, they hoped to end child labor in the United States. Meanwhile, they strove to secure the eight-hour day, to require workplace inspections, to set in place and enforce minimum age restrictions for employment, and to promote compulsory education for the nation's youth.

Owen R. Lovejoy aptly characterized the contributions of the committee during the years from 1904 to 1911 in a speech delivered at the 1911 annual NCLC conference. He stated, "We believe the record of the past seven years gives promise that the American people are ready to rally to the establishment of laws which, throughout the nation, shall guarantee to every child an adequate opportunity to play and grow and learn, and that we shall soon permit ourselves to be brought among those nations truly civilized that recognize in their child-life the most valuable asset among all their treasures" (Rose 2004, 411). Organizations such as the NCLC worked to protect the lives and rights of the nation's children, especially in instances where they were required to hold employment.

20-cent stamp acknowledged Alger by paying tribute to his ties to the historic urban figure of the newsboy.

Alger's influence on American culture remains pervasive, as frequent references to raising oneself "by the bootstraps" recall the struggles of his fiction's urban youth to refuse vice, take responsibility for one's own circumstance in life, and make the most of the nation's much-touted possibilities for social mobility.

Providing for Children at Risk

The harsh realities of American life during the years from 1900 to 1909 meant that many children would become orphans. While there were some informal arrangements for foster homes to house such children, they were far from sufficient to address the scale of the problem. The Children's Aid Society tried to place some of these children with new families by sending them west on "orphan trains." Notices would be posted at the trains' destinations, alerting potential adoptive parents to the arrival of the orphans. Nonetheless, in 1910, there were hundreds of thousands of children living in the nation's orphanages.

Even for those who did have parents, urban environments and the conditions characterizing them during this period in American history did not always bring out the best behavior in youth. Homeless children wandered the streets and sought opportunities, not always legal ones, where they might. Poor boys and girls might steal what they lacked. Young people whose parents worked long hours were largely unsupervised by adults and so were at risk for a whole range of misbehaviors. The problem of wayward youth was less a matter of a want of discipline than a paucity of opportunity. Still, a walk through the any major American city during the first decade of the 20th century would reveal how many children spent the bulk of their time occupying urban streets. Some found employment there selling matches, delivering messages, or distributing newspapers. The rest had to meet their needs through other means, such as picking pockets.

Given the concern for children and their involvement in criminal behavior, cities began to put in place a juvenile justice system designed to address the unique needs of minors as defendants. It was in 1899 that the first juvenile court was established in Chicago. By 1909, 20 states had similar arrangements in place. Denver municipal court judge Benjamin Barr Lindsay was a particularly staunch supporter of the juvenile court system. The era's reformatories were facilities to detain and rehabilitate wayward youth, attempting to rescue troubled children from a life of crime. The concept of juvenile delinquency began to take hold, distinguishing between adults who chose to commit crimes and youth who succumbed to bad impulses or influences.

White House Conference on the Care of Dependent Children

The 1909 White House Conference on the Care of Dependent Children was the first event of its kind in the United States. The conference, called by President Theodore Roosevelt, represented a concerted effort to take a comprehensive look at the needs of the nation's youth, particularly the disadvantaged. At this meeting, 200 concerned Americans gathered to discuss the possibilities for improving child welfare.

This conference came about because attorney James E. West, who was himself orphaned during childhood, who longed to see changes in the way the nation cared for children in crisis. His acquaintance with President Theodore Roosevelt made it possible for West to vet this concept with someone well positioned to make a difference. Although it took time, persuasion, and the assistance of high-profile reformers such as Jane Addams, Homer Folks, Florence Kelley, and Lillian Wald, West convinced Roosevelt to call for a national conference on the status of dependent children in the United States. The meeting also signaled the shift toward federal involvement in programs serving youth.

Until this time, such children had either been overlooked or served through institutional care at facilities such as residential hospitals. The January 1909 conference, however, argued that home environments were the best setting for the development of children. Family care provided a more personal experience than institutional care could offer. The attendees at the meeting favored home-based foster care for this reason. Boys and girls who were orphaned or removed from households needed the kind of attention that child welfare reformers argued could only occur in home settings. For the same reason, adoption became a preferred strategy to orphanages.

Because of meetings such as this one, the United States developed more and stronger home-based care programs for the nation's youth in need of assistance. Among these efforts were improvements in America's systems in place for children without homes or parents. In addition, the conference advocated for licensure and regular inspection of child care facilities. Such events as the 1909 White House Conference also established the groundwork for government entities such as the U.S. Children's Bureau, founded in 1912. While the Children's Bureau was not charged with reforms in child welfare, the information the Bureau gathered regarding American children helped make the case for their needs. Although the Children's Bureau was not authorized to enforce the rights of children, its data empowered others to do so. Were it not for the 1909 White House Conference on the Care of Dependent Children, many more children would have suffered neglect or languished in institutions.

Compulsory Education

For many American families, there was a double bind when it came to the fate of sons and daughters. Parents of limited means experienced a direct conflict between the need to earn a living and the desire to educate their children. If the children of a working-class family were to escape the adversity of their parents, they would need to stay in school. If the children were to continue schooling, however, the family would need the means to house and nourish them. Often, this support relied upon the earnings of school-age youth. The cycle was easy to discern but difficult to break.

Child laborers themselves articulated the seemingly intractable dilemma in their workplace protests. During a1903 protest at a textile plant in Philadelphia, for example, children displayed banners bearing slogans that demonstrated how well such youth understood their plight. With saying such as "We Want to Go to School!" and "More Schools Less Hospitals!" these young protesters made plain their wishes.

As one coal miner put it, "Our boys are not expecting automobiles and membership cards in clubs of every city, but they want their fathers to earn enough to keep them at school until they have a reasonably fair education" (Katzman

1982, 147). Many states had specified by law a minimum number of years of education for children. In 1906, these figures varied, from Maryland's requirement of four years to a minimum of nine years in such states as Illinois and Connecticut (Shifftlett 1996, 52). Statistics of actual school attendance periods are much lower, however, because there was little enforcement of these regulations. On average, American students spent a period of from three to five years attending school during this era (Edwards 2006, 53). Predictably, some populations tended to receive the least schooling, such as the urban poor or rural youth needed to work the farms.

Given the urban crowding, not even all students who attempted to enroll in the public school systems in place in American cities could be accommodated. The flow of population toward the nation's cities complicated planning by the school system. In 1905, for instance, the New York City schools turned away between 60,000 to 75,000 immigrant children (Shifftlett 1996, 128).

Persistence and graduation rates at America's public schools were quite low. Only a portion of those youth who started school were retained. According to a 1908 study of city schools, conducted by the Russell Sage Foundation, for every 1,000 children enrolling in first grade, only 263 would reach eighth grade and just 56 would reach their senior year in high school. Still fewer went on to advanced study.

Over the period from 1900 to 1909, the national percentage of children ages 5–17 enrolled in school did not improve significantly, moving from 78 percent in 1910 to just 79 percent in 1910. If compulsory education laws were to be enforced, restrictions would need to be set in place concerning child labor.

G. Stanley Hall on Adolescence

Social reformers of the Progressive era took special note of the circumstances that affected young people in the United States, presumably on the premise that the nation's youth were the most vulnerable members of the society and deserved special protection. Americans had not always regarded the young as entirely different from their parents. For many purposes, they were simply treated as small adults until they reached maturity. It was only relatively recently that the society had started to regard youth as a separate category within the population, requiring special treatment.

The concept of adolescence as a distinctive phase of human development stemmed from the research of psychologist G. Stanley Hall, who studied with William James at Harvard University. Hall went on to teach at the college level, establishing what some have termed the first psychology laboratory. Halls interests were in child development, but his special focus was on the teenage years.

G. Stanley Hall became best known for his unconventional ideas about the guidance and instruction of adolescents. Hall advocated education for young people that dealt squarely with the developmental needs of this age group. If successful, this argument would shift the emphasis of high school curricula away from college preparation, at least to some degree. Hall's ideas found dissemination through his publications, which include *Adolescence* (1904) and *Aspects of Child Life and Education* (1921).

Hall rose to prominence in his field, including being named the founding president of the American Psychological Association. Hall held this position until his death in 1924. He also established the *American Journal of Psychology,* a central venue for scholarship in the discipline. His work probed the sources of human behavior, and he was particularly instrumental in establishing the area of educational psychology.

The Playground Association of America

The Playground Association of America (PAA), founded in 1906, was part of a vast movement concerned with the living conditions of the nation's youth. The PAA received some instrumental initial funding from the Russell Sage Foundation, a nonprofit organization designed to support social science research. Reformers who participated in this movement viewed environment as a crucial influence on human character. Of particular concern was the fate of city children,

Children in the Carnegie Playground on 5th Avenue in New York City. (Library of Congress)

who frequently lacked access to the most basic public facilities of recreation. Playground activists such as Clara B. Arthur, Luther Gulick, and Joseph Lee wanted to make sure that young people had sufficient and safe places to spend their leisure.

The playground movement sought to bring policy changes at the national level, avoiding a situation where cities and localities might rule differently in the matter. Active play conducted outdoors became a priority. Parks and playgrounds would provide healthy alternatives for children who would otherwise be left to play in city streets. Green spaces with swings, teeter-totters, and other equipment designed for children became an urban priority. Members of the playground movement fought to secure legislation that would set in place and maintain public parks for America's children. By 1909, 20 of the nation's cities had pledged themselves to the care of outdoor recreation facilities for use by children. With the help of private donations, 77 of the major cities in the United States had constructed playgrounds (Flanagan 2007, 67). In 1910, the PAA launched a monthly publication, *The Playground,* to promote their cause. Playground activists believed that investments in appropriate leisure opportunities for America's youth would bring with them civic dividends. The PAA became was renamed in 1911 to reflect the group's interest in activities such as arts and crafts and athletics, becoming the Playground and Recreation Association of America.

THE FOOD SUPPLY AND TRADE

The years from 1900 to 1909 were pivotal in terms of the way Americans thought about the foods and drinks they ingested. This interest was part of the overall preoccupation with making the nation healthy, both inside and out. In an important sense, it was at this time that the United States shifted definitively from a nation of citizens producing all or most of their own food to one in which citizens purchased a significant portion of their food needs from retail stores. This was also the point in the nation's history at which consumers were at great risk as consumers of commercially prepared foods, beverages, and over-the-counter drugs. These areas of commerce were not subject to many regulations in terms of the ingredients in, handling of, packaging for, advertising about, and marketing of such consumer goods. In a reform-minded era, it seemed inevitable that this zeal would extend to a campaign for the integrity of the nation's food supply and trade.

In fact, as Americans shifted their behavior away from foods prepared at home "from scratch," they had good reason to wonder what was in the food items they purchased. During the first decade of the 20th century, for example, frankfurters were newly on the market. When the sandwich-sized sausages were dubbed "hot dogs," many consumers worried that they contained dog meat. These

Table 5.2. Food Expenditures for Working-Class Family, 1900s

The following information describes the food spending by a longshoreman's family during a typical four-week period between 1900–1909. The family consisted of two adults and eight children. The family's annual income totaled $810.00. With an average weekly food expenditure of $9.29 and an average weekly income of $15.58 to meet all expenses, the family ran a chronic budget deficit. Given the size of the family, quantities of food were also insufficient.

Food	Amount	Cost	Cost per week
Beef, veal, mutton	Not given	$5.90	$1.48
Pork, ham, bacon	Not given	3.13	.78
Fish, clams	Not given	1.93	.48
Butter	9 1/2 lbs.	2.86	.72
Cheese	Not given	.15	.04
Eggs	Not given	.15	.04
Condensed milk	24 cans	3.60	.90
Fresh milk	26 qts.	1.30	.32
Buttermilk	Not given	.05	.01
Total animal food		$19.07	$4.77
Vegetables, fresh	Not given	$1.29	$0.32
Vegetables, canned	Not given	.20	.05
Vegetables, dried	Not given	.70	.18
Potatoes	22 qts.	2.79	.70
Bread and rolls	Not given	8.09	2.02
Sugar	Not given	.90	.23
Tea	4 lbs.	1.40	.35
Coffee	Not given	.05	.01
Cereals (oatmeal, rice)	Not given	.54	.14
Cake	Not given	.63	.16
Fruit	Not given	.20	.05
Sundries	Not given	.53	.13
Flour and macaroni	Not given	.74	.18
Total vegetable food		$18.06	$4.52
Total for all food		$37.13	$9.29
Cost per person per day			.22

Source: More 1907, 222–223.

fears are satirized in cartoons of the era, such as those of artist T. A. Dorgan. While hot dogs were not made from dog meat, they likely did contain ingredients that, if known, would be less than palatable to American consumers. The same was true for many commercially marketed food products during this era.

During the first decade of the 20th century, people of the United States confronted consumer fraud and called for legislative changes that would protect

Americans from unsafe and impure retail products. In a wide range of issues related to the rights of ordinary people, both as laborers and as consumers, this reform movement flourished. The American people started to demand that they be treated equitably in the marketplace, including at the grocery store. They also adapted traditional foodways to accommodate the pace of urban life and employment outside the home. Quality, cleanliness, speed, convenience, and thrift became the watchwords of America's consumers and their advocates.

Changing Foodways

An analysis of the nation's consumer culture should examine those items Americans actually consumed in the form of food and drink. At the turn of the century, the American diet reflected some of the changes in the nation's way of life. Whereas in the past most Americans farmed or otherwise produced their own food, urbanization meant that an increasing number of the nation's residents relied on commercially grown or produced foods. Cook stoves replaced cast iron stoves, so foods could be heated with the flip of a switch.

The trend was toward convenience. With industrialization came more prepared foods, and a study of shopping habits during the years from 1900 to 1909 reveals several corresponding shifts in food habits. Bulk sales of grains and crackers started to give way to sale of packaged goods. Enhancements in packaging seals, such as the wax paper closures developed by the National Biscuit Company, helped ensure the freshness of foods sold on this basis. While home canning had long been an option for preserving food, commercially canned foods became much more common during this decade. Tinned items from condensed milk to vegetables had a shelf life and proved convenient ways to keep such foods on hand. Canned peas, in particular, were such a favorite purchase among the nation's consumers that the industry devised specialized machines for packaging them (Hooker 1981, 316–317). Commercially baked goods were becoming more common in American homes, favored because they saved kitchen time and fuel. With Jell-O gelatin available in retail groceries, jellied salads grew in both convenience and popularity.

For those who could afford it, meat and potatoes were the staples of family dining, supplemented with breads, dairy, and produce as available. The midday

Table 5.3. Soda Fountain Beverage Prices in Junction City, Kansas, ca. 1905

Item	Price in cents
Buttermilk	.05
Coffee (hot or iced)	.10
Egg drinks	.10
Grape lemonade	.15
Ice cream soda	.10
Lemon phosphate	.05
Orangeade	.05
Plain soda	.05
Root beer float	.05
Tonic water	.10

Source: Browne 1969, 136.

America's Sweet Tooth

During the years from 1900 to 1909, Americans increased their interest in and consumption of foods containing sugar. While such items were not new to the American diet, they were starting to represent a greater share of the nation's total food intake. In particular, white sugar or refined sugar became more of a staple of both American food production and consumption. Upward trends in the consumption of refined sugar continued throughout the decade of the 1900s, with candy, soda pop, cake, and other sweets providing welcome treats when the family budget could stretch enough to include them.

From chewing gum to breakfast cereal, commercially produced items containing sugar satisfied the cravings of American consumers. New sugar-laden treats marketed for the first time during these years included Nabisco's Animal Crackers and Wrigley chewing gum.

Outside the home, there were also more opportunities to gratify America's sweet tooth. In 1903, for example, the nation's first soda fountain, established as part of a drugstore's counter service opened at Philadelphia's Broad Street Pharmacy (Hooker 1981, 330–331). Sweet beverages of this kind offered a new avenue by which to market sugar to American consumers.

The growth in American sugar production was dramatic. Production of refined sugar in the United States leapt from 4,859,000 pounds in 1900 to 6,986,000 pounds in 1909 (U.S. Department of Commerce 1989, 690).

meal was often the main meal of the day, particularly on Sundays. Sweets were popular treats for those who could afford them.

While some Americans continued to can their own food products and bake their own bread, the period from 1900 to 1909 represented an era during which an increasing number of Americans came to rely upon access to commercially produced canned goods, baked items, and other store-bought foodstuffs.

Merchandising Sentiment, Marketing Mother's Day

The title of a popular song during the first decade of the 20th century captures the era's high regard for motherhood: "Next to Your Mother, Who Do You Love?" While hardly the world's first celebration of motherhood, Mother's Day has a distinctively American origin. This annual holiday, held on the second Sunday in May, honors the virtues and contributions of the nation's mothers.

At least two women are credited, separately, with originating the yearly observance. Julia Ward Howe issued her own "Mother's Day Proclamation" in 1870. Howe, a poet who framed the lyrics to "The Battle Hymn of the Republic," had

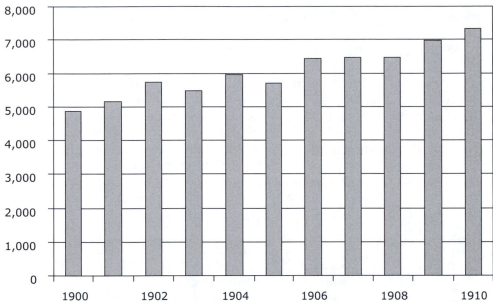

Figure 5.1 *United States Production of Refined Sugar, 1900–1910 (in millions of pounds).* Source: *U.S. Department of Commerce 1989, 690.*

a history of activism in the causes of antislavery and women's suffrage. Her proclamation of Mother's Day was a pacifist statement, issued in reaction to the Civil War and on behalf of mothers throughout the nation. The second name associated with the emergence of Mother's Day is Anna Jarvis (1864–1948), an individual who first conceived of the campaign as a way of carrying forward efforts by her mother, Sunday school teacher Anna Reese Jarvis, to establish a day of recognition for American mothers.

The first observance of Mother's Day, held on May 10, 1908, was a tribute to Jarvis's mother, who had died three years previous. The church service honored the character and accomplishments of Anna Reese Jarvis, and as a tribute to all mothers, attendees received the fallen matriarch's favorite flower, the white

Late-19th- or early-20th-century trade card for Domino Sugar. (Hulton Archive/Getty Images)

Weekly Menu for a Working-Class Family, 1900s

The following information describes the food spending by a longshoreman's family during a typical four-week period between 1900–1909. The family consisted of two adults and eight children. (This is the same family documented in the table of food expenditures, above.) Their average diet is scant in terms of the quantities of food needed to nourish a family of this size. While there is an effort to achieve food variety, the menu emphasizes animal proteins (meat and dairy) and starches. In that respect, it typifies family meal planning documented for the era, although this menu is particularly heavy in terms of consumption of bread products.

Day		Meals
Saturday	Breakfast:	Oatmeal, milk rolls
	Dinner:	Pork chops, rice
	Supper:	Codfish, bread, butter, milk
Sunday	Breakfast:	Coffee cake, bread, butter, tea
	Dinner:	Lamb, peas, potatoes, bread, and butter
	Supper:	Leftovers from dinner, bread
Monday	Breakfast:	Rolls, bacon
	Dinner:	Meat stew, bread, beer
	Supper:	Pancakes, bread, butter, tea
Tuesday	Breakfast:	Bacon, bread, and milk
	Dinner:	Meat soup, potatoes
	Supper:	Hash, bread, and butter
Wednesday	Breakfast:	Rolls, bread, and milk
	Dinner:	Bacon and beans, potatoes, bread
	Supper:	Bloaters, bread, and milk
Thursday	Breakfast:	Rolls, bread, tea, and milk
	Dinner:	Pork chops, potatoes, turnips, bread
	Supper:	Bread, butter, and tea
Friday	Breakfast:	Oatmeal, milk, bread
	Dinner:	Soup (with rice) and potatoes
	Supper:	Bread and milk

carnation. As the holiday developed, although carnations remained the standard flower of the day, white flowers were used to honor deceased mothers and red carnations were presented to living ones.

After a sustained effort, complete with a letter-writing campaign and founding of a Mother's Day International Association in 1912, Anna Jarvis succeeded in establishing a national day of recognition for American motherhood. In 1914, President Wilson endorsed, and Secretary of State William Jennings Bryan proclaimed, a national observance of Mother's Day. Since then, mothers have received greeting cards and gifts such as boxes of chocolate on this day each year.

As the story has it, Jarvis would later take vigorous exception to the subsequent commercialization of Mother's Day. Her objections reached the level of legal action against profit-oriented celebrations, and Jarvis was even arrested at a convention where carnations were being sold in conjunction with Mother's Day. It is said that the woman behind Mother's Day became so outraged by the merchandizing of the holiday that she would ultimately come to regret her involvement in its establishment. A day that had its beginnings in antiwar thinking and reverence for maternity has since become associated in the national consciousness with sentimentality too often expressed through commerce.

The Pure Food and Drug Act Movement

As early as the 1870s, the American public expressed concern about the quality of the grocery merchandise available for purchase. During the first decade of the 20th century, this grassroots movement gained momentum as the scientific evidence of the legitimate cause for that concern became unmistakable.

There were several related problems that came to the attention of the American consumer. One of these was product substitution. Disreputable producers, distributors, and retailers engaged in this fraudulent practice. In most cases, the tactic involved using look-alike packaging or sound-alike product names to fool customers into thinking they were buying their preferred items or brands.

Another major problem faced by United States consumers was additives. Without informing the buying public, producers of food incorporated such elements as artificial colors, artificial flavors, preservatives, fillers, or flavor enhancers. One especially compelling dramatization of the problem of food additives appeared at the 1904 Louisiana Purchase Exposition in St. Louis, Missouri. Pure food activists there wanted fairgoers to be fully convinced that commercial food production introduced such additives to their diets. In order to be persuasive on this point, they took retail foods containing artificial coloring, extracted the color and used it to dye fabrics such as wool and silk.

In addition, there was an issue of adulteration of ingredients in retail food products. Works such as Samuel Hopkins Adams's *The Great American Fraud* (1906), based upon his pieces for *Collier's* magazine, tried to shed light on the situation by disclosing the actual and complete contents of food and medicines on American store shelves. The results were sobering. Boric acid was found in beef, flour was found to contain chalk or sawdust as filler, and formaldehyde was present in pork and beans. Other staples were also suspect. Milk was not yet pasteurized, and was highly susceptible to bacteria growth if not kept cold enough. Additionally, the cows furnishing the milk were sometimes afflicted with undetected diseases because testing was not routinely performed. In a 1902 effort to assess milk hygiene, the New York City Health Commission determined that 52.77 percent of the milk samples tested were adulterated products (Bettmann 1974, 115).

Finally, there were problems of the cleanliness of product manufacture and handling. Dr. Harvey W. Wiley a chemist with the United States Department of Agriculture, helped lead the way in resolving these issues in favor of the consumer. Wiley, the man the *New York Sun* had named the "chief janitor and policeman of the people's insides," worked with his "poison squad," as his team of volunteers came to be known, to take tainted products off the market (Sullivan and Rather 1996, 235). Food inspection and regulation policies tightened, and the American public enjoyed better protections against consumer fraud.

As part of the larger movement for public health reforms, the pure food movement did not begin and end with Upton Sinclair's publication of *The Jungle*. Sinclair's main concern had not been with cleaning up the meat industry, but during the first decade of the 20th century, the public was ready to assert their rights as consumers. Sinclair himself may have put it best when discussing the impact of *The Jungle* on the American public: "I aimed at the public's heart, and by accident I hit it in the stomach" (Batchelor 2002, 281).

The 1906 Pure Food and Drug Act was a landmark piece of legislation for reformers concerned with drug purity and food hygiene in the United States. This public health measure was clear in "preventing the manufacture, sale, or transportation of adulterated or misbranded or poisonous or deleterious foods, drugs, medicines, and liquors, and for regulating traffic therein." This act enlisted the services of the U.S. departments of Agriculture, Commerce, and the Treasury to conduct federal inspections of American foods, beverages, and drugs to ensure that they remained unadulterated and accurately labeled.

The Automat Arrives

There is a scene in Charlie Chaplin's film *Modern Times* in which his signature character, the Little Tramp, works as a laborer at a factory. One day while on duty, he is required to test an automatic feeding machine under consideration by the factory's owner/manager. This new-fangled device applies the principle of the assembly line to meeting human needs. True to Chaplin's comic reputation, high jinks ensue as the machine malfunctions and ultimately must be abandoned as a source of efficiency or economy. Of course, the factory owner is less concerned with nourishing his workers than reducing the time workers spend away from their tasks. While Chaplin's scene is a parody of corporate greed and labor's exploitation by management, the American public was curious about what automation might mean for everyday life. In a time infatuated with technology and an era when the public was increasingly sensitive to food hygiene, the automatic restaurant seemed to be a perfect innovation. The gleam of automat glass and chrome quickly attracted clientele with its sleek appearance and the suggestion of cleanliness.

American automats got their start in Philadelphia in 1902, turning up in other cities in subsequent years. Joseph Horn and Frank Hardart developed the automat concept. The automat, with its windowed walls of vending, involved a new restaurant configuration. Cold and room-temperature foods were dispensed using vending apparatus installed in the walls of the restaurant. Staff working behind the scenes restocked these items as they were sold. Warm and hot foods were served buffet style from steam tables. All selections were sold à la carte. Customers entering the automat exchanged regular currency for their equivalent in automat tokens. Once that was done, diners assembled their preferred meal or snack and seated themselves at whatever freshly wiped table they wished.

With money tight for most Americans, the prices at the automat were relatively affordable. In addition, the self-service design of the automat permitted people to dine out without the added expense of a gratuity. In fact, automats were popular with the cost-conscious Americans of every economic class. Horn and Hardart's automats were estimated to have served 800,000 meals a day (Cohen 1986, 50). In time, Horn and Hardart extended their business to include locations in New York as well as Philadelphia.

In addition to thrift, patrons dining at such establishments realized several additional benefits. With the quickening pace of urban life, the automat was a fast alternative to table service at traditional restaurants. At the automat, patrons could find a wide range of food choices. The automat kept food and drink secure until the customer was ready to consume them. Customers could see the food before they decided to buy it, and finicky ones could select desired items singly rather than accepting fully plated meal combinations. Automats helped customers transcend language barriers because diners did not have to read menus or place orders with wait staff. These new-style cafeterias were also a welcome development for customers such as artists and performers, whose irregular schedules often made it difficult to dine at conventional restaurants with fixed meal times. They could eat and run or, if they preferred, linger as long as they liked. Some customers socialized routinely there.

Automats provided a humble version of the dining out experience with fewer risks and uncertainties than might be involved with food acquired from street vendors. That is, the "waiterless restaurant," as the automat was dubbed, was something of a misnomer because each automat had significant staffing needs to stock foods, exchange money, bus tables, and clean the restaurant. Horn and Hardart maintained high standards of food service and cleanliness, as regulated with an operator's manual in use at all of the pair's automats. According to historical accounts, they also sampled food items at their automats daily to ensure taste and quality control. Customers voted with their feet—and their tokens—establishing the American automat as an urban institution for decades to come.

EMERGING CONSUMER CONSCIOUSNESS

From 1900 to 1909, a tremendous variety of consumer goods appeared for the first time on the market in the United States. In addition to the products customers were used to seeing on store shelves, they had new choices to consider as purchases. Swift's bacon, Schlitz beer, Sanka decaffeinated coffee, and Lipton's Tea are just a few of the new brand-name items newly available to American consumers during this era. In addition, many familiar consumer products began to enjoy increased sales at this time. For instance, trends in food preparation meant that canned goods and commercially baked goods were on the rise. Disposable goods, such as Hugh Moore's Dixie Cups, entered popular use at the time. Other merchandise, though not entirely new to the American consumer, arrived in more convenient forms. For example, Lux marketed flaked soap, which offered a handy alternative to bar soap for many household cleaning tasks. At the turn of the 20th century, consumers were interested in finding ways to make their lives more efficient, economical, and easy. They also wanted assurances that the items they purchased would be fresh, wholesome, and of high quality. Companies producing and marketing products during this period were happy to oblige, flooding the market with merchandise that promised whatever it might take to convince customers to buy. Thus, Americans were required to become more discerning shoppers or suffer the consequences. It was during this period, energized as it was by the Progressive era's zeal for reform, that American customers organized to demand safer merchandise, more responsible marketing, and respect for the buying public. Middle-class consumers, in particular, formed organizations such as the General Federation of Women's Clubs' "Kitchen Front" and the National Consumers League to protect and exercise the rights of customers in commerce.

Advertising Boom

In 1900, sellers of goods and services in the United States spent $95 million on advertising, compared with $95,000 in 1865 (Schlereth 1992, 157). A share of this advertising content was informational and helped consumers understand the items available for purchase. The majority of the cost of and effort devoted to advertising at this point, however, was designed not to educate the consumer but rather to persuade the public that they needed new items and that they should purchase specific brands, deal with particular purveyors, or contract with a given service provider.

Part of the rise of consumer culture in America involved the introduction of goods and services not previously available to the nation's public. By 1900, for example, American mothers of infants routinely purchased specialty items for babies, including powders, shampoos, lotions, and oils. Adults started to incorporate new toiletries of their own, including toothpaste and deodorant. In addition, the advertising industry faced the larger challenge of selling expensive products that everyone could live—better and longer—without, such as alcohol and tobacco. As G. S. Dickerman, a contributor to a 1913 issue of *Atlantic Monthly*, posed the temptation of such vices as drinking and smoking, "Do we understand the extent to which these artificial appetites are being cultivated and what this means? . . . The prices of flour and meat may advance, but somehow the cost of whiskey and tobacco is kept within the reach of even the most poor. Cigarettes to-day do not cost more than half what they did ten years ago, and three or four times as many of them are used" (Nash 1970, 29). This capacity of sellers to entice Americans to buy unnecessary products only served to underscore the need for consumer awareness.

With national marketing under way in the United States, advertisers faced greater possibilities, but they also encountered impediments, such as increased competition. Market positioning and product differentiation become more important for a product to sell well. At this time, there was also a problem of product substitutions, situations in which grocers or merchants offered inferior alternative goods in place of known brands and preferred products. Some unscrupulous store operators would replace butter with oleo, cut bulk goods with lesser ingredients or filler, or substitute premium merchandise with goods of inferior quality. For that reason, brand names and brand advertising increased during this era, and customers were urged to ask for items by name. Instead of soap they were directed to ask the grocer for Ivory Soap; in place of corn cereal they were instructed to demand Kellogg's Toasted Corn Flakes. Company trademark statutes helped protect consumers and companies that produced "the genuine article" from look-alike packaging or sound-alike product names designed to fool customers. This era also marked the emergence of target marketing, singling out those prospective customers most likely to become steady customers. Merchandising using characters from popular culture, such as the cigarettes linked to *New York World* comic, "Yellow Kid" that started to become common (Batchelor 2002, 159).

"Plain Facts for Old and Young": Dr. John Henry Kellogg on Health and Hygiene

Although his family name became linked inextricably to the breakfast cereal business, John Kellogg was not a conventional businessman. For one thing, he attended New York University Medical College, graduating with a medical degree in 1875. After completing his studies, Kellogg worked at a Battle Creek, Michigan, sanitarium. He taught classes on such topics as healthy food practices. Kellogg had many enthusiasms regarding healthful living, including exercise, sunlight, and a vegetarian diet.

In 1897, he joined his brother in forming a breakfast cereal company, the Sanitas Food Company. They advocated whole grains as an alternative to the traditional heavy morning meals of starch and animal protein that were favored during this era among those who could afford them. John Kellogg and his brother eventually ceased their business partnership, and so it was not John but Will Kellogg who sold toasted corn flakes and established the Kellogg Company.

John Kellogg remained a person of strong ideas about reform and continued his efforts to promote American health. In general, his beliefs about physical vitality involved personal restraint. He advised people to avoid stimulants of all kinds and to practice moderation even in terms of eating. Kellogg also devoted some of his energies to promoting the benefits of soy-based products and other organic foods. He also lent his voice in support to other causes, such as foster care, adoption, and the campaign against tobacco use in America.

The Problem with Home Remedies

Just as Americans were concerned with the ways in which foods were regulated, they became interested in knowing what over-the-counter drugs they were purchasing. Both by custom and necessity, most American families made sparing trips to see physicians. Given the tight budgets of American families during the early 20th century, doctor's visits were reserved for those conditions that did not respond to home remedies. Whenever possible, they treated injuries and illnesses themselves. This was particularly the case for rural Americans for whom visits to doctors were longer trips.

In accomplishing home treatment, Americans had access to an impressive array of home remedies. A shopper during the first decade of the 20th century could choose from an array of elixirs, syrups, tonics, and pills. These retail products, available without prescription, were known as patent medicines. With grand claims, these medicines promised increased or restored health. Many were marketed for multiple purposes, as remedies for a wide range of ailments. According to Mark Sullivan and Dan Rather, Americans purchased more than $59.6 million worth of patent medicines in 1900 alone. (Sullivan and Rather 1996, 230).

Because there were few regulations in place regarding the ingredients of these nostrums or the credibility of advertising claims made for these products, patent drug companies did largely as they pleased. Packages did not bear labels disclosing ingredients or providing safety warnings. Patent medicines might contain dangerous substances, such as cocaine, heroin, morphine, or opium. Alcohol content was also high in many of these products, with some consisting of as much as 80 percent alcohol. At this time, even regular beverages might incorporate unexpected stimulants. During the second half of the 19th century, for example, Coca-Cola had made no secret of the fact that their popular drink contained cocaine. Pharmacist John Pemberton had developed the formula, and it was not until 1900 that the substance was removed from Coca-Cola.

Many patent medicines were sold using advertising, with magazine ads being one of the most extensively used techniques for marketing patent medicines. In fact, one of the categories of consumer products most routinely advertised in American periodicals of this time was patent medicine. Advertisements featuring product endorsements from doctors proved persuasive to mothers trying to treat illnesses and injuries at home.

Edward Bok Takes on the Patent Medicine Industry

Since traditional gender roles suggested that women preside over the use of home cures, popular magazines for women were a favorite venue for home remedy advertisements. Take, for example, the *Ladies' Home Journal,* founded in 1883. The magazine catered to a readership of middle-class American women. In the pages of the *Ladies' Home Journal,* readers could find selections from prominent writers such as William Dean Howells, Mark Twain, and Sarah Orne Jewett. By 1902, this magazine's circulation reached the million mark (Batchelor 2002, 145).

At that point, the editor of the *Ladies' Home Journal* was Edward William Bok. Bok had come to Brooklyn from the Netherlands at the age of seven. During the 1870s, Bok held jobs with a bakery and a telegraph company. He then worked as a stenographer before becoming editor of *The Brooklyn Magazine* in 1884. Bok landed the editorship of the *Ladies' Home Journal* in 1889. Since magazines relied on both their subscriptions and their sponsors to cover the costs of publishing, Bok dedicated himself to thinking creatively about the role advertising could play in his venture.

In the years from 1900 to 1908, a national market for consumer goods, rather than a local or regional one, was taking shape. Advertisers viewed magazines as a sound investment in the sales of their products. The *Ladies' Home Journal* was a prime example of the venue sought by marketers of consumer merchandise.

In 1892, just a few years into his tenure as editor, of the *Ladies' Home Journal,* Bok made the decision to refuse to carry advertisements for patent medicines in the pages of his magazine. He took vigorous exception to the industry's practices and did not want to be complicit in the harm such products might cause his readers. For instance, long after the originator of Lydia Pinkham's Compound died, the company urged readers of their ads to write letters to Pinkham seeking help with their health questions. Those who posted such letters received replies bearing what purported to be the signature of Lydia Pinkham. Such deceptive practices offended Bok's sense of proper conduct in business.

The Rexall Company and the Chain Drugstore

In an era during which department stores and chain stores posed serious threats to the remaining "mom and pop" commercial establishments in the United States, small store owners had to become more resourceful about how they approached their businesses. In 1902, an enterprising individual named Louis Liggett spearheaded an effort to preserve the nation's small drug stores and keep them financially viable. He convinced each of 40 independent drugstore operators to invest $4,000 in a joint venture. Together, they formed a retailers' cooperative, known under the shared name of United Drug Stores. At drugstores operated by members of the cooperative, patrons could purchase the Rexall brand of products. A reliable brand was especially important to customers during a time in American history when the customer could not always be assured of the ingredients of a product or of their purity. Later on, the drugstore cooperative offered franchise opportunities. In this way, participating drugstore operators not only had the opportunity to sell Rexall merchandise but they could also establish stores using the licensed Rexall name and logo (Schlereth 1992, 153).

His act of conscience did not stop there. In 1904, Bok was determined to expose the risks of patent medicines to the American public. Through a partnership with the Women's Christian Temperance Union (WCTU), Bok revealed the ingredients present in some of these home remedies. The antipatent campaign had an effect on the way Americans viewed nostrums. By 1908, for example, patent medicines no longer appeared in the Sears and Roebuck catalog. In addition, legislation passed during the first decade of the 20th century would place more strictures on commercially produced drugs and treatments.

Truth in Trade? The Good Housekeeping Institute

Like Bok's *Ladies' Home Journal, Good Housekeeping* was a periodical directed to America's women. As its title suggests, during the period from 1900 to 1909, the magazine typically offered articles on nutrition, cooking, health, and family life.

At the turn of the 20th century, American consumers had growing doubts about retail merchandise and about the advertising claims made in its promotion. Because magazine advertising was widely perceived as an effective strategy for marketing consumer goods, the era's magazine readers often wondered whether they could believe the advertising copy appearing in popular periodicals. Therefore, although *Good Housekeeping* magazine was founded in 1885, one of its most distinctive features, the Good Housekeeping Institute, debuted in 1900.

Bush's drug store, Benton, Arkansas, between 1900–1920. (Library of Congress)

As concerns about the integrity of products advertised in the magazine's pages grew, *Good Housekeeping*'s publishers determined to take the matter into their own hands by committing time and resources to the cause. The Good Housekeeping Institute was the first laboratory of its kind, operating as a test site at which researchers employed by the magazine tested the products advertised in *Good Housekeeping*. At this facility, first dubbed an "Experiment Station," representatives of the magazine assessed a variety of products for fitness and for the credibility of their promotional claims. By verifying the quality of the items marketed in the pages of their magazine, *Good Housekeeping* demonstrated a commitment to their readers. The institute was also the origin of the Good Housekeeping Seal of Approval, an emblem of the magazine's endorsement of a consumer product. In addition, *Good Housekeeping* implemented a policy guaranteeing products bearing their institute's seal. For a period of two years, the magazine would refund the cost or replace the product if it fell short of the consumer's expectations. In addition to providing a service to readers, the institute helped differentiate its brand from other American magazines for women.

The Good Housekeeping Institute represented an important development in the era's trends toward educating consumers and holding sellers accountable for their merchandise quality and marketing conduct. In particular, *Good Housekeeping* magazine became involved with the nation's campaign for pure food, which landed an important victory with the 1906 passage of the Pure Food and Drug Act. As a reflection of the emerging consumers' movement and a step toward corporate responsibility, the Good Housekeeping Institute helped to change the climate of expectation for America's buyers and sellers alike.

National Consumers' League

The years from 1900 to 1909 were a time during when consumers joined forces to protect themselves and their interests. One such group, the National Consumers' League (NCL), founded in 1899, came to prominence during the first decade of the 20th century. The NCL grew from 30 leagues in 1901 to 64 leagues in 1906, distributed among 20 states (Flanagan 2007, 183). This organization's goal was to advance legislation that added to the rights and bettered the condition of ordinary Americans. Their agenda included instituting a minimum wage, regulating child labor, and inspection labeling for American-made products. In addition to promoting legislation, the National Consumers' League sought to enforce those laws, investigate injustice, and educate the public about their findings. Among the techniques the NCL used to achieve leverage was the consumer boycott. Groups such as this one helped to bring changes that individual consumer decisions could not. They also signaled a shift in the way Americans thought about their own agency. Consumer groups, like other reform movements of the Progressive era in the United States, demonstrated that ordinary people could stand together and that by doing so they could stand up against social problems such as corruption, corporate greed, and threats to the public health.

BIOGRAPHIES

Nannie Helen Burroughs, 1883–1961

Nannie Helen Burroughs was born in 1883 in Orange, Virginia. Her mother worked as a domestic servant, as did many African American women of the time. After her mother was widowed, the family relocated to the District of Columbia. As she grew up, Burroughs endeavored to get the best possible education. Her high school studies emphasized domestic science and business. Burroughs planned to become a domestic science teacher but was thwarted repeatedly in that goal when the D.C. Board of Education declined to hire her. These refusals would in time lead her to open her own school.

On October 18, 1909, she opened and became the first president of the National Trade and Professional School for Women and Girls, located in Lincoln Heights. This institution taught the "3 Bs," which Burroughs regarded as the basics necessary to establish students as exemplars of Christian womanhood: Bible, bath, and broom. The curriculum combined traditional education in academic subjects with vocational education in subjects such as social work or domestic science. In addition, all students enrolled at the school took a course in African American history.

Another educational venture Burroughs promoted was the Women's Industrial Club, a residential facility for African American women who wished to learn household management. In addition to her work as an educator, Burroughs was also a writer, editor, and leader in the Baptist faith. She was a strong advocate for educational and occupational opportunities for African American women.

Nannie Helen Burroughs, educator, writer, and religious leader (1883–1961). (Library of Congress)

Katharine Bement Davis, 1860–1935

Born in Buffalo, New York, Katharine Bement Davis taught school until she had the means to complete her Vassar degree. Davis later became involved in social work, including a stint working at a Philadelphia settlement house. In 1900, she received a University of Chicago Ph.D. in political economy. During the years from 1901 to 1914, Davis served as the superintendent of a women's reformatory in Bedford Hills, New York. She went on to become the first female corrections commissioner for New York City.

With her education and her background in social work, Davis implemented numerous penal reforms during her career. Numerous of these programs were based on Davis' belief in the tenets of eugenics, a theory that generalizes about human differences across population groups. For example, Davis argued that prisoners deemed to possess mental defects should be held in prison indefinitely, and if released, they should be prevented from procreating. She also established a prison hospital to address problem prisoners and study pathological ones. Such notions about the inferiority of whole categories of people typified the medical model of prison reform during the Progressive era. Diagnosis of one or more conditions or deficiencies was used as a rationale for detaining and, in some cases, sterilizing, inmates.

Katharine Bement Davis was an influential prison reformer, social worker, and writer during the late 19th and early 20th centuries. (Library of Congress)

Elizabeth Gurley Flynn, 1890–1964

Elizabeth Flynn was a native of New Hampshire but relocated to New York with her family in 1900. While just a teenager, Flynn launched a lifelong career as an activist, writer, and orator. Her decision to be outspoken at this early age resulted in her expulsion from high school.

Flynn was not dissuaded, however, and in 1907, she became a labor organizer for the Industrial Workers of the World (IWW). She lent her voice to a wide range of causes including birth control, women's rights, the labor movement, and gender equality within trade unions. She also raised funds for legal defense in key cases of suspected political imprisonment, such as the trial of Sacco and Vanzetti. Flynn helped found the American Civil Liberties Union (ACLU). She also served for a time on the organization's national board.

Over time, Flynn's social and political convictions only became stronger. She came to be well known for her association with leftist and radical politics. Flynn eventually became active in the American Communist Party. While her politics made her unpopular with some, others viewed her as a champion of the nation's downtrodden. Folk hero Joe Hill's song "Rebel Girl" was dedicated to Flynn as a tribute to her contributions to radical causes.

Lucy Page Gaston, 1860–1924

Lucy Page Gaston was born to Ohio parents with long-standing commitments to reform, particularly as pertains to the causes of abolition and temperance. As she matured, Gaston joined these efforts to improve society, including joining her mother as a member of the Women's Christian Temperance Union (WCTU). Typically, this organization argued for abstinence from alcohol rather than moderation in its consumption. The membership of the WCTU also tended to perceive direct connections among substance uses, such as drinking and smoking, and it educated consumers accordingly.

With time, Gaston turned her attentions as a reformer chiefly to the anti-smoking cause, playing a similar role in that regard to the role Carry Nation served in the temperance movement. Gaston founded the Anti-Cigarette League, an organization that boasted 300,000 members by 1901 (Tate 1999, 39). Despite the specificity of its name, this organization opposed all forms of tobacco use. The group name's emphasis on cigarettes was largely the result of a dramatic and recent growth in this segment of the tobacco industry at the point the league was founded. Gaston was especially distressed to see America's minors adopting the smoking habit, and she led the fight against such tobacco consumption by youth one child at a time. Armed with print materials pointing out the hazards of smoking, Gaston urged the nation's boys and girls to take the Clean Life Pledge, meaning that they would promise to stop smoking if they had tried tobacco or to avoid tobacco if they had not.

Alice Lakey, 1857–1935

Born in Ohio on October 14, 1857, Alice Lakey spent her childhood in Chicago. As an adult, she resided in a community in New Jersey. While there, Lakey prompted a host of reforms in terms of new municipal services and programs. She helped to improve the quality of daily life by establishing new sanitation standards and provision of senior housing. Her best-known role as a reformer, however, was within the food purity movement. In 1903, Lakey became a sponsor of a piece of legislation that protected consumers from impurities in grocery and pharmacy products. She spearheaded a letter-writing campaign that secured the support of President Theodore Roosevelt; it also resulted in passage of the Pure Food and Drug Act in 1906. She also let her advocacy to the campaign for standards in weights and measures in consumer merchandise. For her efforts as a progressive reformer, Lakey was recognized by *Who's Who,* the first woman to be so honored.

Susan La Flesche Picotte, 1865–1915

Susan La Flesche Picotte was born the daughter of Chief Joseph La Flesche (Iron Eyes) and Mary La Flesche (One Woman) in 1865, and she grew up on the

Omaha reservation in Nebraska. While a young girl, she witnessed the death of an Indian woman when a white physician refused her medical treatment. This experience created an awareness of social injustice that motivated Picotte to pursue a career in medicine. She attended Hampton Institute and the Women's Medical College of Pennsylvania. In 1889, Picotte earned the distinction of being the first Native American woman physician. Picotte went on to become what she termed a "medical missionary" in Nebraska, ministering to the needs of the residential population on the Omaha reservation from 1889–1893.

By the end of the 19th century, Picotte's general health was deteriorating. She began a transition to private medical practice in Bancroft, Nebraska. Picotte did not stray from her commitment to protecting the health of residents of the Omaha reservation. She traveled to the District of Columbia in 1906, where she and her delegation called for a ban on alcoholic beverages on the reservation. Furthermore, in 1907, she wrote a letter to the Commissioner of Indian Affairs, Francis E. Leupp, imploring him to assist her in the efforts to combat disease on the Omaha reservation. Among the problems Picotte highlighted in her appeal to Leupp was the prevalence of tuberculosis, which she described as a "white-plague." Susan La Flesche Picotte culminated her career as both a doctor and an advocate by establishing a reservation hospital in Walthill, Nebraska in 1913.

James E. West, 1876–1948

Orphaned in 1882, James E. West was subsequently placed in the District of Columbia's Washington City Orphan Home. The following year, West contracted tuberculosis. By 1885, he suffered a disability that limited his mobility. So began an arduous childhood. Still, West persevered and accomplished more than others expected of him. After graduating with honors from high school in 1895, West assisted the general secretary of the YMCA. Meanwhile, he attended National Law School, earning a master's degree in 1901, and then entering the District of Columbia bar.

As a relatively new attorney, West helped establish the nation's juvenile courts. He also became active in a variety of groups formed to benefit America's youth, including the Boys' Brigade, National Child Rescue League, and Playground Association of America. West was also the inspiration behind President Theodore Roosevelt's call for the 1909 White House Conference on Dependent Children. As an orphan himself, West knew first-hand the importance of making available quality programs and services for American children in need of assistance. West went on to develop a lifelong affiliation with the newly formed Boy Scouts of America (BSA), an organization dedicated to promoting the moral and spiritual health of the nation's young people. West's influence on scouting included additions to the Scout Law and the BSA constitution. He extended this impact through involvement in the international scouting movement.

REFERENCES AND FURTHER READINGS

American Memory Collection, Library of Congress. http://www.memory.loc.gov.

Anti-Saloon League Museum. http://www.wpl.lib.oh.us/AntiSaloon/.

Ayala, César J. 1999. *American Sugar Kingdom: The Plantation Economy of the Spanish Caribbean, 1898–1934*. Chapel Hill: University of North Carolina Press.

Barbuto, Domenica M. 1999. *American Settlement Houses and Progressive Social Reform: An Encyclopedia of the American Settlement Movement*. Phoenix: Oryx Press.

Batchelor, Bob. 2002. *The 1900s: American Popular Culture through History*. Westport, Conn.: Greenwood Press.

Bell, David, and Joanne Hollows. 2006. *Historicizing Lifestyle: Mediating Taste, Consumption and Identity from the 1900s to 1970s*. Burlington, Vt.: Ashgate.

Bettmann, Otto L. 1974. *The Good Old Days—They Were Terrible!* New York: Random House.

Bowne, Ezra, ed. 1969. *This Fabulous Century, 1900–1910*. Alexandria, Va.: Time-Life Books.

Brobeck, Stephen, ed. 1997. *Encyclopedia of the Consumer Movement*. Santa Barbara, Calif.: ABC-CLIO.

Buenker, John D., and Edward R. Kantowicz, eds. 1988. *Historical Dictionary of the Progressive Era, 1890–1922*. Westport, Conn.: Greenwood Press.

Buenker, John D., and Joseph Buenker, eds. 2005. *Encyclopedia of the Gilded Age and Progressive Era*. Armonk, N.Y.: Sharpe Reference.

Cahalan, Margaret Werner. 1987. *Historical Corrections Statistics in the United States, 1850–1984*. Washington, DC: U.S. Department of Justice/Bureau of Justice Statistics.

Campbell, Ballard C., ed. 2000. *The Human Tradition in the Gilded Age and Progressive Era*. Wilmington, Del.: SR Books.

Cavallo, Dominick. 1981. *Muscles and Morals: Organized Playgrounds and Urban Reform, 1880–1920*. Philadelphia: University of Pennsylvania Press.

Cohen, Daniel. 1986. "For Food Both Hot and Bold, Put Your Nickels in the Slot," *Smithsonian* 16 (January): 50–60.

Cohn, David Lewis. 1940. *The Good Old Days: A History of American Morals and Manners as Seen through the Sears, Roebuck Catalogs, 1905 to the Present*. New York: Simon and Schuster.

Cohn, Jan. 1989. *Creating America: George Horace Lorimer and the* Saturday Evening Post. Pittsburgh: University of Pittsburgh Press.

Crichton, Judy. 1998. *America 1900: The Sweeping Story of a Pivotal Year in the Life of the Nation.* New York: Henry Holt.

Cross, Gary S. 1993. *Time and Money: The Making of Consumer Culture.* New York: Routledge.

D'Antonio, Michael. 2006. *Hershey: Milton S. Hershey's Extraordinary Life of Wealth, Empire, and Utopian Dreams.* New York: Simon and Schuster.

Diehl, Lorraine B., and Marianne Hardart. 2002. *The Automat.* New York: Clarkson Potter/Publishers.

Diggins, John Patrick. 1999. *Thorstein Veblen: Theorist of the Leisure Class.* Princeton: Princeton University Press.

Edwards, Rebecca. 2006. *New Spirits: Americans in the Gilded Age, 1865–1905.* New York: Oxford University Press.

Engs, Ruth Clifford. 2000. *Clean Living Movements: American Cycles of Health Reform.* Westport, Conn.: Praeger.

Eyewitness to History. http://www.eyewitnesstohistory.com/20frm.htm.

Flanagan, Maureen A. 2007. *America Reformed: Progressives and Progressivisms, 1890s–1920.* New York: Oxford University Press.

Gilmore, Glenda Elizabeth. 2002. *Who Were the Progressives?* New York: Bedford/St. Martin's.

Ginger, Ray. 1975. *The Age of Excess: The United States from 1877 to 1914.* New York: Macmillan.

Goodman, Douglas J., and Mirelle Cohn. 2004. *Consumer Culture: A Reference Handbook.* Santa Barbara, Calif.: ABC-CLIO.

Goodwin, Lorine Swainston. 1999. *The Pure Food, Drink, and Drug Crusaders, 1879–1914.* Jefferson, N.C.: McFarland.

Gregory, Ross. 1995. *Modern America, 1914 to 1945.* New York: Facts on File.

Gross, Ernie. 2003. *The American Years.* New York: Scribner.

Heimann, Jim, ed. 2005. *1900–1919: All-American Ads.* London: Taschen.

Hold, Hamilton, ed. 1990. *The Life Stories of Undistinguished Americans, as Told by Themselves.* New York: Routledge.

Hooker, Richard J. 1981. *Food and Drink in America: A History.* New York: Bobs-Merrill Co..

Hunter, Richard. 1912. *Poverty.* New York: Macmillan.

Katz, William Loren, and Laurie R. Lehman, eds. 2001. *The Cruel Years: American Voices at the Dawn of the Twentieth Century.* Boston: Beacon Press.

Katzman, David M., and William M. Tuttle Jr., eds. 1982. *Plain Folk: The Life Stories of Undistinguished Americans.* Urbana: University of Illinois Press.

Keller, Morton. 1994. *Regulating a New Society: Public Policy and Social Change in America, 1900–1933*. Cambridge, Mass.: Harvard University Press.

Kent, Noel Jacob. 2000. *America in 1900*. Armonk, N.Y.: M. E. Sharpe.

Kurian, George Thomas. 2001. *Datapedia of the United States, 1790–2005: America Year by Year*. Lanham, Md.: Bernan Press.

Lears, T. J. Jackson. 1981. *No Place of Grace: Antimodernism and the Transformation of American Culture, 1880–1920*. Chicago: University of Chicago Press.

Levenstein, Harvery A. 1988. *Revolution at the Table: The Transformation of the American Diet*. New York: Oxford University Press.

Littman, Mark S. 1998. *A Statistical Portrait of the United States: Social Conditions and Trends*. Lanham, Md.: Bernan Press.

Lutz, Tom. 1991. *American Nervousness, 1903: An Anecdotal History*. Ithaca: Cornell University Press.

Macleod, David. 1983. *Building Character in the American Boy: The Boy Scouts, YMCA, and Their Forerunners, 1870–1920*. Madison: University of Wisconsin.

Macleod, David. 1998. *The Age of the Child: Children in America, 1898–1920*. New York: Twayne.

Maddow, Ben. 1979. *A Sunday between Wars: The Course of American Life from 1865 to 1917*. New York: Norton.

McGerr, Michael. 2003. *A Fierce Discontent: The Rise and Fall of the Progressive Movement in America, 1870–1920*. New York: Free Press.

Middlemas, Keith. 1977. *The Pursuit of Pleasure: High Society in the 1900s*. New York: Gordon and Cremonesi.

More, Louise Bolard. 1907. *Wage-Earners' Budgets: A Study of Standards and Cost of Living in New York City*. New York: H. Holt.

Nash, Roderick, ed. 1970. *The Call of the Wild: 1900–1916*. New York: G. Braziller.

National Digital Newspaper Program, National Endowment for the Humanities. www.neh.gov/projects/ndnp.html.

National Geographic, ed. 1998. *National Geographic: Eyewitness to the Twentieth Century*. Washington, DC: National Geographic Society.

Okun, Mitchell. 1986. *Fair Play in the Marketplace: The First Battle for Pure Food and Drugs*. Dekalb: Northern Illinois University Press.

Patsouras, Louis. 2004. *Thorstein Veblen and the American Way of Life*. New York: Black Rose Books.

Perry, Elisabeth Israels, and Karen Manners Smith. 2006. *The Gilded Age & Progressive Era: A Student Companion*. New York: Oxford University Press.

Polacheck, Hilda Satt. 1991. *I Came a Stranger: The Story of a Hull-House Girl,* ed. Dena J. Polacheck Epstein. Urbana: University of Illinois Press.

Project Gutenberg (online access to numerous classic examples of Progressive Era muckraking). http://www.gutenberg.org.

Rose, Cynthia, ed. 2004. *1900–1909*. Vol. 1 of *American Decades: Primary Sources*. Detroit: Gale.

Schlereth, Thomas J. 1992. *Victorian America: Transformations in Everyday Life, 1876–1915*. New York: HarperPerennial.

Schlup, Leonard, and James G. Ryan, eds. 2003. *Historical Dictionary of the Gilded Age*. Armonk, New York: M. E. Sharpe.

Shannon, David A., ed. 1966. *Progressivism and Postwar Disillusionment, 1898–1928*. New York: McGraw-Hill.

Shifftlet, Crandall. 1996. *Victorian America: 1876 to 1913*. New York: Facts on File.

Smith, Jessie Carney, and Carrell Horton. 1995. *Historical Statistics of Black America*. New York: Gale Research.

Stage, Sarah. 1979. *Female Complaints: Lydia Pinkham and the Business of Women's Medicine*. New York: Norton.

Stave, Bruce M. 1972. *Urban Bosses, Machines, and Progressive Reformers*. Lexington, Mass.: D. C. Heath and Company.

Stolley, Richard B., and Tony Chiu, eds. 1999. Life: *Our Centuries in Pictures*. New York: Bulfinch Press.

Storrs, Landon R. Y. 2000. *Civilizing Capitalism: The National Consumers' League, Women's Activism, and Labor Standards in the New Deal Era*. Chapel Hill: University of North Carolina Press.

Sullivan, Mark, and Dan Rather. 1996. *Our Times: America at the Birth of the Twentieth Century*. New York: Scribner.

Surface, George Thomas. 1910. *The Story of Sugar*. New York: Appleton.

Tate, Cassandra. 1999. *Cigarette Wars: The Triumph of "The Little White Slaver."* New York: Oxford University Press.

Tompkins, Vincent, ed. 1996. *American Decades: 1900–1909*. Detroit: Gale Research.

U.S. Department of Commerce, Bureau of the Census. 1989. *Historical Statistics of the United States, Colonial Times to 1970*. White Plains, N.Y.: Kraus International Publications.

Wagenknecht, Edward. 1982. *American Profile, 1900–1909*. Amherst: University of Massachusetts Press.

Wattenberg, Ben J. 1976. *Statistical History of the United States: From Colonial Times to the Present*. New York: Basic Books.

Weinberg, Arthur, and Lila Weinberg, eds. 1961. *The Muckrakers: The Era in Journalism that Moved America to Reform, the Most Significant Magazine Articles of 1902–1912*. New York: Simon and Schuster.

West, Elliott. 1996. *Growing Up in Twentieth-Century America: A History and Reference Guide*. Westport, Conn.: Greenwood Press.

Insurgency

OVERVIEW

"'You chump," seven-year-old Billy announces at the beginning of *The Harbor,* Ernest Poole's novel about the far-reaching changes that transformed the United States as the 19th century drew to a close and the new century got under way. Billy, the novel's protagonist and narrator, was expressing his contempt for Henry Ward Beecher, the most influential Protestant minister and preeminent symbol of respectable Victorian America during these years. The novel traces Billy's efforts to come to terms with the modern world, as represented by the transformation of New York's harbor, especially the industrialization of shipping and the growing power of large corporations. By the turn of the century, many Americans, just like Billy, questioned the adequacy of 19th-century Victorian values, a moral code rooted in self-control, industriousness, self-improvement, patriarchy, and the sanctity of motherhood. Different characters in *The Harbor* represent the diverse critics of Victorianism: from Billy's sister Sue, who identifies with the bohemian culture of Greenwich Village; to Joe Kramer, Billy's friend, an outspoken radical who takes part in a strike among the immigrant stokers and other workers in the engine rooms of the great commercial steamships; and to Billy himself, who as a journalist experiences a personal evolution. By the end of the novel, Billy hears the "voice" of the modern harbor pronouncing the birth of a new democracy: "Make way for me. Make way, all you little men. Make way, all you habits and all you institutions, all you little creeds and gods. For I am the start of the voyage. . . . I am reality—I am life! I am the book that has no end!" (Poole 1915, 340).

Much like Billy's declaration at the end of *The Harbor,* the rejection of Victorianism by early-20th-century insurgents was more a matter of outlook than a clearly defined system of ideas. In *The End of American Innocence,* the cultural historian Henry May labels the modernists' abandonment of Victorianism "the Liberation," a revolution in American thought in the pre–World War I era that expressed ideas that, if "easy to taste and observe," are nevertheless hard to define (May 1959, 219). Historians who study the emergence of the insurgent impulse tend to concentrate on the ideas and actions of particular individuals, especially the writers and other "romantic rebels" who began gathering in Greenwich Village after 1890. For the bohemians who collected in Greenwich Village early in the 20th century, insurgency represented less an organized movement than it did the adoption of a nonconformist lifestyle as a self-conscious alternative to the accepted standards of personal and social behavior.

The "restlessness of women" against the constraints imposed by Victorian society became a cause célèbre for Greenwich Village bohemians (Stansell 2000, 226). The Victorian cult of domesticity, pronounced from the pulpit and the political platform and found in the stories of women's magazines through the 19th century, rooted a woman's place in marriage and family. The true woman, as its leading modern chronicler Barbara Welter has observed, judged herself and was judged by others based on her "piety, purity, submissiveness and domesticity" (Welter 1966, 152). In opposition to the conventions of true womanhood, the so-called sex radicals of Greenwich Village such as Emma Goldman denounced in the name of free love the Victorian constraints of respectable femininity. Sexual experimentation, the assertion of a woman's right to sexual pleasure, and a belief in personal independence were intended to challenge the boundaries proscribed by the domestic ideology (Chambers 1992, 101–102).

The largely middle-class bohemians of Greenwich Village were hardly the only Americans to question Victorian strictures at the turn of the century. Working-class men and women increasingly sought relief from the growing intensity of urban industrial life and work in America. They found escape in commercialized entertainments at dance halls, music halls, cheap theaters, brothels, saloons, and amusement parks like Coney Island (Kasson 1978, 100). Dancing took place in community centers, in neighborhood saloons, and in the dance halls run by entrepreneurs seeking to take advantage of the "dance madness" spreading among working-class youth (Peiss 1986, 182). Of course, simply the unchaperoned freedom of association exhibited by young working-class men and women on a Sunday revel at Coney Island likewise challenged middle-class Victorian sensibilities.

Rebel women became, as the author and journalist Hutchins Hapgood noted, the raison d'être for "Greenwich Village which existed not only in New York but all over the country" (Stansell 2000, 226). "New Men" like Hapgood, Floyd Dell,

Max Eastman, and John Reed joined independent "New Women," the growing number of female college-educated professionals, not only in breaking with Victorian taboos but also in playing an increasing role in social reform in the women's suffrage movement and in the workplace.

Not surprisingly, the insurgent uprising against Victorianism that arose after the turn of the century generated intense opposition. Custodians of culture— journalists, academics, ministers, and politicians, as well as businessmen—formed a powerful antimodern phalanx in defense of traditional values. Antimodernism enabled the WASP elite to become "a unified and self-conscious ruling class" during these years (Lears 1981, 301). Animus aroused by the idea of women as voters led to an organized opposition movement against the women's suffrage movement. Insisting that voting placed an unbearable burden on women, whose place was in the home, women of means and social position in the mid-1890s formed organizations such as the Massachusetts Association Opposed to the Further Extension of Suffrage to Women (Flexner 1959, 296). Still, many anti-suffragists were themselves active outside the home in civic charitable, educational, and philanthropic associations. Nevertheless, they insisted, as Mrs. Barclay Hazard offered in a 1907 lecture to the New York State Federation of Women's Clubs, that "intelligent, self-sacrificing women" could best fulfill their maternal responsibilities in American society "untrammeled by any political obligations" (Thurner 1995, 212).

For many women coming of age around the turn of the century, economics, that is, the right to labor and to secure an independent livelihood, mattered as much if not more than did politics. In the decade before 1900, the U.S. Department of Labor surveyed the members of almost 1,300 women's clubs and found that their members believed that "the science of economics is at the bottom of nearly all their problems" (Buhle 1983, 59). In *Women and Economics: A Study of the Economic Relation between Men and Women as a Factor in Social Relations* published in 1898, the feminist author and socialist Charlotte Perkins Gilman argued that the sexual relationship between men and women was in essence also an economic relationship. The key to women's emancipation and liberation from sexual oppression, according to Gilman, lay in the formation of collectivized systems of cleaning, cooking, and child care (Matthews 2003, 79–84). Even before *Women and Economics* had appeared in print, Gilman, the great-niece of Harriet Beecher Stowe, who, ironically, had celebrated the domestic role of woman, had embraced the collectivist ideals outlined by Edward Bellamy in his utopian novel *Looking Backward* (1888). Bellamy described a utopia in which public kitchens and dining rooms, and nurseries and day schools for children managed by the state enabled women to work and achieve their full potential (Buhle 1983, 79–80).

Representing the many strands of anticapitalist thought in America, more than 100 men and women gathered in Indianapolis, Indiana's Masonic Hall in the intense heat of late July 1901 to found the Socialist Party of America (SPA). In his history of the Socialist Party, David A. Shannon observes that the economic philosophy of many of the delegates drew more on Bellamy's *Looking Backward* than on Karl Marx's *Das Kapital*. Singing the anthem of revolution, the "Marseillaise," the SPA's founders proclaimed the ballot box to be the requisite instrument for replacing capitalism's exploitative wage system with the cooperative commonwealth. Optimistic, they were convinced that, as Julius A. Wayland, the editor of the socialist weekly newspaper *Appeal to Reason,* asserted, "Socialism is coming. It's coming like a prairie fire and nothing can stop it. . . . The next few years will give this nation to the Socialist Party" (Shannon 1967, 4).

Just a year before the founding of the SPA, the labor leader–turned-socialist Eugene V. Debs had been the standard-bearer for the Social Democratic Party (SDP) in the presidential election. Socialism was for Debs "something more than a mere labor question. It is a demand for equalizing of burdens and an equalizing of benefits throughout the whole society" (Salvatore 1982, 165). A recent convert to socialism and, beginning in 1904, the SPA's candidate for president in four national elections, Debs attempted to straddle the movement's factions. On the socialist left stood the leader of the Socialist Labor Party, Daniel De Leon, who boycotted the founding of the SPA and condemned the American Federation of Labor (AFL) as "labor fakirs" and the AFL's president Samuel Gompers as a "labor lieutenant of capitalism." De Leon insisted that socialism had to remain true to its revolutionary nature (Dubofsky, "Hillquit, Morris"). Opposition to De Leon came from the "kangaroos," a faction that included the leader of New York City's socialists, the attorney Morris Hillquit. Hoping to convert trade unions to socialism, the followers of Hillquit and other "gradualists" were still willing to work within the AFL. In the political sphere, they put great emphasis on winning votes and endorsed immediate improvements in capitalism that they hoped would benefit workers and farmers (Shannon 1967, 10).

After 1905, according to Morris Hillquit, socialism became "almost a fad." During these years, socialists spoke out at many public forums including radical salons; tent meetings and encampments in the southern Great Plains; protest marches and giant public rallies on the streets of many leading cities; Union Square in New York City; college campuses through the auspices of the Intercollegiate Socialist Society; organized socialist clubs like the Workmen's Circle, which became a national club in 1900; and at even more informal gatherings (Weinstein 1969, 80). A profusion of socialist publications such as the *Appeal to Reason,* one of the most widely circulated newspapers in the world, and the *National Rip Saw,* a monthly aimed primarily at farmers, as well as many local newspapers and trade union papers disseminated socialist ideals. Americans also learned about socialism by reading the works of such popular authors as Jack London and Upton Sinclair.

Although only eight women were delegates to the Socialist Party's founding convention and no one there spoke on behalf of women's issues, by 1904 there was a small but sturdy network of independent socialist women's clubs. Born in

Kansas, Kate Richards O'Hare became one of socialism's most popular speakers, spreading the word in rural towns and socialist summer encampments throughout the Midwest and Southwest. Josephine Conger, who began life in Centralia, Missouri, became the leading editor of the socialist women's movement and an ardent promoter of socialist political victory. Active in urban industrial centers like New York, Chicago, Milwaukee, and St. Louis, socialist women recruited immigrant members and actively took part in auxiliaries such as sick-and-benefit societies, choirs, and union label leagues. In 1908, the party launched the Woman's National Committee, which provided socialist women with an official bureau within the party. Although sympathetic to suffrage and other issues important to its female members, the SPA held that class struggle was the "sole solution to the woman question" (Buhle 1983, 152). Moreover, leading socialist women like O'Hare, who after becoming a socialist continued to speak out against the evils of "race suicide" and divorce as well as against the liquor traffic, tended to be almost Victorian in their thinking about women and family (Dawley 1991, 100).

In June 1905, committed to militant direct action against the capitalist order and to organizing skilled and unskilled workers together into industrial unions, the radical leaders of the Western Federation of Miners (WFM), Charles Moyer and William D. "Big Bill" Haywood, joined with Debs and representatives of the Socialist Party's left wing, such as National Executive Committee member Algie Simons and Daniel De Leon of the Socialist Trade and Labor Alliance in Chicago, and almost 200 other delegates to found the Industrial Workers of the World (IWW). Debs called on workers to sever their ties to their old unions and help the IWW "hasten the emancipation of the working class and the brighter, happier day for all humanity" (Cantor 1978, 36). Haywood told the delegates that they had gathered in a "Continental Congress of the working class," which aimed at putting "the working class in possession of the economic power, the means of life, in control of the machinery of production and distribution, without regard to capitalist masters" (Dubofsky 1969, 81). Founded on the idea of class struggle, the IWW looked to organize whole industries into One Big Union.

Although unity prevailed during the first few days of the IWW's founding convention, the delegates adopted confusing compromises on politics and on the fledgling organization's structure because the lack of precision enabled each individual to interpret the outcome to his or her own satisfaction (Dubofsky 1969, 83–87). Over the next few years, the IWW sorted out its political and philosophical commitments. In 1906, the WFM and the socialists lost control to the "anarchists" allied with De Leon. Then, having made little headway in organizing workers, partly because of an economic downturn that followed the Panic of 1907, the IWW convention the following year expelled De Leon and fully endorsed Haywood's program of revolutionary industrial unionism. Rejecting politics altogether, the IWW defined direct action as any struggle, including conventional strikes and sabotage, undertaken by workers at the point of production.

Ultimately, direct action came to mean a general strike, an event that, although never precisely defined, sought to displace capitalists from power and put the means of production in the hands of workers. In 1908, the WFM withdrew from the IWW, and Debs quietly let his membership lapse.

In 1909, the IWW took charge of a strike by steelworkers at McKees Rocks, Pennsylvania. Employing the techniques of Frederick Winslow Taylor, the Pressed Steel Car Company, a subsidiary of U.S. Steel, had imposed a new piece-rate pay system intended to increase worker efficiency and output. In a 45-day strike marked by violent clashes, the IWW, using multilingual organizers and newspapers to unite the immigrant workforce, won a victory against the steel trust. During the previous year, the IWW, now actively organizing among the migratory workers in the lumber camps and mines of the West, had led the first of many "free speech" fights in Spokane, Washington. When local authorities arrested the IWW's soapbox orators, the prisoners filled the city's jails and the passersby heard them singing out the words they had added to a Gospel tune, "Hallelujah, I'm a bum." In 1909, the IWW paper the *Industrial Worker* called on its readers to "quit your job. Go to Missoula, Fight with the Lumber Jacks for Free Speech." These battles brought great attention to the IWW as the standard-bearer for revolutionary class-consciousness and for the possibility of organizing the nation's neglected immigrant and casual workers (Green 1980, 67–69).

TIMELINE

1900   Carrie Chapman Catt is elected president of the National American Women's Suffrage Association.

The Workmen's Circle is founded.

1901   The Socialist Party of America is founded.

1902   Elizabeth Cady Stanton dies.

The Spirit of the Ghetto by Hutchins Hapgood is published.

1903   The Women's Trade Union League is founded.

1905   The Industrial Workers of the World is founded.

The Intercollegiate Socialist Society is founded.

1906   Susan B. Anthony dies.

1907   Harriot Stanton Blatch organizes the Equality League of Self-Supporting Women.

1908	Socialist Party of America candidate Eugene V. Debs campaigns for president on the "Red Special."
	The Iron Heel by Jack London is published.
	Work by "The Eight" is exhibited at the Macbeth Gallery in New York.
1909	Industrial Workers of the World leads a free speech fight in Spokane, Washington.
	Sigmund Freud delivers Five Lectures on Psychoanalysis at Clark University.
	The first White House Conference on the Care of Dependent Children takes place.
	Martin Eden by Jack London is published.

REBELS IN BOHEMIA

The rebels who congregated in New York's Greenwich Village at the turn of the century self-consciously engaged in a cultural rebellion against middle-class standards of propriety (Fishbein 1982, 4). In their nonconformism, the bohemians created informal connections that counterbalanced the loss of community experienced in modern industrial America. Although the more formal institutions contrived by the Village's freethinkers—the Liberal Club, Mabel Dodge's salon, and the Armory Show—were products of the next decade, during the early years of the 20th century Greenwich Village's bohemians combined a belief in sexual equality, feminism, and socialism to create a lifestyle—a sense of connectedness and a shared perspective. The content of that lifestyle is most intimately revealed in the personal biographies of the Village's most prominent residents in these years, Hutchins Hapgood, Neith Boyce, Floyd Dell, Max Eastman, Mary Heaton Vorse, Emma Goldman, and others.

Located in lower Manhattan, Greenwich Village was bounded on the north by 14th Street, on the east by Fourth Avenue and the Bowery, on the west by the Hudson River, and on the south by Houston Street. Socially, the area below Houston was home to the Jewish Lower East Side, which encompassed bohemian and radical cultures of its own and a working-class population that lived in proximity to Union Square, a focal point for mass protest in New York, on 14th Street. By the turn of the century—near the elegant townhouses built around Washington Square Park at the foot of Fifth Avenue, the urban campus of New York University, fine hotels, shopping emporia, and theaters—the Village contained deteriorating old brick row houses and winding streets inhabited by recently arrived German, Irish, and Italian immigrants who found employment in

A 1903 view of Washington Arch, located in Washington Square Park at the center of Greenwich Village in New York City. (Hulton Archives/Getty Images)

the breweries, warehouses, and coal and lumberyards near the Hudson and in the garment manufacturing lofts such as the Triangle Waist Company located southeast of Washington Square Park. The lower rent of the older houses and the crowded multifamily dwellings were what first attracted the bohemian population. Although there was little contact between the newly arrived artists and writers and either their wealthy or immigrant neighbors, by the end of the first decade of the 20th century, Greenwich Village was well known for its tolerance of unfamiliar customs, radicalism, and nonconformity (Jackson 1995, 506–508).

By 1910, Village bohemians had created an informal community, a haven for like-minded people who saw themselves surrounded by a respectable and hostile Victorian world. Having just graduated from Harvard, the journalist and author Walter Lippman celebrated Greenwich Village's spirit: "Instead of a world once and for all fixed, with a morality finished and sealed, we have a world bursting with new ideas, new plans, and new hopes" (Stansell 2000, 44). "New" was the key word—New Woman, New Man. Yet the Village as a community existed more as an opportunity for individual self-expression than as a formal space or an organized movement. The writer Floyd Dell recalls the experience of "manufacturing a Bohemia for myself" (Stansell 2000, 49). During the first decade of the 20th century, Greenwich Village emerged as a subculture within the larger society, an island for self-expression.

The Ashcan School

At the end of the 19th century, a group of newspaper and magazine illustrators in Philadelphia that included William Glackens, George Luks, Everett Shinn, and John Sloan gathered around Robert Henri, a painter whose credo was that "art cannot be separated from life" (Chilvers 1998, 37). Arriving in New York City between 1896 and 1904, these artists shared an intense interest in recording modern urban life. In 1907, Henri withdrew two of his paintings from the National Academy of Design in protest over the conservative Academy's refusal of to exhibit the works of "progressive" artists such as Glackens, Luks, and Sloan (*New York Times,* April 12, 1907). The following year he organized an independent exhibition at the Macbeth Gallery in New York of "The Eight"—a title accepted by the group but one that was not of their making—which included

the works of Arthur B. Davies, Ernest Lawson, and Maurice Prendergast as well as Glackens, Luks, Shinn, Sloan, and Henri. Although this show would be the only time that The Eight exhibited together, during the year it circulated to nine other venues. Along with other painters, such as George Bellows, who was known for his muscular boxing pictures and scenes of the urban poor and who in 1904 had been a student of Henri, The Eight would have the sobriquet the Ashcan School applied to them in 1934 in *Art in America in Modern Times* edited by Holger Cahill and Alfred H. Barr (Chilvers 1998, 37).

Robert Henri crusaded for an independent and more realistic American art free from academic restriction (Homer 1969, 53). Rebelling against "art for art's sake," Henri insisted that art should grow from life and not theories. Like their fellow Greenwich Village bohemians, the

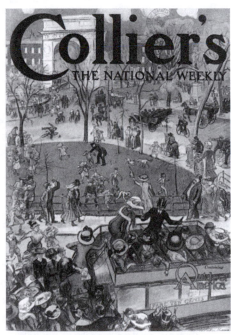

A Spring Morning in Washington Square, New York, *by William Glackens, a leading member of the Ashcan School. (Library of Congress)*

Ashcan School was less a formal group than a collection of like-minded persons who indicted the art of the National Academy as "effete" for favoring the wealthy and the beautiful as subjects. Expressing a preference for earthy themes like "Lusty Luks's" *The Wrestlers,* realist Ashcan School artists recorded scenes of people from the city's poorest neighborhoods: residents sitting on benches, children playing in the city's parks, a gang of mostly naked boys swimming off a decaying Hudson River pier, outdoor markets, riding the ferry, and a dock strike. (Brooklyn Museum). Called the "revolutionary black gang," Ashcan artists were neither avowedly reformist like the era's muckrakers nor openly political (although Sloan ran as Socialist for the New York State Assembly in 1910 and was an illustrator for the radical monthly journal *The Masses*) (Chilvers 1998, 37). In their work, Ashcan artists worried less about social issues than they did about representing the vitality and spontaneity of lower-class lives.

Sexual Modernism

Throughout most of the 19th century, Greenwich Village remained a quaintly picturesque and ethnically diverse neighborhood in lower Manhattan. Yet by the turn of the century, an avant-garde of artists and writers noted for their modern work in books and, especially, in "little magazines" published by small presses had been drawn to the area. Principally in private acts of rebellion, Greenwich Villagers openly proclaimed their assault against Victorianism. They went swimming in the nude to free themselves of the "stupid codes of ordinary people" who were "ashamed and afraid" of the human body (Humphrey 1978, 237). Villagers generally conducted themselves, according to the writer Floyd Dell, in "a gay and riotous abandon" intended to arouse the antipathy of their sober middle-class neighbors (Jackson 1995, 108).

The Villagers' lack of inhibition about sexual behavior represented a self-conscious rejection of the Victorian "conspiracy of silence" (Fishbein 1982, 74). Critics of the new sexual license worried that "our former reticence in matters of sex is giving way to a frankness that could even startle Paris" (Fishbein 1982, 74). Heirs to the 19th-century free love radicals Victoria Woodhull and Tennessee Claflin, who proclaimed their right to love whomever they pleased, Village bohemians acclaimed women's sexuality and would not be bound by monogamy in marriage. Floyd Dell recounted that his 1906 story "I Doubted Not," an intense account of a young girl's experience of orgasm, set a high standard for the male: "Physically as well as spiritually, love is a responsible and egalitarian relationship" (Fishbein 1982, 81). Rejecting the domestic ideology that glorified purity in women as erecting barriers between the sexes, Village rebels demanded an end to prudery and the opportunity for men and women to achieve unrestrained sexual fulfillment (Humphrey 1978, 242).

Greenwich Village proved attractive to women as a place where they could enjoy pleasures that were until then generally limited to men. Art Young, a Village resident and cartoonist for radical magazines, observed that in the Village, "a woman could say 'damn' right out loud and still be respected" (Humphrey 1978, 241). Women could smoke in public (in contrast, in 1904 a woman in a car driving along New York's Fifth Avenue was arrested for smoking), drink in bars, dress as they pleased, and entertain men in their apartments. Village rebels rejected as hypocrisy the double standard of morality that characterized a woman's but not a man's sexual activity outside of marriage as sinful. At the climax of her lectures on sexual equality, the anarchist Emma Goldman would dare any man "who had no premarital sexual experience to stand up" (Fishbein 1982, 75). Few men apparently did.

The sisterly bond that drew female Village rebels to support working-class immigrant women who labored in the predatory garment factories in Lower Manhattan was connected to a sense of alienation generated by modern work in the new industrial order. Most members of the bohemian community agreed with Emma Goldman when she complained that mass society was destroying pride in craftsmanship and creating a class of "brainless, incompetent automatons who turn out enormous quantities of things, valueless to themselves, and generally injurious to the rest of mankind" (Fishbein 1982, 67). Attempting to lead simple lives free of bourgeois trappings, Village bohemians embraced the craftsman ethic advanced by the English radicals John Ruskin and William Morris as well as by Hull House's Jane Addams, who, in 1902, contributed examples of handicraft to the Chicago Arts and Crafts Exhibition (Fishbein 1982, 66). For Village bohemians, art collectives and cooperative publishing provided a personal alternative to the competitive demands of the art market or commercial publishing. Other more radical Villagers like Hutchins Hapgood sought a more political solution to the problem of alienation. Looking to achieve an ideal society led many workers, according to Hapgood, to become anarchists, trade unionists, free lovers, and socialists.

Writers and Bohemians

Hutchins Hapgood is but one example of the outsiders who came to New York drawn by the bohemian lifestyle of Greenwich Village. In the 1890s, Hapgood first worked in New York as a reporter for the *Commercial Advertiser,* which was edited by the muckraker Lincoln Steffens. Practicing the kind of "personal journalism" championed by Steffens, Hapgood wrote a series of newspaper sketches about the lives of Jewish immigrants on the Lower East Side whom he had learned about the from a fellow reporter, Abraham Cahan; these stories were published as *The Spirit of the Ghetto: Studies of the Jewish Quarter of New York* (1902) (Jackson 1995, 521). Supplemented by the illustrations of Jacob Epstein, who was more familiar with this Jewish neighborhood than was the reporter, Hapgood's vivid portraits captured the lives and pursuits of the push-cart peddlers and sweatshop workers, the intellectual life of the cafés, and the

Portrait of reporter and novelist Neith Boyce who, along with her husband Hutchins Hapgood, was part of the Greenwich Village bohemian scene. (Library of Congress)

combativeness of Jewish unionists and socialists.

While working at the *Commercial Advertiser,* Hapgood met fellow reporter Neith Boyce whom he married in 1899. Boyce, who kept her name, and Hapgood thought of themselves as members of a newly liberated generation that had abandoned outmoded Victorian constraints. Boyce continued to write, publishing four novels as well as many newspaper articles that captured the women characters' conflicts with men as well as their struggle against repressive mores. Her marriage to Hapgood mirrored the cultural clashes about which Boyce wrote. But Hapgood and Boyce only partially succeeded in achieving a marriage based on free love. Boyce would write to her friend Mabel Dodge, whose salon was the linchpin of the Village's social and intellectual life in the second decade of the 20th century, that "both Hutch and I feel that we are free to love other people—but that nothing can break or even touch the deep vital passionate bond between *us* that exists now as it always has" (Fishbein 1982, 97). Hapgood too would be dissatisfied with the "sexual friendships" he formed with other women. An archive of personal correspondence has been preserved that captures the tensions between Hapgood and Boyce as they failed to achieve the free love ideal they set for themselves.

The Hapgood and Boyce union would not be the only partnership to fall short of achieving the bohemian ideal. Although the novelist Floyd Dell did not move to Greenwich Village until 1913, he had already adopted a bohemian lifestyle, first in Davenport, Iowa, and later in Chicago. Born in Barry, Illinois, Dell moved to Davenport in 1904 at age 17. By the early 20th century, a cosmopolitan intellectual core flourished on the fringes of mostly respectable Davenport, a small city on the Mississippi. This group consisted of professionals, trade unionists, members of the two branches of the Socialist Party, and such New Women as novelist Susan Glaspell and Mollie Price Cook, who, before coming to Davenport, had worked as an assistant on Emma Goldman's journal *Mother Earth*. In Davenport, Dell, the son of a failed butcher, had attracted the attention of "an intelligentsia who knew books and ideas" and who helped him get a job as a reporter on the local newspaper (Humphrey 1978, 210). He also became a socialist while in Davenport and produced poetry that celebrated free love. In 1908, with the support of his mentors, Dell moved to Chicago, where he again took a job as a reporter. A year later, he married Margery Currey, a graduate of Vassar College and an ardent suffragist.

According to his "First Impressions," which he started writing just after his arrival in Chicago, Dell moved freely among the Second City's bohemians, its extensive immigrant populations, and the luminaries of its high and popular culture as well as the literati who frequented its bookstores and cafés. Chicago had already produced an urban salon, the Little Room, where the local artists, playwrights, and writers who entered passed under a doorway sign that proclaimed "All Passes—ART Alone Endures" (Stansell 2000, 52). By 1908, the center of Chicago's "real" bohemia had shifted to the Jackson Park area of South Chicago and the avant-garde Little Theater and to the Dells' home, where Currey founded a salon that attracted artists, theater people, and such writers as Sherwood Anderson, Theodore Dreiser, and Margaret Anderson (founder of the *Little Review*). A friend wondered in verse about Currey: "Why does all of sharp and new; / That our modern age can brew; / Culminate in you?" (Stansell 2000, 53).

Many of the participants in Currey's salon moved on to Greenwich Village during the second decade of the 20th century. Dell also relocated there after Currey, who had grown impatient with his numerous infidelities, had ended their marriage. Dell endeavored to achieve public acceptance of free unions, which he believed provided a healthy outlet for sexual desires. As a feminist, he rejected the Victorians' identification of women's moral power with their domestic roles. Christine Stansell in *American Moderns: New York and the Creation of a New Century,* observes that Dell rejected Victorian maternalism: "'It is the setting of mothers free that concerns people now" (233-234). In his book of essays, *Women as World Builders* (1913), Dell saluted the English feminist Dora Marsden, the editor of the *Freewoman,* as a representative of "a band of capable females, knowing what they want and taking it, asking no leave from anybody, doing things and enjoying life" (Stansell 2000, 233–234). Yet Dell was also aware of his tendency to be jealous and would become disenchanted with the idea of free love. He concluded later in life, "Free love, that beautiful ideal of the utopian mind, is indeed a delusion and a snare. . . . Jealousy is a human reality, and so is the deep craving of both men and women for permanence and security in love" (Fishbein 1982, 98–99). In the 1910s, Dell became a prominent figure in Greenwich Village, working as an assistant editor of *The Masses,* a magazine edited by the writer and socialist Max Eastman that mixed radical politics with art and literature (Clayton, American National Biography Online).

Born in upstate New York in 1883, Max Eastman first came to New York City in 1907 to study philosophy under John Dewey at Columbia University. Soon after, Eastman settled in Greenwich Village with his sister, Crystal, a Vassar graduate who studied industrial labor law at New York University law school and was well known among the area's radicals, reformers, and feminists. The historian Robert Humphrey credits Crystal "and her liberated friends" for prying Max away from Columbia, the "knowledge foundry," and thrusting him "into bohemianism and political rebellion" (Humphrey 1978, 167). Max also apparently followed his sister's lead, along with that of other emancipated Village women such as Inez Milholland and Ida Rauh, in becoming an outspoken suffragist. Indeed, Milholland would ride down Fifth Avenue on a white horse at the head of a 1909 suffrage parade that, as secretary of the Men's League for Woman Suffrage, Max Eastman had organized. For several years afterward, Eastman toured the nation giving popular lectures on suffrage. Committed to women's equality, Eastman insisted that "the question of sex equality, the economic, social, political independence of woman, stands by itself parallel and equal in importance to any other question of the day" (Stansell 2000, 229). After a brief romance with Milholland ended, in 1911 Eastman married Rauh, a socialist, feminist, actress, and artist. After a trip to Europe, the Eastmans returned to Greenwich Village and Max became editor of *The Masses,* which, in the years before the federal government shut it down in 1917, mixed political and sexual radicalism with modern graphics, labor journalism, and poetry and fiction (Stansell 2000, 166). Under Eastman, *The Masses* expressed a more politically radical side of the Village bohemian rebellion against Victorian America (Gilbert 1968, 32).

Yet as Leslie Fishbein, a leading chronicler of this community, notes, before *The Masses* politicized the bohemian rebellion against gentility, the artists and radicals of Greenwich Village were "ready to respond to the appeal of Freudianism" (Fishbein 1982, 84). Villagers looked to Freud as an ally in their struggle to free themselves from the sexual and personal inhibitions of prudish Victorianism. In the aftermath of Freud's 1909 visit to Clark University in Worcester, Massachusetts, Eastman and Dell became leading members of a sizable movement of "popularizers" of Freud's theories among Americans.

Freud Comes to America

In September 1909, in his first and only visit to the United States, Sigmund Freud presented five lectures on the origin and development of psychoanalysis at Clark University as part of the school's 20th anniversary celebration. Invited by Clark president G. Stanley Hall, a pioneer in the new study of adolescence, Freud was pleasantly surprised by the warmth of his reception in America. As he later recalled, "As I stepped on to the platform at Worcester to deliver my *Five Lectures on Psychoanalysis* it seemed like the realization of some incredible day dream: psychoanalysis was no longer the product of delusion, it had become a valuable part of reality" (Hale 1971, 3–4). Among those in the audience was an uninvited guest, Emma Goldman, whom the *Boston Evening Transcript* referred to as "Satan" and who happened to be in Worcester on a speaking tour. For her part, Goldman viewed Freud as a confederate whose theories proved that sexual repression had crippled intelligence in women (Hale 1971, 22).

The Clark Conference was a turning point in the reception of psychoanalysis in the United States. Because of his lectures Freud established long-term relationships with, among others, Hall, a founder of developmental psychology, and William James, a Harvard psychologist and philosopher who was an old friend of Hall, as well as with Franz Boas, who was transforming the discipline of anthropology and challenging accepted ideas about race. Citing specific cases, Freud's Clark lectures revealed his techniques, which concentrated on talking with patients without using hypnosis, the analysis of dreams, and sublimation as an alternative to repression, all of which he believed demonstrated practical approaches to the treatment of nervous disorders. At this point, Freud had yet to formulate such key concepts as the id and the superego. At Hall's behest, the lectures were published in 1910 in the *American Journal of Psychology.*

Freud's most controversial lecture, on the sexual impulses of the child, produced shock and, even among supportive colleagues, a sense that he was exaggerating the importance of sex. In ways that elicited a more sympathetic response from the Greenwich Village community, Freud denounced accepted domestic pieties and current sexual taboos. He would later write that he found the extreme sexual morality in America to be "very contemptible" (Hall 1971, 13). Often exaggerating elements of Freud's theories, Greenwich Village's rebels like Max Eastman and Floyd Dell, both of whom would be treated by American Freudians, became popularizers of psychoanalysis. Noting with approval the claims of American analysts, Eastman observed, "You see . . . it is a kind of 'magic' that is rapidly winning the attention of the most scientific minds in the world of medicine" (Hall 1971, 400). A few years after Freud's Clark lecture, Dell identified neurotic symptoms, which both he and Eastman had experienced, as the "inability to achieve results in one's work commensurate with the efforts put forth; infelicity in personal relationships, and a sense of not being able to get at grips with the realities of life," that could be cured by psychoanalysis (Hall 1971, 401). For Village bohemians like Eastman and Dell, Freudianism provided "a convenient tool" with which to escape the American Puritanism and sexual repression (Fishbein 1982, 87). Eastman would even develop a Freudian interpretation of the origins of World War I, although his theory failed to impress Freud. Although Eastman and, to a lesser extent, Dell considered themselves to be a socialists, they were still attracted to Freudianism as an explanation for the personal problems in their lives.

Greenwich Villagers as Free Spirits

Among the free spirits who populated Greenwich Village at the start of the 20th century there was likely no more colorful a figure than Emma Goldman. For many in the audiences across the country who attended Goldman's speaking tours she came to represent "Bohemian Greenwich Village" (Stansell 2000, 120). Goldman, in the 1890s merely one anarchist agitator among many in the Lower East Side, transformed herself during the following decades into a modernist symbol, at once vilified and adored, who embodied "both celebrity and politics, spectacle and radicalism, universality and self-aggrandizement" (Stansell 2000, 121). In 1906, Goldman began publishing *Mother Earth,* which she dedicated to those who "breathe freely only in limitless space; . . . The Earth free for the free individual!" (Goldman 1906, 1). By 1910, Goldman divided her time between living in the Village in a cooperative housekeeping arrangement and traveling across the United States delivering public lectures, sometimes two or three times a week, on a variety of topics. Gradually Goldman's lectures began to focus on support for the Industrial Workers of the World, birth control, women's emancipation, free speech, and free love (Stansell 2000 124–125).

Next to Goldman, Mary Heaton Vorse, an outspoken feminist, journalist, and labor reformer, was the Village's reigning New Woman during the early years of the 20th century. Looking to "escape from conformity," Village bohemians spent their time, Vorse observed, "more in the realities of life than in that soul-racing game known as keeping up appearances" (Humphrey 1978, 6). Born in New York City in 1874 but raised in genteel Amherst, Massachusetts, where she first began her rebellion against polite mores, Vorse "was the core around whom many of the young [Greenwich Village] intellectuals gathered" (Garrison 1989, 63). A recent graduate of the Art Students' League, Mary Heaton married Albert Vorse, a newspaperman, in the winter of 1898 and the new couple settled into an eighth-floor Greenwich Village apartment. After brief stays in Europe and Provincetown, Massachusetts, Bert and Mary returned to New York in 1906 to live in the A Club, a cooperative housing venture just blocks from Washington Square that was home to radicals, reformers, and writers like Ernest Poole, who recalled, "With most of us writing books, stories, or plays and all of us dreaming of reforms and revolutions of divers kinds, life in that house was a quick succession of intensities, large and small . . . but through it all ran broad fresh river of genial humor and relish in life" (Garrison 1989, 37). As a feminist, Vorse expressed gratitude to the previous generations of American women "who were the real revolutionaries . . . [they] shattered convention, belled sacred cows, and tweaked the beards of stuffed shirts" (Garrison 1989, 16). Because of their efforts, women of her day were living in a golden age: "We had the feeling that we were important civic factors who could put a thumb almost anywhere and pull out a plum, ranging from voices for women to a fine new building" (Stansell 2000, 245–246). Already somewhat a senior citizen to the young radicals and artists who gathered in Greenwich Village before 1910, Vorse would be intimately connected to many of the groups, such as *The Masses* coterie, the Liberal Club, the Heterodoxy Club, and Mabel Dodge's Fifth Avenue salon, that made the Village the political center for nonconformity just prior to World War I.

Open in matters of sex, Village bohemians during the early years of the 20th century advanced a right to pleasure independent of reproduction and family. Proponents of a woman's need for sexual fulfillment, Villagers rejected the double standard and accepted diverse sexual identities including homosexuality (Trimberger 1983, 132–133). Bohemians were influenced, as were other Americans, by the writings of the English sexologist Havelock Ellis, who in his major work, *Studies in the Psychology of Sex* (six volumes of which were published between 1897 and 1910), championed heterosexual gratification and referred to what he called "sexual inversion," or homosexuality, as natural and inborn. Ellis insisted that what the world needed was "not more restraint but more passion" (D'Emelio and Freedman 1988, 224). In modern America, as men and a few women lived apart from their families, an uncertain number came to view their homosexual desires as an expression of independence from the majority, and an underground sexual subculture was established in many large cities in the United States (D'Emelio and Freedman 1988, 227). Like its resident heterosexual bohemians, lesbians and gay men found the Village's cheap rents and inexpensive food, as well as the community's tolerance for "eccentricity," congenial (Chauncey 1994, 229). In fact, as historian George Chauncey notes in *Gay New York: Gender, Urban Culture, and the Making of the Gay Male World, 1890–1940,* "gay people were initially drawn to the Village primarily as bohemians rather than as homosexuals" and did not appear to have any interest in developing distinctly gay institutions until the 1920s (Chauncey 1994, 232).

Working-Class Liberation

At the turn of the 20th century, Greenwich Villagers' rebellion against repression and their desire to pursue their sexual yearnings spread far beyond the borders of their bohemian community. The young women and men who labored for wages in the New York City's sweatshops and factories also wanted to liberate themselves from the constraints imposed by Victorian society and to gain greater independence in their personal interrelations. An urban subculture emerged and spread, oriented around commercial amusements such as the dance hall and Coney Island. The success in the 1890s of dances run by social or pleasure clubs encouraged entrepreneurs to build halls for dancing that attracted growing numbers of working-class youth, especially single young women from all the immigrants groups in New York. According to a survey conducted in 1901, one dance hall or dance academy could be found for every two-and-a-half blocks of the Lower East Side (Peiss 1986, 177–179).

The new dances encouraged greater freedom of sexual expression and physical contact. "Spieling," or "pivoting," a popular dance found in the commercial halls, parodied the self-control of the more acceptable fast waltz. Wild spinning promoted "a charged atmosphere of physical excitement, often accompanied by

Coney Island

At the turn of the century, Coney Island became another commercialized venue for "loose" and unregulated social contact between young working-class men and women. During these years, commercial entrepreneurs constructed three amusement parks—Steeplechase, Luna Park, and Dreamland—that transformed the amusement industry. Contemporary commentators observed that "Coney Island has a code of conduct which is all her own" (Kasson 1978, 41). Coney Island broke with the severe middle-class constraints imposed on the interactions between single young men and women. Each of the parks featured mechanical rides, such as the Tunnel of Love, that provided ample opportunities for "spooning" and "petting," or such activities as the Blowhole Theater, at the end of which clowns paddled customers while others watched and laughed in an atmosphere of freedom and sexual license. Throughout Steeplechase, jets of air shot up from beneath iron grates sending women's dresses flying upward. As a beach resort, Coney Island encouraged looser dress and freer deportment. Period photographs reveal the "noticeably more relaxed postures" and "dramatic poses" in which beachgoers are "exuberantly mugging for the camera. Lifting and supporting one another, arms and bodies interlinked, they display a solidarity and mutual pleasure in the release of social constraints" (Kasson 1978, 45–46). In one stereopticon image, five smiling women are caught in a "naughty" pose bending over so that the short skirts of their bathing costumes lifted up (Kasson 1978, 49). Although the promoter George C. Tilyou insisted that the carnival spirit at Steeplechase was not spontaneous but was carefully manufactured, visitors to Coney's parks and beach found themselves among strangers caught up in a festival atmosphere that challenged conventional standards of propriety.

shouts and singing" (Peiss 1986, 182). The sexuality of these dances was made even more objectionable by the custom of "treating." Many of the working-class women who attended these dance halls earned less than 10 dollars a week, a wage that barely covered their basic living costs. As one investigator found, "The acceptance on the part of the girl of almost any invitation needs little explanation when one realizes that she often goes pleasureless unless she does accept 'free treats'" (Peiss 1983, 80). Working-class women who accepted treating and traded sexual favors became known in the contemporary slang as "charity girls." For example, when "Dottie," needed "a new pair of shoes she had found it easy to 'earn' them in the way that other girls did." Dottie, the investigator noted, was now a respectable married woman (Peiss 1983, 81–82). What working-class girls thought about this process of negotiation is unknown, but obviously, they did not measure respectability by strict middle-class standards of chastity.

The "promiscuity" of unattached young men and women caught the attention of Progressive era reformers. One vice investigator deplored the sexual license

Bathers romp on Coney Island, ca. 1903. Coney Island became a place where men and women of all social classes could meet free of Victorian social constraints. (Library of Congress)

he found in a Turnverein ball, "I saw one woman smoking cigarettes, most the young couples were hugging and kissing . . . they were all singing and carrying on, they kept running around the room and acted like a mob of lunatics, let lo[o]se" (Peiss 1986, 180–181). A Committee on Amusements and Vacation Resources of Working Class Girls of New York City had been formed during the first decade of the 20th century to suppress such "tough" dances as the "slow rag," "lovers' two-step," and the "bunny hug." The committee condemned the dance halls that had "sprung up" within the last few years "in every city throughout the country" where "immoral" dances, in conjunction with "liquor drinking," had become "the principal means through which girls are now being led astray, seduced or procured" (Peiss and Paterson 2001, 282–283).

THE RISE OF THE NEW WOMAN

By offering women and men freedom from the restraint of propriety, Greenwich Village provided a context for the emergence of modern feminism (Fishbein 1982, 136). By 1900, feminism, which would not become synonymous with women's rights until the second decade of the 20th century, was already identified with, in addition to sexual freedom, economic independence and a release from the domestic obligations of wifehood, motherhood, and daughterhood. Inspired by the writings of Charlotte Perkins Gilman, women sought alternatives to traditional domestic arrangements through the establishment of communal kitchens and professionalized housework (Evans 1989, 162). Liberation from domestic responsibilities also came through work outside the home. During the last decade of the 19th century women increased their participation in the labor force at a faster rate than that for men. That so many women had "forsaken the traditions of the hearth and are competing with men in the world of paid labor" meant, according to the journalist Rheta Childe Dorr, that "women are rapidly passing from the domestic control of their fathers and husbands. Surely this is the most important economic fact in the world today" (Fishbein 1982, 142). By 1910, some 8 million women were working for wages, almost one quarter of the wage-earning population in the United States (Green 1980, 43).

Economic independence was the goal of numerous college-educated women who resided in Greenwich Village during the early years of the 20th century. As one example, Ida Rauh, the daughter of a well-to-do uptown German-Jewish Manhattan family, graduated from New York University law school in 1902. At NYU, she undoubtedly met Crystal Eastman, an active suffragist who would become her sister-in-law, and Jessie Ashley, whose father was the dean of the law school. In 1903, these women joined Rauh in founding the Women's Trade Union League and battled as "allies" in the 1909 shirtwaist makers' strike (Stansell 2000, 244–245). Female Village residents were more likely to become full-time activists than to practice their professions. For many women, "professional" in these years often meant a job as an executive secretary to a male literary editor or other low-paid work. As one woman recalls, women "could force their way into the professions only against great obstacles that prevented all but the most determined and brilliant from keeping up the struggle" (Stansell 2000, 245). Even so, in 1900, there were almost 9,000 women physicians and, in 1910, 1,500 female lawyers; the names of 204 women could be found in the 1910 Directory of American Scientists (Matthews 2003, 41–42).

Whatever their profession, and however public the activity, women in the early 20th century were still largely understood to be operating within a separate sphere. Women's pursuits outside the home were justified by the promise of expanding their motherly and selfless influence in society (Ryan 1975, 136). Hence, many of the social services provided by Hull House involved and aided women in the surrounding immigrant community, and the "white label" campaigns of the National Consumers League mobilized women as consumers to improve the conditions of women as workers. The Illinois Woman's Alliance, a cross-class umbrella organization of 30 women's unions and voluntary societies joined with the female residents of Hull House to press the state legislature to regulate sweatshop industries (Muncy 1991, 26). In 1905, Kelley proclaimed that the "care and nurture of childhood [was] a vital concern of the nation" (Muncy 1991, 38). Four years later, President Theodore Roosevelt convened the First White House Conference on the Care of Dependent Children, which called for the formation of a federal children's bureau. Within three years, the Children's Bureau was established under the direction of Hull House veteran Julia Lathop, who staffed the agency only with women. The prominence of women and women's organizations in social reform during the Progressive era provided the basis for what Robyn Muncy has characterized as the emergence of a "female dominion." During the early years of the 20th century, the New Woman as a professional gained considerable control over family and child policy, areas of growing concern for which a woman's alleged unique qualities endowed her with expertise and legitimized a particularly feminized version of professionalism (Muncy 1991, xii–xv). After 1900, the network of women's organizations and the accompanying emergence of the New Woman provided considerable impetus to a revitalized women's suffrage movement.

Independent Women

In the late-19th and early-20th centuries, a growing revolt arose among middle-class and upper-class women against the Victorian assumption that economic dependency was the natural condition for women. In *Women and Labor* (1911), Olive Schreiner, a South African writer, exposed the fallacy of what she labeled "female 'parasitism': the condition of performing no 'active conscious social labor. . . . The result of this parasitism has invariably been the decay in vitality and intelligence of the female'" (Mathews 2003, 88). Both Schreiner and Charlotte Perkins Gilman expressed the helplessness of women in terms of evolution. Because women were "continually bred for physical and mental weakness, women had over time become totally economically dependent upon men" (Matthews 2003, 81). To break this cycle of dependency and enable women to develop physically, mentally, and even morally, Gilman, an admirer of Jane Addams, conceived, in a 1904 magazine article, of an apartment building in which both wives and husbands, members of the professional and business class, would work outside the home. Cooking would take place at a central kitchen with meals being served in the apartments or in common dining rooms. Housework would be carried out by professionals and, similarly, child care would be provided by well-trained professional nurses and teachers in a kindergarten.

The socialist Henrietta Rodman, a disciple of Gilman, attempted to realize her mentors' vision but never successfully raised the requisite funding for an apartment house to be constructed in New York (Matthews 2003, 83–84).

Hull House and Economic Independence

Born in 1860, the youngest of five children of the wealthiest man in Cedarville, Illinois, Jane Addams is typical of middle-class women of her generation who anticipated going to college and then on to medical school. The death of her father upset her plans, but in 1887, while traveling in England with Ellen Gates Starr, Addams visited London's Toynbee Hall Settlement House and discovered her true "mission," the project that would give purpose to her life. On returning to the United States, Addams and Starr established Hull House in Chicago as a settlement that, in Addams's words, would serve as "an experimental effort to aid in the solution of the social and industrial problems which are engendered by the modern conditions of life in a great city" (Addams 1910, 95). Women comprised most of the resident workers at Hull House. Whenever Addams identified a need in the community, she immediately sought out a wealthy sponsor

A group of immigrants, ranging from children to senior citizens, singing in a Hull House choir, Chicago, Illinois, ca. 1910. Photo by Lewis Hine. (Hulton Archive/Getty Images)

Table 6.1. High School and College Graduates, 1890–1910

Year of graduation	High school			College		
	Total	Men	Women	Total	Men	Women
1890	43,791	18,549	25,182	14,306	10,157	4,149
1900	94,883	38,075	56,808	25,324	17,220	8,104
1910	156,429	63,676	92,753	34,178	22,557	11,621

Source: Adapted from Federal Security, Office of Education. *Biennial Survey of Education.* Cited in *Statistical Abstract of the United States,* 1952, 127.

to donate the requisite funds to pay the settlement workers' salaries. In addition to generating needed services to assist the surrounding immigrant community, what Addams called the "fellowship system" was intended to provide women settlement house workers with an income that enabled them to be self-supporting (Muncy 1991, 17).

The fellowship system enabled women to transform what had previously been volunteer work into the new professions of social worker and social investigator (Muncy 1991, 18). Long associated with the "Lady Bountiful" relief and charity activities that were largely carried out by women in religious and other voluntary associations, social work in the first decade of the 20th century emerged as an occupation recognized by federal enumerators in the 1910 census. Women constituted between two-thirds to three-quarters of the staffs of the "classic" settlements like Hull House and other settlements across the United States (Walkowitz 1999, 27–39). Florence Kelley, another college graduate and resident of Hull House, was a pioneer social investigator and key figure in the development of early welfare policy. Born in the Germantown section of Philadelphia a year before Addams, Kelley was the daughter of a patrician Quaker and Unitarian family. In 1886, she left her abusive husband and moved with her two children into Hull House. Faced with the need to support herself and her children, Kelley began working for the Illinois Bureau of Labor Statistics and the U.S. Department of Labor on a study of working conditions in Chicago, research that became the basis of *Hull House Maps and Papers* (1895). While at Hull House, she also became active in antisweatshop campaigns that led to her appointment in 1893 as chief factory inspector in Illinois. Six years later, she began her life's work as secretary of the National Consumers' League (NCL), a voluntary social reform agency that promoted protective labor legislation for women and children. Between 1900 and 1907, Kelley spent much of her time traveling, inspecting workshops, awarding the NCL's "white label" to manufacturers that maintained fair conditions, and helping build local leagues. Muncy summarizes Kelley's strategy for reform as consisting, in equal measure, of research, publicity, organization, and lobbying (Muncy 1991, 62).

Table 6.2. White-Collar Women, 1900–1910

Job Category	1900		1910	
	Number of women	% of Total employed in occupation	Number of women	% of Total employed in occupation
Clerical workers[a]	187,053	25.4	588,609	34.2
Teachers[b]	325,485	73.5	478,027	79.8
Trained nurses	11,946	93.6	76,508	92.9
Social welfare, and religious workers[c]	3,373	3.0	8,889	55.7
Artists, sculptors, and teachers of art	11,021	44.3	15,429	45.2
Musicians, and teachers of music	52,359	56.8	84,478	60.6
Lawyers, judges, and justices; abstracters, notaries, and justices of the peace	1,010	0.9	1,343	1.1

[a]Includes agents, collectors, and credit men; bookkeepers, cashiers, and accountants; clerks (except clerks in stores); messengers, errand and office boys and girls; stenographers and typists.

[b]Includes college presidents and professors 1900, although given the data for subsequent years, it is unlikely they ever amounted to more than 2% of the total.

[c]Includes clergy for 1900.

Source: Adapted from Alba Edwards, *Comparative Occupational Statistics for the United States, 1870 to 1940;* Part of the Sixteenth Census of the United States: 1940 (Washington: Government Printing Office, 1943).

New Women's Work

By 1900, 10 percent of medical students were female; 10 years later women comprised 6 percent of medical practitioners. Yet even though in 1900 "medical women," according to one woman physician, appeared to be "accepted as a fact of civilization," changes were already under way, including the closing of medical schools that trained women and the imposition of quotas that limited the number of female applicants to the remaining "male" schools (Matthews 2003, 41). As a result, after 1910, the proportion of women in medicine declined. Moreover, even as pioneers, most women physicians accepted the domestic ideology's belief in the moral superiority of women and placed great faith in women's intuitive qualities as natural healers. For example, Elizabeth Blackwell, who had established the Woman's Medical College of the New York Infirmary in 1869, expressed the conviction that medicine was a moral enterprise that would be greatly enhanced by the "spiritual power of maternity" (Morantz-Sanchez 1985, 57–58).

In addition to doctors, throughout the late-19th and into the early-20th centuries women also became lawyers, academicians, social workers, teachers, librarians, and nurses. Although the first woman was admitted to the bar in 1872, there were still only 1,500 women lawyers in the United States by 1910, and most of these women worked for government agencies, edited legal journals, or worked in their husbands' offices. Similarly, most female academics worked mainly for women's colleges or in such "women's specialties" as home economics or social work. Women also easily found positions open in the "semiprofessions," ones burdened by lesser prestige and lower pay. By 1910, 75 percent of schoolteachers were women who earned less than half the pay of their male colleagues. In that year, more than three-quarters of librarians were female, and the field of nursing was completely female. As for business, women entered the corporate offices in growing numbers but mainly as secretaries or in other clerical positions. Yet by identifying a niche market, some women, such as Madame C. J. Walker, who developed hair-care products for African American women, or Katherine Gibbs, who opened schools to train young women to use the typewriter, achieved a measure of success and great wealth in smaller-scale independent enterprises (Matthews 2003, 49).

Women in Business: Madame C. J. Walker

There is no better example of the growing ability of women to achieve economic independence than in the rags-to-riches narrative of Madame C. J. Walker. Yet her story is one not only of individual advancement but also of the collective opportunities that her hair-care business provided for African American women in the early 20th century. Born Sarah Breedlove, the daughter of former slaves in the Louisiana Delta in 1867 and orphaned at age seven, she and her sister moved to Vicksburg, Mississippi, in 1878, where they eventually found work as maids. At age 14 she married Moses McWilliams, as she observed later in her life, "to get a home of my own" (Bundles 2001, 40). In 1885, she gave birth to a daughter, Lelia. A few years later, McWilliams was killed, possibly, her biographer and great-great-granddaughter, A'Lelia Bundles, speculates, lynched during a race riot. Now 20 years old, Sarah left Mississippi with Lelia and, like a growing number of African American women in the latter decades of the 19th century, headed north, ending up in St. Louis, where her brothers lived.

Settled in the Gateway City, which unlike her native South had a "colored aristocracy" consisting of self-employed barbers and other modest entrepreneurs, Sarah worked as a laundress, washing for "families in St. Louis," she later told a reporter (Bundles 2001, 45). She also became active in St. Paul African Methodist Church (AME) and as a member of the Court of Calanthe, the women's auxiliary of the Knights of Pythias. Such affiliations provided personal and material support for Sarah and her daughter and, after she became a businesswoman, were the community institutions that she initially contacted whenever she began a campaign in a new town. A second and unfortunate marriage to John Davis ended in 1903. At some point during her years in St. Louis, Sarah, who was going bald, most likely as a result of her long hours spent over steaming washtubs filled with chemicals, had a "dream," as she would claim, in which "a big black man appeared to me" and gave her the formula for the hair products that became the basis of her business enterprise (Bundles 2001, 60). The dream, with its claim of divine providence and African origins, proved to be, as her great-great-granddaughter acknowledges, "an ingenious marketing device" (Bundles 2001, 60). Whether such a dream ever happened, Sarah blithely ignored the two years of training in the hair treatment business that she had received earlier while working as an agent for another businesswoman, Annie Pope-Turnbo, and began selling a hair product called Wonderful Hair Grower. In 1906, after relocating to Denver, Colorado, Sarah embarked on a third marriage to Charles J. Walker, and reinvented herself as Madame C. J. Walker, hiring a tutor in standard English and creating a more fashionable and refined appearance as she launched her own beauty products company (Peiss 1998, 80).

After first selling Wonderful Hair Grower in Denver "house-to-house . . . among people of my race," Walker began her travels to every section of the country teaching African American women how to treat their hair and sell her products. These recruits, or agents, trained others (Peiss 1998, 70,76). Within a few years, thousands of African American women, most of whom—especially in the South—could expect to work as washerwomen or domestics and be paid perhaps one or two dollars a week, now earned, according to the Walker Company, "from three to five dollars a day" as company agents. Top saleswomen could make as much as $100 a week (Peiss 1998, 91). Having relocated her business to Pittsburgh in 1908, Madam Walker earned $6,672 that year, nearly double what she had made the previous year. In 1909, her income grew by another 25 percent, to $8,782 (or to just over $150,000 in 21st-century dollars) (Bundles 2001, 96). In 1910, Walker settled her business in Indianapolis, which she believed would be favorable spot for national distribution (Peiss 1998, 70).

A controversy about Madame C. J. Walker's phenomenal success centers on whether she was selling products to enable her clients to, as she wrote, "imitate white folk" (Bundles 2001, 20). Walker bristled at the impression, promoted in white newspapers, that she was the "de-kink queen." She told one reporter, "Right here let me correct the erroneous impression held by some that I claim to straighten hair. . . . I have always held myself out as a hair culturist. I grow hair" (Bundles 2001, 20). Walker refused to sell skin bleaches and never spoke of hair straightening as an aspect of her beauty system. As Peiss observes in her history of America's beauty culture, Walker emphasized the impact of her products on the improved sense of inner worth of women who were usually demeaned and ill-treated by the larger society. Peiss continues, Walker embedded her business in "the daily life of black communities linked by kin, neighbors, churches," community institutions, and schools (Peiss 1998, 89–90). One company advertisement linked better appearance with "Pride of Race" and "Applied

Industry." As the ad concluded, "Look your best . . . you owe it to your race" (Peiss 1998, 204). For many African American women in the early 20th century, the Walker Company held out hope when little else in America did that they could improve their circumstances and provided them with the means to do so.

SUFFRAGE RENAISSANCE

In her groundbreaking study, *Century of Struggle: The Women's Rights Movement in the United States,* Eleanor Flexner has described the early years of the 20th century as "the doldrums," a period in which each of the few state referenda on women's suffrage failed and the federal suffrage amendment "appeared moribund" (Flexner 1959, 256). First introduced in 1879 and debated in Congress eight years later, the national suffrage, or Susan B. Anthony, amendment would ensure that the right of all citizens of the United States to vote could "not be abridged . . . or denied by any state on account of sex" (Baker 2005, 10). In 1890 an earlier rift in the women's suffrage movement between leaders such as Anthony and Elizabeth Cady Stanton, who supported the federal amendment, and those like Lucy Stone, who promoted state-by-state actions, had been bridged with the formation of the National American Women's Suffrage Association (NAWSA). Despite the lack of progress on state and federal fronts, historian Sara Hunter Graham has found a renewal of the women's suffrage movement in these years that rested on a greater solidarity among women achieved through the creation of a new, more respectable political culture, one that focused on suffrage as a single issue and was more appealing to mainstream American women (Graham 1995, 159).

In 1900, Carrie Chapman Catt was elected to succeed Anthony as president of NAWSA. As head of NAWSA's Business Committee during the previous decade, Catt had helped revitalize local suffrage clubs and appealed to the "best people" to join the suffrage movement. As president, she launched NAWSA's "society plan," which recruited respectable middle-class women, especially influential clubwomen, as well as ministers and wealthy men to the suffrage cause. In 1904, NAWSA recommended that suffragists become more involved in the civic, charitable, or educational work of their communities. Through these efforts, the association would attract an already active and experienced group of wealthy and middle-class women who could be counted on to devote time and money to suffrage campaigns. As a way of welcoming respectable women who were unlikely to attend a public rally, NAWSA began to hold parlor meetings in private homes at which a suffrage advocate would speak: "While we were drinking tea, I gave them a little talk and they asked questions about what was going on" (Graham 1995, 162–163). Although Catt would remain active in the suffrage movement, developing a decade later what she called "The Winning

American suffragettes use parasols to advertise their support for votes for women, ca. 1910. (Hulton-Deutsch Collection/Corbis)

Plan," her husband's deteriorating health led her to resign in 1904 as NAWSA president.

During the first decade of the 20th century, the two most celebrated leaders of the women's suffrage movement passed from the scene: Elizabeth Cady Stanton died in 1902, and four years later, Susan B. Anthony was also dead. A new generation of leaders quickly emerged—Carrie Chapman Catt, Harriot Stanton Blatch, and Alice Paul. As had Blatch, Paul, a native of New Jersey, returned to America in 1910 from England with a strategy for winning the vote based on the more activist and confrontational tactics of the British suffrage movement, tactics that invigorated the suffrage movement in the United States. Although the movement for women's suffrage again fractured during the second decade of the 20th century, the years surrounding World War I provided the requisite political impetus for ratification in 1920 of the 19th Amendment, which guaranteed that the right of all citizens to vote could not be "denied or abridged" on account of sex.

Harriot Stanton Blatch, the Women's Trade Union League, and Women's Suffrage

Not all suffragists were enthusiastic about the attention NAWSA was extending to society women. Elizabeth Cady Stanton's daughter Harriot Stanton Blatch chafed, pronouncing that the suffrage movement in New York was "in a rut. . . . It bored its adherents and repelled its opponents. Most of the ammunition was being wasted on its supporters in private drawing rooms" (Flexner 1959, 250). The elitism of the society plan repelled Blatch, and in 1907, she founded the Equality League of Self-Supporting Women "to recognize the importance of the vote to wage-earning women and the importance of wage-earning women to winning the vote" (DuBois 1995, 222). The Equality League looked to unite the "talents of educated professionals" with "the power and political sagacity of trade-union women" to develop "a new and aggressive—indeed militant—style of activism" in the suffrage movement (DuBois 1995, 222).

Blatch saw work outside the home in factories and offices as a means for the psychological as much as the material emancipation of women. Still, the issues of class and gender, the exploitation of laboring women, and the impact of paid work on the place of women in society needed to be worked out. Hence, for Blatch, suffrage was just as necessary for working-class women as it was for middle-class and wealthy women. In fact, she believed that "it is the women of the industrial class . . . who have been the means of bringing about the altered attitude of public opinion toward women's work in every sphere of life" (DuBois 1995, 231). Whereas Blatch's mother, Elizabeth Cady Stanton, argued for suffrage based on the natural right of every citizen in America, Blatch emphasized the economic contribution and the significance of women as a group (DuBois 1995, 231). In 1902, shortly after she returned to the United States from England where she had participated in the militant suffrage movement, Blatch became active in the Women's Trade Union League (WTUL), a coalition of working-class and elite women who hoped to draw wage-earning women into the trade union movement. As head of the WTUL's Equality League of Self-Supporting Women, Blatch engaged female professionals to support the 1909 shirtwaist workers' strike. Leaders of the WTUL walked the picket lines, and some, such as WTUL president Mary Drier, were arrested during the strike (Green 1980, 72). Leonora O'Reilly, a labor organizer and leading member of the New York Suffrage League, informed the antisuffrage politicians that the 8 million working women in the United States did not have "the protection that we should have. You have been making laws for us and the laws you have made have not been good for us" (Davis 1983, 143). The WTUL, which in 1908 had established a Suffrage Department, emphasized enfranchisement as a prerequisite for gaining better working and living conditions for working-class women.

Attracted by the greater militancy of the British "suffragettes," as they had come to call themselves, Blatch encouraged open-air parades and public demonstrations as the best means to gain much-needed publicity for the suffrage movement. Acknowledging "the value of publicity or rather the harm of the lack of it," Blatch employed attention-getting tactics to encourage the mainstream press to acknowledge the suffrage movement (DuBois 1995, 239). Having rejected the genteel traditions identified with NAWSA's society plan, Blatch was often pictured and quoted in the growing newspaper coverage of the increasingly outrageous and controversial events. In an October 1908 story headlined "Women Suffragists

Plan Hot Campaign," *The New York Times,* attempting to clarify the state of the suffrage movement for its readers, distinguished between the "old-line suffrage organizations who don't want to be confused with the suffragettes or street variety, lately imported from England. 'Don't get us mixed,' they say. 'You see there are suffragettes and suffragists and then there are Hattie Blatch's 14,000 self-supporting women'" (*New York Times,* October 25, 1908). Yet the tactics employed by the militants, who became a distinct wing of movement in New York, would soon be adopted by mainstream suffrage groups throughout the United States.

Socialists and Women's Suffrage

Although convinced that support of working women was necessary to the success of the suffrage movement, Harriot Stanton Blatch nevertheless regarded class-related issues as secondary to enfranchisement. Membership in unions, historian Nancy Schrom Dye points out, was for Blatch only one component of a multifaceted campaign for women's rights, one that could not be an end in itself (Dye 1977, 239). Yet based on their "materialist" analysis of modern capitalism, women active in the Socialist Party of America (SPA), many of whom had participated in the suffrage movement, would turn Blatch's priorities on their head. To them class struggle was primary and the political rights of women secondary. Rather than merely gaining the right of women to participate in the process, socialists wanted to overthrow the existing political system. Lines from "The Socialist and the Suffragist," a contemporary poem by Charlotte Perkins Gilman capture the nature of this debate: "'A lifted world lifts women up,'/ The Socialists explained./ 'You cannot lift the world at all/ While half of it is kept so small,'/ The suffragist maintained" (Buhle 1983, 214).

For a brief moment toward the end of the first decade of the new century, the divide that kept socialists and suffragists apart would be bridged. Following the 1907 call by the worldwide socialist movement, the Second International, to agitate "strenuously" for woman suffrage, American socialists in their convention the following year created the Woman's National Committee (WNC), whose main task was to formulate a strong suffrage plank in the Socialist Party's platform. In 1909, the National Executive Committee of the SPA called on locals to hold mass meetings on behalf of women's rights on Woman's Day, the last Sunday in February. That year the WNC also participated in a NAWSA-led mass petition drive. This effort was one of the last cooperative ventures sponsored by the WNC. In the aftermath of the great strikes of 1909, New York socialists inveighed against political agitation for the vote as drawing attention away from the class-conscious goal of organizing factory workers. During the next decade, even though the suffrage movement's more militant tactics had appealed to such

African American Women and Suffrage

African American women had only a tenuous relationship to the suffrage movement. Tensions had first surfaced in the late 1860s at the time of the political debate over the 15th Amendment, which expanded suffrage to include former slaves but not women and resulted in Elizabeth Cady Stanton and Susan B. Anthony dissociating themselves from "Negro suffrage" (Terborg-Penn 1995, 139). By the turn of the century, despite the National American Women's Suffrage Association's lack of solidarity with African American women, Mary Church Terrell, president of the National Association of Colored Women (NACW), called on "my sisters of the dominant race, [to] stand up not only for the oppressed sex, but also for the oppressed race!" (Terborg-Penn 1995, 145). The NACW had already established a suffrage department to increase the understanding of governmental affairs among African American women so they would "be prepared to handle the vote intelligently and wisely" (Davis 1983, 144). African American women persisted in their struggle for universal suffrage even as NAWSA, looking to build its movement among Southern white women, sanctioned permitting state suffrage organizations to endorse white supremacy.

leading socialists as Florence Kelley, cross-class coalitions between socialists and suffragists took place only on the state and local levels (Buhle 1983, 222–239).

Antisuffrage Activism

Opposition to suffrage had long been expressed by businessmen in the liquor-making and dispensing industries, proponents of the Victorian cult of domesticity, and Southern states' rights advocates. By the first decade of the 20th century the "antis"—women and men organized in opposition to women suffrage—had developed a formidable campaign against the involvement of women in politics. Some assumed that women's alleged essential emotionalism or their supposed delicate physical constitution or nervousness prevented women's involvement in the practical and competitive world of politics. Antisuffrage politicians, in particular, regularly invoked the sentimental vision of Home and Mother as precluding any female engagement in the public sphere (Kraditor 1971, 12–15). In *Women in the Republic* (1897) Helen Kendrick Johnson, a writer of children's stories who was, along with her journalist husband, Rossiter Johnson, a leading activist in the anti–women's suffrage movement in upstate New York, agreed that a woman's sacred place in her separate, domestic sphere was essential for maintenance of the American republic. She also insisted that women did not need the vote to obtain their full legal and economic rights. Other antis believed that a woman's participation in politics could only diffuse the energy that she more appropriately employed in meeting "the demands of society, the calls of charity, the church, and philanthropy" (Thuner 1995, 210). By 1900, there were organized antisuffrage groups in Massachusetts, New York, Illinois, South Dakota, Washington, and Oregon.

Yet, the antis did not so much oppose active participation by women in public affairs as insist that it be "without the ballot," that is, carried out by disinterested nonpartisan women (Thurner 1995, 203). Only by their independence, "freed from party affiliations, untrammeled by any political obligation," Mrs. Barclay Hazard told the New York State Federation of Women's Clubs in 1907, could women assert their appropriate influence on society (Thurner 1995, 212). Much like their sisters in the suffrage movement, turn-of-the-century antisuffragists insisted on the distinctive contribution that women could make to improving society. But for the antis, a woman's role as a public advocate was diminished rather than enhanced by the vote.

"As American as Apple Pie"? Labor Radicalism in the United States

Although launched in the early 1870s as a temperance group dedicated to ending the pernicious influence of alcohol by closing down the retail liquor trade and reforming individual drunkards through moral suasion, the Women's Christian Temperance Union (WCTU) under the leadership of Frances Willard expanded and redefined its mission in the 1880s and 1890s. To advance Willard's motto, "Do Everything," the WCTU extended its philanthropic endeavors beyond charity into social action. As she began to understand that poverty and poor working conditions bred intemperance (rather than the other way around) among the working classes, Willard endorsed the eight-hour workday and became a supporter of trade unions and the reformist Knights of Labor. By the 1890s, her reading of Edward Bellamy's utopian novel *Looking Backward* led Willard, like Gilman, to embrace "gospel socialism" and to advocate such fundamental reforms of the economic system as the five-and-a-half-day week and the nationalization or municipal ownership of the railroads, the telegraph, public utilities, and factories. Willard addressed her "Beloved Comrades" at the 1897 WCTU convention in Buffalo, New York, telling them that socialism "is the higher way; it enacts into everyday living the ethics of Christ's gospel. Nothing else will do it" (Weinstein 1969, 53). Although she would be unsuccessful in leading the WCTU to embrace socialism, by 1900, "Do Everything" encompassed support for women's suffrage and the WCTU had become a substantial political and social force in the United States (Bordin 1990, 95–139).

By 1900, socialism had attracted a diverse group of adherents, some of whom, like Willard, had first embraced the nationalist program of Bellamy or the ideals of Christian socialism, whereas others, such as Daniel De Leon, the head of the Socialist Labor Party, had come to socialism through an orthodox reading of Karl Marx. Eugene V. Debs is said to have been converted to socialism during his stay in Woodstock Prison, where he had been incarcerated for his leadership of the 1894 Pullman strike. Yet, even though the Milwaukee socialist Victor Berger had brought Debs a copy of *Das Kapital* while the labor leader was in prison, Debs's advocacy of socialism was less an epiphany than a deepening conviction that the growing concentration of economic and political power of the nation's largest corporations fundamentally threatened America's democratic traditions. Debs proposed a counterrevolution that would marshal the political power of the people to end the competitive wage system and replace it with a cooperative commonwealth, that is, a social and economic order that equalized the benefits of work and ensured the dignity of each individual. In 1900, running under the banner of the Socialist Democratic Party in his first campaign for president, Debs spoke before cheering crowds, condemning capitalism and invoking socialism as the sole means by which Americans would be able to redeem their revolutionary heritage (Salvatore 1982, 147–188).

In July 1901, more than 100 delegates gathered in a Unity convention in Indianapolis to launch the Socialist Party of America (SPA). Julius A. Wayland predicted in his weekly socialist newspaper *Appeal to Reason* in 1902 that "the next few years will give this nation to the Socialist Party" (Shannon 1967, 4). Facing the future with great hopes, the party's founders attempted, with some success, to overcome the internal dissension and factional strife that had splintered radical movements during the latter decades of the 19th century. At least through the next decade, the growth of socialism would appear to justify the party leaders' optimism. Debs would run as the SPA's candidate in the 1904, 1908, and 1912 elections, and each time the party's membership and vote totals rose dramatically. In 1904, the SPA had more than 20,000 members (about twice the number as at its founding) and Debs polled more than 400,000 votes, or four times his 1900 totals. By the next presidential election, SPA membership had again doubled, but the vote for Debs remained almost the same. The high point for the socialist movement was reached in 1912 when party membership almost tripled, and Debs's votes totaled 6 percent of the popular vote (Shannon 1967, 4–5). In that year, some 1,200 socialists held office in 340 municipalities across the United States, including 79 mayors in 24 states (Weinstein 1969, 93–103).

Although frequently rent by factional struggles during its early years, the SPA remained a coalition of regional groups who gained strength from their diversity. The Lower East Side of Manhattan, especially the neighborhoods around Union Square and in the garment district, was one center for socialism. David Shannon, in his history of the SPA, observes that socialism in these neighborhoods "was a way of life" that extended out of the workplace into the streets and homes. "You grew up a reader of Abraham Cahan's *Jewish Daily Forward,* in Yiddish, or the *Call,* in English," he adds (Shannon 1967, 8). Linked to the largely immigrant and class-conscious unions like the Amalgamated Clothing Workers and the International Ladies' Garment Workers' Union, socialists also formed numerous benevolent and fraternal societies such as the Bund, the Jewish Socialist Federation, and the Workmen's Circle. The socialist movement thrived in the tenements, cafés, dance halls, and theaters as well as in the parades, in the crowds that responded to Union Square soapbox orators, and in such strikes as the "Great Revolt" among cloak makers in 1910 that were carried out as public celebrations of solidarity. One observer of a march during this strike describes a "sea of people surging from all side streets to Fifth Avenue. . . . In my mind I could only picture to myself such a scene taking place when the Jews were led out of Egypt" (Leinenweber 1977, 155). During the 1908 campaign for Congress of the socialist labor leader Morris Hillquit, who grew up on the Lower East Side, an average of 25 street meetings were held each night. Unable to break the influence of Tammany Hall, the Democratic political machine, over the neighborhood's immigrant community, Hillquit lost this election, as he had two years earlier (Howe 1976, 313).

The Workmen's Circle (Arbeiter Ring)

Founded in 1892 as a Jewish social and cultural fraternal society, the Workmen's Circle provided its members with mutual aid health and death benefits and was allied with Jewish unions, the Yiddish labor press, and the Socialist Party. The roots of this organization lay in the ambition of two Jewish cloak makers, Sam Greenberg and Harry Lasker, who joined together with a small group of other workers in March 1892 to launch the Workingmen's Circle Society of New York. Answering the self-posed question, "What is the Workmen's Circle?" one member announced in 1894 that the order attempts to make known to each member that "he has a right to enjoy, to which he is entitled as a human being, rather than to exist as a slave, a creative slave, who creates for others what he may not have for himself" (Shapiro 1970, 33). After branch lodges had been established in Harlem and Brooklyn, both in 1898, the 300 members decided two years later to reorganize the society as the Workmen's Circle. At the time that the new group met in its first convention in March 1901, there were 9 branches in three states with a combined membership of 644. Two years later, the Workmen's Circle had 27 branches with a total of 1,500 members. The association would continue to grow through the rest of the decade, enrolling almost 40,000 members by 1910.

Among those who joined the Workmen's Circle in the first decade of the 20th century were the socialist members of the General Jewish Workers' Bund of Russia and Poland who fled to America in the aftermath of the Kishineff Pogroms of 1903 and the aborted Russian revolution of 1905. Coming with an active ideological background sympathetic to the left wing of the international socialist movement, the new members looked to forge a Jewish working-class identity rooted in the class struggle. For them, the Workmen's Circle's active involvement in strikes, like that of the shirtwaist workers in 1909, was not simply a victory for workers who happened to be Jews but one "for *Jewish* workers" (Howe 1976, 294). An active lecturer for the Workmen's Circle, Baruch C. Vladeck, noted that it was "no exaggeration to suggest that during the lecture season, no less than one thousand lectures are held at branches of the Workmen's Circle" (Howe 1976, 357). The wide-ranging topics included the history of ancient Greece, Yiddish literature, religion, free love, and socialism. Vladack worried that the Circle's success as a mutual benefit association drew too many members who were more interested in practical services than in radicalism and social change (Shapiro 1970, 46–47). Despite such "faults," in 1910 one leader was certain that the more the Workmen's Circle grew, "the more [it would] be inspired by its great calling—to win for socialism the entire Jewish working population of America." To aid this cause, the Circle opened in New York in 1906 its first socialist Sunday school, and by 1911, there were 10 such schools with an enrollment of 1,500 pupils in the city. With its lectures, classes, and comfortable settings in which to meet and gossip while enjoying a glass of tea, its insurance benefit program that offered members at least some security, and its active support for unions and the Socialist Party, the Workmen's Circle enabled Jewish immigrants in these years to feel that even as they adjusted to life in America they could retain a socialist consciousness.

"One Step at a Time": Evolutionary Socialism in the Early 20th Century

An orthodox Marxist, Morris Hillquit became a leader of New York's socialist community. Having fallen out with Daniel De Leon over the formation in 1898 of the Socialist Trade and Labor Alliance as a rival to the American Federation of Labor, Hillquit was instrumental three years later in bringing together radical and conservative socialists to found the SPA. Hillquit believed that to flourish socialists required "the cooperation of persons from other classes" (Weinstein 1969, 10). As a supporter of immediate reforms, such as public health clinics and the regulation of hours and wages that would help workers but did not necessarily challenge the basic capitalist order, he was what is often referred to as an "evolutionary" socialist. In 1908, Hillquit wrote to a progressive reformer that "we do not expect the Socialist order to be introduced by one sudden and great political cataclysm, . . . nor [do we] expect it to be established by a rabble made desperate by misery and starvation" (Dubofsky, American National Biography Online). Historian James Weinstein highlights the similarities between Hillquit's political and economic program and that supported by Debs. Both socialist leaders endorsed industrial unionism—the representation of all workers, including the unskilled, in an industry by one union rather than by craft—as was the policy of the AFL. Each supported political action, and, although Debs supported the formation of the Industrial Workers of the World (IWW) in 1905 and Hillquit did not, both labor leaders opposed the use of violence by labor unions (Weinstein 1969, 10).

Still another supporter of the "one step at a time" evolutionary approach, Victor Berger, had helped Debs found the Social Democratic Party in 1897 and then left the Socialist Labor Party with Hillquit to launch the SPA (Shannon 1967, 16). Berger, a publisher of German- and English-language socialist newspapers, helped turn Milwaukee into another regional center of socialism in the United States. In contrast to most other industrial cities, Milwaukee's heavily German and Old Stock American labor movement was staunchly socialist. Like Hillquit, Berger opposed AFL president Samuel Gompers but not the Federation itself, and he criticized socialists who attended the founding of the IWW for being well meaning but misguided. Having helped establish a powerful political organization in Milwaukee, Berger was in 1910 elected as the first socialist to serve in Congress. As a representative of Wisconsin's Fifth Congressional District, Berger sponsored legislation that would provide old-age pensions, abolish child labor, and develop public works projects for the relief of the unemployed (Shannon 1967, 21–25). Berger's "step at a time" reformism was based on his belief that the economic concentration of capital in America would lead to the eventual triumph of socialism through the nationalization of industry. However committed he may have been to a peaceful transition to socialism, Berger was personally bombastic and egotistical and very much at the center of the sectarian battles that roiled the Socialist Party during its first decade (Miller, "Berger").

Grassroots Socialism

During the first decade of the new century, a radical and emotional offshoot of socialism emerged in the Great Plains and in the South and Western states of Texas, Oklahoma, Louisiana, Alabama, Kansas, and Missouri. Outspoken critics of the evolutionary approach endorsed by Berger and Hillquit, which they derided as "slowcialism," the socialist movement in these states was a grassroots campaign among poor farmers and workers, many of whom had been militant Populists in the 1890s (Shannon 1967, 16). Employing rhetoric based more in religious revivalism than in Marxism, the indebted farmers and impoverished tenants of the agrarian countryside united in class struggle against wealthy absentee landlords and businessmen, the "parasites" of the cities and towns. Socialist Party leaders, organizers, editors, and lecturers in these states acted as a "cadre of professional agitators" who galvanized the local militants who had already developed a radical brand of moral and natural rights socialism (Green 1978, xi–xx). These socialists were Debs's natural constituency.

The socialist word spread through the Southwest and Great Plains at encampments, lively outdoor meetings that lasted about a week and attracted large crowds, often numbering 5,000 people, who came in covered wagons from as far as 70 miles away. The weeklong activities included music, classes in history and economics, and speeches from Debs and other activists, including Kate Richards O'Hare, who published the *National Rip-Saw;* Caroline Lowe, a former Kansas City schoolteacher; and Oscar Ameringer, a socialist journalist and organizer. These fiery speakers exhorted the crowd to struggle to build the cooperative commonwealth. Standing in a grove of trees or under a large tent, the socialist disciples sang "I Will Join the Party, Mother," with lyrics that announced "Yes, I'll join the party mother, Join it body and soul / With my comrades, like a brother, Fighting e'er to gain a goal" (Shannon 1967, 26–27). Impassioned socialist orators frequently quoted chapter and verse from the Bible as inspiration for socialism. One Texas socialist preacher spoke on "Socialism and the Bible" to "prove that capitalist rent, interest, and profit [were] condemned by the word of God" (Green 1978, 151–152). Debs explained the encampment audience's "genuine ardor and enthusiasm": after listening to "the gospel from the party's best preachers" they would "wend their way homeward . . . feeling that they [had] refreshed themselves at a fountain of enthusiasm" (Green 1978, 158).

Two men in Yellow Medicine County, Minnesota, with Socialist Party pennants. Socialism attracted widespread interest in the United States during the early 20th century. (Ole Mattiason Aarseth/Minnesota Historical Society)

Getting Out the Word

However colorful and inspiring they may have been, socialist encampments took place only once a year. Thus, the main vehicle for steady, everyday communication and education was the socialist press, a vast array of weekly and monthly newspapers and magazines circulated nationally, daily and weekly, including local newspapers, trade union newspapers, foreign language papers, and other

"Red Kate"

Looking back later in life on her experiences traveling on the Southwestern encampment circuit with Eugene Debs, Kate Richards O'Hare captures the gatherings' revivalist spirit. The crowds responded to them, she recalls, as "Jesus of Nazareth and Martha, burdened by many cares, speaking to the harried Jews in Palestine" (Green 1978, 154). Having come of age in a time of despair caused by her family's desperate circumstances, O'Hare explains in "How I became a Socialist Agitator," published in *Socialist Woman* in October 1908, how she was drawn into the "church and religious work" by her faith that God would not have "abandoned his children to such hopeless misery and sordid suffering. There was nothing uplifting in it, nothing to draw the heart nearer to him, only forces that clutched and dragged men and women down into the abyss of drunkenness and vice" (O'Hare 1908). Yet even as she embraced religion, O'Hare, much like Frances Williard of the Women's Christian Temperance Union, came to understand that intemperance and vice "did not cause poverty, but that poverty was the mother of the whole hateful brood" of suffering that she hoped to eliminate (O'Hare 1908). In the mid-1890s, while working as an apprentice in her father's machine shop in Kansas City, Kansas, O'Hare was initially introduced to socialism by Mother Jones, the labor organizer and radical agitator, and a short while later by Julius A. Wayland, the editor of *Appeal to Reason*. Now, "All the universe pulsated with a new life that swept away the last vestige of the mists of creed and dogma and old ideas and beliefs," she recalled. "Recreated, I lived again with new aims, new hopes, new aspirations and the dazzling view of the new and wonderful work to do" (O'Hare 1908). Even though throughout her life her rhetoric remained evangelical, O'Hare was an evolutionary socialist who believed that socialism would inevitable replace capitalism peacefully through reform, political action, and the education of workers (Miller, "O'Hare").

On New Year's Day, 1902 Kate Richards married Frank O'Hare, a fellow student in the International School of Social Economy run by Walter Thomas Mills, "the little professor" and the author of *The Struggle for Existence,* a textbook on "scientific socialism" (Green 1978, 41). The new couple began their lives as itinerant socialist lecturers "on the street corner and in the pulpit, at the shop door and in the college assembly room, in the country school houses and trades union hall, in the legislative chambers and temples of justice" (O'Hare 1908). During these "glorious years of battle with the forces of ignorance," O'Hare looked ahead optimistically, believing that as a result of socialism's already impressive gains, in the United States and around the world there "glows the spark of human brotherhood, ready to spring at our call into living flame" (O'Hare 1908).

O'Hare is often referred to as the second most effective socialist lecturer after Debs. Preaching, like Debs, a secular socialism that attacked capitalism from a materialist basis, O'Hare used a revivalist approach to inspire her audiences to, in the words of another encampment lecturer, adopt "socialism like a new religion" (Green 1978, 162). In 1909, O'Hare took over the leadership of the state Socialist Party in Kansas and the following year ran unsuccessfully for Congress. During the following decade, she held top party positions, was an editor of the *National Rip-Saw,* and would, like Debs, be jailed for opposing American entry into World War I.

publications (Weinstein 1969, 84–85). One of the most influential socialist papers, *Appeal to Reason,* cost subscribers only 25 cents a year and, in 1907, reached a circulation of more than 300,000 (Green 1978, 39). The newspaper's editor, Julius Wayland, proudly proclaimed that "more people have had the subject [socialism] thrust upon their attention by the *Appeal* than all other influences combined. . . . It goes into new places or into new homes in old places and prepares the ground for the work of organizers and other literature" (Shannon 1967, 28). Louis Klamroth was one of 80,000 "salesmen-soldiers" in the *Appeal*'s army; riding his bicycle around the countryside, he sold more than 100,000 subscriptions and thousands of socialist pamphlets (Shannon 1967, 29). James Weinstein has uncovered at least 50 weekly and monthly socialist periodicals that began publishing before 1910. Although the great majority had fewer than 5,000 subscribers, in 1912 the *Appeal* had an average weekly circulation of 761,741; the *National Rip-Saw* reached around 150,000: the *Jewish Daily Forward,* 142,000; and *International Socialist Review,* 42,000. Although few of these papers or magazines were directly owned or published by the SPA, the socialist press was a main source for education in socialism and current information about socialist, labor, and farmers' movements (Weinstein 1969, 84–102).

One journal, *The Intercollegiate Socialist,* was a quarterly publication of the Intercollegiate Socialist Society (ISS), which served as a forum for socialist students and intellectuals. The society's organ, *The Intercollegiate Socialist,* provided a place to discuss the "possible methods of socializing industry," the activities of Victor Berger in Congress, and other tactical matters (Weinstein 1969, 75). Started in September 1905 by Upton Sinclair, the ISS had 70 chapters 10 years later. The adventure novelist and socialist author Jack London toured the nation's campuses on behalf of the ISS, urging undergraduates to social action, to move beyond a "passionless pursuit of passionless intelligence." Possibly London inspired the journalist and later communist John Reed, who says of his introduction to socialism during his years at Harvard (1905–1910) that he learned that "there was something going on in the dull outside world more thrilling than college activities" (Cantor 1978, 44). Another center for socialist education was the Rand School of Social Science founded in New York in 1906 with funds from the will of Mrs. Carrie Rand, the wealthy mother-in-law of the Christian socialist George D. Herron. The Rand School focused on worker education and offered courses in public speaking, English grammar and composition, and American history and government as well as socialist theory and history (Shannon 1967, 9).

Eugene V. Debs: Socialist Citizen

The most powerful voice spreading the socialist message in the early 20th century remained that of Eugene V. Debs. Unlike Hillquit, Berger, and other socialist leaders, Debs focused less on getting elected than on using his campaigns as

Jack London

The critic Alfred Kazin encapsulated Jack London's literary output in his remark that the "greatest story Jack London ever wrote was the story he lived" (Kazin 1942, 85). London's popular adventure stories such as *The Call of the Wild* (1903) and *The Sea Wolf* (1904), as well as his socialist works, the collection of essays *The War of the Classes* (1905), *The Iron Heel* (1908), and *Martin Eden* (1909), all draw on his turbulent life. London grew up in poverty, the illegitimate son of a spiritualist mother and an astrologer father who left his wife when he learned that she was pregnant. London was forced to work from an early age, even after his mother married John London, an unsuccessful businessman. The boy sold papers and did odd jobs. As he got older, he worked in a cannery, labored long hours in a jute mill, shoveled coal on the Oakland Street Railway, and marched on Washington with Coxey's Army (a protest by the jobless during the 1890s depression). He finished high school, where he read Karl Marx's *The Communist Manifesto,* and joined the Socialist Labor Party. Following high school, London unsuccessfully sought to make his fortune extracting gold in the Klondike. In 1902, he spent six weeks in the slums of London and finally found his vocation in writing the stories and books that translated these life experiences into popular fiction and active involvement with the socialist cause.

Although London pointed to his reading of *The Communist Manifesto* as the key to his conversion to socialism, his ideas were more an amalgam of influences, including those of Charles Darwin and Herbert Spencer on the ideas of evolution and the survival of the fittest. From these authors and from his life he came to view society as a struggle in the "Social Pit," a conflict "of man against man, as the domination of the weak by the strong" (Rideout 1956, 41). *The Iron Heel* depicts the long reign of a capitalist oligarchy that stamps out democracy and free institutions before being ultimately swept away by "the Brotherhood of Man." In *Martin Eden,* which ends with the suicide of the protagonist, a stand-in for the author, the hero is a common laborer and sailor who struggles to become a writer and free himself from middle class authority (Rideout 1956, 45).

In 1901 and 1905, London, "The Boy Socialist," as the newspapers dubbed him, ran unsuccessfully for mayor of Oakland, California, on the Socialist Party ticket. Already a famous author, he became the first president of the Intercollegiate Socialist Society (ISS) in 1905 and in October traveled across the Midwest and the East lecturing on the coming revolution. At Yale, he lectured on "Revolution," telling the undergraduates, "The capitalist class has been indicted. It has failed in its management and its management is to be taken away from it. . . . The revolution is here, now. Stop it who can" (Rideout 1956, 39). London was a complicated figure whose own radicalism was undercut by a racialism drawn from his sympathy with Spencer and Social Darwinism. London's body of work combines both "a glorification of the superior individual over the mass" and a warm-hearted embrace of the brotherhood of man (Rideout 1956, 42).

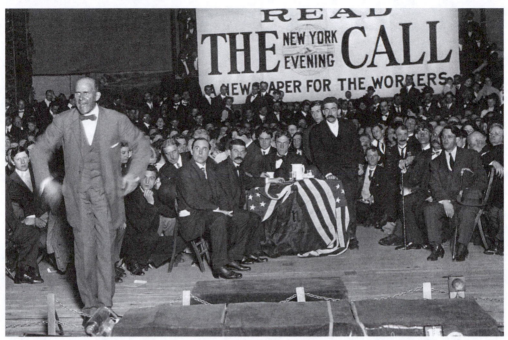

The socialist Eugene V. Debs speaks to a rally in support of his bid to become president of the United States. (AP/Wide World Photos)

vehicles for mass education. A native son who was capable of attracting a large and devoted following, Debs saw the key to eventual socialist success not in "the mere accumulation of votes" but instead in the "profound transformation of individual voters" (Salvatore 1982, 186–187). In 1904, the SPA nominated Debs for president and Benjamin Hanford, a New York printer, for vice president. Listening to Debs speak at one campaign stop, Ralph Chaplin, a young socialist, was impressed with Debs's earnestness: "I shall always remember the resonance, flexibility and volume of that voice. . . . You feel he really cared when he talked about the misery and injustice afflicting the world" (Green 1978, 31). The Socialist Party secured the ballots of more than 10,000 voters in 13 states in 1904, which doubled the socialist total from four years earlier. The most impressive gains were made in the American heartland—Ohio, Iowa, and Kansas— where the socialist vote increased by almost 1,400 hundred percent (Salvatore 1982, 190).

Socialists entered the 1908 presidential campaign with great hopes. Since their last campaign, Socialist Party membership had doubled and the number of locals had grown to 2,500 (Bell 1967, 68). The country and capitalism were still reeling from the economic dislocation caused by the Panic of 1907; the popular and dynamic Roosevelt had been replaced by William Howard Taft as the Republican nominee; and Socialist Party membership had continued to surge,

The "Red Special"

The 1908 Socialist Party convention featured a tumultuous struggle between the left, which united behind Eugene V. Debs, and the right, led by Victor Berger and Morris Hillquit. After adopting a platform that made concessions to both factions, the party endorsed Debs for president and Benjamin Hanford for vice president, the same ticket that it had nominated in the 1904 election. Debs, who was in Girard, Kansas, during the convention, told a local crowd that he opposed capitalism because it was "a system in which labor is simply merchandise; in which the man who works the hardest and longest has the least to show for it" (Morgan 1962, 94). To reach as many people as possible, national party secretary J. Mahlon Barnes proposed outfitting a special train, which was dubbed the "Red Special," to carry Debs across the country as he campaigned for the presidency (Ginger 1949, 285–286). From August 30, 1908, through Election Day, the Red Special conveyed Debs along with a brass band and a car loaded with campaign literature to more than 300 communities in 33 states (Salvatore 1982, 223). Having recently recovered from throat surgery, Debs made between 5 and 20 speeches a day for 65 consecutive days. At stops in larger cities, Debs spoke in auditoriums and convention centers, as he did at the Hippodrome in New York City before an audience of 10,000 who, *The New York Times* reported, held aloft a "red sea of waving" flags whenever they became enthusiastic (*New York Times,* October 5, 1908).

The Red Special began its journey in Chicago. At each stop, local party officials wearing their red lapel buttons boarded the train and then introduced Debs to cheering crowds waiting alongside the track. Debs said of the Red Special, "The enthusiasm it inspires everywhere is a marvel to me" (Morgan 1962, 101). In Des Moines, Iowa, Debs excoriated the Republicans for being tied hand and foot to Wall Street and derided William Jennings Bryan, the Democratic Party candidate, for claiming that he would represent both workers and employers: "Such a feat . . . was just as impossible as it would be 'to ride two horses at the same time, going in opposite directions'" (Ginger 1949, 292). In Grand Junction, Colorado, more than 1,800 people, half the town's population, jammed the largest hall to hear Debs attack capitalism (Morgan 1962, 101–102). Wearing his nightshirt, Debs spoke to a huge throng in Santa Barbara, California, who had come out to greet him when he arrived at four o'clock in the morning. Heading east, the Red Special arrived in New York's Grand Central Station to a crowd "eager to touch so much as the hem of his garment" (Morgan 1962, 106). After speaking at the Hippodrome, Debs toured the Lower East Side, where Morris Hillquit was running for Congress. The novelist Ernest Poole captures the Debs charisma, "I stood near him for hours one night on a truck that slowly plowed its way through a roaring ocean of people as far as the eye could see, all up and down dark tenement streets. . . . The truck stopped and Debs leaned out with both arms raised, smiling over the roaring crowd. Stillness came. And then only his voice was heard— a voice that could do with a crowd what it willed, not because of the mind behind it but because of the great warm heart which the crowd felt speaking there. . . .

The "Red Special", Continued

I listened to him, tingling deep. What could I myself do for the cause?" (Ginger 1949, 299).

Not everyone greeted Debs's Red Special campaign with enthusiasm. Noting the "spirit of revolution" that Debs sought to inspire, *The New York Times* observed that he "would make a fine campaigner in Russia or Turkey, where the constituencies have something to revolt against. . . . But nobody who retains coherency of thought believes that our troubles are remediable by revolution in any correct sense of the word" (*New York Times,* August 21, 1908). In response to the Socialist Party candidates' attacks against him, Samuel Gompers, president of the American Federation of Labor denounced Debs as "the Apostle of Failure" and pronounced that "a vote for the Socialist or Independent Party is one lost to the Democratic candidate" Bryan, whom Gompers had endorsed (Morgan 1962, 110). Despite of the high hopes that Debs inspired, the Socialist Party did little better in this election than it had in 1904. Undaunted, the *Appeal to Reason* countered, "Taft is elected; Bryan defeated; Debs victorious" (Ginger 1949, 301). Debs, who worried less about vote totals than about educating the public "in the true spirit of Socialist comradeship," was satisfied that the Red Special had triumphed (Ginger 1949, 302).

---

reaching in 1908 41,000 dues-paying members in more than 3,000 locals. Yet the results of the election were disappointing. Despite impressive gains in the West and Southwest, Debs polled fewer than 20,000 more votes than he had in the 1904 campaign. Working against the Socialists was Samuel Gompers's public support of the Democratic candidate, William Jennings Bryan, the first political endorsement the labor leader had made in 22 years. In addition, both traditional parties had supported economic and political reforms in their platforms, which preempted the insurgent appeal of the socialists (Salvatore 1982, 220–224). Able to inspire intense personal fervor for himself, Debs never quite convinced working- and middle-class voters in the United States to break with the traditional parties and adopt a more class-conscious approach to politics (Salvatore 1982, 267–269).

Samuel Gompers, the American Federation of Labor, and Socialism

At the American Federation of Labor's (AFL) 1903 convention in Boston, socialist trade unionists introduced 10 different resolutions aimed at bringing about "some phase" of the cooperative commonwealth. These resolutions represented the latest maneuver in a more than decade-long effort by socialists to persuade the AFL and Samuel Gompers to commit to independent political action on behalf of a radical restructuring of American society. To this effort, Gompers responded: "I want to tell you, Socialists, that I have studied your philosophy; read your works upon economics . . . studied your standard works. . . . I know, too, what you have up your sleeve. And I want to say that I am entirely at variance with your philosophy. I declare to you, I am not only at variance with your doctrines, but with your philosophy. Economically, you are unsound; socially you are wrong; industrially you are an impossibility" (Gompers 1:1967, 397). Although in his youth Gompers had been deeply impressed by Marxian and radical ideas, by 1903 his understanding of history had left him with little patience for all "isms"; as Gompers saw it, the principal task of American trade unions was to achieve better wages and conditions for workers within the existing order. At least in the short run, Gompers prevailed and the convention rejected the socialist resolutions by a margin of five to one.

In the 1890s, Gompers twice surmounted socialist challenges to his pure-and-simple trade union philosophy, although in the second instance he won at the cost of a brief hiatus in his presidency of the AFL. At the 1890, AFL convention the conflict between federation members affiliated with the Socialist Labor Party (SLP) and the federation's leadership came to a head. Daniel DeLeon, a lawyer and former law professor who led the SLP and a supporter of industrial unionism and class-based political action, branded Gompers a "labor faker." Despite DeLeon's attack, Gompers succeeded at this convention in excluding SLP representatives from membership in the AFL. But the socialists continued to challenge Gompers. At the AFL convention in 1893 and then again in 1894, Thomas J. Morgan, a prominent socialist from Chicago, offered resolutions in support of a political program that, in its most controversial plank, called for "the collective ownership by the people of all the means of production and distribution" (Greene 1998, 62). Debate centered on a resolution that would commit the AFL to organizing an independent labor party. Put to a vote in 1893, the resolution lost by only 71 votes out of 2,400 cast. The following year, Gompers more successfully maneuvered to defeat the socialists' challenge to his leadership, but he did not emerge unscathed. With socialist backing, the convention replaced Gompers as AFL president with John McBride, the head of the United Mine Workers Union.

The late 19th century witnessed the emergence of socialism as an organized political force in the United States. When Eugene Debs, the president of the American Railway Union, got out of jail in 1897, after the Pullman strike, he helped found Social Democracy of America, a political party that endorsed socialism. In 1900, Debs was that party's candidate for president of the United States. For his part, Gompers, having returned to office in 1895 as president of the AFL, began a process of accommodation to the modern corporate structure of America by making a clean break with his socialist and radical past. Gompers, who later labeled Debs the "Apostle of Failure," wrote in an editorial in the *American Federationist,* the AFL's official journal, that he saw nothing "new or novel" in the founding of the Socialist Democracy Party. All such utopian efforts lose sight of the incontrovertible fact that "modern industry and commerce admits of no side show or small competitor. The struggle for the attainment of labor's rights, for justice to the toilers, must be waged *within* modern society and upon the field of modern industry and commerce" (Kaufman 1986-1998, 4: 361). Abjuring socialism, Gompers embraced the National Civic Federation (NCF). A tripartite conservative reform association founded by financial and corporate leaders in 1900, the NCF brought these business leaders together with representatives of trade unions and the public. Gompers was named vice president at the founding of the NCF and held this position until his death on December 13, 1924.

Gompers came to believe that opposition by the labor movement to the concentration of corporate economic power in the United States was futile. To be effective, workers had to fashion trade unions as counterorganizations capable of dealing with capital on an equal footing. This would not happen, in Gompers's view, until unions centralized authority and developed a practical administrative system in addition to focusing on winning tangible benefits for their members. Only when trade unions achieved a balance of power with capital could they, through collective bargaining, secure members' material needs: higher wages, shorter hours, and better working conditions. Even though Gompers, during the first decade of the 20th century, would amend his adamantine opposition to party politics, he remained steadfast in his opposition to socialism (Greenberg 1996, 270–286).

American Exceptionalism and the "Why Is There No Socialism" Question

Much historical scholarship on the history of socialism in the United States takes as its point of departure the question first posed in 1906 by the German historical economist Werner Sombart as the title of his book *Why Is There No Socialism in the United States?* Why, Sombart wondered, was the United States the only industrial nation in the world without an entrenched mass-based socialist political movement? The historians and political scientists who have tried to explain American exceptionalism offer variations on the following "objective" factors that Sombart identified: (1) lacking a feudal past and a hereditary aristocracy, Americans have viewed themselves from the beginning as free citizens and have believed that the class distinctiveness that afflicted Europe and the Old World is absent in the United States; (2) the success of capitalism and the material prosperity of Americans subvert socialist class consciousness; (3) greater opportunity for upward social mobility has encouraged Americans to work for individual success rather than for collective advance; (4) geographic mobility, especially the open frontier, has served as a safety valve mitigating discontent in the more established areas of the nation; and (5) the American two-party system has made it difficult for insurgent parties like the Socialist Party to effectively contend for political power, especially because the existing parties tend to appropriate for their purposes elements of the third parties' reform programs (Howe 1985, 110–111). Sombart found most compelling the idea that "on the reefs of roast beef and apple pie" all "socialistic utopias are sent to their doom" in America (Howe 1985, 117).

Sombart's formula for the failure of socialist consciousness to take root in America rested on external factors, that is, on the character and consciousness of the American political and economic system. The labor historian Selig Perlman noted that the massive waves of immigrants who came to United States created deep cleavages within the working class that made it difficult to develop a unified class consciousness (Howe 1985, 111). Historian Stephen Thernstrom, in *Poverty and Progress: Social Mobility in a Nineteenth Century City* (1971), concluded that in the late 19th century, the working-class families of Newburyport, Massachusetts, had been "persuaded by the uniqueness of American social arrangements," especially the opportunity for economic advance (Thernstrom 1971, 186). In his biography *Eugene V. Debs, Citizen and Socialist,* Nick Salvatore observed that the inability of the Socialist Party candidate to gain greater electoral success was not a shortcoming "of party tactics and leadership or capitalist repression." Despite the anxiety they felt over "emerging class distinctions," Americans remained, Salvatore concludes, "resistant to a permanent class consciousness" (Salvatore 1982, 267–269).

There have been voices of dissent. Since the late 1960s, many New Labor Historians, as they are called, question the consensus that formed around working-class Americans' alleged lack of class consciousness. Prominent among this group was Herbert Gutman, whose scholarship concentrated on workers' oppositional movements and workers' resistance to acquisitive capitalist individualism. Gutman rejected as inappropriate the "why no socialism in America" question. "Once we free ourselves from the notion that it should have happened in one particular way," he insisted, "then we stop looking for the reasons why it didn't happen that way" (MARHO 1979, 200–201). For Gutman, what was important was how working men and women "interpreted and then dealt" with their experiences (MARHO 1979, 203). Also writing in the 1960s, James Weinstein determined in *The Decline of Socialism in America, 1912–1925* that through the first decades of the 20th century "a broadly based movement for socialism did exist in the United States" (Weinstein 1969, ix). Weinstein considered the reason for the decline of socialism in the United States to be internal, specifically, the splintering of the radical movement in the aftermath of the 1917 Russian Revolution. Only in the mid-1920s did a mass movement give way to narrow sectarianism and bitter infighting. If the Socialist Party of the early 20th century never quite convinced a majority of Americans to adopt their program for collective action, the socialist movement left a formidable legacy.

One Big Union

Militant class struggle activated the just more than 200 delegates who gathered in Chicago in June 1905 to found a national revolutionary labor union, the Industrial Workers of the World (IWW). Debs was among them. An avowed supporter of industrial unions, Debs vilified the AFL for its policy of craft unionism and, in a plea for a united front, called on each delegate "to take by the hand every man, every woman, who comes here, totally regardless of past affiliation" (Dubofsky 1969, 82–83). The unity that prevailed at the militant IWW's founding did not last long. Within a few years, although he never formally withdrew, Debs had dissociated himself from the IWW.

The impetus for the founding of the IWW came out of the West, in particular the Western Federation of Miners and its longtime secretary, William D. "Big Bill" Haywood. The IWW called for organizing all workers—skilled and unskilled, native-born and immigrant, women and men, black and white—into One Big Union. In the "Manifesto" adopted at its founding convention, the IWW derided the AFL for promoting craft divisions that divide workers "at the ballot box as well as in the shop, mine and factory . . . [whereas] one great industrial union embracing all industries should be founded on the class struggle" (Cantor 1978, 36). The IWW subscribed to the tactics of militant direct action: strikes against employers, slowdowns in the workplace, sabotage, and the general strike, an ill-defined assault on capitalist power that would place the means of production in workers' hands (Dubofsky 1969, 158–159).

By 1908, the broad-based coalition of groups and individuals on the left that had founded the IWW has splintered into factions with discordant agendas. As champion of the "overalls brigade," the growing number of transient workers from the West, Haywood defeated his critics and emerged victorious. Delegates to the 1908 IWW convention formally rejected politics and dedicated the radical union to organizing the mass of unorganized workers (Dubofsky 1987, 55). The following year, representing the unskilled immigrant workers long ignored by the AFL, the IWW assumed the leadership of a strike against the Pressed Steel Care Company in McKees Rocks, Pennsylvania. Yet, in a pattern that would be repeated in later years, victory soon turned into defeat as the employer successfully exploited the skill and ethnic differences among workers and the IWW failed to sustain the organization created by the strike (Dubofsky 1969, 199–209).

During the second decade of the 20th century the IWW went on to battles like the famous "Bread and Roses" textile workers' strike in Lawrence, Massachusetts, that burnished the Wobblies' (the nickname given to members of the IWW) reputation for militant industrial unionism and made the organization a target of vigilante violence and government suppression during World War I. Despite the fear that the IWW and the Socialist Party engendered among political leaders and employers during the first decade of the 20th century, neither of these radical groups was in the end able to contest effectively the class realities of capitalist America. Nevertheless, both the Socialists and the Wobblies in these years generated a mass following among those Americans whose experiences and beliefs belied the much-celebrated and self-congratulatory sense of the United States as a land of unlimited promise.

The Spokane Free Speech Fight

As the first decade of the 20th century came to a close, the insurgent spirit of the Wobblies was present in the "free speech" battle in Spokane, Washington. Migratory workers who gathered in Spokane during the winter would be hired in the spring to labor in the Far West's agricultural, mining, railroad, and lumber industries. "General" J. H. Walsh, who came to Spokane after the IWW's 1908 convention, quickly organized these hard-bitten workers. With some 1,500 dues-paying members, the IWW in Spokane had a new headquarters by April 1909 that included reading rooms, offices, and an assembly hall that could seat several hundred. Responding to employers' complaints, Spokane's city council passed an ordinance prohibiting "revolutionary" soapbox orators from holding street-corner meetings. The next day, rising to the challenge, Walsh mounted a soapbox and was arrested. Many other Wobblies quickly followed suit, and the city's jails began to fill with Wobblies singing revolutionary songs, holding meetings, and making speeches while refusing to work the jail rock pile. This first battle came to a close as the weather warmed and city officials released the migratory workers who left Spokane for work across the West (Dubofsky 1969, 175–177).

The end of summer brought the migratory workers back to Spokane and to a renewed free speech struggle as IWW soapboxers again took to the streets. The arrests continued even after the city's ban had been declared unconstitutional in November. Once again, Spokane's jails filled with Wobblies. To make Spokane a testing ground for passive resistance and confrontation, the IWW advised members not to resist arrest. On November 3, city officials, hoping to paralyze the organization, raided the IWW headquarters and arrested the leaders on criminal conspiracy charges. In jail the Wobblies confronted harsh conditions, club-wielding police officers, and, after arrest, ice-cold showers and unheated cells. According to the IWW, as a result of such conditions most of the men arrested during the second Spokane battle from November 1909 through March 1910 had to treated in hospital emergency rooms a total of 1,600 times (Dubofsky 1969, 177–180).

Yet the IWW endured, helped by the many volunteers drawn to Spokane by the free speech fight. Among them was a 19-year-old girl, only recently released from a jail in Missoula, Montana, where another free speech battle was raging. The daughter of immigrant Irish parents, Elizabeth Gurley Flynn, who would forever be memorialized as the "Rebel Girl," was an agitator who over the next decade would be at the forefront of the IWW's battles. Despite city official's hopes of breaking the IWW, in March 1910 Spokane's authorities negotiated a compromise that permitted the IWW to freely hold indoor meetings and out-door rallies as long as they remained peaceful. The officials also recognized the right of the IWW to sell the *Industrial Worker* on the city's streets. For IWW's leaders, the Spokane free speech fight was a complete victory for direct action and passive resistance. Nevertheless, victory in the free speech battle did not advance organization of the migratory workers who had struggled there. Only later would the IWW be able to unite the timber and other itinerant workers throughout the United States (Dubofsky 1969, 180–184).

BIOGRAPHIES

Oscar Ameringer, 1870–1943

Newspaper Editor and Humorist

Born in Germany, Oscar Ameringer grew up in a lower-middle-class family discontented from the religious fervor and anti-Semitism that characterized his Lutheran background. Ameringer left Germany for America at age 16 as soon as he could get away. Endowed with musical talent and a keen sense of humor, he became active in labor and socialist movements in his adopted country. By the first years of the 20th century he had become a writer and a newspaper ed-itor. Settling finally in Oklahoma in 1907, Ameringer was a very popular story-teller and performer at socialist encampments. Known as the "Mark Twain of American Socialism," he was praised by the poet Carl Sandburg as a crusader, philosopher, and humorist. Ameringer's comic history of the United States, *Life and Deeds of Uncle Sam: A Little History for Big Children,* sold 500,000 copies and was translated into 15 languages.

Victor Louis Berger, 1860–1929

Socialist Politician and Newspaper Editor

The child of innkeepers in a region of the Austro-Hungarian empire that is now Romania, Victor Berger immigrated to Bridgeport, Connecticut, in 1878 after at-tending universities in Europe. Three years later, he moved to Milwaukee, where he became a schoolteacher and was active in the Turnverein, an educational and athletic club popular among Germen immigrants in the Wisconsin city. An orthodox Marxist, in 1897 Berger helped found the Social Democratic Party, and in 1901, with Eugene V. Debs, Morris Hillquit, and others, he launched the Socialist Party of America. Berger became the editor and publisher of a number of German-language newspapers in Milwaukee. He also fashioned a formidable political empire as the leader of the Milwaukee branch of the Socialist Party. With the endorsement of the Milwaukee Federated Trades Council, Berger was elected to the City Council in 1910 and, later that year, to the U.S. House of Representatives, becoming the first socialist to serve in Congress. Although a leading "gradualist" within the factional divides of the Socialist Party, Berger opposed AFL president Samuel Gompers. He believed that in working cooperatively within the AFL he could win the labor federation's support for socialism. Convicted of violating the Espionage Act during World War I, Berger was denied his congressional seat in 1919. His conviction was overturned by the U.S. Supreme Court in 1921, and Berger went on to serve in Congress until 1926, when he was defeated for reelection.

Carrie Chapman Catt, president of the National American Woman Suffrage Association from 1900 to 1904 and after 1915, helped lead the fight for the Nineteenth Amendment, which gave women the right to vote in 1920. (Library of Congress)

Carrie Chapman Catt, 1859–1947

Women's Suffrage Leader

The daughter of farmers, Carrie Clinton Lane was born in Ripon, Wisconsin, and at age seven moved with her family to Charles City, Iowa. While attending Iowa State Agricultural College she organized a debate on woman suffrage and joined a public-speaking society, an activity not yet seen as appropriate for respectable women. After graduation, Carrie became a teacher and school administrator in Mason City, Iowa. In 1885, she married Leo Chapman with whom she coedited the *Mason City Republican*. After Leo died of typhoid fever, Carrie returned to Charles City where she became active in the Women's Christian Temperance Union and then, in 1889, in the Iowa state suffrage movement. In May 1890, she attended the first convention of the reunited National American Woman Suffrage Association (NAWSA) and the following month married George Catt, a successful engineer and supporter of women's suffrage. Two years later, the Catts moved to New York City where Carrie became active in local suffrage campaigns. She also served as head of NAWSA's business committee, recruiting and educating new members through a network of organizer lecturers. In 1900, Catt was elected NAWSA president, and two years later, she was a founder of the International Woman Suffrage Alliance. Although she remained active in the suffrage movement during the decade, Catt resigned as NAWSA president in 1904 when her husband's health failed. She again became president of NAWSA in 1915 and developed what she called the "Winning Plan," a strategy that combined suffrage action on the state level with a concerted push for a federal amendment. Although a pacifist, she supported American entry into World War I, hoping that NAWSA's patriotism would win the support of President Woodrow Wilson and the American public for suffrage. After a number of states passed suffrage amendments, Congress finally passed the 19th Amendment in 1919, which guaranteed the right of women to vote. The following year, after ratification by the requisite 36 states, the 19th Amendment was adopted as part of the constitution.

Daniel De Leon, 1852–1914

Socialist Leader

The son of a wealthy Sephardic Jewish family in the Dutch West Indies, Daniel De Leon moved with his mother to Europe after his father died in 1864. Ten years later, he immigrated to the United States, settling in New York City. After graduating from Columbia University Law School in 1878, De Leon moved to Brownsville, Texas, where he married and practiced law. He returned to New York in 1883 and, while teaching at Columbia, became active in Henry George's 1886 United Labor mayoral campaign and other radical causes. After a brief association with the Nationalist Movement founded to advance the utopian vision associated with Edward Bellamy's novel *Looking Backward,* De Leon became a socialist. He joined the Socialist Labor Party in 1890 and through the 1890s served as a national lecturer and editor of the party's paper, the *People.* To further the cause of revolutionary socialism, in 1895 De Leon founded the Socialist Trade and Labor Alliance. De Leon was an avowed opponent of the conservative labor policies of Samuel Gompers and the American Federation of Labor, and he helped found the Industrial Workers of the World in 1905. De Leon's increasingly narrow sectarianism and dominating personality isolated him; at the time of his death in 1914, he had only a few loyal followers.

Crystal Eastman, 1881–1928

Greenwich Village Bohemian and Suffrage Leader

The daughter of Congregational ministers, Crystal Eastman was born in Marlboro, Massachusetts, and moved with her family in 1894 to Elmira, New York.

She graduated from Vassar College in 1903 and the next year earned a master's degree in sociology from Columbia University. In 1907, she was awarded her doctorate from New York University Law School. As a resident of Greenwich Village, she became active in the social settlement movement in New York. In 1907–1908, Eastman became the principal investigator for a study of workplace accidents funded by the Russell Sage Foundation that was published in 1910 as *Work Accidents and the Law*. New York governor Charles Evans Hughes appointed her in 1909 to the state's Employers' Liability Commission. Based on the commission's recommendations, the New York legislature created the nation's first workers' compensation program in 1910. Eastman, an active suffragist, joined with Alice Paul and Lucy Burns in 1913 to found the Congressional Union for Woman's Suffrage. She also helped institute the Woman's Peace Party during World War I and in the 1920s actively supported groups pursuing the Equal Rights Amendment, access to birth control, peace, and other social justice goals. Married twice, Eastman was critical of the deadening effect of conventional marriage on sexual feeling. She held that spouses should have separate residences in order to preserve the intimacy of a love affair.

William Dudley "Big Bill" Haywood, 1869–1928

Radical Labor Leader

William Haywood was born in Salt Lake City, Utah, in 1869. After his father died in 1872, his mother remarried a hard rock miner four years later. William received little formal education; by 1889 he had become a skilled hard rock miner in the copper mines around Bingham Canyon, Utah, and then in Silver City, Idaho. Having joined the Western Federation of Miners (WFM) in 1896, four years later he became president of the local and a member of the WFM's general executive board. A veteran of the violent class wars in Colorado between the WFM and the mine owners and their allies in state government, Haywood became an outspoken revolutionary socialist. In June 1905, Haywood presided over a convention in Chicago of what he called the "Continental Congress of the Working Class," the founding convention of the Industrial Workers of the World (IWW). The following year Haywood was arrested, charged with being an accomplice in the assassination of Frank Steunenberg, a former governor of Idaho. Defended by Charles Darrow, Haywood was exonerated. In 1908, after sectarian battles led the WFM, Eugene V. Debs, and others to withdraw from the IWW, Haywood took complete control over the radical industrial union. A proponent of direct action against the bosses and the capitalist class, Haywood became increasingly critical of the Socialist Party as means for realizing revolutionary change in the United States. In 1912, the IWW successfully led a strike among immigrant workers in the textile mills of Lawrence, Massachusetts, but the following year, it lost a strike among silk workers in Paterson, New Jersey.

After this defeat, Haywood successfully organized migratory workers in the West. During World War I, the IWW suffered severe losses due to government repression. Haywood, facing jail for his alleged subversive activities during the war, went into exile in 1921 in the Soviet Union, where he died seven years later.

Mary Harris "Mother" Jones, 1837–1930

Radical Activist

The daughter of Richard Harris, a laborer, and Ellen Cotter, Mary Harris fled Ireland during the potato famine. In 1860, she became a teacher in Monroe, Michigan, and then a dressmaker in Chicago; just before the Civil War, she relocated to Memphis, Tennessee, where she married George Jones, an iron molder and union member. After her husband and four children died of yellow fever in 1867, she moved back to

The "grandmother of all agitators" Mother Jones, labor leader and community activist, in 1902. (Library of Congress)

Chicago where she began her career as a union organizer and socialist activist. Having already become a paid organizer for the United Mine Workers, she became widely known as Mother Jones at around the turn of the century after she began using that name for her articles published in the *International Socialist Review*. Her fiery rhetoric and confrontational tactics made her a well-known national labor figure. She co-founded the IWW in 1905, helped organize the shirtwaist workers in 1909, and remained active in numerous labor campaigns throughout her life.

Julius A. Wayland, 1854–1912

Socialist Newspaper Editor

Julius Wayland was born in Versailles, Indiana, in 1854, and his father died in a cholera epidemic soon after his birth. His mother, Micha Wayland, supported the family by taking in sewing and washing. J. A., as he became known, worked odd jobs until apprenticing at age 16 as a "rolling boy" at the local weekly newspaper. At 19 he bought his first newspaper, which would be followed over the next decade by the purchase of other weekly papers. During the early 1890s,

Wayland became increasingly involved in politics, first as a Populist and then as a committed socialist. Believing in what he called the "One-Hoss Philosophy," Wayland drew on such disparate influences as Thomas Jefferson, Andrew Jackson, Abraham Lincoln, and Edward Bellamy in the struggle against the forces that he felt were overwhelming small-town America. After a slow start, Wayland, in the late 1890s, successfully built the *Appeal to Reason* into the largest-circulation socialist publication in America. By 1912, promoted by a vast army of "salesmen-soldiers of the revolution," the *Appeal* was read by far more than its half million subscribers. Wayland committed suicide in 1912, not long after the death of his second wife.

References and Further Readings

Addams, Jane. 1910. *Twenty Years at Hull-House with Autobiographical Notes.* Reprint edition, edited with an introduction by Victoria Bissell Brown. Bedford Series in History and Culture. Boston: Bedford/St. Martin's, 1999. Page references are to the 1999 edition.

American National Biography Online. http://www.anb.org/articles/15/15-00737-print.html

Baker, Jean H. 2005. *Sisters: The Lives of America's Suffragists.* New York: Hill and Wang.

Bell, Daniel. 1967. *Marxian Socialism in the United States.* Princeton: Princeton University Press.

Bordin, Ruth. 1990. *Woman and Temperance: The Quest for Power and Liberty, 1873–1900.* New Brunswick, N.J.: Rutgers University Press.

Brooklyn Museum. "Urban Views: Realist Prints and Drawings by Robert Henri and His Circle." http://www.brooklynmuseum.org/exhibitions/urban_views.

Buhle, Mari Jo. 1983. *Women and American Socialism, 1870–1920.* Urbana: University of Illinois Press.

Bundles, A'Lelia. 2001. *On Her Own Ground: The Life and Times of Madam C. J. Walker.* New York: Washington Square Press.

Cantor, Milton. 1978. *The Divided Left: American Radicalism, 1900–1975.* New York: Hill and Wang.

Chambers, John Whiteclay, II. 1992. *Tyranny of Change: America in the Progressive Era, 1890–1920,* 2nd ed. New York: St. Martin's Press.

Chauncey, George. 1994. *Gay New York: Gender, Urban Culture, and the Making of the Gay Male World, 1890–1940.* New York: Basic Books.

Chilvers, Ian. 1998. *A Dictionary of Twentieth-Century Art*. New York: Oxford University Press.

Clayton, Douglas. "Floyd Dell." American National Biography Online. http://www.anb.org/articles/16/16-00446.html.

Davis, Angela Y. 1983. *Women, Race and Class*. New York: Vintage Books.

Dawley, Alan. 1991. *Struggles for Justice: Social Responsibility and the Liberal State*. Cambridge: Harvard University Press.

D'Emelio, John, and Estelle B. Freedman. 1988. *Intimate Matters: A History of Sexuality in America*. New York: Harper and Row.

Dubofsky, Melvyn. "Hillquit, Morris." American National Biography Online. http://www.anb.org/articles/06/00276.html

Dubofsky, Melvyn. 1987. *"Big Bill" Haywood*. New York: St. Martin's Press.

Dubofsky, Melvyn. 1969. *We Shall Be All: A History of the Industrial Workers of the World*. Chicago: Quadrangle Books.

DuBois, Ellen Carol. 1995. "Working Women, Class Relations, and Suffrage Militance: Harriot Stanton Blatch and the New York Woman Suffrage Movement, 1894–1909." In *One Woman, One Vote: Rediscovering the Woman Suffrage Movement,* ed. Marjorie Spruill Wheeler, 221–244. New York: New Sage Press.

Dye, Nancy Schrom. 1977. "Creating a Feminist Alliance: Sisterhood and Class Conflict in the New York Women's Trade Union League, 1903–1914." In *Class, Sex, and the Woman Worker,* ed. Milton Cantor and Bruce Laurie, 225–245.Westport, Conn.: Greenwood Press.

Edwards, Alba. 1943. *Comparative Occupational Statistics for the United States, 1870 to 1940*. Washington D.C.: Government Printing Office.

Evans, Sara M. 1989. *Born for Liberty: A History of Women in America*. New York: The Free Press.

Fishbein, Leslie. 1982. *Rebels in Bohemia: The Radicals of The Masses, 1911–1917*. Chapel Hill: University of North Carolina Press.

Flexner, Eleanor. 1959. *Century of Struggle: The Woman's Rights Movement in the United States*. New York: Atheneum.

Garrison, Dee. 1989. *Mary Heaton Vorse: The Life of an American Insurgent*. Philadelphia: Temple University Press.

Gilbert, James Burkhart. 1968. *Writers and Partisans: A History of Literary Radicalism in America*. New York: John Wiley and Sons.

Ginger, Ray. 1949. *Eugene V. Debs: The Making of an American Radical*. New York: Collier Books.

Goldman, Emma. 1906. *Mother Earth* 1 (March). http://dwardmac.pitzer.edu/Anarchist_Archives/goldman/ME/mev1n1.html#me.

Gompers, Samuel. 1925. *Seventy Years of Life and Labor: An Autobiography*. 2 vols., NewYork: Augustus M. Kelley. Page references are to the 1967 edition.

Graham, Sara Hunter. 1995. "The Suffrage Renaissance: A New Image for a New Century, 1896–1910." In *One Woman, One Vote: Rediscovering the Woman Suffrage Movement,* ed. Marjorie Spruill Wheeler, 157–178. New York: New Sage Press.

Green, James R. 1978. *Grass-Roots Socialism: Radical Movements in the Southwest, 1895–1943*. Baton Rouge: Louisiana State University Press.

Green, James R. 1980. *The World of the Worker: Labor in Twentieth Century America*. New York: Hill and Wang.

Greenberg, Brian. 1996. "Samuel Gompers and the American Federation of Labor." In *American Reform and American Reformers,* ed. Randall M. Miller and Paul A. Cimbala, 270–286. Wesport, Conn.: Greenwood Publishing Group.

Greene, Julie. 1998. *Pure and Simple Politics: The American Federation of Labor and Political Activism, 1881–1917*. New York: Cambridge University Press.

Hale, Nathan G. 1971. *Freud and the Americans: The Beginnings of Psychoanalysis in the United States, 1876–1917*. Vol. 1. New York: Oxford University Press.

Homer, William Innes. 1969. *Robert Henri and His Circle*. Ithaca, N.Y.: Cornell University Press.

Howe, Irving. 1985. *Socialism and America*. San Diego: Harcourt Brace Javonovich.

Howe, Irving. 1976. *World of Our Fathers: The Journey of the East European Jews to America and the Life They Found and Made*. New York: Simon and Schuster.

Humphrey, Robert E. 1978. *Children of Fantasy: The First Rebels of Greenwich Village*. New York: John Wiley and Sons.

Jackson, Kenneth T., ed. 1995. *Encyclopedia of New York City*. New Haven, Conn.: Yale University Press.

Kasson, John F. 1978. *Amusing the Million: Coney Island at the Turn of the Century*. New York: Hill and Wang.

Kaufman, Stuart, et al. 1986–1998. *The Samuel Gompers Papers*. 7 vols. Urbana: University of Illinois Press.

Kazin, Alfred. 1942. *On Native Grounds: An Interpretation of Modern American Prose Literature*. Garden City, N.Y.: Doubleday and Company.

Kraditor, Aileen S. 1971. *The Ideas of the Woman Suffrage Movement, 1890–1920*. Garden City, N.Y.: Anchor Books.

Lears, T. J. Jackson. 1981. *No Place of Grace: Antimodernism and the Transformation of American Culture, 1880–1920*. New York: Pantheon Books.

Leinenweber, Charles. 1977. "Socialists in the Streets: The New York City Socialist Party in Working Class Neighborhoods, 1908–1918." *Science and Society* (Summer): 152–171.

MARHO, The Radical Historians Organization. 1979. *Visions of History*. Manchester, UK: MARHO.

Matthews, Jean V. 2003. *The Rise of the New Woman: The Women's Movement in America 1875–1930*. Chicago: Ivan R. Dee.

May, Henry F. 1959. *The End of American Innocence: A Study of the First Years of Our Own Time, 1912-1917*. Chicago: Quadrangle Paperbacks.

Miller, Sally M. "Berger, Victor Louis." American National Biography Online. http://www.anb.org/articles/06/06–00040.html.

Miller, Sally M. "O'Hare, Kate Richards." American National Biography Online. http://www.anb.org/articles/15/15-00808.html.

Morantz-Sanchez, Regina Markell. 1985. *Sympathy and Science: Women Physicians in American Medicine*. New York: Oxford University Press.

Morgan, H. Wayne. 1962. *Eugene V. Debs: Socialist for President*. Syracuse, N.Y.: Syracuse University Press.

Muncy, Robyn. 1991. *Creating a Female Dominion in American Reform, 1890–1935*. New York: Oxford University Press.

O'Hare, Kate Richards. 1908. "How I Became a Socialist Agitator." In *Socialist Woman* October. http://historymatters.gmu.edu/d/43/.

Peiss, Kathy. 1983. "'Charity Girls' and City Pleasures: Historical Notes on Working-Class Sexuality, 1880–1920." In *Powers of Desire: The Politics of Sexuality,* ed. Ann Snitow, Christine Stansell, and Sharon Thompson, pp. 74–87. New York: Monthly Review Press.

Peiss, Kathy. 1986. "Dance Madness: New York City Dance Halls and Working-Class Sexuality, 1900–1920." In *Life and Labor: Dimensions of American Working-Class History,* ed. Charles Stephenson and Robert Asher, 177–189. Albany: State University of New York Press.

Peiss, Kathy. 1998. *Hope in a Jar: The Making of America's Beauty Culture*. New York: Metropolitan Books.

Peiss, Kathy, and Thomas Paterson, eds. 2001. *Major Problems in the History of Sexuality: Documents and Essays*. Boston: Houghton Mifflin.

Poole, Ernest. 1915. *The Harbor*. Reprint New York: Sagamore Press, 1957. Page references are to the 1957 edition.

Rideout, Walter B. 1956. *The Radical Novel in the United States, 1900–1954: Some Interrelations of Literature and Society*. New York: Hill and Wang.

Ryan, Mary P. 1975. *Womanhood in America: From Colonial Times to the Present*. New York: New Viewpoints.

Salvatore, Nick. 1982. *Eugene V. Debs: Citizen and Socialist*. Urbana: University of Illinois Press.

Shannon, David A. 1967. *The Socialist Party of America: A History*. Chicago: Quadrangle Books.

Shapiro, Judah Joseph. 1970. *The Friendly Society: A History of the Workmen's Circle*. Bridgeport, Conn.: Media Judaica.

Stansell, Christine. 2000. *American Moderns: Bohemian New York and the Creation of a New Century*. New York: Metropolitan Books.

Statistical Abstract of the United States. Washington, D.C.: Government Printing Office, 1952.

Terborg-Penn, Rosalyn. 1995. "African American Women and the Woman's Suffrage Movement." In *One Woman, One Vote: Rediscovering the Woman Suffrage Movement,* ed. Marjorie Spruill Wheeler, 135–156. New York: New Sage Press.

Thernstrom, Stephan. 1971. *Poverty and Progress: Social Mobility in a Nineteenth-Century City*. New York: Atheneum.

Thurner, Manuela. 1995. "'Better Citizens Without the Ballot': American Anti-suffrage Women and Their Rationale During the Progressive Era." In *One Woman, One Vote: Rediscovering the Woman Suffrage Movement,* ed. Marjorie Spruill Wheeler, 203–220. New York: New Sage Press.

Trimberger, Ellen Kay. 1983. "Feminism, Men, and Modern Love: Greenwich Village, 1900-1925." In *Powers of Desire: The Politics of Sexuality,* ed. Ann Snitow, Christine Stansell, and Sharon Thompson, 131–152. New York: Monthly Review Press.

Walkowitz, Daniel J. 1999. *Working With Class: Social Workers and the Politics of Middle-Class Identity*. Chapel Hill: University of North Carolina Press.

Weinstein James. 1969. *The Decline of Socialism in America, 1912–1925*. New York: Vintage Books.

Welter, Barbara. 1966. "The Cult of True Womanhood, 1820–1860." *American Quarterly* 18 (Summer): 151–174.

Mass Consumption
and Leisure

OVERVIEW

Leisure pursuits and patterns of consumption in the United States at the turn of the 20th century represent a rich area of research, especially for historians who specialize in interpreting the lives and choices of everyday Americans. Scholars of consumer culture, for example, make a study of both consumption practices and their symbolic meanings. Researchers Douglas Goodman and Mirele Cohn articulate this distinction clearly, noting that "while consumption is an act, consumer culture is a way of life" (Goodman and Cohn 2004, 2). Behind these behaviors stand American attitudes, preferences, and outlooks about the good life. For this reason, social historians have carefully examined the process by which the United States became a nation of consumers of both entertainment and merchandise.

During the period from 1900 to 1909, America was producing an impressive range of consumer goods as well as high quantities of them. According to Edward Wagenknecht, "The United States was producing more than half the world's cotton, corn, copper, and oil; more than one-third of its steel, pig iron, and silver; about a third of its coal and gold" (Wagenknecht 1982, 5). In addition to its natural resources, the nation was generating goods to satisfy new desires among consumers. America was home to several major centers in food production, especially when it came to making sweets. In Atlanta, Georgia, the Coca-Cola Company bottled its soft drinks. In upstate New York, Jell-O gelatin was made.

Philadelphia produced Whitman's Chocolates. The Wrigley Company of Chicago produced spearmint and fruit-flavored chewing gums, and the New England Confectionary Company manufactured NECCO wafers. New products stimulated new appetites among American consumers.

There were economic reasons for this stunning growth in sales of consumer goods in the United States. According to scholar David Nasaw, "Between 1870 and 1900, real income for non-farm employees increased by more than 50 percent, while the cost of living, as measured by the consumer price index, decreased by 40 percent. This increase in wages was accompanied by a steady decrease in work hours" (Nasaw 1993, 4). With both more income and more leisure time in which to dispose of it, Americans were ready to embrace consumerism as not only a lifestyle but also as an expression of personal identity.

Producers, merchants, and marketers encouraged American consumers to approach their purchases as a means to improve their lives. The rise of the mail-order catalogue exemplified this change in American consumer practices. The relatively new form of commerce linked customers across geographic areas and demographic categories. Particularly for rural populations in America, retail purchasing by mail provided an alternative to reliance on homemade or locally purchased consumer goods. In the years from 1900 to 1909, the nation's residents could browse mail-order catalogues for a wide array of merchandise, including such goods as books, cherry pitters, bicycles, buggies, and cutlery. Companies from Montgomery Ward to Sears, Roebuck & Company vied for the business of America's consumers, and the catalogues they offered could be 1,000 pages in length.

For urban residents, department stores such as Macy's and Marshall Field's served a similar function. New arrivals to America's cities, including immigrants, looked to consumption of manufactured goods as an important way to signal their assimilation to the nation's urban culture, complete with its markers of lifestyle and status. By patronizing the urban core districts, shoppers could access a variety of goods and services. At major department stores, consumers could travel to one location to satisfy a whole range of buying needs and desires. The era's trend was toward packaged, prepared, and ready-made consumer goods, freeing Americans from the time and labor necessary to make their own clothes or other items.

It was at the turn of the 20th century that the United States shifted from an emphasis on production to a focus on consumption, and that American conduct turned from a work ethic to a leisure habit. As described by social historian David Nasaw, the period from 1900 to 1909 in America was a "story of the varnished world of phonograph and kinetoscope parlors; of vaudeville halls and ten-twenty-thirty-cent melodrama theaters; of world's fair midways; of amusement parks, ballparks, dance halls, and picture palaces (Nasaw 1993, 2). With reduced work hours, increased discretionary cash, and time saved through store-bought goods, consumers launched an era of mass culture.

TIMELINE

1900   Kodak introduces the Brownie, a box camera pre-loaded with film and retailing for one dollar.

On April 16, the U.S. Postal Service commences sales of postage stamps by the book.

More than 1.3 million telephones are in operation across the nation.

The American League of professional baseball teams is formed.

Louis Lassen begins serving beef patties on buns at the diner he operates in New Haven, Connecticut, creating the sandwich to become known as the hamburger.

The nation employs 100,000 stenographers.

America has approximately 4,000 millionaires.

Four billion cigarettes are produced in the United States.

1901   The Cadillac automobile company is established on August 22.

The electric typewriter appears on the American market.

Paper clips receive a U.S. patent as a means for fastening pages.

New York City's theater district at Times Square starts to be known as "The Great White Way," after the title of an Albert Paine play.

The "wireless," a technology developed by Marconi's Wireless Telegraphy Co., Ltd., begins to supplant the telegraph.

1902   Theodore Roosevelt's decision against shooting a captured bear brings him unexpected attention as stuffed animal toys are then marketed as "teddy bears."

Inventor Willis Carrier offers a prototype for the air conditioner.

Philadelphia becomes the site of the first automat.

Gasoline-powered lawn mowers are first introduced to retail.

The Pepsi-Cola Company is established.

The first marketing of Nabisco's animal crackers gets under way.

The electric hairdryer is invented.

Scott Joplin publishes his musical composition, "The Entertainer."

Both Marshall Field's and Macy's open vast new department stores.

Buster Brown and his dog, Tige, appear as new characters in comic strips.

The first Rose Bowl is held on January 1.

On April 2, Los Angeles opens the first movie theater, "The Electric Theatre."

1903   Crayola crayons are first produced for sale.

The state of Massachusetts becomes the first in the United States to issue license plates for automobiles.

Gillette markets disposable shaving blades.

A fire at Iroquois Theater kills 600, for although the structure was supposedly "fireproof," its contents were not.

The Automobile Association of America (AAA) is founded on March 4.

Luna Park, an amusement park in New York, is illuminated with electricity at night.

Edwin S. Porter's "The Great Train Robbery," an Edison film, becomes first exhibited narrative film and excites popular interest in motion pictures.

The first World Series in baseball is held, with Pittsburgh's team beating Boston's.

Redbook magazine is founded.

1904   The first comic book is released.

A major fire strikes Baltimore, Maryland.

As a celebration of the centennial of the Louisiana Purchase (1803), the St. Louis World's Fair takes shape.

St. Louis is the site of the Third Olympic Games.

A woman becomes subject to arrest for public smoking when she lights up on New York City's Fifth Avenue.

Phonograph rolls achieve popularity in American as sound recordings.

Cy Young, of the Boston Americans, pitches the first perfect game in major league baseball on May 5.

1905   The entertainment trade publication, *Variety,* gets its start.

The Rotary Club is founded.

The first nickelodeon opens in Pittsburgh, Pennsylvania.

Charlotte Perkins Gilman publishes *Women and Economics*.

Portland, Oregon, hosts the Lewis and Clark Centennial Exposition.

1906   Lux introduces boxed soap chips to the consumer market.

An early version of the jukebox is conceived.

The term "hot dog" becomes a familiar way to refer to a sandwich-sized sausage served on a bun.

1907   A July 28 fire at New York's seaside resort, Coney Island, causes $1.5 million of damage.

Ringling Brothers acquires the Barnum and Bailey circus on October 22.

The "Ziegfield Follies" opens in New York.

Dallas, Texas, becomes the site of the first retail store of Neiman Marcus.

On November 15, Bud Fisher's "Mr. A. Mutt" is the first daily comic strip in the United States, running in the *San Francisco Chronicle;* later that same year, the strip evolves into "Mutt and Jeff," featuring two characters who engage in get-rich-quick schemes.

The first electric washing machine becomes available.

1908   A ball drops for the first time at New York's Time Square, heralding the arrival of a new year and launching an annual tradition.

The electric razor first becomes offered for sale.

A screen adaptation of Robert Louis Stevenson's *Dr. Jekyll and Mr. Hyde* becomes the first horror film.

The National Board of Review of Motion Pictures is established.

On December 24, 550 nickelodeons are forced to surrender their licenses for morals violations.

General Electric secures a patent for the electric iron.

Winsor McKay's "Gertie the Dinosaur" becomes the first animated cartoon to enter the marketplace.

1909   The 10th Amendment is ratified, thereby establishing a federal income tax.

Lipton's Tea appears on the market.

The electric toaster debuts.

Newsreels begin to appear.

Seattle, Washington, becomes the home of the Alaska-Yukon-Pacific Exposition (June 1–October 16).

A new fabrication material and precursor to plastic, Bakelite, receives a patent; it replaces hard rubber and celluloid for most products.

Jigsaw puzzles become popular.

A blimp bearing the logo for Coca-Cola floats over the nation's capital.

The Kewpie doll appears on the American market and subsequently becomes a popular souvenir item.

1904 St. Louis World's Fair

In 1900, St. Louis was the fourth largest city in the nation (Batchelor 2002, 480). When it was selected as the site for the 1904 World's Fair, St. Louis was not quite as large as New York or Chicago, but it was nonetheless an important urban center. With the attention and capital that such a high-profile event would likely attract to this Midwestern city, St. Louis prepared for its entrance onto the world stage.

The theme of the event was a celebration of the centennial of the Louisiana Purchase Treaty, signed on April 30, 1803. Through the Louisiana Purchase, the United States had acquired a vast expanse of land that would become all or portions of the following states: Arkansas, Colorado, Iowa, Kansas, Louisiana, Minnesota, Missouri, Montana, Nebraska, North Dakota, South Dakota, Oklahoma, and Wyoming. Because the exposition buildings and grounds were not ready in time to open on the 100th anniversary of the signing of the treaty, St. Louis postponed the event until the following April.

From April 30 to December 1, 1904, St. Louis received an influx of exposition visitors. The lyrics of a popular song of the day issued this invitation: "Meet me in St. Louis, Louis, meet me at the Fair." Adults paid an admission of 50 cents, and children were charged 25 cents. Although this pricing was comparable to that used at previous expositions in the United States, the St. Louis Exposition was a much larger event and covered more land area than the 1893 fair in Chicago or the 1903 Pan-American Exposition in Buffalo. The site was so vast that the era's physicians counseled those with nervous disorders to stay away from the expanse and overstimulation of the Fair (Edwards 2006, 277). In fact,

At the St. Louis World's Fair, visitors were greeted by an array of impressive-looking buildings constructed specifically for the event. Since expositions were short in duration, the structures were often impermanent. Exposition architecture, though visually imposing, was seldom built to last. (Library of Congress)

the event was not without casualties. Fiction writer Kate Chopin experienced heart failure following a tour of the fair (Edwards 2006, 277).

The Design of the Site

Visitors to the Louisiana Purchase Exposition found the experience there a memorable one. Among the most remarked features of the site were its architecture, the grounds, the observation wheel, and the midway. These elements of the exposition design created a sense of wonder for crowds who came to the exposition.

As is consistent with previous fairs and expositions, the major buildings of the St. Louis Exposition were designed to create an imposing appearance. They were large, ornate, and arranged to provide vistas for spectators. Structures at the site typically were named to reveal their contents as well as their grandeur, such as the "Palace of Forestry" and the "Palace of Agriculture." An idyllic woodland park of over 1,100 acres, known as "Forest City," also made up part of the grounds.

The observation wheel installed at the St. Louis Exposition employed the same George Ferris design that had graced the Columbian Exposition of 1893. Flatbed rail had transported the apparatus from Chicago to St. Louis for the occasion. The attraction had 36 cars, each accommodating 60 passengers for a total capacity of 2,160 riders on each boarding. The Ferris wheel, as it was known, made one revolution every 15 minutes. Standing 265 feet tall, the observation wheel permitted passengers to look out over the exposition and its environs. As it had been in Chicago, the St. Louis wheel was extremely popular. More than 3 million tickets to the observation wheel were sold at the St. Louis Exposition ("The World's Fair").

The midway at St. Louis was known as "The Pike," and was approximately one mile long. Its expanse inspired the popular phrase, "coming down the pike," to suggest a long anticipated journey. For a fee, a visitor to the midway could take in 50 shows plus other attractions. Midways became standard components of subsequent world's fairs and expositions and a favorite among the visiting public.

The Content on Display

The spectacles to behold at the St. Louis Exposition were many, but some of the most successful elements were items and products on view there. Some simple pleasures included the public's introduction to hot dogs, iced tea, ice cream cones, and T-shirts.

Inventors and retailers showcased their latest innovations and developments, as had been done at previous fairs and expositions. In 1904, these technological triumphs included the air conditioner, the dishwasher, and the automatic player piano. Historical artifacts on view included the Liberty Bell. Even human beings were on display at the Louisiana Purchase Exposition, such as the Native American leaders Geronimo and Chief Joseph. Scott Joplin performed ragtime at the St. Louis Exposition and is said to have composed his tune "The Entertainer" as a tribute to the event. The exposition also had its share of oddities and novelties, such as the exhibit of a butter sculpture of Theodore Roosevelt. There were also demonstrations of social progress at home. Exhibits were devoted to such topics as physical culture and the settlement house movement.

In addition, this exposition featured the ethnological exhibits that had been customary in prior expositions. The Philippine Reservation was a prime example of these displays, delivered at a cost exceeding $1 million (Edwards 2006,

279). The reservation consisted of three different components, representing the Philippines' past, present, and future. Visitors were invited to travel through the history of the Philippines, starting with the era of Spanish colonialism. The overall perspective these displays invited visitors to inhabit was laudatory, applauding America's involvements internationally and its role in countering Philippine independence. President Theodore Roosevelt personally directed the specifications for attire of Philippine natives presented in the Reservation's tribal display.

Ethnologist William John McGee hoped to secure his reputation by playing a major role in the 1904 Louisiana Purchase Exposition in St. Louis, at which he presided over the fair's rather extensive ethnological exhibits. The ethnological and anthropological displays at the 1904 Louisiana Purchase Exposition were framed to support arguments of racial hierarchy and portrayed people of color as exotic yet inferior beings. Meanwhile, Chinese visitors to the exposition were subjected to fingerprinting and the required wearing of numbered tags to ensure that they left the country after their time at the fair.

The Message: Pageant of Conspicuous Consumption

There is a scene in the film adaptation of John Steinbeck's novel *The Grapes of Wrath* in which a Midwestern family loses their farm and packs up to find work in California. As they prepare to leave their homestead, the family members must take only what they can carry in the car with them. The family matriarch, Ma Joad, finds it hard to part with a souvenir commemorating the 1904 exposition. From postcards to soapstone carvings, souvenirs became a big part of the exposition experience. Merchandising the events helped make fairs and expositions profitable. World's fairs and expositions of this era in American history both embodied and promoted acts of consumption.

Furthermore, the exhibits, displays, and demonstrations at the St. Louis Exposition touted the nation's material progress and prosperity. From mechanical inventions to imperialist conquests, the message at the Louisiana Purchase Exposition affirmed the rightness of American acquisitiveness. It is telling that the initial capital investment required to initiate the Louisiana Purchase Exposition equaled the original outlay for the Louisiana Purchase itself: $15 million (Rydell 1984, 157).

Proponents of the St. Louis Exposition were unhindered by humility in their claims for the event's singular importance. Most striking, perhaps, among these assertions were the words of fair official David Francis, who stated that "so thoroughly does [the event] represent the world's civilization that if all man's other works were by some unspeakable catastrophe blotted out, the records here established by the assembled nations would afford all necessary standards for the rebuilding of our entire civilization" (Rydell, Findling, and Pelle 2000, 53). With the material gathered for the St. Louis Exposition, organizers hoped to celebrate the best portrait of human progress and American success to date.

The Louisiana Purchase Exposition had an impact on numerous subsequent events but especially on the 1905 Lewis and Clark Centennial and American Pacific Exposition and Oriental Fair in Portland, the 1907 Jamestown, Virginia, Tercentennial, and the 1909 Alaska Yukon Pacific Exposition in Seattle.

Jingle All the Way—Commercializing Christmas

During the years from 1900 to 1909, Americans embraced Christmas as a consumer-driven celebration. The holiday is older than the United States, but the United States nearly didn't establish it based upon the disapproval of such faith groups as the Puritans felt toward its pagan origins. In the latter part of the 17th century in Massachusetts, a financial penalty could be levied against any-one found observing Christmas. Over the years, however, those with profound spiritual objections to Christmas yielded to the views of others who embraced the holiday. By 1890, all states and the District of Columbia afforded legal recog-nition to Christmas. Since that time, Americans have celebrated Christmas with customs of display, entertaining, and gift-giving that frequently befit Thorstein Veblen's concept of conspicuous consumption.

Many traditional practices associated with Christmas, such as the custom of exchanging greeting cards, originated in England. Innovations in printing and, especially lithography, made the exchange of holiday cards fashionable during the latter portion of the 19th century. German native Louis Prang, who rose to prominence for his card designs during the 1870s, is widely regarded as the chief proponent of this practice in the United States.

While the United States did not originate the celebration of Christmas, its resi-dents have continued many older traditions from other lands, modified others, and added still more practices of its own to the day's observance. As the holi-day became more commercial, its suggestions became more secular.

Labor Day Becomes a National Observance

Celebrated on the first Monday of September each year, Labor Day honors the hard work performed by Americans all year long. Labor Day had its begin-nings in the American labor movement and was tied directly to the struggles of the industrial working class. It was particularly closely tied to the 19th-century battle for the eight-hour workday. Like many U.S. national holidays, Labor Day was established because of the devoted efforts of its champions. Organized la-bor got behind the concept of acknowledging the contributions of workers to

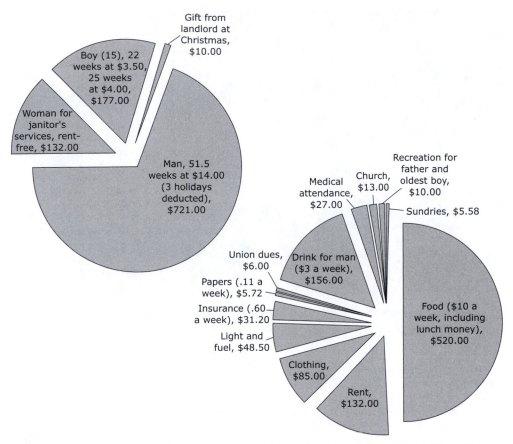

Figure 7.1. *Average Annual Budget for Working-Class Family in 1900s. The following information describes income and expenditures by a New York City glassworker's family for the one-year period from July 1904 to July 1905. The household consists of eight members, including six children younger than 16 years of age. The wife works as tenement janitor, in exchange for which the family receives rent credit toward three ground-floor rooms. She purchases her husband's alcoholic beverages daily at the saloon, reckoning that he spends less if drinking at home.* Source: *More 1907, 185–187.*

the American way of life. In particular, Peter J. McGuire and Matthew MacGuire, a labor leader and a machinist, respectively, saw to it that the Central Labor Union in New York City celebrated the first such occasion in 1882 with a parade, picnic, and other festivities. Two years later, the Knights of Labor called for Labor Day to become an annual observance. Individual states began to honor the day officially, starting with Oregon in 1887. Others followed, until all 50 states and the District of Columbia joined in recognizing Labor Day. In 1894, President Grover Cleveland made it a national holiday. In the first decade of the 20th century, Labor Day traditions were becoming established. Early celebrations of Labor Day included speeches, processions, and other public festivities, some of which continue today. Religious services also marked the event in its original form.

Women on a float of the Women's Auxilliary Typographical Union during the Labor Day parade in New York, 1909. (Library of Congress)

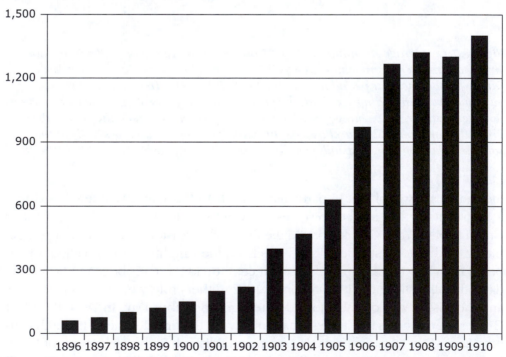

Figure 7.2 *Bowling Teams in the United States, 1896–1910.* Source: *Wattenberg 1976, 225.*

What Role Did American Men Play in the Emerging Consumer Culture?

Most scholarship devoted to the social history of consumption in America, particularly during the early 20th century, has concentrated chiefly on the role of women as consumers. The emphasis is understandable. If occupying the traditional role of a female head of household, an American woman would not only prepare most of the food and drink consumed in the home, she would also preside over a good deal of the purchasing for the home and family, from furnishing to clothing. For that reason, historians examining American consumer culture have tended to focus on the shopping behaviors of, and influence on acquisitions by, American women.

A preoccupation with women's consumption, however, could mislead researchers investigating the period from 1900 to 1909 in the United States. At the turn of the 20th century, consumer activities and patterns reflected a considerable degree of gender differentiation. The nation's men were active consumers during this era but have been overlooked by scholars for one main reason: most of their spending took place outside the family home.

Between work and leisure activities, men of this period in United States history were frequently away from home. Of course, men needed wardrobes and purchased clothes and accessories according to their habits. Some of men's other typical spending was related to work, such as the payment of union dues. Other costs involved membership in groups, such as fraternal organizations, men's clubs, and volunteer fire companies. Additional purchases were made at establishments where men congregated and socialized, such as barbershops, tobacconist shops, bathhouses, and saloons. Still other spending money went to diversions available at rifle ranges, gyms, bowling alleys, spectator sports venues, dime museums, billiard and gaming halls, minstrel shows, and brothels. Most of these consumer patterns involved the purchase of services rather than goods and therefore left behind fewer traces for social historians to find.

When considering everyday life in the United States at the turn of the 20th century, it is important to look at the entire budget of a household—funds allocated by or for women, men, and children—to establish a comprehensive picture of how the United States developed as a nation of consumers. Consumer spending by American males was hardly secondary to women's purchasing. In fact, the scholar Lawrence B. Glickman contends that "American men consumed about twice as many recreational and leisure goods as women and spent about 30 percent of the family's disposable income in doing so" (Glickman 1999, 233).

Origins of Father's Day Celebrations in the United States

It was during the first decade of the 20th century that Americans first began to celebrate Father's Day. Father's Day is an American holiday that follows Mother's

Table 7.1. Popular Fraternal Organization Memberships, 1900 (in thousands)

Group	Members
American Legion of Honor	8
Ancient Order of Foresters	38
Ancient Order of United Workmen	420
Benevolent and Protective Order of Elks	100
Brith Abraham Order	19
Catholic Benevolent Legion	42
Catholic Knights of America	24
Foresters of America	195
Freemasons	903
Improved Order of Heptasophs	52
Improved Order of Red Men	260
Independent Order of B'nai Brith	30
Independent Order of Foresters	187
Irish Catholic Benevolent Union	14
Junior Order of United American Mechanics	104
Knights of the Golden Eagle	70
Knights of Honor	60
Knights of Maccabees	228
Knights of Malta	26
Knights of Pythias	517
Ladies' Catholic Benevolent Association	72
Modern Woodmen of America	643
Mystic Circle	17
National Union	60
New England Order of Protection	29
Odd Fellows	1,027
Order of United American Mechanics	47
Royal Arcanum	227
Royal Templars of Temperance	24
Sons of Temperance	33
Star of Bethlehem Order	18
Tribe of Ben Hur	67
United Ancient Order of Druids	17
United Order of Pilgrim Fathers	23
Woodmen of the World	252
Other	43
Total	6,103,000

Sources: The World Almanac, 1902, 328; Shifftlet 1996, 275.

Day, both in terms of chronology of origin and the sequence on the calendar each year. Like many holidays, its beginnings are somewhat unclear, and more than one name and locality have been credited with its design. Around 1900, there appear to have been several local movements toward declaration of a day to honor America's fathers, including efforts conducted in Illinois and West Virginia. Perhaps the most widely known among these efforts, whether it was truly the first, was spearheaded by Washington State's Sonora Louise Smart Dodd. As the story goes, a Mother's Day sermon inspired Dodd to build and promote an equivalent holiday to honor the nation's fathers. Dodd sought to pay formal tribute to fathers, especially her own. William Jackson Smart, a Civil War veteran, raised Dodd, along with five other children, on a Spokane farm following the death of his wife during childbirth. In 1910, Spokane, Washington, celebrated Father's Day on the third Sunday in June, the birth month of Dodd's beloved father. At that time, Dodd sought to establish the custom of Father's Day celebrants wearing a red rose to thank a living father, and a white rose to honor a deceased one.

Formal designation of Father's Day as a holiday in the United States took time. From Spokane, the celebration spread through Washington State. Several states appear to have been marking Father's Day. In 1916, President Woodrow Wilson signaled public approval for the concept, and in 1924, President Coolidge encouraged states to hold their own observances. It was not until 1966 that President Johnson made the third Sunday in June a national father's holiday by annual presidential proclamation, and not until 1972 that President Nixon made June's third Sunday a permanent holiday like its counterpart, Mother's Day.

MECHANIZED LEISURE

In 1893, orator Annie Wood Besant spoke to the hardships experienced by America's hard-working population. Besant wrote of a country of people too busy making ends meet to concern themselves with recreation or discretionary spending. She asserts, "They have no leisure for cultivating the intellectual powers, the artistic faculties, or the imaginative potencies of the human mind. They are condemned to a life of labor—the price of which merely purchases them the right to live" (Walter 1992, 165). When they did have time or money to spend on leisure, Americans wanted to make sure they found as much benefit as possible.

At the turn of the 20th century, mechanized leisure celebrated America's technological ingenuity. It was also a form of entertainment that families and people of all ages might enjoy. In this regard, there was substantial enthusiasm for emerging forms of recreation that provided alternatives to alcohol or other temptations. Even where the forms of leisure available were of somewhat questionable moral content, as was the case for early motion pictures, many still welcomed them as a counterpoint to drinking as a form of leisure in itself. The period from 1900 to 1909 offered Americans a variety of inexpensive forms of mechanized entertainment, including vitascopes, kinetescopes, peep shows, penny arcades, and nickelodeons.

The Rise of Amateur Photography

Photography is a meaningful element of both material and popular culture in America. The commercialization of photography for nonelite consumption has made photography a shared life experience and presence for many. If not since photography's arrival in 1839 then certainly since the turn of the century with Kodak's role in the rise of amateur photography, photographs have chronicled the lives of ordinary life in persons. In this sense, the camera was a technological tool of democratization. As an artifact that occurs in a context, a literal and figurative frame, the photograph may be considered for the subtle information it holds about the human condition.

After the hand camera freed photographers of some of the costly and cumbersome tripods and dangerous flash units once required, more travel and quicker exposures became possible. This revolution in technology had an impact on both the photographic subjects and the manner of their presentation. Pictures became affordable and plentiful, as well as less formally posed. Studio portraits purchased from professionals began to give way to candid images taken by family members and friends.

In addition, photograph albums joined scrapbooks as some of the most prized possessions of the American home. In these albums, ordinary Americans collected, captioned, and narrated the experiences those images recall. People assign their own meanings to images, and yet, when viewed in large numbers, snapshots of a given era begin to form patterns that provide insights into everyday life.

Nickel Madness: Nickelodeons Launch the Motion Picture Industry

The remarkable commercial success of short motion pictures released at the turn of the 20th century helped create a new form of leisure in the United States: the nickelodeon. At small storefront locations, entrepreneurs set up the equipment necessary to transform other businesses into nickel-viewing theaters, or nickelodeons. Usually, this meant up to 200 hard chairs assembled for viewers to occupy. Films were short, lasting on average 15 to 20 minutes each, and would be screened continuously during the hours of operation, usually from 8 a.m. to midnight. Audiences would turn over quickly, and sing-alongs were sometimes conducted while the projectionist changed reels. By 1908, approximately 10,000

"You Press the Button": Kodak's Brownie Camera Inspires a Nation of Popular Photographers

As a relatively new medium of communication, photography remained largely the province of the affluent during the 19th century. In 1900, however, the Kodak Company changed that by introducing to the marketplace an affordable camera that was easy to operate. This box camera, known as a Brownie, sold for one dollar and came pre-loaded with film. The advertising slogan used to sell the Brownie conveyed the appeal of its easy use: "You press the button, we do the rest." This innovation, both in terms of cost and operation, enabled a much wider population of Americans to take their own photographs. Promotions of the new camera targeted youth in particular, seeking in that way to popularize photography as an American avocation. Kodak's ad campaigns highlighted the Brownie as both a Christmas gift and activity. During the first year of availability, the Brownie sold some 250,000 pieces (National Geographic 1998, 23). This new product democratized the medium of photography because aspiring photographers no longer needed to be especially rich, artistic, or technically proficient. This immensely popular box camera, as well as its many single-use successors, changed the way Americans viewed cameras, photographs, and themselves. In this way, the snapshot was born.

commercial concerns had transformed into nickelodeons, seeking to cash in on the public enthusiasm. The theaters were so named because customers surrendered a fee of five cents to screen a short film in the company of other viewers.

Audiences at nickelodeons represented a mixture of people, of varying backgrounds and age groups. For the most part, however, the clientele was downscale because nickelodeons provided affordable and passive recreation at locations convenient for slum and tenement dwellers. Immigrants and members of the working class composed the majority of the audiences. A significant portion of the customers consisted of unsupervised children.

The features covered a wide range of subject matter but tended to make the most of the medium's signature feature of motion. Physicality dominated the productions, with chase scenes and other features that highlighted the motion picture's ability to capture movement. For the most part, the content of the nickelodeon offerings tended toward sensationalism and escapist fare. Viewers purchased an experience capable of making them forget the boredom or adversity of everyday life, if only for a short while. The most popular films were exciting, action-packed presentations. Tales of adventure, crime, and romance were especially welcome.

Progressive reformers looked askance at the role nickelodeons played in the lives of ordinary Americans. The screening areas were crowded, smelly, noisy, and frequented by undesirables such as pickpockets. Many films contained violent, criminal, or sexual content of questionable appropriateness for children. The morality of the stories themselves came into question, as did the conduct of some patrons sharing the darkened space of the nickelodeons. Indeed, on December 24, 1908, 550 nickelodeon-operators lost their licenses for morals violations. Although some had transgressed the legal standard by showing films on Sunday, others tolerated sexual activity during screenings. When, in 1907, Jane Addams attempted with a program described as "uplift theater" at Hull House to provide a more wholesome alternative to the commercially furnished nickelodeon experience, the experiment failed. Viewers did not find the settlement house's literary adaptations and nature films sufficiently compelling, and they returned to the familiar genre films of the nickelodeons.

As concerns about the morality of the nickelodeon escalated, cities attempted to regulate their content and presentation. In 1909, New York City's People's Institute formed the National Board of Review of Motion Pictures. This body would charge producers a fee to preview films for their compliance with moral standards. The findings of the National Board of Review, however, were provided in terms of suggestions only and could not be enforced.

During the period from 1900 to 1909, the nation experienced "nickel madness," and nickelodeons sold an average of 7,000 tickets daily (National Geographic 1998, 47). By 1910, *Scientific American* magazine contended that the 20,000 nickelodeons in the United States served 240,000 audience members each day (Shiftlett 1996, 280). These ventures helped seed the motion picture industry, launching many of the individuals who would later be associated with Hollywood pictures. Louis B. Mayer, the Warner brothers, and Adolph Zukor got their start in the nickelodeon business.

Popular Nickelodeon Films, 1900–1909

The Life of an American Fireman	*Great Lion Hunt*
	Boss Away, Choppers Play
The Ex-Convict	*Cheekiest Man on Earth*
The Kleptomaniac	*Attack on an Agent*
The Great Train Robbery	*Fatal Hand*
A Mother's Sin	*Roof to Cellar*
Johnny's Run	*Village Fire Brigade*
The Car Man's Danger	*A Woman's Duel*
The Pirates	*Catch the Kid*
The Coroner's Mistake	*Wizard's World*
The White Slave	*Knight Errant*

(Patterson 1907, 10, 11, 38; Ashby 2006, 157)

The Great Train Robbery

Although many films were screened during this era, few nickelodeon shows achieved the pinnacle of popularity reached by director Edwin S. Porter's 11-minute, single-reel feature, *The Great Train Robbery*. The 1903 film's story was based on an actual 1900 Union Pacific railway robbery committed in Wyoming and attributed to Butch Cassidy's Hole in the Wall Gang. As was typical of nickelodeon films, *The Great Train Robbery* enticed viewers with its fast-paced action and a sustained element of danger. In one of its most startling effects, one of the film's characters raises a gun, points it directly at the viewing audience, and then discharges the weapon. The film's performances were steeped in the traditions of melodrama, with broad visual choices in acting and clearly delineated heroes and villains. This Edison-produced film is probably the best known of all nickelodeon titles, both in terms of its sales and its innovations in use of the medium. By some accounts, it was the first narrative film and the first screen

A woman kneels over the bound and gagged telegraph operator in a scene from The Great Train Robbery. *Filmed in 1903, the movie is an innovative landmark, being the first narrative film and the first Western, setting the standard for years to come.* (Corbis)

Western. Many also credit the film with the first camera close-up. Filmed in part in a Paterson, New Jersey, freight yard, *The Great Train Robbery* evoked the Wild West and its much-storied outlaws. It also helped launch the Western as a film genre in the United States.

Coney Island Culture and America's Amusement Parks

With romantic names such as Dreamland (opened in 1904), Luna Park (opened in 1903), and Steeplechase (opened in 1897), amusement parks of this era permitted Americans to step away from their everyday habits and cares to enter a world of whimsical possibilities. Visitors enjoyed attractions with names such as "Helter Skelter," "Mountain Torrent," and "Shoot the Chutes." While the particulars at each of these locations varied, a site such as Atlantic City afforded vacationers arcades, a boardwalk, carousels, mutoscopes (or peep shows, as they were also known), penny arcades, and hotels. Enthusiasm for amusement parks was not limited to New York or the Northeast. Cities across the nation were building such parks. Denver had Manhattan Beach, Chicago had Riverview Park, San Francisco had The Chutes, and Atlanta had Ponce de Leon Park. When World War I got under way, the United States boasted approximately 2,000 of these "meccas for the millions" (Girodano 2003, 16).

The same forces that favored urbanization and industrialization also hastened the development of the American amusement park. Crowding in cities provided an ample customer base. Mechanization made possible many of the rides and decorations. Sweltering summer heat inspired urban residents to escape to seaside resorts for bathing, sand play, and other diversions. During the years from 1900 to 1909, such seashore locations often also featured an amusement park for visitors to frequent. At sites from Coney Island to Atlantic City, vacationers at the shore could explore the array of attractions available at the era's amusement parks: rides, concessions, fortune-tellers, peep shows, vaudeville shows, circuses, freak shows, carousels, and, of course, the midway. There, park visitors could play games of chance or skill, win prizes, view oddities, and socialize informally within a whole swirl of strangers.

The area of Long Island known as Coney Island was convenient for city dwellers, just nine minutes from Manhattan by trolley or other public conveyance. From May to September each year, working-class Americans often ventured there for a respite from daily routines and a release from customary social inhibitions. On a weekend day or holiday in 1900, Coney Island usually welcomed between 300,000 and 500,000 guests (Giordano 2003, 16). In 1909 alone, more than 20 million people visited Coney Island (Nasaw 1993, 3). At this amusement complex, composed of Coney Island itself and companion sites, Steeplechase Park and Luna Park, patrons found a place to play.

Fred Thompson's Luna Park

Frederick Thompson was the man behind Luna Park, one of several amusement areas located at New York's Coney Island. The park had its origins in a ride Thompson had designed with his partner, Elmer Dundy, to be featured at the 1901 Pan-American Exposition in Buffalo, New York: "A Trip to the Moon." At this fairground attraction, passengers boarded a vessel equipped with flapping wings. The ride enjoyed considerable popularity among Buffalo fairgoers.

Thompson and Dundy parlayed this success into a greater one the following year by moving the ride to New York's Steeplechase Park. "A Trip to the Moon" was warmly received, and it was not long until the two entrepreneurs acquired a property that had been the prior home of Sea Lion Park. They transformed this land into a whole new amusement park, Luna Park.

Inspired in part by the dramatic architecture that characterized world's fairs, Luna Park's architecture was rather eye-catching. Thompson and Dundy took another cue from the site of the Pan-American Exposition of 1901, dotting the exteriors of these structures with electric lamps. This newly devised approach to festival sites particularly enhanced the appearance of the park for visitors present after dark. On opening day in 1903, Luna Park commanded some 45,000 admissions.

Based on the success of Thompson's venture, other parks opened under the same name in locations around the world. They adapted the Luna Park's design and attractions to meet the needs of their own settings and customers.

POPULAR AMUSEMENTS

In the early years of the 20th century in the United States, leisure activities took many forms. Against the backdrops of bars, saloons, and other unsavory recreational environments stood those organizations and establishments designed to provide more wholesome entertainment. Professional athletic competitions, such as the nation's favorite pastime of baseball, provided leisure activities suitable for the entire family. Professional sports were popular, and the period from 1900 to 1909 saw both the first Rose Bowl in football and the first World Series in baseball. Recreational sports— from stickball played in vacant city lots

Table 7.2. Baseball Attendance in the United States, 1901–1909

Year	American League	National League
1901	1,684	1,920
1902	2,206	1,683
1903	2,345	2,390
1904	3,024	2,664
1905	3,121	2,734
1906	2,938	2,781
1907	3,399	2,640
1908	3,611	3,512
1909	3,740	3,496

In thousands.

Source: Kurian 2001, 182.

Table 7.3. Baseball Champions, National League and American League, 1900–1909

Year	National League champions	American League champions
1900	Brooklyn	—
1901	Pittsburgh	Chicago
1902	Pittsburgh	Philadelphia
1903	Pittsburgh	Boston
1904	New York	Boston
1905	New York	Philadelphia
1906	Chicago	Chicago
1907	Chicago	Detroit
1908	Chicago	Detroit
1909	Pittsburgh	Detroit

Source: Based on Frank G. Menke, *The Encyclopedia of Sports* (1969), 81–82, as reprinted in Shifftlet 1996, 283.

to tobogganing on snow-covered hillsides in the country—continued to be favorites among youth.

At this point in American history, improvements in transportation made it easier for entertainers to take their performances on the road. An increasing number of leisure opportunities circulated across the country, touring to provide the nation's entertainment. Festivals, circuses, freak shows, and Wild West shows did very well at this time in the history of the United States.

Some leisure facilities even dedicated themselves to uplifting participants. At public libraries and fine arts museums, Americans had the opportunity to experience the world's treasures of art and literature. National parks and forests provided Americans with safe settings in which to experience the grandeur of the natural landscape. Phenomena such as the Chautauqua movement, with its goal of adult education, attempted to inspire Americans to self-improvement.

Popular Theater

Popular theater was vibrant during the period from 1900 to 1909 in the United States. It was the era of music halls, burlesque, and dazzling productions such as the much-touted Ziegfeld follies. On the vaudeville circuit, performers such as magician and illusionist Harry Houdini entertained the nation. Before they entered the world of cinema, personalities such as W. C. Fields and Mae West thrilled live audiences with their irreverence.

Vaudeville theater got its start in America's saloons. Early in vaudeville's history, performers were hired to entertain the patrons while they drank and socialized. For this reason, the entertainers had to capture the audience's attention to be noticed. The shows became known for tantalizing audiences by incorporating elements of risqué display and ribald humor. By 1900, however, the emphasis within most vaudeville was on the stage rather than the bar. Although the barroom shows continued, a more refined version of vaudeville grew in popularity with customers seeking slightly more respectable leisure. The tone shifted from sensational to sentimental to accommodate a wider public. Variety shows provided audiences with samples of many stage artists, and at the turn of the 20th century, the content and cost of these entertainments began to appeal to more women. Even children might attend the stage performances of this more family-friendly version of vaudeville.

Popular theater did not enjoy the respectability of the legitimate stage. In many cases, these theaters were not the formal venues of Broadway, but rather neighborhood establishments where working-class people could enjoy themselves informally. Ethnic and immigrant theater thrived at this time, serving audiences by providing theatrical productions in the spectator's first language, from Chinese to Yiddish.

These trends in popular theater—variety entertainment, ethnic and immigrant theater, and stage performance for both men and women—coincided with a sharp growth in affordable theater venues. During the years from 1896 to 1909, seating in theaters charging modest admissions (15 cents or less) increased more than 100 percent (Nasaw 1993, 37). Inexpensive theater admissions, increases in the number of venues, and theater forms catering to a wider audience made it attractive and possible for more Americans to experience live entertainment.

Dance Halls

During the years from 1900 to 1909, ordinary Americans frequented leisure establishments such as juke joints, honky-tonks, and dance halls to socialize, hear the latest music, and dance with one another. People of color and those residing outside the nation's cities often went to hear live music and dance at juke joints and honky-tonks. In the nation's cities, dance halls met some of these needs. At this point in American life, major cities each had hundreds of such halls. New York City led the trend with 500 dance halls, while Chicago boasted 400, San Francisco had 300, and Cleveland hosted 130 (Giordano 2003, 12).

Musical styles at America's dance halls varied with the clientele, but ragtime was often favored for its fast pace and lively syncopation. Patrons also enjoyed the so-called animal dances: Bunny Hug, Turkey Trot, and Chicken Scratch, to name a few. These novelty steps were fun to perform or watch, and they enabled dance hall patrons to abandon the decorum of polite society for the sake of an evening's enjoyment.

With the physicality of dance and the fanciful motions associated with the dance steps originating during this era, dance halls were sometimes regarded with suspicion by moralistic onlookers. Detractors saw such environments as dance halls as a bad influence on youth and an immoral form of recreation. There was talk of "charity girls," or young working women reputed to flirt—or more—in exchange for the price of an evening's enjoyment. Reformers, such as Jane Addams, did not necessarily oppose dancing but nonetheless sought to promote safer dance halls for young women. Dance halls afforded urban Americans a respite from their day-to-day responsibilities and created opportunities,

The most famous American composer and bandmaster of his day, John Philip Sousa and his ensemble were tremendously popular for years while the energetic composer wrote operettas, songs, and band suites. Many of his marches, such as "The Stars and Stripes Forever," remain popular to this day. (National Archives)

especially for young people, to mingle and meet one another.

Popular Music

From 1900 to 1909, Americans enjoyed a variety of popular music genres. With the emergence of mass culture, sheet music, and phonographs exposed Americans to performances by a wide array of musical artists. In additional to traditional tunes, listeners during this period could sample everything from the patriotic marches of John Philip Sousa to the ragtime compositions of Scott Joplin. The most successful songs, such as "In the Good Old Summer Time," might sell one million copies in the first year (Time-Life 1969, 181). This was the era of Tin Pan Alley, a movement within popular music that got its start on 28th Street in New York City. Using an assembly line approach to musical composition, Tin Pan Alley writers produced popular tunes the way factories produced toasters, then published it as sheet music. This explosion of musical writing and its distribution through mass media created increased choices of musical accompaniment to live performances, home enjoyment of recorded music, and rapidly cycling fashions of popular music featured at America's dance halls and other leisure locations. In 1910, for example, 2 billion copies of sheet music were sold in the United States (Time-Life 1969, 181).

Did the Phonograph Democratize Music?

During the late 19th century, Americans regarded music as an important part of an ideal domestic environment. The Victorian parlor organ or piano, for those families who could afford one, emblematized the ennobling influences of a cultured mother and a moral home. During the 1800s, however, if a family wanted to hear the sounds of music in the home, they had to learn how to play the in-

Scott Joplin's "Treemonisha" as Ragtime Opera

Musical composer Scott Joplin is best known for short works of ragtime, such as "Maple Leaf Rag" and "The Entertainer." In addition to writing popular tunes in the style he made famous, however, Joplin also applied those innovations to the musical form of opera. The result was a 1910 composition, "Treemonisha: An Opera in Three Acts."

In this piece, Scott Joplin explored a story about the tension between modern and traditional cultures for African Americans of the era and place where it was set, Arkansas in 1884. The period of Reconstruction forms the backdrop for this opera. At the center of the opera is a tale about a childless couple who adopt a daughter, whom they name Treemonisha. Treemonisha pursues an education and, as a consequence, seeks to bring back to her community the benefits of that learning.

The dilemma comes when Treemonisha takes a stand against the folk beliefs and customs that formed an integral part of that community. In particular, she challenges the tradition of conjuring, a set of practices by which some African Americans of the time used roots and rituals for the purpose of influencing the course of human events. Treemonisha regards such attempts to attract good fortune as mere superstition and at odds with a life informed by modern schooling.

When conjurers approach Treemonisha's mother in the attempt to sell her an object purported to bring good luck, she opposes them. In an act of reprisal, the conjurers kidnap and attempt to harm her. Ultimately, Treemonisha's suitor frees her from this captivity. In the aftermath of this incident, she is able to share her education with the rest of the community.

Joplin's "Treemonisha" is remarkable for the manner in which he combines elements of classical music with features of ragtime, thereby creating a new hybrid musical form, the ragtime opera.

struments themselves. To play the popular tunes of the age, they would purchase the necessary sheet music and learn to play the notes for themselves.

By the turn of the 20th century, however, the advent of recorded sound began to make it possible for more Americans to enjoy music at home. It was no longer essential to perform the music one played at home. The mass production of phonographs ushered in the era of recorded music. Even those who were not proficient as singers or players of musical instruments could enjoy listening to others sing and play.

There were several advantages to this new medium, including cost, convenience, and unlimited access to strong musical production values. While it is true that only a portion of the nation's residents possessed the discretionary income for such purchases, prices fell as the technology took hold. In this sense, the phonograph was an affordable way for owners to hear a wide range of musical

Table 7.4. Hit Songs, 1900–1909

1900	"A Bird in a Gilded Cage"
	"Down South"
	"The Gladiator's Entry"
	"Goodbye Dolly Gray"
	"I Can't Tell You Why I Love You, But I Do"
	"Just Because She Made Dem Goo-Goo Eyes"
	"Ma Blushin' Rose"
1901	"Stars and Stripes Forever"
	"I Love You Truly"
	"Finlandia"
	"Hiawatha"
	"Just A-Wearyin' for You"
	"Mighty Lak' a Rose"
	"Serenade"
1902	"Bill Bailey, Won't You Please Come Home"
	"The Entertainer"
	"Because"
	"In the Good Old Summer Time"
	"In the Sweet Bye and Bye"
	"Pomp and Circumstance"
	"Under the Bamboo Tree"
	"Oh, Didn't He Ramble"
	"Please Go 'Way and Let Me Sleep"
	"On a Sunday Afternoon"
1903	"Toyland"
	"Always Leave them Laughing When You Say Goodbye"
	"Bedelia"
	"Dear Old Girl"
	"Kashmiri Love Song"
	"The March of the Toys"
	"Ida, Sweet as Apple Cider"
	"I Can't Do the Sum"
	"Good Bye, Eliza Jane"
1904	"(I Am) The Yankee Doodle Boy"
	"Give My Regards to Broadway"
	"Goodbye, Little Girl, Goodbye"
	"Please Come Play in My Yard"
	"Stop Yer Tickling, Jock!"
	"Teasing"
	"You're the Flower of My Heart (Sweet Adeline)"

	"Come Take a Trip on My Airship"
	"Meet Me in St. Louis, Louis"
1905	"In My Merry Oldsmobile"
	"I Don't Care"
	"Nobody"
	"Will You Love Me in December (as You Do in May)?"
	"I Want What I Want When I Want It"
	"Clair de Lune"
	"Mary's a Grand Old Name"
	"Everybody Works But Father"
	"Tammany"
	"The Whistler and His Dog"
	"Forty-Five Minutes from Broadway"
	"In the Shade of the Old Apple Tree"
	"Kiss Me Again"
	"Rufus Rastus Johnson Brown (What You Goin' to Do When the Rent Comes Round)"
	"My Gal Sal (They Call Her Frivolous Sal)"
	"So Long Mary"
	"Wait 'til the Sun Shines, Nellie"
1907	"Budweiser's a Friend of Mine"
	"Will the Circle Be Unbroken?"
	"Maxim's"
	"Red Wing"
	"Harrigan"
	"Glow Worm"
	"The Merry Widow Waltz"
	"Vilia"
	"It's Delightful to Be Married"
	"On the Road to Mandalay"
	"Wal, I Swan!, or Ebenezer Frye, or Giddiap Napoleon, It Looks Like Rain"
	"School Days"
	"Bell Bottom Trousers"
1908	"Get on the Raft with Taft"
	"Shine On, Harvest Moon"
	"Sweet Violets"
	"Smarty"
	"Cuddle Up a Little Closer, Lovey Mine"
	"Take Me Out to the Ball Game"

Table 7.4. Hit Songs, 1900–1909, *Continued*

1909	"Meet Me Tonight in Dreamland"	"I've Got Rings on My Fingers"
	"Put on Your Old Grey Bonnet"	"Heaven Will Protect the Working Girl"
	"Has Anybody Here Seen Kelly?"	
	"Casey Jones"	"From the Land of the Sky Blue Water"
	"My Hero"	"Yip-I-Addy-I-Ay!"
	"By the Light of the Silvery Moon"	"I Love My Wife, But Oh You Kid"
	"My Pony Boy"	"On Wisconsin"
	"That's A Plenty"	"I Wonder Who's Kissing Her Now"

Source: Based on Barnet, Nemerov, and Taylor 2004; Lax and Smith 1984, 20–36.

genres and performers. Even those who lacked the means to attend concerts and other musical events could, in this way, access recorded music. By acquiring one record at a time, consumers could sample different musical artists and forms. Not only popular music but also classical and orchestral music reached a wider audience through this distribution process.

The phonograph also provided customers with a measure of convenience. No longer did Americans need to wait for a scheduled recital; unlike live music, their recorded music would be ready whenever they were. With the help of the phonograph, people could also experience those musical productions again and again. Because the songs were prerecorded, listeners could obtain music in an exactly repeatable form. If they liked a record, they could hear it as many times as they wished and it would be perfect every time.

In relative terms, phonographs were also portable devices, and so the experience could be conveyed to new locations at will. Schools, churches, hospitals, and other sites could make use of recorded music for the education or uplift of their populations. With these shared uses of musical recordings beyond the home, Americans of all ages could encounter music that would otherwise be unknown to them.

By most accounts, American music listenership widened because of the phonograph. Its arrival stimulated music appreciation, and inspired some to learn to play and perform music. Some phonograph models permitted users to record their own musical efforts at home. On the other hand, the availability of prerecorded music appears to coincide with a reduction in the amount of live musical performance by family members within the home. The option of passive musical experience may have proved too tempting, and as the phonograph—and later the radio—became increasingly more common in the nation's households, sales of pianos and sheet music dropped. As one cultural observer noted, "It's everywhere, this Victrola: in the tenements, the restaurants, the ice-cream parlors, the candy stores. You lock your door at night and are safe from burglars, but not from the Victrola" (Ashby 2006, 168–169).

Table 7.5. Illiterate Residents of the United States, 1880–1910, by Race (percent)

Year	Total	White, native	White, immigrant	People of color
1880	17.0	8.7	12.0	70.0
1890	13.3	6.2	13.1	56.8
1900	10.7	4.6	12.9	44.5
1910	7.7	5.0	12.7	30.5

Source: U.S. Department of Commerce 1989, 382.

CROSSCURRENTS IN AMERICAN LEISURE: ALTERNATIVES TO CONSUMER CULTURE

At the same time that consumer culture was growing and flourishing in the United States, there emerged alternatives to the usual entertainments, more highbrow opportunities for the American public to spend their leisure time and money. There were even some sites, such as public libraries and fine arts museums, where Americans could enjoy activities and entertainments free of charge. Other forms of leisure were available at nominal costs, such as national parks and chautauquas. Therefore, while consumer culture became a pervasive presence in everyday life in America, it was far from the only source of recreation for the nation's people. If, as the saying would have it, "the best things in life are free," even those of the most modest means could borrow much of the best of what the nation had to offer, even if they could not afford to buy it.

Reading Culture

The first decade of the 20th century marked a time in which a higher percentage of Americans had achieved literacy than ever before in the nation's life. Consequently, reading culture flourished in the form of magazines, newspapers, and books. In 1900, the nation's people purchased 200,000 magazine subscriptions. Some were general audience periodicals, such as the *Atlantic, Century, Harper's, McClure's,* and *Saturday Evening Post.* Others targeted women readers in particular, such as *Good Housekeeping, Ladies' Home Journal, McCall's, Redbook,* and *Woman's Home Companion.* Still others appealed to more specific populations, such as hobbyists. Pulp magazines, so named for the paper stock on which they were printed, also flourished during this era. The genre of stories carried in pulp magazines was fairly formulaic, tending toward action and adventure. In a process that approximated mass production, "fiction factories" churned out tales to satisfy the American public's appetites for such stories.

The United States had 1,600 daily newspapers in 1900, with a total circulation of 2.8 million readers. By 1910, however, there were 2,600 dailies and a circulation of 24.2 readers (Giordano 2003, 11). Although newspapers of this era were local and regional rather than national, they were just beginning to include such elements as a travel section, indicative of the readership's increased prospect for leisure.

Book readers during the years from 1900 to 1909 had the good fortune to live during a rich era in the history of American fiction. They could sample the works of such writers as Jack London, Edith Wharton, Frank Norris, Henry James, Upton Sinclair, and Theodore Dreiser. They could also read serialized fiction in the pages of popular magazines such as *Collier's* and *Scribner's*. Far from all of the fiction published during this era was so literary; a good deal of it consisted of what H. L. Mencken termed "mush for the multitude"; that is, commercially motivated fiction tended toward the formulaic and the sentimental.

Fans of nonfiction also had a wealth of reading choices at this time. It was during this period that many of the landmark texts in Progressive era's explorations of social science first appeared. Edward A. Ross, Jane Addams, Simon Nelson Patten, and Lester Frank Ward were among the figures who published sociological texts at this time.

Table 7.6. Featured Content of Periodicals, 1902

Content category	Percent
Personal, social, local	28.6
Business	26.9
Political/governmental	17.7
Criminal, sensational, trivial	14.3
Intellectual, scientific, religious	12.5

Source: Based on John Cotton Dana's "What People Read," *Public Libraries* 7 (June 1902): 230, as it appears in Carrier 1985, 46.

Building the Nation's Public Library System

At the turn of the 20th century, there were roughly 2,000 public libraries in the United States (Martin 1998, 11). The role of libraries in American life was growing. Both the numbers of libraries and the size of their collections rose during this era. According to scholar Esther Jane Carrier, "By 1900 there was one library to every 14,718 persons in the United States, and 45,000,000 library volumes, or fifty-nine books to every one hundred people, whereas in 1875 libraries had contained only 11,0000,000 volumes, or one book to every four persons" (Carrier 1985, 4).

In the first 10 years of the 20th century, the literacy rate in America grew by 3 percent. As the literacy rate in the United States rose and reading culture flourished, the time became right for establishing a full-fledged public library system. The movement for growth of the nation's libraries was a campaign to elevate

Table 7.7. Selected Fiction and Nonfiction Books Published, 1900–1909

1900	Theodore Dreiser, *Sister Carrie*
	L. Frank Baum, *The Wonderful Wizard of Oz*
	Charlotte Perkins Gilman, *Concerning Children*
1901	Frank Norris,*The Octopus*
	Edward A. Ross, *Social Control*
	Booker T. Washington, *Up from Slavery*
	Upton Sinclair, *Springtime and Harvest*
1902	Owen Wister, *The Virginian*
	Henry James, *The Wings of the Dove*
	Jane Addams, *Democracy and Social Ethics*
1903	W. E. B. Du Bois, *The Souls of Black Folk*
	Jack London, *The Call of the Wild*
	Simon Nelson Patten, *Heredity and Social Progress*
	Kate Douglas Wiggin, *Rebecca of Sunnybrook Farm*
1904	Lincoln Steffens, *The Shame of the Cities*
	Ida Tarbell, *The History of the Standard Oil Company*
1905	Edith Wharton, *The House of Mirth*
	Thomas Dixon Jr., *The Clansman*
1906	Upton Sinclair, *The Jungle*
	Ellen Glasgow, *The Wheel of Life*
	Lester Frank Ward, *Applied Sociology*
1907	Jane Addams, *Newer Ideals of Peace*
	Henry Adams, *The Education of Henry Adams*
	William Graham Sumner, *Folkways*
	Edward A. Ross, *Sin and Society*
1908	John Fox Jr., *The Trail of the Lonesome Pine*
	Jack London, *The Iron Heel*
	Mary Roberts Rinehart, *The Circular Staircase*
1909	William Vaughn Moody, *The Faith Healer*
	Jane Addams, *The Spirit of Youth and City Streets*

Source: OCLC Worldcat Database, OCLC, http://www.worldcat.org.

the American people through reading, as well as to supplement the education available to the nation's children. Industrialist and philanthropist Andrew Carnegie was instrumental in bringing such a system to the nation. Carnegie wanted to reward initiative among Americans motivated for self-improvement. He stated, "I chose free libraries as the best agencies for improving the masses of the people, because they only help those who help themselves" (Martin 1998, 19).

With the help of Carnegie's donations, new libraries started to appear in America. Free loans of materials from public libraries made it possible for those without the means to purchase books and magazines to read on a regular basis. Children who could not attend school might still get to develop their abilities as readers. Those striving to learn English for the first time could access resources to help them accomplish that goal. Individuals who wanted to raise their station in life could conduct self-directed learning. In this sense, the public library functioned in a manner that inspired some to dub it "the People's University."

Carnegie libraries were often located in areas where he had established business concerns so they might conceivably benefit his own workers. Of course, there were practical limits to the use they might make of such a facility. As social worker Margaret Byington expressed with reference to the steelworkers of Homestead, Pennsylvania, "They appreciate what the library and manual training offer to them and their children, but they resent a philanthropy which provides opportunities for intellectual and social advancement while it withholds conditions which make it possible to take advantage of them" (quoted in Edwards 2006, 131). Although some communities declined Carnegie's form of help, many accepted his money toward the establishment of public libraries.

The Rise of Popular Fiction

Just as the nation's working and leisure practices were changing during the years from 1900 to 1909, so were the public's reading habits. In an article written for a 1906 issue of the *Library Journal,* novelist W. D. Howells remarked on these shifts, satirizing their trend. He wrote, "The reading public is not the old reading public, with a critical taste of more or less refinement and the wish, more or less conscienced, to read good things. What we have to satisfy is not a palate, it is a maw, asking to be filled with whatever will produce an agreeable feeling of distention" (quoted in Carrier 1985, 30). As the criticism made by Howells suggests, American readers of the early 20th century did not limit their interests to so-called serious books. Although public libraries such as those sponsored by Andrew Carnegie had been established for purposes of education and uplift, recreational reading was also an important component of patron use of libraries at this time.

Evidence of the reading public's enthusiasm for fiction survives in the library research conducted by John Cotton Dana. In one of his research projects, Dana gathered information about borrowing patterns at the Newark library over the course of a period of 15 days in 1903. Of items borrowed from the library during that period, 70 percent were fiction. Approximately 6,000 different novels circulated from the library during the period documented.

Given the ardor for fiction reading, American librarians of the era engaged in debates regarding what fiction should be acquired for public library collections.

Table 7.8. Visits to National Parks in the United States, 1900–1909

Year	Number of parks	Area (acres)	Visits
1900	7	3,286,000	—
1902	8	3,445,000	—
1904	10	3,457,000	—
1906	12	3,251,000	31,000
1908	12	3,449,000	69,000
1909	12	3,449,000	86,000

Source: Based on U.S. Department of Commerce, 1989, 396.

Often, these debates dramatized competing notions of the guiding purpose behind establishment of a public library system. Were librarians arbiters of morality? Were libraries to be cultural gatekeepers, barring entrance to all but the most distinguished writings available? Were library patrons themselves the best judges of what they needed or wanted from libraries? While some librarians argued that only the works deemed to be of highest literary quality and enduring value be placed in libraries, others sought to consider the public's appetite for popular fiction. Most libraries tried to strike a balance among highbrow, middlebrow, and lowbrow forms of fiction.

The first decade of the 20th century positioned public libraries as largely democratic institutions. Accessibility emerged as the library system's greatest virtue. Librarians such as Minerva Sanders became exponents of open shelves, permitting library visitors to move freely through the holdings and to retrieve books for themselves. Aiding them in this process were the printing services of the Library of Congress. Starting in 1902, the Library of Congress began distributing preprinted entries for the card catalogues of public libraries (Martin 1998, 29). The volumes available there reflected diverse topics, genres, and tastes. Public library collections anticipated the needs of a wide range of American readers, regardless of region, background, or station.

America's National Parks

In 1900, the national park system in the United States consisted of just 7 sites. By 1909, that figure rose to 12 national parks. Over this decade, the number of visitors to national parks increased steadily, as parks provided an affordable, family-friendly recreation for Americans who could access them. Because automobiles were not yet commonly owned by ordinary citizens, public transportation played a role in the development of a park-going American public. For instance, one contributing factor to the growth in visitor rates at national parks was the advertising campaigns conducted by railroads with lines serving the areas in which parks were located. For instance, the Northern Pacific Railway's advertisements extolled the beauty of a location within their service area, Yellowstone National Park. By highlighting the attractions riders could experience via rail travel, the railroads hoped to increase their own business. It was during this era that the Audubon Society got its start and congressional measures began to protect endangered species. The United States Senate also took steps to preserve the dwindling population of buffalo in America.

The Chautauqua Movement

As a counterpoint to the tawdrier forms of mass entertainment, the chautauqua movement emphasized self-improvement as its goal for participants. The trend started in 1874, when a group of Sunday school teachers gathered at New York's Lake Chautauqua to discuss pedagogy. The camp maintained at that site became a summer colony welcoming a wider range of visitors. While there, participants enrolled in courses on art, crafts, music, and household science. By 1900, traveling chautauquas made the circuit, bringing the experience to the

A prospector or guide at Yellowstone National Park, 1903. Photo by Francis Benjamin Johnston. (Library of Congress)

rest of the nation. A stop along the way of such a tour might last from three days to a week, and many attendees traveled to participate. These tent shows provided a self-respecting form of leisure, combining lectures on such subjects

Chautauqua assembly in Clarinda, Louisiana, ca. 1908. (Library of Congress)

Niagara's Declaration of Principles, 1905

Progress: The members of the conference, known as the Niagara Movement, assembled in annual meeting at Buffalo, July 11th, 12th and 13th, 1905, congratulate the Negro-Americans on certain undoubted evidences of progress in the last decade, particularly the increase of intelligence, the buying of property, the checking of crime, the uplift in home life, the advance in literature and art, and the demonstration of constructive and executive ability in the conduct of great religious, economic, and educational institutions.

Suffrage: At the same time, we believe that this class of American citizens should protest emphatically and continually against the curtailment of their political rights. We believe in manhood suffrage; we believe that no man is so good, intelligent, or wealthy as to be entrusted wholly with the welfare of his neighbor.

Civil Liberty: We believe also in protest against the curtailment of our civil rights. All American citizens have the right to equal treatment in places of public entertainment according to their behavior and deserts.

Economic Opportunity: We especially complain against the denial of equal opportunities to us in economic life; in the rural districts of the South this amounts to peonage and virtual slavery; all over the South it tends to crush labor and small business enterprises; and everywhere American prejudice, helped often by iniquitous laws, is making it more difficult for Negro-Americans to earn a decent living.

Education: Common school education should be free to all American children and compulsory. High school training should be adequately provided for all, and college training should be the monopoly of no class or race in any section of our common country. We believe that, in defense of our own institutions, the United States should aid common school education, particularly in the South, and we especially recommend concerted agitation to this end. We urge an increase in public high school facilities in the South, where the Negro-Americans are almost wholly without such provisions. We favor well-equipped trade and technical schools for the training of artisans, and the need of adequate and liberal endowment for a few institutions of higher education must be patient to sincere well-wishers of the race.

Courts: We demand upright judges in courts, juries selected without discrimination on account of color and the same measure of punishment and the same efforts at reformation for black as for white offenders. We need orphanages and farm schools for dependent children, juvenile reformatories for delinquents, and the abolition of the dehumanizing convict-lease system.

Public Opinion: We note with alarm the evident retrogression in this land of sound public opinion on the subject of manhood rights, republican government and human brotherhood, and we pray God that this nation will not degenerate into a mob of boasters and oppressors, but rather will return to the faith of the fathers, that all men were created free and equal, with certain unalienable rights.

Health: We plead for health—for an opportunity to live in decent houses and localities, for a chance to rear our children in physical and moral cleanliness.

Niagara's Declaration of Principles, 1905, Continued

Employers and Labor Unions: We hold up for public execration the conduct of two opposite classes of men: The practice among employers of importing ignorant Negro-American laborers in emergencies, and then affording them neither protection nor permanent employment; and the practice of labor unions in proscribing and boycotting and oppressing thousands of their fellow-toilers, simply because they are black. These methods have accentuated and will accentuate the war of labor and capital, and they are disgraceful to both sides.

Protest: We refuse to allow the impression to remain that the Negro-American assents to inferiority, is submissive under oppression and apologetic before insults. Through helplessness we may submit, but the voice of protest of ten million Americans must never cease to assail the ears of their fellows, so long as America is unjust.

Color Line: Any discrimination based simply on race or color is barbarous, we care not how hallowed it be by custom, expediency, or prejudice. Differences made on account of ignorance, immorality, or disease are legitimate methods of fighting evil, and against them we have no word of protest; but discriminations based simply and solely on physical peculiarities, place of birth, color of skin are relics of that unreasoning human savagery of which the world is and ought to be thoroughly ashamed.

"Jim Crow" Cars: We protest against the "Jim Crow" car, since its effect is and must be to make us pay first-class fare for third-class accommodations, render us open to insults and discomfort and to crucify wantonly our manhood, womanhood, and self-respect.

Soldiers: We regret that this nation has never seen fit adequately to reward the black soldiers who, in its five wars, have defended their country with their blood, and yet have been systematically denied the promotions which their abilities deserve. And we regard as unjust, the exclusion of black boys from the military and naval training schools.

War Amendments: We urge upon Congress the enactment of appropriate legislation for securing the proper enforcement of those articles of freedom, the thirteenth, fourteenth and fifteenth amendments of the Constitution of the United States.

Oppression: We repudiate the monstrous doctrine that the oppressor should be the sole authority as to the rights of the oppressed. The Negro race in America stolen, ravished, and degraded, struggling up through difficulties and oppression, needs sympathy and receives criticism; needs help and is given hindrance, needs protection and is given mob violence, needs justice and is given charity, needs leadership and is given cowardice and apology, needs bread and is given a stone. This nation will never stand justified before God until these things are changed.

Continued on next page

Niagara's Declaration of Principles, 1905, Continued

The Church: Especially are we surprised and astonished at the recent attitude of the church of Christ—of an increase of a desire to bow to racial prejudice, to narrow the bounds of human brotherhood, and to segregate black men to some outer sanctuary. This is wrong, unchristian, and disgraceful to the twentieth century civilization.

Agitation: Of the above grievances we do not hesitate to complain, and to complain loudly and insistently. To ignore, overlook, or apologize for these wrongs is to prove ourselves unworthy of freedom. Persistent manly agitation is the way to liberty, and toward this goal the Niagara Movement has started and asks the cooperation of all men of all races.

Help: At the same time we want to acknowledge with deep thankfulness the help of our fellowmen from the Abolitionist down to those who today still stand for equal opportunity and who have given and still give of their wealth and of their poverty for our advancement.

Duties: And while we are demanding, and ought to demand, and will continue to demand the rights enumerated above, God forbid that we should ever forget to urge corresponding duties upon our people:

The duty to vote.

The duty to respect the rights of others.

The duty to work.

The duty to obey the laws.

The duty to be clean and orderly.

The duty to send our children to school.

The duty to respect ourselves, even as we respect others.

This statement, complaint, and prayer we submit to the American people, and Almighty God.

as home canning and morality with entertainments such as vocal performance and bell ringers. When the featured speakers included someone prominent, such as William Jennings Bryan, crowds would grow considerably. These traveling chautauquas continued throughout the decade, reaching many Americans with their message of education and uplift.

Fine Arts Museums in America

Although collecting original art remained the province of the cultural elite in the United States, the period from 1900 to 1909 witnessed the opening of a number of major fine art museums to the public at locations across the country. At such institutions as the Metropolitan Museum of Art in New York and the National

The Advent of the Niagara Falls Honeymoon

In a decade during which the nation's progress was measured in an important sense through the use of electrical energy, it might not be surprising that Niagara Falls took on additional symbolic importance. Its hydroelectric power made it not only a site of reverie but also a force for industry. A visit to Niagara Falls simultaneously offered afforded visitors a renewed sense of nature's unspoiled splendor and a glimpse at the industrial progress ahead.

During the years from 1900 to 1909, Niagara Falls also hosted important events and gatherings. One such occasion was the 1905 founding meeting of the Niagara Movement. At this time, persons concerned with the struggle for civil liberties assembled to form a group that would later become the NAACP.

At the turn of the 20th century, Niagara Falls had long been recognized as a natural wonder. It had established itself as the resort and recreation site for those who lived in the region or for those affluent enough to venture distances for its spectacle. As early as the 19th century, members of the economic elite began to regard the falls as an appropriate vacation spot, including for newly married couples. As roads improved and automobile travel became more pervasive, Niagara Falls also became a destination of choice for middle-class tourists visiting from other regions. This was particularly true for newlyweds.

Although during the years from 1900 to 1909 it was still relatively few America's newlyweds who had the means to travel or the luxury of time off from work to celebrate their nuptials with a vacation trip, an increasing number of middle- and upper-class couples in the United States started to think of post-wedding travel as, if not a custom, an ideal. The beauty of the setting at Niagara Falls appealed to such Americans, and it grew sharply in its popularity as a place to spend one's honeymoon. At first, Niagara Falls was a secluded opportunity for communion with both nature and one's new spouse. Later, as tourism redefined the atmosphere, it became a traditional approach to honeymooning. In fact, it was during the first half of the 20th century that this location declared itself the "honeymoon capital of the world."

Collection of Fine Arts in the District of Columbia, visitors could see first-hand the works of great artists, both past and present, free or for a nominal fee.

In addition, at major gatherings such as world's fairs and expositions, entire buildings were commonly reserved for displays of artworks. At these displays, even those Americans who might not otherwise venture into a museum encountered original works of fine art.

During the years from 1900 to 1909, a group of American artists known as the Ashcan School changed the way Americans thought about appropriate subject matter for visual art. Although the customary subject matter for painting involved traditional notions of beauty, members of this group of artists experimented with another aesthetic entirely. Ashcan School painters created images of subjects less elevated and rarified. Instead, they portrayed scenes from everyday life, even if those realities were not pretty. In particular, they depicted unvarnished versions of the urban environment in the United States. George Bellows painted boxing matches while John Sloan showed us the smoky interiors of saloons and the bleak backyards of New Yorkers.

CRITICS OF MASS CULTURE

Although mass culture was just emerging at the turn of the 20th century, the central tools of its promotion—advertising, marketing, and sales—had accompanied earlier appeals to the nation's consumers. In fact, P. T. Barnum, a 19th century American showman whose name became associated with a traveling circus, was widely known for his assertion that "there is a sucker born every minute." In order to attract business, sellers and advertisers spent vast sums of time and money trying to convince consumers that they wanted and needed things they had not even thought of yet. Whether selling merchandise or promoting services, capitalists sought ways to persuade Americans to indulge in new purchases rather than simply to make do with the possessions they already had. By the middle of the 19th century, a few dissenting voices, such as Henry David Thoreau, spoke to the importance of eschewing industrial culture and its trappings. With his classic 1854 text, *Walden,* Thoreau advocated simplicity in lifestyle. In effect, he coached readers on ways to avoid becoming the "sucker" that hucksters such as P. T. Barnum relied upon for their livelihoods.

Commentators Then

For the most part, turn-of-the century critics of consumer culture invoked some version of a social control argument. That is, they maintained that the problem with consumption was the tendency to become more closely identified with the role of customer than with the citizen. They did not want individuals to confuse the thrill of shopping with the power exercised by voting. Such critics cautioned Americans against substituting interest for influence, excitement for agency. These commentators warned of advertising illusions that might cause people to confuse consumer choice with personal autonomy. As George Penderevo, one of the characters in H. G. Wells' *Tono-Bungay* (1908), a character, who was both an aeronautical engineer and the nephew of a lion in the patent medicine industry, observed: "In these plethoric times when there is too much coarse stuff for everybody and the struggle for life takes on the colour of competitive advertisement and the effort to fill your eye, when there is no urgent demand either for personal courage, sound nerves or stark beauty, we find ourselves by accident" (Lears 1993, 1595).

Although the Wells character was fictional, there were countless critics of consumer culture in the lived world of turn-of-the-20th-century America. One of these dissenting voices was Charlotte Perkins Gilman (1860–1935). Gilman was part of the famous Beecher family and so was related to published authors Catharine Beecher and Harriet Beecher Stowe.

In addition to developing a career as an author, Gilman maintained an active life as a social critic, speaker, and activist. She was strongly linked to the field of academic sociology, particularly its reformist branches. Gilman called herself a "humanist," and was particularly attuned to the condition of women in America. Her nonfictional works reflect this commitment: *Women and Economics* (1898), *Concerning Children* (1900), *The Home* (1903), and *The Man-Made World* (1911). Gilman's writings portrayed a social world in which women were beholden to men for financial security. Within such a marital economy, women outfitted themselves lavishly in order to compete for the attention of male suitors. Gilman's portrayals of this dynamic suggested a form of courtship in which Darwin's model of evolution, "survival of the fittest" became "survival of the finest." For example, women with the means dressed in impractical attire and ornaments. The 1905 Sears catalog featured 75 varieties of ostrich feathers, intended to adorn elaborate hats (Time-Life 1989, 159). Gilman argued that such absurd efforts to attract and maintain the visual interest of men demeaned women and pitted them against one another.

As an advocate of economic independence for women, Charlotte Perkins Gilman made a major intellectual contribution to the American feminist movement of her day. (Library of Congress)

In many cases, Charlotte Perkins Gilman's fictional worlds embody some of her views about social and cultural conventions of the day. For instance, in one of Gilman's short stories, "If I Were A Man," a husband and wife are at odds about her spending patterns. Frustrated by the extent to which her husband dominates the financial decisions for her household, the woman wishes she were a man. At this point, she suddenly experiences a transformation in which she retains her awareness of being a woman while simultaneously inhabiting the mind and body of a man. In this new shape, the character finds out what it feels like to live as a man in an androcentric (male-centered) society. In this way, Gilman's story confounds the oppositions of the era's gender roles, revealing them to be invented rather than inherent. She also highlights the absurdity of gender roles that require men and women to exaggerate personal attributes or feign identities in order to meet conventional gender expectations.

With her writings, Charlotte Perkins Gilman not only exposed issues of gender inequality in America, she also attempted to imagine alternatives to these conditions. Often cast as a feminist for this reason, Gilman contributed new ideas to improve the living conditions of the nation's women. For example, in some of her writings, Gilman proposed architectural designs for "kitchenless" homes that might free women from the isolation of domestic labor by rendering food preparation communal. Whether she was writing fiction or nonfiction, Gilman's work brought insight to the status of women in the United States.

Scholars Since

In the years since 1909, many scholars have examined the implications of American consumer culture. They have advanced multiple theories about what effect consumerism has on everyday life in the United States. At times, researchers have focused on the passive nature of many consumer and leisure activities. When watching motion pictures or spectator sports, for example, viewers are still and seated. They enjoy a vicarious experience rather than encountering life firsthand. Sedentary leisure, while relaxing, tends to render consumers spectators in the deeds of others.

Scholars also have questioned the character of mass cultural entertainments. By this argument, popular culture forms must appeal to a wide range of customers. Consequently, they might cater to base instincts and coarse tastes, and so tending toward the lowest common denominator. Such amusements may be mindless, asking little of, and accomplishing even less for, consumers.

This notion of cheap thrills is another objection to mass culture at the turn of the 20th century. Some cultural observers contend that commercial entertainments do not promote quality or complexity, instead favoring sensation over substance. Other critics of consumer culture object to its proclivity for escapism. In the effort to please the widest possible public, mass entertainments may emphasize showiness over aesthetics. They frequently overstimulate consumers with artificial sights and fleeting pleasures.

Mass culture and leisure detractors also argue that standardizing entertainments and consumer practices promote social conformity. In the cultural equivalent of mass production of goods, mass leisure creates desires and delivers pleasures that are predictable and uniform. In fact, some cultural observers claim that mass consumption and leisure actually subdue the public by seducing them with merchandise. Within this analysis, commodities and entertainments appear therapeutic. They have a palliative effect and so not only distract people from their problems but also create the illusion of satisfaction.

Theodore Dreiser's *Sister Carrie*

With his 1900 novel *Sister Carrie,* Theodore Dreiser crafted a narrative that emblematized the appeal and the hazard of life in the city. Carrie, a young person from a small town, arrives in the city of Chicago. Once there, she finds a setting that offers both temptations and dangers. The experience corrupts her, making the novel among other things a cautionary tale.

Dreiser's Carrie makes a common journey for young people of her time, from small-town life to factory. She arrives to find a glittering cityscape that outshines the reality of life in a shoe factory. In time, she is dismissed from the factory and becomes an actress. At this point in American history, people in the theater were not regarded as highly moral individuals. In fact, some at the time viewed actors and actresses as little more than prostitutes.

Dreiser's portrait of the city is a landscape of competing desires. Carrie functions as an object of desire, but she also has enthusiasms of her own. In a scene that effectively captures the spectacular impact of the era's department store displays and the acquisitive impulses they excited in patrons, Carrie finds herself overwhelmed with material desires. "There was nothing there which she could not have used—nothing which she did not long to own" (Wagenknecht 1982, 169). She seems to be hypnotized by this palace of consumption and filled with lust for its commodities. Within the context of *Sister Carrie,* readers must often discern key elements of character psychology from their longings for objects and the relationships they seem to imply. In this way, Dreiser's novel offers a compelling, if somewhat melodramatic, critique of American materialism and popular leisure.

BIOGRAPHIES

William Edward Burghardt "W. E. B." DuBois, 1868–1963

W. E. B. DuBois was born February 23, 1868, in Great Barrington, Massachusetts. He attended Fisk University where he received a bachelor of arts in 1888. DuBois then attended Harvard University where he earned a second bachelor's degree in 1890 and a master of arts degree in 1891. In 1896, DuBois became the first African American to receive a Ph.D. from Harvard in 1896.

DuBois was a prolific writer and published plays, poems, novels, autobiography, and critical articles. He was also a skilled editor and correspondent. DuBois' published writings include *The Philadelphia Negro* (1899), *The Star of Ethiopia* (1913), *The Negro* (1915), *Dark Water: Voices from within the Veil* (1920), *The Brownies' Book* (1920), *Black Reconstruction* (1935), *Black Folk Then and Now* (1939), and *Dusk of Dawn* (1946). DuBois also composed nonfiction. In 1909, for example, he published a biography of the abolitionist John Brown.

By far his most famous work, however, was *The Souls of Black Folk* (1903). This landmark work dealing with the value of cultural consciousness. It is within this text that DuBois articulated his concepts of "twoness" and "double consciousness." That is, he contended that in terms of survival, African Americans had no choice but to cultivate awareness of both African American and white cultural outlooks. The final chapter of this book employs the African American folk song to symbolize a rich heritage of folk traditions. In fact, DuBois argued that this music, such as spirituals, represented the only true national legacy in America. This approach separated DuBois from more conciliatory figures such as Booker T. Washington.

In addition to his life as a figure in African American letters, DuBois also achieved distinction as editor of *Crisis,* a publication of the NAACP, from approximately 1910 to 1935. In time, DuBois would be named to the faculty of several institutions, including Wilberforce College, University of Pennsylvania, and Atlanta University.

Geronimo, 1829–1909

Geronimo was a famous figure within Native American resistance efforts. Born in 1829, Geronimo was part of an Apache group, the Chirocahuas. His name was a war cry, and the circumstances in his life could make anyone fierce. He experienced many tragedies, including the murders of his mother, wife, and children. In addition, like many other Native Americans, Geronimo had to contend with Indian Removal campaigns. As a warrior against efforts to relocate his population, Geronimo led them in resistance. This period, from 1881–1886, marked the height of his fame. The events were alternately described as "Geronimo's Resistance" or the "Apache Wars." He and his people struggled mightily against removal, spending some time in hiding and some time on reservations in the process. Finally, in September 1886, Geronimo surrendered to Anglo American forces and became a prisoner of war. He was then sent into exile in Florida and later Alabama. He died on an Oklahoma reservation in

Geronimo was a legendary Apache leader and medicine man. (National Archives)

1909. Although he did not escape the fate of life on the reservation, Geronimo became an icon of courage in battle. In fact, Theodore Roosevelt invited him to appear in the inaugural parade when Roosevelt assumed the U.S. Presidency in 1905. Geronimo was also placed on display at the St. Louis Louisiana Purchase Exposition in 1904.

Charles Dana Gibson, 1867–1944

Educated at Manhattan's Arts Students League, Charles Dana Gibson became a successful artist and illustrator for American periodicals during the 1880s. Although he furnished a wide range of pen and ink images for such magazines as *Scribner's, The Century, Collier's,* and *Harper's,* Gibson became best recognized for his satirical depictions of the members of America's upper classes. Of these figures, the recurring image of a female beauty who came to be known as the "Gibson Girl" appeared for the first time in the pages of *Life* magazine and captured America's popular imagination. With her hourglass figure, upswept coiffures, and self-possessed demeanor, the Gibson Girl came to represent ideals of American womanhood at the turn of the 20th century. At the height of her popularity, the Gibson Girl adorned merchandise from vanity sets to wallpaper. Various women, from artist's model Minnie Clark to actress Jobyna Howland, were rumored to be the basis for Gibson's stylized female character. Novelist and journalist Richard Harding Davis is believed to be the model for Gibson's male character of the dandy, the Gibson Girl's counterpart. Although his illustrations were intended to reflect the leisure class, Americans nonetheless embraced the images as icons.

Frances Benjamin Johnston, 1864–1952

Frances Benjamin Johnston was born into privilege, and she grew up in the District of Columbia. Through her family, Johnston had contact with people of power and influence. George Eastman, the man behind Kodak, provided Johnston with her first camera. The director of photography at the Smithsonian Institution, Thomas Smillie, taught her the fine points of taking and developing photographs. Johnston studied art at Paris' *Academie Julian* and established her own photographic studio in the 1890s. Early in her career, Johnston became White House photographer. In this capacity, she photographed presidents Benjamin Harrison, Grover Cleveland, William McKinley, Theodore Roosevelt, and William H. Taft.

Not only was Johnston one of very few women working as a photographer at this point in history but she was also a remarkably active photojournalist. She photographed celebrities and noted individuals of the day, including Mark Twain,

Photographer Frances Benjamin Johnston at Yellowstone National Park in 1903. (Library of Congress)

Susan B. Anthony, Joel Chandler Harris, Geronimo, and John Philip Sousa. She captured images of events from the Pan-American Exposition to the Louisiana Purchase Exposition. Johnston also traveled extensively in order to document Americans at such locations as the Carlyle Indian School, Tuskegee Institute, and the Hampton Institute. Later in her career, Johnston became well known for her documentary photographs of architecture. These images were extremely useful to historic preservationists. Johnston photographed throughout her life, and her photographs offer a valuable record of the country's history and culture.

Chief Joseph, 1840–1904

Chief Joseph distinguished himself as a Native American tribal leader and champion of harmony in relations between indigenous people and Euro-Americans. Born Hin-mah-too-yah-lat-kekt in Oregon's Wallowa Valley in 1840, Joseph became a well-known member of the Nez Percé. His name meant "thunder coming up over the land from the water," and true to his name, he would become a powerful force. The name by which the man became widely known, Joseph, was derived from his father, who took the name Joseph when he converted to Christianity in 1838. Both Joseph the Senior and Joseph the Younger had advocated peace with white populations. This outlook changed, however, when an 1860 gold rush caused the federal government to violate an 1855 treaty by seizing some 6 million acres of Nez Percé territory. This move had the effect of reducing the tribe's land by 90 percent. While they had cooperated with formation of a reservation, this dramatic tightening of its boundaries put an end to that support. As a consequence, Joseph the Elder refused the treaty establishing the smaller version of a reservation and declined to relocate the group away from their traditional hunting grounds.

As son succeeded father with Joseph the Elder's death in 1871, he became known as Joseph the Younger, or simply as Joseph. Like his father before him, Joseph resisted the federal government's attempts to commandeer land and constrict his tribe's available area. The tribe became engaged in the homeland wars, and their new chief helped lead Native American resistance. A long struggle ensued, during which the tribe held off a U.S. force nearly three times its own number, and the defiant tribe staged a long march—some 1,500 miles—toward Canada by way of Oregon, Idaho, Wyoming, and Montana. Finally, Joseph relented when he had reached a position fewer than 40 miles from the border. On October 5, 1877, he issued a formal surrender. His speech on this occasion proved memorable, most notably his declaration that "I will fight no more forever." Following the surrender, Chief Joseph and his people were sent to a series of reservations, never to see their homeland again.

Joseph remained outspoken about the historic injustice done to his tribe, pointing out the irony of an America that sought its own people's independence at the expense of another's. Although he even made his case to President Rutherford B. Hayes, Chief Joseph died while still confined on the Colville Reservation in Washington State in 1904. While he had been permitted to resume residence to the Pacific Northwest, Joseph was never allowed to revisit the ground that held the bones of his parents and other tribal ancestors. In the final year of his life, Chief Joseph was placed on exhibit at the 1904 Louisiana Purchase Exposition. Despite such indignities, Chief Joseph's protests against the U.S. government's mistreatment of Native Americans earned the respect of human and civil rights advocates.

Thorstein Bunde Veblen, 1857–1929

Thorstein Veblen was born to Norwegian immigrants residing in Wisconsin. He learned to speak and write English while in his teens. Veblen attended Carleton College, Johns Hopkins University, and Yale University. He earned a Ph.D. in political economy at Cornell University. At each campus, he both studied and critiqued the leading social and economic theories of his day. In 1892, Veblen joined the faculty at the University of Chicago. He later taught at such institutions as Stanford University, the University of Missouri–Columbia, and the New School for Social Research. Of all his works, Thorstein Veblen is most known for his influential 1899 volume, *The Theory of the Leisure Class*. This work cast a skeptical eye at the conduct of America's affluent. Using terms such as "conspicuous consumption," Veblen discussed the theatricality with which the wealthy, particularly those with new money, chose to demonstrate the full measure of their purchasing power. Through excessive buying and ostentatious display, Veblen's leisure class reasserted and reinforced their claims to membership in a cultural elite. With its emphasis on human motivation as well as conduct, Veblen's theory drew not only on economics but also on a variety of ideas from the social sciences. He became interested in the interplay between business practices and anthropological concepts such as ceremony. Veblen's analysis of the behaviors by which the rich exercised pageantry shaped subsequent investigations and critiques of consumer culture within the United States.

"Madam C. J. Walker"/Sarah Breedlove, 1867–1919

Sarah Breedlove was born the daughter of ex-slaves residing in Louisiana. She lost both her mother and her father by the age of seven. Consequently, she began work in the cotton fields of the American South. She married young, gave birth to a daughter, and lost her husband just two years after that. Breedlove took daughter A'Lelia to St. Louis to live. After an illness cost her most of her hair, Breedlove became familiar with the products of African American businesswoman Annie Malone. Breedlove worked for a time for Malone but eventually adopted the name "Madam C. J. Walker" and initiated a career as a hair care entrepreneur. She developed and sold products including scalp treatments intended to grow hair. Walker traveled extensively to market her hair products, and she built a highly successful business concern. Financial security enabled to contribute her time and funds to worthy causes, including the NAACP's campaign against lynching.

REFERENCES AND FURTHER READINGS

American Memory Collection, Library of Congress. http://www.memory.loc.gov.

Andrist, Ralph K. 1972. *American Century: One Hundred Years of Changing Life Styles in America*. New York: American Heritage Press.

Aron, Cindy S. 1999. *Working at Play: A History of Vacations in the United States*. New York: Oxford University Press.

Ashby, LeRoy. 2006. *With Amusement for All: A History of American Popular Culture Since 1830*. Lexington: University Press of Kentucky.

Barnet, Richard D., Bruce Nemerov, and Mayo R. Taylor. 2004. *The Story behind the Song: 150 Songs that Chronicle the Twentieth Century*. Westport, Conn.: Greenwood Press.

Batchelor, Bob. 2002. *The 1900s: American Popular Culture through History*. Westport, Conn.: Greenwood Press.

Bell, David, and Joanne Hollows. 2006. *Historicizing Lifestyle: Mediating Taste, Consumption and Identity from the 1900s to 1970s*. Burlington, Vt.: Ashgate.

Benson, Susan Porter. 1986. *Counter Cultures: Saleswomen, Managers, and Customers in American Department Stores, 1890–1940*. Urbana: University of Illinois Press.

Braden, Donna R. 1988. *Leisure and Entertainment in America*. Dearborn, Mich.: Henry Ford Museum and Greenfield Village.

Brooks, Tim. 2004. *Lost Sounds: Blacks and the Birth of the Recording Industry, 1890–1919*. Urbana: University of Illinois Press.

Butsch, Richard, ed. 1990. *For Fun and Profit: The Transformation of Leisure into Consumption*. Philadelphia: Temple University Press.

Carrier, Esther Jane. 1985. *Fiction in Public Libraries, 1900–1950*. Littleton, Colo.: Libraries Unlimited.

Cohen, Daniel. 1986. "For Food Both Hot and Bold, Put Your Nickels in the Slot." *Smithsonian* 16 (January): 50–60.

Cohn, Jan. 1989. *Creating America: George Horace Lorimer and the* Saturday Evening Post. Pittsburgh: University of Pittsburgh Press.

Cross, Gary S. 2004. *Encyclopedia of Recreation and Leisure in America*. Farmington Hills, Mich.: Charles Scribner's Sons.

Cross, Gary S. 1993. *Time and Money: The Making of Consumer Culture*. New York: Routledge.

Diggins, John Patrick. 1999. *Thorstein Veblen: Theorist of the Leisure Class*. Princeton: Princeton University Press.

Dubinsky, Karen. 1999. *The Second Greatest Disappointment: Honeymooning and Tourism at Niagara Falls*. New Brunswick: Rutgers University Press.

"Early Motion Pictures of World's Fairs and Expositions." Corrales, N.M.: New Deal Films, 1997.

Edwards, Rebecca. 2006. *New Spirits: Americans in the Gilded Age, 1865–1905*. New York: Oxford University Press.

Emergence of Advertising in America, 1850–1920, Digital Scriptorium, Duke University Library. http://scriptorium.lib.duke.edu/eaa.

Eyewitness to History. http://www.eyewitnesstohistory.com/20frm.htm.

Forsher, James. 2003. *The Community of Cinema: How Cinema and Spectacle Transformed Downtown*. Westport, Conn.: Praeger.

Fox, Stephen. 1984. *The Mirror Makers: A History of American Advertising and Its Creators*. New York: William Morrow.

Fox, Timothy J., and Duane R. Sneddeker. 1997. *From the Palaces to the Pike: Visions of the 1904 World's Fair*. St. Louis: Missouri Historical Society Press.

Gelber, Steven M. 1999. *Hobbies: Leisure and the Culture of Work in America*. New York: Columbia University Press.

Giordano, Ralph. 2003. *Fun and Games in Twentieth Century America: A Historical Guide to Leisure*. Westport, Conn.: Greenwood Press.

Gleason, William A. 1999. *The Leisure Ethic: Work and Play in American Literature, 1840–1940*. Stanford: Stanford University Press.

Glickman, Lawrence B., ed. 1999. *Consumer Society in American History: A Reader*. Ithaca, N.Y.: Cornell University Press.

Goodman, Douglas J., and Mirelle Cohn. 2004. *Consumer Culture: A Reference Handbook*. Santa Barbara: ABC-CLIO.

Gregory, Ross. 1995. *Modern America, 1914 to 1945*. New York: Facts on File.

Grover, Kathryn, ed. 1992. *Hard at Play: Leisure in America, 1840–1940*. Amherst: University of Massachusetts Press.

Heimann, Jim, ed. 2005. *1900–1919: All-American Ads*. London: Taschen.

Hill, Daniel Delis. 2002. *Advertising to the American Women, 1900–1999*. Columbus: Ohio State University Press.

Horowitz, Daniel. 1992. *The Morality of Spending: Attitudes toward the Consumer Society in America, 1875–1940*. Chicago: I. R. Dee.

Kasson, John F. 1978. *Amusing the Million: Coney Island at the Turn of the Century*. New York: Hill and Wang.

Katz, Mark. 1998. "Making America More Musical through the Phonograph, 1900–1930." *American Music* 16 (4, Winter): 448.

Katz, William Loren, and Laurie R. Lehman, eds. 2001. *The Cruel Years: American Voices at the Dawn of the Twentieth Century*. Boston: Beacon Press.

Kenney, William Howland. 1999. *Recorded Music in American Life: The Phonograph and Popular Memory, 1890–1945*. New York: Oxford University Press.

Kent, Noel Jacob. 2000. *America in 1900*. Armonk, N.Y.: M. E. Sharpe.

Kurian, George Thomas. 2001. *Datapedia of the United States, 1790–2005: America Year by Year*. Lanham, Md.: Bernan Press.

Lax, Roger, and Frederick Smith. 1984. *The Great Song Thesaurus*. New York: Oxford University Press.

Lears, T. J. Jackson. 1993. "Mass Culture and Its Critics." In *Encyclopedia of American Social History,* ed. Mary Kupiec Cayton, Elliot J. Gorn, and Peter W. Williams, 1591–1609. New York: Charles Scribner's Sons.

Littman, Mark S. 1998. *A Statistical Portrait of the United States: Social Conditions and Trends*. Lanham, Md.: Bernan Press.

Martin, Lowell Arthur. 1998. *Enrichment: A History of the Public Library in the United States in the Twentieth Century*. Lanham, Md.: Scarecrow Press.

May, Lary. 1980. *Screening Out the Past: The Birth of Mass Culture and the Motion Picture Industry*. New York: Oxford University Press.

McBee, Randy D. 2000. *Dance Hall Days: Intimacy and Leisure among Working-Class Immigrants in the United States*. New York: New York University Press.

Middlemas, Keith. 1977. *The Pursuit of Pleasure: High Society in the 1900s*. New York: Gordon and Cremonesi.

More, Louise Bolard. 1907. *Wage-Earners' Budgets: A Study of Standards and Cost of Living in New York City*. New York: H. Holt.

Nasaw, David. 1993. *Going Out: The Rise and Fall of Public Amusements.* Cambridge, Mass.: Harvard University Press.

National Digital Newspaper Program, National Endowment for the Humanities. www.neh.gov/projects/ndnp.html.

National Geographic, ed. 1998. *National Geographic: Eyewitness to the Twentieth Century.* Washington, DC: National Geographic Society.

Ohmann, Richard. 1996. *Selling Culture: Magazines, Markets, and Class at the Turn of the Century.* New York: Verso.

Patsouras, Louis. 2004. *Thorstein Veblen and the American Way of Life.* New York: Black Rose Books.

Patterson, Joseph Medill. 1907. "The Nickelodeons: The Poor Man's Elementary Course in the Drama," *The Saturday Evening Post,* November 23, pp. 10, 11, 38.

Peiss, Kathy Lee. 1986. *Cheap Amusements: Working Women and Leisure in Turn-of-the-Century New York.* Philadelphia: Temple University Press.

Register, Woody. 2001. *The Kid of Coney Island: Fred Thompson and the Rise of American Amusements.* New York: Oxford University Press.

Riess, Steven A. 1980. *Touching Base: Professional Baseball and American Culture in the Progressive Era.* Westport, Conn.: Greenwood Press.

Rose, Cynthia, ed. 2004. *1900–1909.* Vol. 1 of *American Decades: Primary Sources.* Detroit: Gale.

Rydell, Robert W., John E. Findling, and Kimberly D. Pelle. 2000. *Fair America: World's Fairs in the United States.* Washington, DC: Smithsonian Institution Press.

Rydell, Robert W. 1984. *All the World's a Fair: Visions of Empire at American International Expositions, 1876–1916.* Chicago: University of Chicago Press.

Schlereth, Thomas J. 1992. *Victorian America: Transformations in Everyday Life, 1876–1915.* New York: HarperPerennial.

Shifflet, Crandall. 1996. *Victorian America: 1876 to 1913.* New York: Facts on File.

The [St. Louis] World's Fair: Looking Back at Looking Forward, Missouri Historical Society. http://www.mohistory.org/content/fair/wf/html/index_flash.html.

Strasser, Susan. 1995. *Satisfaction Guaranteed: The Making of the American Mass Market.* Washington, DC: Smithsonian Institution Press.

Time-Life, ed. 1969. *This Fabulous Century, 1900–1910.* Alexandria, Va.: Time-Life Books.

Tompkins, Vincent, ed. 1996. *American Decades: 1900–1909.* Detroit: Gale Research.

U.S. Department of Commerce, Bureau of the Census. 1989. *Historical Statistics of the United States, Colonial Times to 1970*. White Plains, N.Y.: Kraus International Publications.

Wagenknecht, Edward. 1982. *American Profile, 1900–1909*. Amherst: University of Massachusetts Press.

Waller, Gregory A. 1995. *Main Street Amusements: Movies and Commercial Entertainment in a Southern City, 1896–1930*. Washington, DC: Smithsonian Institution Press.

Walter, Dave. 1992. *Today Then: America's Best Minds Look 100 Years into the Future on the Occasion of the 1893 World's Columbian Exposition*. Helena, Mont.: American and World Geographic Publishing.

Wattenberg, Ben J. 1976. *Statistical History of the United States: From Colonial Times to the Present*. New York: Basic Books.

West, Elliott. 1996. *Growing Up in Twentieth-Century America: A History and Reference Guide*. Westport, Conn.: Greenwood Press.

"The World's Fair and Exposition Information and Reference Guide, St. Louis World's Fair." Earth Station 9. http://www.earthstation9.com/index.html?1904 _stl.htm

"The World's Greatest Fair." Saint Louis: Technisonic Studios/PBS Home Video, 2004.

People and Events
in the 20th Century

THE 1900s

THE 1910s

THE 1920s

THE 1930s

THE 1940s

The 1950s

THE 1960s

THE 1970s

THE 1980s

THE 1990s

1900s Index

About the Authors

Brian Greenberg is the Jules Plangere Chair in American Social History at Monmouth University. Among his many works in labor and social history are *Worker and Community: Response to Industrialization in a Nineteenth-Century American City, Albany, New York, 1850–1884* (1985) and, with Leon Fink, *Upheaval in the Quiet Zone: A History of Hospital Workers' Union, Local 1199* (1989). A second and updated edition of *Upheaval in the Quiet Zone* is forthcoming.

Linda S. Watts, professor of American Studies in the Interdisciplinary Arts and Sciences Program at the University of Washington, Bothell, is author of *Rapture Untold: Gender, Mysticism, and the "Moment of Recognition" in Writings by Gertrude Stein* (1996), *Gertrude Stein: A Study of the Short Fiction* (1999), and *Encyclopedia of American Folklore* (2006).